ZAGAT ®

Chicago
Restaurants
2007/08

Including
Milwaukee

LOCAL EDITORS
Alice Van Housen and Ann Christenson
LOCAL COORDINATOR
Jill Van Cleave
STAFF EDITOR
Allison Lynn

Published and distributed by
Zagat Survey, LLC
4 Columbus Circle
New York, NY 10019
T: 212.977.6000
E: chicago@zagat.com
www.zagat.com

ACKNOWLEDGMENTS

We thank Bill Rice, Brenda and Earl Shapiro, Laura Levy Shatkin, Steven Shukow and Tom Van Housen, as well as the following members of our staff: Kelly Stewart (assistant editor), Sean Beachell, Maryanne Bertollo, Deirdre Bush, Sandy Cheng, Reni Chin, Larry Cohn, Alison Flick, Jeff Freier, Caroline Hatchett, Roy Jacob, Natalie Lebert, Mike Liao, Christina Livadiotis, Dave Makulec, Andre Pilette, Becky Ruthenburg, Carla Spartos, Kilolo Strobert, Liz Borod Wright, Sharon Yates and Kyle Zolner.

Contents

About This Survey

This **2007/08 Chicago Restaurants Survey** is an update reflecting significant developments since our last Survey was published. It covers 1,110 restaurants in the Chicago area and in Milwaukee, including 118 important additions. We've also indicated new addresses, phone numbers, chef changes and other major alterations.

WHO PARTICIPATED: Input from 4,842 avid diners forms the basis for the ratings and reviews in this guide (their comments are shown in quotation marks within the reviews). Collectively they bring roughly 804,000 annual meals worth of experience to this Survey. We sincerely thank each of these participants – this book is really "theirs."

HELPFUL LISTS: Whether you're looking for a celebratory meal, a hot scene or a bargain bite, our lists can help you find exactly the right place. See Most Popular (page 7), Key Newcomers (page 7), Top Ratings (pages 9–14) and Best Buys (page 15). We've also provided 42 handy indexes.

OUR LOCAL TEAM: Special thanks go to our local editors for this update, Alice Van Housen, a freelance writer and editor; and Ann Christenson, the dining critic for *Milwaukee Magazine*; and to our coordinator Jill Van Cleave, a cookbook author and food consultant.

ABOUT ZAGAT: This marks our 28th year reporting on the shared experiences of consumers like you. What started in 1979 as a hobby involving 200 of our friends has come a long way. Today we have over 300,000 surveyors and now cover dining, entertaining, golf, hotels, movies, music, nightlife, resorts, shopping, spas, theater and tourist attractions worldwide.

SHARE YOUR OPINION: We invite you to join any of our upcoming surveys – just register at **zagat.com,** where you can rate and review establishments year-round. Each participant will receive a free copy of the resulting guide when published.

AVAILABILITY: Zagat guides are available in all major bookstores, by subscription at **zagat.com** and for use on a wide range of mobile devices via **Zagat To Go.**

FEEDBACK: There is always room for improvement, thus we invite your comments and suggestions about any aspect of our performance. Just contact us at chicago@zagat.com.

New York, NY
July 11, 2007

Nina and Tim Zagat

What's New

Chi-town's status as a world-class dining destination continued to grow this year with a spate of red hot newcomers. No wonder that 83% of surveyors are eating out as much as or more than they did three years ago.

THE HOT LIST: Chicagoans welcomed sizzling neophytes Aigre Doux, Chalkboard, Marigold, Republic Pan-Asian and Room 21, and the high-style dining scene grew in the suburbs too, with the arrival of Niche, Osteria di Tramonto and Quince. And speaking of hot, Hot Doug's made headlines for fighting the city's foie gras ban – and the law won, hitting the hot dog emporium with a citation, fine and confiscation of the illicit liver.

 CUISINE CONVERSION: The sushi and small-plates surges seem to be slowing as surveyors cited Italian as their favorite cuisine. On that note, a passel of pizza joints opened, like Coalfire, Frasca Pizzeria & Wine Bar, Sapore di Napoli, Spacca Napoli and the organic Crust. Pedigreed Latin/Mex cantinas were popular too, with DeLaCosta (from top toque Douglas Rodriguez), Tepatulco (Geno Bahena's return) and Xel-Há (a Dudley Nieto production) drawing diners. Gastropubs were a third trend, with BB's, Cooper's and The Gage serving haute bar fare and brews.

DRAMATIC DEPARTURES: A number of classics closed, most importantly old favorite Ambria. We also bid adieu to Pasteur, the Ritz-Carlton Dining Room, del Toro, Papa Milano's, Rushmore and X/O.

FUTURE FEEDING FRENZIES: Next year should be even more heated, with the launch of the comfort-food specialist Otom from the Moto folks, Shikago from Kevin's Shikami brothers, a Follia spin-off called Tocco, an outpost of New York's Brasserie Ruhlmann and a kosher Wolfgang Puck cafe in the Spertus Institute. Celeb chefs Terrance Brennan (of NYC's Picholine) and Laurent Gras (ex NYC's Bistro du Vent) are setting up shop too – and rumor has it that Joël Robuchon and Alain Ducasse are also scouting locations. Hometowner Charlie Trotter has already found his: The Elysian, a luxury Gold Coast hotel where, come 2008, he will helm both fine-dining and casual restaurants.

MILWAUKEE MOVES ON UP: Disproving its stereotype as a strictly meat-and-potatoes town, Milwaukee welcomed a stylish Cajun-Creole in the form of the East Side's Bayou, and two prominent Downtown hotel eateries offered creative, unstuffy, high-end fare – the Pfister's Mason Street Grill and Intercontinental Milwaukee's Kil@wat. On the economical end, newcomers North Star American Bistro and Il Mito Enoteca are luring in budget-conscious diners who also crave white-tablecloth flair.

THE TALLY: At $33.75, the average cost of a Chicago meal is just above the national average of $33.28. Still, that didn't stop 61% of reviewers from opining that the city's dining is reasonably priced.

Chicago, IL
Milwaukee, WI
July 11, 2007

Alice Van Housen
Ann Christenson

Downtown Chicago

W. Division St.
SEWARD PARK
N. Elm St.
N. Orleans St.
N. Franklin St.
N. Wells St.
W. Maple St.
Original Pancake House*
Gibsons Steakhouse
Hugo's Frog & Fish
OAK BEACH PARK
Morton's*
Bellevue Pl.
W. Oak St.
N. La Salle Dr.
N. Clark St.
N. Dearborn St.
N. State St.
N. Rush St.
E. Walton St.
Café Spiaggia
Spiaggia
Lake Michigan
W. Locust St.
W. Chestnut St.
mk
Delaware St.
E. Chestnut St.
N. Wabash Ave.
Michigan Ave.
Cheesecake Factory*
E. Pearson St.
Lake Shore Dr.
W. Chicago Ave.
Café Iberico
NoMI
N. State St.
E. Superior St.
41
MILTON LEE OLIVE PARK
W. Huron St.
Fogo de Chão
Wildfire*
Maggiano's*
Chicago Chop House
N. Rush St.
Tru
Pizzeria Due
E. Huron St.
E. Erie St.
E. Ontario St.
W. Ontario St.
W. Ohio St.
Heaven on Seven*
E. Ohio St.
Frontera Grill
Topolobampo
P.F. Chang's*
Pizzeria Uno
E. Grand Ave.
Navy Pier
Lou Malnati's*
Joe's Seafood
E. Illinois St.
W. Kinzie St.
E. Hubbard St.
Shaw's Crab House
N. Water St.
W. Carroll Ave.
Brasserie Jo
Bin 36
Ruth's Chris
Chicago River
Turning Basin
E. Wacker Dr.
W. Wacker Dr.
N. Wabash
E. Wacker Dr.
S. Water St.
W. Lake St.
N. Michigan Ave.
41
South Branch Chicago River
Giordano's*
N. La Salle Dr.
N. Clark St.
Heaven on Seven*
E. Randolph St.
DALEY BICENTENNIAL PLAZA
W. Washington Blvd.
S. Wacker Dr.
W. Madison St.
Rosebud*
S. Dearborn St.
S. State St.
Michigan Ave.
0   1/4 mi
S. Wells St.
S. Franklin St.
W. Adams St.
W. Jackson Blvd.
W. Van Buren St.
Everest
Congress Pkwy.
W. Harrison St.

Check for other locations

W. Diversey Pkwy.
N. Halsted St.
N. Clark St.
North Pond
Lake Michigan
Lou Malnati's*
Mon Ami Gabi
LINCOLN PARK
North Branch Chicago R.
John F. Kennedy Expwy.
W. Fullerton Pkwy.
N. Racine Ave.
Charlie Trotter's
Café Ba-Ba-Reeba!
W. Armitage Ave.
N. Clybourn Ave.
Alinea
W. North Ave.
N. Larabee St.
N. Clark St.
64
Bin Wine Café
Spring
90
94
GOOSE ISLAND
41
W. Division St.
N. Milwaukee Ave.
N. Ashland Ave.
N. Damen Ave.
Japonais
W. Chicago Ave.
N. State St.
Avec
Blackbird
Chicago
W. Randolph St.
N. Jefferson St.
N. Michigan Ave.
W. Madison St.
Francesca's*
290
W. Taylor St.
Dwight D. Eisenhower Expwy.
W. Jackson Blvd.
W. Roosevelt Rd.
0   1/2 mi

60
45
21
McKinley Rd.
Sheridan Rd.
Francesca's*
Town Line Rd.
Lake Forest
83
60
94
41
Green Bay Rd.
22
Wildfire*
Lincolnshire
Deerfield Rd.
Highland Park
12
Lake Cook Rd.
P.F. Chang's*
68
14
Dundee Rd.
Northbrook
Ruth's Chris
Palatine
Bob Chinn's
Wheeling
43
Wildfire
Shaw's Crab House
Glenview
Golf Rd.
Skokie
Lou Malnati's*
Schaumburg
58
Dempster St.
Evanston
Lake Michigan
Higgins Rd.
290
294
21
41
Ridge Ave.
Sheridan Rd.
Cheesecake Factory*
Maggiano's*
19
Chicago-O'Hare Int'l Airport
90
Harlem Ave.
14
Peterson Ave.
Park Rd.
20
Gibsons Steakhouse
Rosemont
41
Center inset detail
355
64
12
York Rd.
45
43
Lake St.
North Ave.
Cicero Ave.
94
Downtown top detail
P.F. Chang's*
Mon Ami Gabi
Lombard
Oak Brook
Morton's*
Westchester
Roosevelt Rd.
Ogden Ave.
Ashland Ave.
90
41
Hugo's Frog & Fish
Naperville
294
34
55
Chicago
0   5 mi

Most Popular

Each surveyor has been asked to name his or her five favorite places. This list reflects their choices.

①	Charlie Trotter's	㉑	Original Pancake*
②	Tru	㉒	Mon Ami Gabi
③	Frontera Grill	㉓	Cheesecake Factory
④	Wildfire	㉔	Giordano's
⑤	Morton's Steak	㉕	P.F. Chang's*
⑥	Gibsons Steak	㉖	Café Iberico
⑦	mk	㉗	Chicago Chop Hse.*
⑧	Topolobampo	㉘	Spring
⑨	Everest	㉙	Lou Malnati Pizza
⑩	Joe's Seafood/Steak	㉚	North Pond
⑪	Maggiano's	㉛	Avec
⑫	Spiaggia	㉜	Heaven on Seven
⑬	Shaw's Crab House	㉝	Ruth's Chris Steak
⑭	Alinea	㉞	Bin 36/Bin Wine
⑮	NoMI	㉟	Brasserie Jo
⑯	Blackbird	㊱	Japonais
⑰	Rosebud	㊲	Bob Chinn's Crab
⑱	Fogo de Chão	㊳	Café Spiaggia*
⑲	Hugo's Frog & Fish	㊴	Cafe Ba-Ba-Reeba!
⑳	Francesca's	㊵	Pizzeria Uno/Due*

It's obvious that many of the above restaurants are among Chicago's most expensive, but if popularity were calibrated to price, we suspect that a number of other restaurants would join the above ranks. Given the fact that both our surveyors and readers love to discover dining bargains, we have added a list of 80 Best Buys on page 15. These are restaurants that give real quality at extremely reasonable prices.

KEY NEWCOMERS

Our take on the most notable new arrivals of the past year. For a full list see the Additions index on page 206.

Aigre Doux	Niche
Chalkboard	Osteria di Tramonto
Crust	Pops for Champagne
DeLaCosta	Quince
Gage, The	Republic Pan-Asian
Marigold	Room 21

* Indicates a tie with restaurant above

Ratings & Symbols

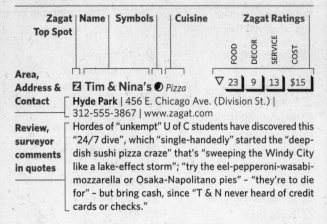

	Zagat Top Spot	Name	Symbols		Cuisine		Zagat Ratings			
							FOOD	DECOR	SERVICE	COST
Area, Address & Contact	**Z**	**Tim & Nina's** ◕			*Pizza*	▽	23	9	13	$15

Hyde Park | 456 E. Chicago Ave. (Division St.) | 312-555-3867 | www.zagat.com

Review, surveyor comments in quotes

Hordes of "unkempt" U of C students have discovered this "24/7 dive", which "single-handedly" started the "deep-dish sushi pizza craze" that's "sweeping the Windy City like a lake-effect storm"; "try the eel-pepperoni-wasabi-mozzarella or Osaka-Napolitano pies" – "they're to die for" – but bring cash, since "T & N never heard of credit cards or checks."

Ratings   **Food, Decor** and **Service** are rated on a scale of 0 to 30.

0 – 9	poor to fair
10 – 15	fair to good
16 – 19	good to very good
20 – 25	very good to excellent
26 – 30	extraordinary to perfection
▽	low response	less reliable

Cost reflects our surveyors' average estimate of the price of a dinner with one drink and tip and is a benchmark only. Lunch is usually 25% less.

For **newcomers** or survey **write-ins** listed without ratings, the price range is indicated as follows:

I	$25 and below
M	$26 to $40
E	$41 to $65
VE	$66 or more

Symbols
Z	Zagat Top Spot (highest ratings, popularity and importance)
◕	serves after 11 PM
S	closed on Sunday
M	closed on Monday
⊄	no credit cards accepted

Top Food Ratings

Ratings are to the left of names. Lists exclude places with low votes.

29 Carlos'	mk*
28 Le Français	Isabella's Estiatorio
Les Nomades	Gabriel's
Tru	Seasons
Alinea	Va Pensiero
Tallgrass	Crofton on Wells
Arun's	Sushi Wabi
27 Topolobampo	Le Titi de Paris
Charlie Trotter's	Joe's Seafood/Steak
Everest	Salbute
Vie	Agami
Spring	Morton's Steak
Barrington Bistro	Kevin
Oceanique	NoMI
Blackbird	Le Lan
26 Courtright's	Naha
Frontera Grill	25 Avec
Spiaggia	Scylla
Mirai Sushi	Michael
Avenues	Moto

BY CUISINE

AMERICAN (NEW)

28 Alinea
27 Charlie Trotter's
Vie
Spring
Blackbird

AMERICAN (TRAD.)

25 Seasons Café
24 Bongo Room
Lawry's Prime Rib
23 Wildfire
West Town Tavern

ASIAN (MISC.)

26 Kevin
Le Lan
24 Shanghai Terrace
23 Yoshi's Café
Opera

BARBECUE

23 Fat Willy's
22 Twin Anchors
Ribs 'n' Bibs
21 Merle's Smokehouse
Hecky's

CAJUN/CREOLE

21 Heaven on Seven
Wishbone
20 Pappadeaux Seafood
19 Dixie Kitchen
Davis St. Fishmarket

CHINESE

24 Lao Sze Chuan
23 Happy Chef Dim Sum
Chens
Emperor's Choice
22 Evergreen

COFFEE SHOPS/DINERS

23 Original Pancake
Manny's
Orange
22 Lou Mitchell's
21 Milk & Honey

ECLECTIC

25 Moto
Lula
23 Aria
Victory's Banner
Orange

FRENCH (BISTRO)

- 27 Barrington Bistro
- 25 D & J Bistro
- Retro Bistro
- 23 Bistro Campagne
- Jacky's Bistro

FRENCH (NEW)

- 29 Carlos'
- 28 Le Français
- Les Nomades
- Tru
- Tallgrass

GREEK

- 22 Roditys
- Pegasus
- 21 Santorini
- Greek Islands
- Artopolis Bakery

HAMBURGERS/ HOT DOGS

- 25 Hot Doug's
- 22 Superdawg Drive-In
- Al's #1 Beef
- 21 Pete Miller Sea/Steak
- 20 Wiener's Circle

INDIAN

- 23 India House
- 22 Tiffin
- Gaylord Indian
- Indian Garden
- 21 Vermilion

ITALIAN

- 26 Spiaggia
- Gabriel's
- Va Pensiero
- 24 Café Spiaggia
- Coco Pazzo

JAPANESE

- 26 Mirai Sushi
- sushi wabi
- Agami
- 25 Kuni's
- Heat

MEDITERRANEAN

- 26 Isabella's Estiatorio
- Naha
- 25 Avec
- Scylla
- 24 Pita Inn

MEXICAN

- 27 Topolobampo
- 26 Frontera Grill
- Salbute
- 24 Salpicón
- 23 Cafe 28

MIDDLE EASTERN

- 24 Pita Inn
- 23 Maza
- 21 Tizi Melloul
- Turquoise
- 20 Kabul House

NUEVO LATINO

- 23 Cuatro
- 22 Nacional 27
- Mas
- Carnivale
- 21 Vermilion

PIZZA

- 24 Lou Malnati Pizza
- Art of Pizza
- 22 Aurelio's Pizza
- Pizza D.O.C.
- Pizzeria Uno/Due

SEAFOOD

- 27 Spring
- Oceanique
- 26 Avenues
- Joe's Seafood/Steak
- 25 Scylla

SMALL PLATES

- 25 Avec
- Green Zebra
- 23 Maza
- BOKA
- 21 Enoteca Piattini

SPANISH/TAPAS

- 23 La Tasca
- Mesón Sabika
- Café Iberico
- 22 Twist
- Cafe Ba-Ba-Reeba!

STEAKHOUSES

- 26 Morton's Steak
- 25 Chicago Chop Hse.
- Gibsons Steak
- 24 Capital Grille
- Tango Sur

THAI

- 28 Arun's
- 22 Thai Pastry
- Spoon Thai
- 21 Vong's
- 20 Ruby of Siam

VEGETARIAN

- 25 Green Zebra
- Lula
- 24 Ethiopian Diamond
- 23 Maza
- Victory's Banner

BY SPECIAL FEATURE

BREAKFAST

- 26 Seasons
- NoMI
- 25 Seasons Café
- Lula
- 24 Bongo Room

BRUNCH

- 26 Frontera Grill
- Seasons
- 25 Magnolia Cafe
- North Pond
- 24 Salpicón

BUSINESS DINING

- 28 Le Français
- Les Nomades
- Alinea
- 27 Topolobampo
- Charlie Trotter's

CHILD-FRIENDLY

- 24 Bongo Room
- Lawry's Prime Rib
- Lou Malnati Pizza
- 23 Original Pancake
- Manny's

HOTEL DINING

- 26 Avenues
  (Peninsula)
- Seasons
  (Four Seasons)
- Va Pensiero
  (Margarita Inn)
- NoMI
  (Park Hyatt)
- 25 Seasons Café
  (Four Seasons)

LATE DINING

- 26 sushi wabi
- Agami
- 25 Avec
- Michael
- Seasons Café

MEET FOR A DRINK

- 26 Frontera Grill
- mk
- Joe's Seafood/Steak
- NoMI
- 25 one sixtyblue

PEOPLE-WATCHING

- 27 Spring
- Blackbird
- 26 Mirai Sushi
- mk
- NoMI

WINNING WINE LISTS

- 29 Carlos'
- 28 Le Français
- Les Nomades
- Tru
- Alinea

WORTH A TRIP

- 29 Carlos'
  Highland Park
- 28 Le Français
  Wheeling
- Tallgrass
  Lockport
- 27 Vie
  Western Springs
- 26 Courtright's
  Willow Springs

BY LOCATION

ANDERSONVILLE/ EDGEWATER

- 24 Ethiopian Diamond
- M. Henry
- 23 Francesca's

- 22 Jin Ju
- 21 La Tache

BUCKTOWN

- 25 Scylla
- 24 Think Café

<u>23</u> Coast Sushi
Café Absinthe
Hot Chocolate

CHINATOWN

<u>24</u> Lao Sze Chuan
<u>23</u> Happy Chef Dim Sum
Emperor's Choice
<u>22</u> Evergreen
Phoenix

GOLD COAST

<u>26</u> Spiaggia
Seasons
Morton's Steak
NoMI
<u>25</u> Seasons Café

GREEKTOWN

<u>22</u> Roditys
Pegasus
Butter
<u>21</u> Santorini
Greek Islands

LAKEVIEW/
WRIGLEYVILLE

<u>24</u> Tango Sur
Art of Pizza
<u>23</u> Chens
Yoshi's Café
Cafe 28

LINCOLN PARK

<u>28</u> Alinea
<u>27</u> Charlie Trotter's
<u>25</u> North Pond
<u>24</u> Sai Café
Lou Malnati Pizza

LINCOLN SQUARE/
UPTOWN

<u>26</u> Agami
<u>25</u> Magnolia Cafe
<u>23</u> Bistro Campagne
<u>22</u> Thai Pastry
Pizza D.O.C.

LITTLE ITALY

<u>24</u> RoSal's Kitchen
<u>23</u> Francesca's
<u>22</u> Al's #1 Beef

Tuscany
Chez Joël

LOOP

<u>27</u> Everest
<u>26</u> Morton's Steak
<u>24</u> Nick's Fishmarket
<u>23</u> Palm, The
Aria

MARKET DISTRICT

<u>26</u> sushi wabi
<u>25</u> Moto
one sixtyblue
<u>23</u> Starfish
Red Light

RIVER NORTH

<u>27</u> Topolobampo
<u>26</u> Frontera Grill
Avenues
mk*
Crofton on Wells

STREETERVILLE

<u>28</u> Les Nomades
Tru
<u>24</u> Capital Grille
<u>23</u> Saloon Steak
Volare

SUBURBS

<u>29</u> Carlos'
<u>28</u> Le Français
Tallgrass
<u>27</u> Vie
Barrington Bistro

WEST LOOP

<u>27</u> Blackbird
<u>25</u> Avec
<u>24</u> Meiji
<u>23</u> La Sardine
<u>22</u> Nine

WICKER PARK

<u>27</u> Spring
<u>26</u> Mirai Sushi
<u>24</u> Bongo Room
<u>23</u> Bob San
Francesca's

Top Decor Ratings

Ratings are to the left of names.

27
NoMI
Tru
Seasons
Signature Room
North Pond
Alinea
Spiaggia

Carnivale
Le Français
Seasons Café
Tizi Melloul
Spring
Carlos'
Canoe Club

26
Everest
Agami
Lobby, The*
Les Nomades
SushiSamba rio
Shanghai Terrace
Avenues
RL
Japonais
Custom House
Zealous

24
Pump Room
Cité
Atwater's
Nine
Le Colonial
mk
Atwood Cafe
one sixtyblue
Arun's
Le Titi de Paris
Wave
Tallgrass
Nacional 27

25
Courtright's
Charlie Trotter's

OUTDOORS

Athena
Cafe Ba-Ba-Reeba!
Feast
Meritage Cafe
Mesón Sabika
Park Grill

Pegasus
Puck's at MCA
Room 21
Smith & Wollensky
SushiSamba rio
Timo

ROMANCE

Avenue M
Bistro Campagne
BOKA
Café Absinthe
DeLaCosta
Everest

Geja's Cafe
Il Mulino New York
Le Colonial
Pops for Champagne
Spring
Tizi Melloul

ROOMS

Alinea
Carnivale
Custom House
Il Mulino New York
Japonais
Marché

NoMI
North Pond
Quince
RL
Saltaus
Shanghai Terrace

VIEWS

Cité
Courtright's
Everest
Flatwater
Fulton's
NoMI

North Pond
Park Grill
Riva
Signature Room
Spiaggia
Tasting Room

Top Service Ratings

Ratings are to the left of names.

<u>28</u> Alinea	Le Titi de Paris
Tru	Spring
Carlos'	Joe's Seafood/Steak
Les Nomades	mk
Le Français	<u>24</u> Capital Grille
<u>27</u> Charlie Trotter's	Brazzaz
Seasons	Morton's Steak
Everest	Barrington Bistro
<u>26</u> Arun's	Café la Cave
Avenues	Fogo de Chão
Courtright's	Oceanique
Moto	Le Lan
NoMI	Scylla
Gabriel's	Naha
Seasons Café	Buona Terra
	Aria
<u>25</u> Spiaggia	<u>23</u> Green Zebra
Shanghai Terrace	Lawry's Prime Rib
Isabella's Estiatorio	Pump Room
Tallgrass*	Saloon Steak*
Va Pensiero	Crofton on Wells
Topolobampo	

Best Buys

In order of Bang for the Buck rating.

1. Cereality Cereal
2. Superdawg Drive-In
3. Potbelly Sandwich
4. Hot Doug's
5. Margie's Candies
6. Wiener's Circle
7. Gold Coast Dogs
8. Mr. Beef
9. Al's #1 Beef
10. Pita Inn
11. Julius Meinl Café
12. Cold Comfort Cafe
13. Victory's Banner
14. Milk & Honey
15. Original Pancake
16. Art of Pizza
17. Irazu
18. Aurelio's Pizza
19. Penny's Noodle
20. Lou Mitchell's
21. Breakfast Club
22. Pompei Bakery
23. Toast
24. M. Henry
25. Orange
26. Nookies
27. My Pie Pizza
28. Tre Kronor
29. Pasta Palazzo
30. Bongo Room
31. Billy Goat Tavern
32. Aladdin's Eatery
33. Ann Sather
34. Artopolis Bakery
35. Medici on 57th
36. Flo
37. Hai Yen
38. Uncommon Ground
39. Duke of Perth
40. Kitsch'n

OTHER GOOD VALUES

Akai Hana
A La Turka
Andies
Baccalà
Bagel, The
Bandera
Best Hunan
Big Bowl
Boston Blackie's
Café Iberico
Club Lucky
Cordis Brothers
Cyrano's Bistrot
D&J Bistro
Dave's Italian
Davis St. Fishmarket
Depot Amer. Diner
Dining Rm. at Kendall
erwin cafe & bar
Fonda del Mar
Francesca's
Greek Islands
Hot Tamales
La Crêperie
Las Tablas
Maiz
Matsuya
Mundial Cocina
Old Jerusalem
Parthenon
Quince
Reza's
Riques
Rose Angelis
Shiroi Hana
Tango Sur
Thai Classic
Thai Pastry
Village, The
West Town Tavern

CHICAGO
RESTAURANT
DIRECTORY

	FOOD	DECOR	SERVICE	COST

Adelle's ☒ *American* | 25 | 22 | 23 | $36 |

Wheaton | 1060 College Ave. (bet. President St. & Stoddard Ave.) |
630-784-8015 | www.adelles.com

A "delightful" "little spot", this "pretty, cozy" Wheaton New American "fills a need" in the Western Suburbs with "hearty yet innovative" "comfort food done well" and offered at a "value price", not to mention a staff that provides "excellent attention to customers"; monthly wine dinners, live jazz on most Thursday nights and "great outdoor dining" are additional incentives.

NEW Adesso *Italian* | - | - | - | M |

Lakeview | 3332 N. Broadway St. (bet. Buckingham Pl. & W. Aldine Ave.) |
773-868-1516 | www.eatadesso.com

Casual neighborhood Italian beckons at this Boys Town spot serving salads and panini for lunch, and a well-rounded, wallet-friendly menu for dinner; the airy space features plenty of windows, soft blue walls and an open kitchen, while friendly types will enjoy the communal table.

Adobo Grill *Mexican* | 21 | 19 | 20 | $32 |

Old Town | 1610 N. Wells St. (North Ave.) | 312-266-7999
Wicker Park | 2005 W. Division St. (Damen Ave.) |
773-252-9990
www.adobogrill.com

Pleased patrons of this "mid-scale Mexican" pair in Old Town and Wicker Park praise the "quality" fare with "bold flavors" and "a nice variety of Latin specialties" ("don't look for tacos or burritos"); the "party atmosphere", "especially on weekends", is "fun" to some, "noisy" to others, and while the "killer" "custom-made guacamole", "potent margaritas" and "impressive tequila list" are widely praised, banditos bemoan that they "seem to be the standouts"; N.B. a Lombard location is set to open in summer 2007.

☑ Agami ● *Japanese* | 26 | 26 | 23 | $38 |

Uptown | 4712 N. Broadway (Leland Ave.) | 773-506-1854

"Incredibly fresh", "flavorful sushi that really pops in your mouth" as well as "inventive" signature dishes are served by a "friendly staff" at this Uptown Japanese; "fish on a video screen" are part of this spot's "over-the-top" "underwater" decor that "Jules Verne would envy", and the "fashionable bar area" offers an "excellent selection of sake."

NEW Aigre Doux *American* | - | - | - | E |

River North | 230 W. Kinzie St. (bet. N. Franklin & Wells Sts.) |
312-329-9400 | www.aigredouxchicago.com

The married cooking duo of Mohammad Islam and Malika Ameen – he's savory, she's sweet – whose culinary pedigree most recently includes LA's Chateau Marmont, helms this sophisticated, borderline-expensive River North New American restaurant (with adjacent bakery) offering a smart, well-priced wine list; located in the former Pili.Pili space, its linear, spartan-chic dining room is lit intimately by rows of dangling exposed bulbs.

	FOOD	DECOR	SERVICE	COST

Akai Hana *Japanese*

| 21 | 12 | 18 | $26 |

Wilmette | 3223 W. Lake Ave. (Skokie Blvd.) | 847-251-0384 | www.akaihanasushi.com

North Suburban sushi stalwarts "crowd" this "reliable", "family-friendly" Japanese in Wilmette that "keeps it simple" with "solid", "bargain"-priced fare in a "low-key", "strip-mall location" and a staff that "means well"; snipers see it "getting tired", though, saying the service is "mixed", the "food hasn't kept up with their escalating prices" and the "cheesy decor" "wasn't even an afterthought."

Aki Sushi ● *Japanese*

| - | - | - | M |

Wicker Park | 2015 W. Division St. (Damen Ave.) | 773-227-8080

Wicker Park's latest Japanese contender in the modern maki maelstrom offers a menu dominated by fresh 'fusion' rolls (with only a few teriyaki cooked selections); laid-back lounge music, candlelight and a rock garden with koi pond set the mood, which is easily enhanced by the swanky sake-cocktail options.

Aladdin's Eatery *Mideastern*

| 17 | 12 | 15 | $14 |

Lincoln Park | 614 W. Diversey Pkwy. (Clark St.) | 773-327-6300 | www.aladdinseatery.com

Charmed champions of this Lincoln Park "treasure" cheer for its "quick", "cheap, healthy Middle-Eastern" eats from a "huge menu" with lots of "vegetarian options", adding that "you can't beat the prices"; still, antis assert that the decor "doesn't draw people in" and insist that the "average cuisine", though "not bad", "isn't exactly what [they] would ask the genie to conjure up."

A La Turka *Turkish*

| 20 | 19 | 19 | $25 |

Lakeview | 3134 N. Lincoln Ave. (Belmont Ave.) | 773-935-6447 | www.alaturkachicago.com

"Savor the flavors" of "Turkey without leaving Chicago" at this "funky", "dim" Lakeview lair, where the "authentic" food is "tasty" and "well prepared", the "Zorba-like owner is charming" and the "beautiful belly dancers" (Thursday–Sunday nights) are "amazing"; so even if "service can be spotty", it adds up to "a fun evening of Turkish food, culture and atmosphere" "at a reasonable price" – "with hookahs to boot!"

NEW Alhambra Palace Restaurant ● *Mideastern*

| - | - | - | M |

Market District | 1240 W. Randolph St. (bet. Elizabeth St. & Racine Ave.) | 312-666-9555 | www.alhambrapalacerestaurant.com

Over-the-top and opulent, this Market District dazzler revives the El Morocco tradition of adult theme park, Arabian Nights–style, with multiple dining rooms and a multilevel nightclub with elevated stage (belly dancing, live jazz) making up 24,000 sq. ft. of dreamy decor, fueled by exotic cocktails; N.B. it's open till 3 AM Fridays.

Alice & Friends Vegetarian Cafe Ⓩ *Asian*

| ▽ 20 | 9 | 15 | $16 |

Uptown | 5812 N. Broadway (Ardmore Ave.) | 773-275-8797

This "unpretentious" Uptown Asian draws plums for its "interesting selections" of "healthful, delicious" vegetarian and vegan fare, in-

cluding "unbeef, unchicken and whatever other unmeat is available" ("good desserts" too), but earns lemons for its so-so service and "low-budget decor" dominated by "spooky TV-evangelism" videos that seem to "run on perpetual loop"; N.B. no alcohol service, and no BYO.

Z Alinea M *American* 28 | 27 | 28 | $168

Lincoln Park | 1723 N. Halsted St. (bet. North Ave. & Willow St.) | 312-867-0110 | www.alinearestaurant.com

Astronomic scores support the "sheer genius" of chef-owner Grant Achatz and the "astonishing flavors" of his "fabulous" "experimental" New American cuisine at this Lincoln Park "thrill ride" that "engages all of your senses" and "expands your concept of fine dining"; the space is "lovely, understated and serene", the nearly 700-bottle wine list is "superb" and the "polished service" (ranked No. 1 in Chicagoland) is near "perfect"; be prepared, though, as this "surreal" "journey" will be "loooong" and "ungodly expensive" - though "worth it"; N.B. open Wednesday-Sunday for dinner only.

Allen's S *American* 24 | 20 | 23 | $50

River North | 217 W. Huron St. (bet. Franklin & Wells Sts.) | 312-587-9600 | www.allenscafe.com

Allen Sternweiler's River North New American "still pleases" with seasonal sustenance that's "inventive but not too busy" and a menu that "satisfies meat eaters and seafood lovers alike" ("especially" the "excellent game" dishes); factor in an "eclectic wine list", "great service" and a "clean modern setting" that's "casual but upscale", and it's "one of the classier options in the area."

Al's #1 Italian Beef *Sandwiches* 22 | 7 | 15 | $9

River North | 169 W. Ontario St. (Wells St.) | 312-943-3222 ◐
Little Italy | 1079 W. Taylor St. (Aberdeen St.) | 312-226-4017 S
NEW **Evanston** | 622 Davis St. (Chicago Ave.) | 847-424-9704
Lincolnwood | Lincolnwood Town Ctr. | 3333 W. Touhy Ave. (McCormick Blvd.) | 847-673-2333
Addison | 1600 W. Lake St. (bet. Lombard & Rohlwing Rds.) | 630-773-4599
NEW **Niles** | 5948 W. Touhy Ave. (N. Lehigh Ave.) | 847-647-1577
Park Ridge | 33 S. Northwest Hwy. (bet. Euclid & Prospect Aves.) | 847-318-7700
Chicago Heights | 551 W. 14th St. (Division St.) | 708-748-2333
Oak Lawn | 10276 S. Harlem Ave. (103rd St.) | 708-636-2333 S
Tinley Park | 7132 183rd St. (Harlem Ave.) | 708-444-2333
www.alsbeef.com
Additional locations throughout the Chicago area

"Are your cholesterol and sodium dangerously low?" - then visit this "quintessential" "Chicago legend", a "cheap-eats" chain spun off from the 1938 "Taylor Street original" that's cheered for Italian beef "sandwiches so juicy there's no neat way to eat them" (plus "delicious burgers and sausages, and even better fries"); "lacking" service and

"nonexistent" decor don't deter the "crowds", though some who swear the kitchen's "getting a little skimpy on the meat" say they "don't get why it calls itself #1."

Amarind's Ⓜ *Thai*   ▽ 25 | 15 | 19 | $24

Far West | 6822 W. North Ave. (Oak Park Ave.) | 773-889-9999

"Gorgeous presentations" and a "good variety" of "imaginative", "fresh" Thai fare at "extremely reasonable" prices please patrons of this "casual", "unpretentious" "jewel" on the cusp of Oak Park that's "worth the trip" to the Far West suburbs; N.B. a bargain prix fixe lunch (Tuesday–Friday) and free parking lot sweeten the pot.

NEW Amarit *Thai*   - | - | - | I

Printer's Row | 600 S. Dearborn St. (Harrison St.) | 312-939-1179 | www.amaritthai.com

A new attitude and modern Printer's Row setting revive a former Gold Coast Thai standby, as does the updated menu, featuring some creative dishes (pepper-garlic quail, mussels with wine and cream) plus various Asian standards like tempura udon and kung pao chicken; lots of angles, earth tones, wood and windows make for an attractive setting.

Amber Cafe *American*   24 | 19 | 20 | $44

Westmont | 13 N. Cass Ave. (Burlington Ave.) | 630-515-8080

Western Suburban locals feel "lucky" to have this "excellent" "seasonal" New American "gem" in Westmont with "a real downtown feel", "inviting atmosphere" and "well-priced wine list", even if it's "still figuring some things" out – including service that seesaws from "warm" to "disappointing"; P.S. the "beautiful patio" is "a nice place to sit out in the summer."

American Girl Place Cafe *American*   12 | 21 | 19 | $28

Gold Coast | American Girl Pl. | 111 E. Chicago Ave. (Michigan Ave.) | 312-943-9400 | www.americangirlplace.com

Home of "charming tea parties for girls big and small" and shows in the adjacent theater, this "enchanting" Gold Coast "kiddie cutie" is a "dream"-come-true, making "great memories" for little ones in "mommy training" (there's even "booster chairs for the dolls"); the "setting is a trip" and almost everyone's "happy and excited to be there" – so what if the "overpriced" Traditional American food is "enough to make one pray for boys"; P.S. "at least they serve alcohol" (wine and beer only).

NEW Amira Ⓢ *Italian/Mediterranean*   - | - | - | M

Streeterville | NBC Tower | 455 N. Cityfront Plaza Dr. (E. Illinois St.) | 312-923-9311

Modern Mediterranean and Italian fare (including brick-oven pizzas and calzones) arrive at Streeterville's NBC Tower in a colorful bistro setting with underlit palm trees and a market area for take-out (on weekdays only) soups, salads and panini; N.B. clubby Thursday nights feature small plates, hookahs and live music with belly dancing after 10 PM.

	FOOD	DECOR	SERVICE	COST

Andies *Mideastern*

	18	15	18	$21

Andersonville | 5253 N. Clark St. (Berwyn Ave.) | 773-784-8616 ◗
Uptown | 1467 W. Montrose Ave. (Greenview Ave.) |
773-348-0654
www.andiesres.com

The "good-size portions" of "fresh, flavorful" Middle Eastern cuisine (including "many vegetarian options") are "a great value" at this "reliable" duo of "casual" "standbys" that regularly draw "crowds"; raters who rank them "run-of-the-mill" regret their "ho-hum atmosphere", uneven service (though the "delivery is dependable") and "inconsistent" kitchens, claiming they "might be better if they did fewer things" and did them well; N.B. the Andersonville location serves a brunch buffet and is open later than Uptown.

Angelina Ristorante *Italian*

	20	18	20	$27

Wrigleyville | 3561 N. Broadway (Addison St.) | 773-935-5933 |
www.angelinaristorante.com

Within the "cozy neighborhood" confines of this "romantic" "little storefront" in Wrigleyville, "surprisingly authentic" Southern Italian fare is offered at "reasonable prices" along with "earnest" "service by the adorable Boys Town set" (plus "now they deliver"); inversely, indifferent in-putters lament that it's "inconsistent"; P.S. the Sunday "champagne brunch is a great deal."

Anna Maria Pasteria *Italian*

	19	19	19	$27

Uptown | 4400 N. Clark St. (Montrose Ave.) | 773-506-2662 |
www.annamariapasteria.com

"Sisters Anna and Maria" do "homey", "hearty" Italian food that's "solid, if not spectacular", and "fairly priced" at this "cute" Uptown "neighborhood spot" that draws a "good mix of straights, gays, singles and families"; regulars also appreciate the "friendly service" and credit the siblings for doing a "nice job relocating" in 2005 from their former Wrigleyville digs.

Ann Sather *American/Swedish*

	19	13	18	$16

Andersonville | 5207 N. Clark St. (Foster Ave.) | 773-271-6677
Lakeview | 929 W. Belmont Ave. (Sheffield Ave.) | 773-348-2378
Ann Sather Café *American/Swedish*
Lakeview | 3416 N. Southport Ave. (Roscoe St.) | 773-404-4475
Wrigleyville | 3411 N. Broadway (Roscoe St.) | 773-305-0024
www.annsather.com

You "can't beat the buns" – cinnamon, that is – at this "nothing-fancy" Traditional American–Swedish sisterhood of "solid" full- and cafe-service "standbys" that are "buzzing on weekends" with fans of their "hugely substantial" "family" or "hangover" breakfasts and brunches; still, a few detractors declare them "bland" and "tired."

NEW Anteprima *Italian*

	-	-	-	M

Andersonville | 5316 N. Clark St. (bet. Berwyn & Summerdale Aves.) |
773-506-9990

Andersonville-sweet on the outside and decorator-funky on the inside, this midpriced Italian with a cool cafe atmosphere uses sea-

	FOOD	DECOR	SERVICE	COST

sonal, local and organic ingredients; its budget-friendly, all-Italian wine list offers vino by the quartino.

Antico Posto *Italian*   23 | 20 | 21 | $30
Oak Brook | Oakbrook Center Mall | 118 Oakbrook Ctr. (Rte. 83) | 630-586-9200 | www.leye.com

Boosters boom *"buono!"* for this "cute", "classy" and "relaxing" West Suburban Italian "tucked away in Oakbrook Center", where an "attentive staff" delivers "fresh, delicious" fare from a "varied menu" paired with "a wine list for all occasions" and followed by "great tiny dollar desserts" – all in all, it's "better than expected from a mall restaurant."

Arco de Cuchilleros *Spanish*   19 | 14 | 17 | $27
Lakeview | 3445 N. Halsted St. (Newport Ave.) | 773-296-6046

Amigos of this "overlooked" Spanish spot "hidden" "in the heart of Boys Town" enjoy sampling its 40-plus menu of "reliably delicious", "cheap tapas" along with "sangria on the patio" (there's also a small Iberian wine list); opposers, though, "say *adios* to" what they call "uninteresting" edibles, "sketchy service" and "cramped quarters."

Aria *American/Eclectic*   23 | 23 | 24 | $50
Loop | Fairmont Chicago Hotel | 200 N. Columbus Dr. (South Water St.) | 312-444-9494 | www.ariachicago.com

Friends of this New American–Eclectic eatery in the Fairmont Chicago Hotel maintain that its "menu is like a trip around the world", its wine list is "well thought out" and its "service has improved" of late; the "posh" Loop location is set up for "sleek comfort", with "a bit of space between you and your dining neighbors", and "the bar is good for cozy dessert and drinks"; N.B. they offer a children's menu.

Army & Lou's *Southern*   ▽ 19 | 14 | 16 | $18
Far South Side | 422 E. 75th St. (Martin Luther King Dr.) | 773-483-3100 | www.armyandlous.com

Supporters swear that "soul food could be defined with a picture of this community fixture" on the Far South Side, a "favorite" for "generous portions" of "down-home" Southern sustenance such as the signature short ribs and peach cobbler, all at "reasonable prices" and served by "the sweetest waitresses"; P.S. live jazz on "Friday nights" and a buffet on the first Sunday of every month are added incentives.

Art of Pizza, The *Pizza*   24 | 6 | 16 | $13
Lakeview | 3033 N. Ashland Ave. (Nelson St.) | 773-327-5600

Pie-sanos praise this Lakeview lair as one of the best pizza joints in town, sighing that they "cannot live without the fabulous buttery, crispy crust" of its "excellent" thin version or the "secret sauce" that made its "delish deep dish" "famous" in Chicagoland; true, the "strip-mall storefront" has "no decor to speak of", hence aficionados "always do delivery" – indeed, some say they've "never been inside."

	FOOD	DECOR	SERVICE	COST

Artopolis Bakery, Cafe & Agora ● *Greek/Mediterranean*

| 21 | 17 | 17 | $18 |

Greektown | 306 S. Halsted St. (Jackson Blvd.) | 312-559-9000 | www.artopolischicago.com

A "wonderful little fusion of a bar and coffee shop", this Greektown Greek-Med makes "marvelous", "lighter-than-average" sandwiches and salads and "beautiful desserts" available for "sit-down or takeout"; it's a "hip" hang that's "fun" and "friendly", hence Hellenophiles "can spend all afternoon here" enjoying the "good people-watching" – and the "late service is a godsend" (midnight weekdays, 1 AM on weekends).

☑ Arun's Ⓜ *Thai*

| 28 | 24 | 26 | $88 |

Northwest Side | 4156 N. Kedzie Ave. (bet. Belle Plaine & Berteau Aves.) | 773-539-1909 | www.arunsthai.com

Arun Sampanthavivat's "completely inventive", "customized" 12-course tasting-only menu of "transcendental" Thai is tantamount to "edible art", "served with care and courtesy" in a "simply" "elegant gallery" setting with a "great wine cellar"; sure, it's "tucked in an industrial/residential neighborhood" on the Northwest Side, but it's "as good as the best in Thailand" and "a whole lot easier to get to", even if it "can seem wildly expensive" – in other words, "make sure this is on your 'things to do before I die' list."

a tavola Ⓢ *Italian*

| 23 | 18 | 23 | $43 |

Ukrainian Village | 2148 W. Chicago Ave. (bet. Hoyne Ave. & Leavitt St.) | 773-276-7567 | www.atavolachicago.com

Connoisseurs of Northern Italian flavors favor this "secret", "quiet" "romance-and-fine-dining" destination "hidden in plain sight" in Ukrainian Village for its "small menu" of "sophisticated" savories (such as its "famous risotto" and gnocchi that are like "little pillows of heaven"); "minimal", "elegant" decor and a "knowledgeable", "attentive staff" round out the experience.

Athena ● *Greek*

| 19 | 20 | 19 | $26 |

Greektown | 212 S. Halsted St. (Adams St.) | 312-655-0000 | www.athenarestaurant.com

"The prices are right" at this "family-oriented" Greektown "standard" with a "nice staff" serving "tasty", "basic" Greek cooking; fans feel affection for the "fabulous garden" with its "skyline and stars" during summer (not to mention "winter indoors by the fireplaces"), but critics crow that the "crowds seem to overlook" faults with the fare just "for a chance to dine" "alfresco."

☑ Atwater's *American/French*

| 21 | 24 | 22 | $46 |

Geneva | Herrington Inn | 15 S. River Ln. (State St.) | 630-208-7433 | www.herringtoninn.com

"Hidden" in the Herrington Inn, this "intimate" Suburban West spot offers a "romantic setting" with a "beautiful river view" (especially from the scenic patio); the "creative" New French–New American cuisine is "great", especially "for hotel dining", and Sunday brunch is offered.

	FOOD	DECOR	SERVICE	COST

☑ Atwood Cafe *American* — 21 | 24 | 21 | $37

Loop | Hotel Burnham | 1 W. Washington St. (State St.) | 312-368-1900 | www.atwoodcafe.com

"You feel like you're part of the city's architectural history" at this Traditional American "oasis" in the Loop's "landmark" Hotel Burnham, where a "big-city experience" is "crowded" into "tiny", "cramped" quarters (though "high ceilings" help) amid "magical" "Mad Hatter's Ball" decor; the "trendy comfort food" is offered with "solid service", so many "do lunch", "pre-theater" or a "State Street shopping stop", or perhaps "dine alfresco and enjoy the passersby."

Aurelio's Pizza *Pizza* — 22 | 15 | 18 | $16

Loop | Holiday Inn | 506 W. Harrison St. (Canal St.) | 312-994-2000
Addison | Centennial Plaza | 1455 W. Lake St. (Lombard Rd.) | 630-889-9560
Chicago Heights | 1545 Western Ave. (south of Lincoln Hwy./14th St.) | 708-481-5040
Homewood | 18162 Harwood Ave. (183rd St.) | 708-798-8050
South Holland | 601 E. 170th St. (South Park Ave.) | 708-333-0310
Homer Glen | 13001 W. 143rd St. (Bell Rd.) | 708-645-4400
Palos Heights | 6543 W. 127th St. (Ridgeland Ave.) | 708-389-5170
Tinley Park | 15901 Oak Park Ave. (Rte. 6) | 708-429-4600
Downers Grove | 1002 Warren Ave. (Highland Ave.) | 630-810-0078
Oak Brook | 17 W. 711 Roosevelt Rd. (Summit Rd.) | 630-629-3200
www.aureliospizza.com
Additional locations throughout the Chicago area

Supporters salivate for the "different", "delicious thin-crust" pies with "sweet tomato sauce" and the "great antipasto salad" at these "favorite" "suburban staples"; traditionalists are true to the family-owned Homewood location (the others are franchises) with its "old-fashioned pizza-parlor decor", saying it offers "the best" chow in the chain (in-the-know "regulars ask for theirs cooked in the old oven").

☑ Avec ◐ *Mediterranean* — 25 | 19 | 22 | $42

West Loop | 615 W. Randolph St. (Jefferson St.) | 312-377-2002 | www.avecrestaurant.com

"The fabulous people" "squeeze into" this "must-dine" Med small-plates specialist for the "incredible flavors" of Koren Grieveson's "fantasy" "peasant cuisine", paired with an "eclectic, affordable wine list" and served by a "knowledgeable staff"; its "metrosexual Paul Bunyan" "wood-lined steam-room" setting with "table sharing" and "bench seating" is "not for the anti-social", who lambaste it as "loud" and "wildly uncomfortable", but extroverts enthuse over the "hip" West Loop "scene"; P.S. "if only they took reservations."

Avenue M ◐ *American* — - | - | - | M

Near West | 691-695 N. Milwaukee Ave. (Huron St.) | 312-243-1133 | www.avenue-m.com

Daniel Kelly (of the defunct d.kelly) cooks seasonal New American fare with a steakhouse sensibility at this swanky Near West eatery with an intimate balcony and an outdoor patio festooned with flow-

ering trees and imported grapevines; curtained off from the main dining room is a late-night lounge designed to lure the pretty people.

☑ Avenues M *French/Seafood* | 26 | 26 | 26 | $88 |

River North | Peninsula Hotel | 108 E. Superior St. (bet. Michigan Ave. & Rush St.) | 312-573-6754 | www.chicago.peninsula.com

A trio of 26s conveys surveyors' praise for this "posh", "gracious" River North New French–seafood sophisticate where boulevardiers are buoyed by Graham Elliot Bowles' "amazing tasting menus" and "innovative, avant-garde presentations" – plus the "champagne cart pre-dinner is a nice touch"; the "well-spaced" tables of its "luxurious" Peninsula Hotel setting provide "beautiful views", and service strikes most as "impeccable" (though a smidge "stuffy" to some); P.S. you might want to "come with an expense account or rich aunt" and, if you're a gent, a jacket is recommended as well.

NEW Azucar M *Spanish* | - | - | - | M |

Logan Square | 2647 N. Kedzie Ave. (bet. Milwaukee & Wrightwood Aves.) | 773-486-6464

The name of this sweet little tapas spot located just across from the Logan Square train station means 'sugar' in Spanish; the romantic space is adorned with old-world touches, a colorful Picasso-style mural and a bar at which to enjoy its modern martini menu or red and white sangrias.

Babylon Eatery *Mideastern* | ▽ 17 | 10 | 15 | $13 |

Bucktown | 2023 N. Damen Ave. (McLean Ave.) | 773-342-7482

Middle-Eastern meals at this casual, cafeteria-style Bucktown BYO are a "tasty", "authentic" option for "quick and cheap" dine-in, or "call in your order ahead of time" and do takeout if you're not a fan of that "sandwich-shop look and feel"; N.B. plans are in the offing to switch to table service, and the hookahs are history unless the outdoor dining area is open.

NEW Baccalà ⑤M *Italian* | - | - | - | M |

Wicker Park | 1540 N. Milwaukee Ave. (North Ave.) | 773-227-1400

John Bubala transformed Wicker Park's former Thyme Cafe into this regional Italian focused on hearty Piedmontese fare; the wallet-friendly compact menu is paired with an affordable all-Italian wine list and Goose Island microbrews, and served in a neighborhood-casual storefront setting with cushioned window seats, long banquettes and walls hung with dozens and dozens of paintings.

Bacchanalia ⊅ *Italian* | ▽ 23 | 13 | 21 | $27 |

Southwest Side | 2413 S. Oakley Ave. (bet. 24th & 25th Sts.) | 773-254-6555 | www.bacchanaliachicago.com

"Mouthwatering" "homestyle" Northern Italian fare (order "anything Vesuvio" and "make sure you have a cannoli") is on the menu at this "down-to-earth" dining depot in the Heart of Italy; the "nothing-special decor" seems "right out of the un-cool '50s" (actually, the place opened in 1979), but "enormous portions" ensure "you'll go home with an entire meal in a doggy bag."

	FOOD	DECOR	SERVICE	COST

Bagel, The *Deli*

18 | 11 | 16 | $16

Lakeview | 3107 N. Broadway St. (Belmont Ave.) | 773-477-0300
Skokie | Westfield Shoppingtown | 50 Old Orchard Ctr. (Old Orchard Rd.) |
847-677-0100
www.bagelrestaurant.com

"If you're having a knish fit", consider this pair of "old-time delis" in Skokie and Lakeview for "big portions" of "nosh-worthy fare" such as "softball-size matzo balls" and "mish-mash soup" that "should be served with a snorkel"; fans find comfort in "decor and clientele reminiscent of Miami Beach in the '50s" and even service that ranges from "friendly" to "crabby", but grouches grump they "can't figure out why" these "inconsistent" "greasy spoons are so popular."

Balagio ⊠ *Italian*

▽ 22 | 21 | 21 | $28

Homewood | 18042 Martin Ave. (Ridge Rd.) | 708-957-1650 |
www.balagio-restaurant.com

South-siders say this is a "satisfying" spot for a "pleasant, relaxing dining experience", with "huge portions" of "tasty" Italian eats ("you can easily share with a friend and still have leftovers") presented amid "beautiful decor" – and a "great piano bar"; still, the charms of this "friendly" "neighborhood favorite" may be lost on non-locals.

Ballo ◐ *Italian*

19 | 17 | 18 | $37

River North | 445 N. Dearborn St. (Illinois St.) | 312-832-7700 |
www.rosebudrestaurants.com

Contributors converge on the "partylike atmosphere" at Alex Dana's (Rosebud) "flashy" River North ristorante, complete with "disco ball", "loud music" and "mob movies playing on plasma TVs"; whether the "hearty", "old-fashioned Italian" eats and "antipasto bar" are "surprisingly good" or "nothing to rave about", the scene "hot" or "cheesy", and the service "friendly" or "in-your-face" – maybe because "you can't hear your waiter" – are your call; P.S. after dinner it "turns into a nightclub for late-night revelers."

Bandera *American*

20 | 20 | 19 | $30

Streeterville | 535 N. Michigan Ave., 2nd fl. (bet. Grand Ave. & Ohio St.) |
312-644-3524 | www.houstons.com

Up "on the second floor of the Mag Mile", this Streeterville "comfort-food heaven" is "one of the best locations in town" for a retail respite, "business lunch" or "romantic" interlude over Southwestern-style Traditional American chow like "great rotisserie chicken", "huge salads" and "melt-in-your-mouth mashed potatoes", all of which are "cheap for this neck of the woods" – no wonder there are "loooong waits" at peak periods (though you can "eat at the bar"); P.S. "live jazz" is offered nightly.

Bank Lane Bistro ⊠ Ⓜ *American*

23 | 18 | 20 | $39

Lake Forest | 670 Bank Ln. (bet. Deerpath Rd. & Market Sq.) |
847-234-8802 | www.banklanebistro.com

"Darling" and "discreet", this "little restaurant" that "looks out onto Lake Forest's beautiful, historic Market Square" is "one of

FOOD · DECOR · SERVICE · COST

the more romantic North Shore" options, with a "helpful staff" serving a "sophisticated but not pretentious menu" of "delicious" New American cuisine (try "the daily degustation with wine pairings"); P.S. summertime porch tables are a great way to enjoy this "refreshing choice."

NEW Barcello's Ⓜ Italian/Pizza   — — — M

Wicker Park | 1647 N. Milwaukee Ave. (bet. Concord Pl. & W. Caton St.) | 773-486-8444 | www.barcelloschicago.net

New owners have adopted this veteran Wicker Park trattoria, giving it an extreme makeover but keeping its name and Buick-sized '50s-era brick oven, which now bakes specialty pizza with unusual ingredients (salmon, peaches and pomegranate sauce; Beluga caviar with lobster, chives and crème fraîche) that complement hearty Italian entrees; the face-lift exposed the original brick walls and created a loftlike space accented with mango-hued walls, a black granite bar and red leather chairs.

Bar Louie ◐ American   15 14 15 $19

River North | 226 W. Chicago Ave. (Franklin St.) | 312-337-3313
Wrigleyville | 3545 N. Clark St. (Addison St.) | 773-296-2500
Bucktown | 1704 N. Damen Ave. (Wabansia Ave.) | 773-645-7500
Hyde Park | 5500 S. Shore Dr. (55th St.) | 773-363-5300
South Loop | 47 W. Polk St. (Dearborn St.) | 312-347-0000
Little Italy | 1321 W. Taylor St. (Ashland Ave.) | 312-633-9393
Evanston | 1520 N. Sherman Ave. (Grove St.) | 847-733-8300
Orland Park | 14335 S. LaGrange Rd. (143rd St.) | 708-873-9999
NEW Oak Park | 1122 Lake St. (Harlem Ave.) | 708-725-3300
Naperville | 22 E. Chicago Ave. (Washington St.) | 630-983-1600
www.barlouieamerica.com
Additional locations throughout the Chicago area

Barflies befriend this bevy of "casual" Traditional Americans as "pit stops" for "meeting friends", "ogling" others, enjoying "late-night dining" or just "hanging and watching a game" while snarfing an "interesting" "variety" of "good" "pub food" along with a "great beer selection"; still, skeptics swat at the "noisy" "chain"-sters' "uneven offerings" and "inconsistent service at the various locations."

ⓩ Barrington Country Bistro Ⓢ French   27 21 24 $42

Barrington | Foundry Shopping Ctr. | 700 W. Northwest Hwy. (Hart Rd.) | 847-842-1300 | www.barringtoncountrybistro.com

Toques off to the "top-quality traditional bistro fare" at this "hidden gem" situated in an "inauspicious" Northwest Suburban mall; "excellent service" is provided within a "pleasant country-French setting", and it's all overseen by a particularly "gracious owner"; P.S. "lunch is a special treat."

Basil Leaf Café Italian   21 16 20 $24

Lincoln Park | 2460 N. Clark St. (Fullerton Pkwy.) | 773-935-3388 | www.basilleaf.com

Neighbors of this "cute", "friendly" Lincoln Park Northern Italian nod to its "wide selection" of "yummy pastas", "first-rate salads" and "fresh soups", all at "reasonable prices" and served in an "un-

	FOOD	DECOR	SERVICE	COST

"pretentious" setting that "reminds [some] of Tuscany"; P.S. "it's fun to sit outside" on the "charming patio."

NEW BB's ●🅱 *Eclectic*

	-	-	-	I

River North | 22 E. Hubbard St. (N. State St.) | 312-755-0007

The initials of the late, great restaurateur Bud Binyon grace this River North gastropub from the owners of Stanley's Kitchen & Tap (one the son of Bud), as does his legendary turtle soup; the comfy-chic setting features antique mirrors, a British phone booth and generous portions of Eclectic, bargain-priced comfort food, including Stanley's rave-worthy mac 'n' cheese.

Bella Bacino's *Pizza*

	21	12	15	$18

Lincoln Park | 2204 N. Lincoln Ave. (Webster Ave.) | 773-472-7400
West Loop | 118 S. Clinton St. (Adams St.) | 312-876-1188 🅱
La Grange | 36 La Grange Rd. (Harris Ave.) | 708-352-8882
www.bacinos.com

This threesome of pie purveyors has its partialists, who peg it as their "local pick" for "great" "thin-crust" and "Chicago stuffed" pizza made from "fresh ingredients" (a special mention for the "heart-healthy spinach" version), plus they serve pasta too; P.S. as an "extra bonus", "the Lincoln Avenue location is especially close to the bars."

Bella Notte *Italian*

	23	17	21	$33

Near West | 1374 W. Grand Ave. (Noble St.) | 312-733-5136 | www.bellanottechicago.com

"Head west on Grand" to this "friendly", "family-run" "favorite" if you favor "huge portions" of "old-school Chicago Italian" ("great seafood pasta dishes", and "the stuffed bone-in filet is the bomb") in a "convivial" Near West "neighborhood place"; the only rift among raters is on the relative merits of the "flashier digs" over the "homey" forerunner (next door).

Benihana *Japanese/Steak*

	19	16	20	$34

Wheeling | 150 N. Milwaukee Ave. (Dundee Rd.) | 847-465-6021
Schaumburg | 1200 E. Higgins Rd. (Meacham Rd.) | 847-995-8201
Lombard | 747 E. Butterfield Rd. (Meyers Rd.) | 630-571-4440
www.benihana.com

Those who score these Japanese steakhouse staples as "sentimental favorites" find "fun" in the "circus" of "well-prepared", "reliable seafood-and-steak" teppanyaki "cooked at your table", adding you can "meet some interesting people" thanks to the "communal arrangement"; still, the unenthused, who find the spots more "tired" than "tried-and-true", "expect" more, maintaining "the projectiles should at least be tasty if they're being thrown at my head" – especially since you'll leave with "that just-fried smell."

Ben Pao *Chinese*

	21	22	19	$31

River North | 52 W. Illinois St. (Dearborn St.) | 312-222-1888 | www.benpao.com

"Pillars and waterfalls" in a "glamorous" setting "put you in a mood for an exotic meal" at this "trendy" Lettuce Entertain You Chinese-

"themed palace" in River North, where supporters savor "surprising twists" on Asian food, with "innovative preparations" of "fresh ingredients"; antis, however, allege that the "Americanized" and "expensive" "Disney[-esque] experience" is "disappointing all around."

Berghoff Cafe 🈂 *German*   - | - | - | M

Loop | 17 W. Adams St. (bet. Dearborn & State Sts.) | 312-427-7399 | www.berghoffcafe.com

Berghoff Cafe O'Hare *German*

O'Hare Area | O'Hare Int'l Airport | Concourse C | 773-601-9180
Fleisch und kartoffel fans heartbroken by the closure of longtime Loop German The Berghoff can rejoice over weekday-only lunch at this latest incarnation on the lower-level of the old space, with a slightly modified cafeteria-style menu that adds salad, sandwich and pasta options to the classic Teutonic choices; the former main room upstairs is now a private event facility (The Century Room), and the historic bar has reopened with a new name (17 West); N.B. the airport outpost has a shortened menu.

Best Hunan *Chinese*   21 | 13 | 17 | $23

Vernon Hills | Hawthorn Fashion Sq. | 700 N. Milwaukee Ave. (Rte. 60) | 847-680-8855 | www.besthunan.com
Friends feast on "good size portions" of "some excellent" "traditional Chinese" dishes (and "lunch specials" that "are a great value") at this "comforting" North Shore Hunan-Mandarin mainstay where they "treat you like one of the family"; still, some foes feel Shanghai-ed by what they call "inconsistent" offerings.

Big Bowl *Asian*   18 | 17 | 17 | $22

River North | 60 E. Ohio St. (Rush St.) | 312-951-1888
Gold Coast | 6 E. Cedar St. (State St.) | 312-640-8888
Lincolnshire | 215 Parkway Dr. (Milwaukee Ave.) | 847-808-8880
Schaumburg | 1950 E. Higgins Rd. (Rte. 53) | 847-517-8881
www.bigbowl.com
While "clearly a 'concept'" chain, this stir-fry setup is a great "your-way" option for fans of "fast", "fresh-tasting blends of Americanized Thai, Chinese and other Asian cuisines" plus "addictive" "fresh-made ginger ale" and "hibiscus iced tea" (it's "great for vegetarians" and "kids love it"); longtime supporters insist it's "back on track now that it's an LEYE operation again" after some "corporate shuffling", but those who "preferred the old menu" believe the "bland" bowls "feel mass-produced"; N.B. a recent shift toward organic and sustainable foods is not reflected in the Food score.

Bijan's Bistro ➊ *American*   19 | 17 | 18 | $26

River North | 663 N. State St. (Erie St.) | 312-202-1904 | www.bijansbistro.com
"Pop in for a warm welcome" at this River North "neighborhood bar with a bit more class" than some and a "good, mixed" New American menu that satisfies "celebs", "locals" and "lots of industry people" who "go there when they get off work"; it's especially valued for weekend brunch and as a "late-night" "hangout" for "drunk vittles" (the

kitchen's open till 3:30 AM), even if "bistro is a bit of a misnomer" – it's more in the "below-fine-dining-but-above-coffee-shop category."

NEW Billy Berk's *American/Eclectic*

| - | - | - | M |

Skokie | Westfield Shoppingtown | 3 Old Orchard Shopping Ctr. (Skokie Blvd.) | 847-763-4600 | www.maxsworld.com

Piano bar sing-alongs provide the Broadway soundtrack to this musical-themed newcomer in a sprawling Northwest Suburban shopping-mall setting; the midpriced menu offers a colossal collection of Eclectic and Traditional American items (including burgers, deli classics and monster desserts) with cutesy names; N.B. there's a marble bar loaded with flat-screen TVs.

Billy Goat Tavern *American*

| 15 | 11 | 14 | $12 |

Loop | 309 W. Washington St. (Franklin St.) | 312-899-1873 🅱️🚭
River North | Chicago Mart Plaza | 350 N. Orleans St. (W. Kinzie St.) | 312-464-1045 🅱️
River North | 430 N. Lower Michigan Ave. (Illinois St.) | 312-222-1525 ◑🚭
Streeterville | Navy Pier | 700 E. Grand Ave. (Lake Shore Dr.) | 312-670-8789
O'Hare Area | O'Hare Field Terminal 1 | Concourse C | 773-462-9368
South Loop | 330 S. Wells St. (Van Buren St.) | 312-554-0297 🅱️🚭
West Loop | 1535 W. Madison St. (Ogden Ave.) | 312-733-9132 🚭
www.billygoattavern.com

Among this herd of Traditional American "joints", the original "shrine" "down in the belly of the el" is a "dingy" "icon" with a "storied past" ("home of the Cubs curse") offering a "salt-of-the-earth Chicago-style" experience famed for "paper-thin" "cheezborgers" and "lousy" service; still, shrinking violets who keep "waiting for the grill man to press a hamburger patty in his armpit" say your "time and money are better spent renting a video of the *Saturday Night Live* skit."

❷ Bin 36 *American/French*

| 20 | 19 | 20 | $39 |

River North | 339 N. Dearborn St. (Kinzie St.) | 312-755-9463 | www.bin36.com

❷ Bin Wine Café Ⓜ *American/French*

Wicker Park | 1559 N. Milwaukee Ave. (Damen Ave.) | 773-486-2233 | www.binwinecafe.com

"Hip" and "happening", these "swanky but approachable" (and sometimes "noisy") River North and Wicker Park New American–French bistro "scenes" feature "fun flights" of "esoteric" *vins*, a "mind-boggling cheese list" and "great appetizers" that are generally considered "better than" the "unremarkable entrees", all served by staffers who "actually know a little bit about the wines" – "all of [which] can be purchased right there"; P.S. insiders assert that the "mini-Bin" cafe may be "even more delightful."

Birch River Grill *American*

| - | - | - | M |

Arlington Heights | 75 W. Algonquin Rd. (Arlington Heights Rd.) | 847-427-4242

Upscale down-home eats issue from the 'American kitchen' of this Northwest Suburban lodge from the team behind Karma and Dine;

if the hearty, moderately priced offerings (e.g. Yankee pot roast, banana cream pie) don't soothe diners, the comfy room with rustic wood-and-leather accents, cushy banquettes and a stone fireplace certainly will; N.B. open for breakfast, lunch and dinner.

Bistro Campagne *French*

23 | 21 | 21 | $38

Lincoln Square | 4518 N. Lincoln Ave. (bet. Sunnyside & Wilson Aves.) | 773-271-6100 | www.bistrocampagne.com

"Hearty, healthy" and "wonderful" "provincial French bistro" cuisine exhibiting chef-owner Michael Altenberg's "commitment" to "working with the best organic farms in the area" delights denizens of this "tiny" (some say "cramped") and "romantic" Lincoln Square "find" where the "beer list is as interesting as the wine list", the service "experienced" and "personable", and the "pretty" "patio transports you to the countryside" – in other words, it's "the kind of place you wish were a secret."

Bistro Kirkou *French*

22 | 18 | 22 | $45

Lake Zurich | 500 Ela Rd. (Maple Ave.) | 847-438-0200

"Creative combinations" of "delicious" French bistro fare, "friendly, efficient service" and a "gracious" host-owner (one of the house's "Le Titi de Paris alumni") make this "small, intimate" setting with multiple rooms, murals and a fireplace "one of the bright spots" in the Northwest Suburbs; still, naysayers nag it's "noisy" and "uninspired"; N.B. lunch is only served on Thursdays and Fridays.

NEW Bistro Monet M *French*

- | - | - | M

Glen Ellyn | 462 Park Blvd. (bet. Crescent Blvd. & Duane St.) | 630-469-4002

Glen Ellyn's Les Deux Autres has been replaced by this midpriced French bistro whose thoughtful menu of Continental comfort food will please classicists – as will the offering of city-illicit foie gras; warm wood paneling still adorns the intimate, refined space, but the fabric wall coverings have been 86-ed in favor of prints by its namesake.

Bistro 110 *French*

20 | 19 | 19 | $39

Gold Coast | 110 E. Pearson St. (bet. Michigan Ave. & Rush St.) | 312-266-3110 | www.bistro110restaurant.com

"For years" this "reliable" Gold Coast "crowd-pleaser" has been a "favorite" of Francophiles who find "comfort" in its "traditional" bistro cooking, including its "signature roasted garlic" ("just hand it over and no one will get hurt"); still, quoters quibble over whether it's "reasonable" or "overpriced", the ambiance is "quaint" or "fake" and the service "friendly" or *trop* "French" in "attitude", while other "disappointed" diners deem it "tired" and "touristy" because of its "prime" "off-Michigan" location.

Bistrot Margot *French*

21 | 19 | 20 | $37

Old Town | 1437 N. Wells St. (bet. North Ave. & Schiller St.) | 312-587-3660

"Authentic French bistro food" "done well" is the draw at this "romantic", "unpretentious" eatery, causing one devotee to exclaim, "Old Town residents are lucky to have this as their neighborhood place", even if the high "noise level" makes it "conversation-challenging"

("try to sit upstairs where tables are not on top of each other");
P.S. check out the outdoor seats and "great" Saturday–Sunday brunch.

Bistrot Zinc *French* | 20 | 20 | 20 | $36 |

Gold Coast | 1131 N. State St. (bet. Cedar & Elm Sts.) | 312-337-1131 |
www.bistrotzinc.com

"Your classic neighborhood bistro" is a "quiet getaway" just "a few
paces from the hubbub of Rush Street", where the "good take on standard" French food and "charming atmosphere" (an "authentic zinc
bar") serve up "a little bit of Paris in the Gold Coast"; P.S. contributors
compliment the "outstanding child-friendly weekend brunch."

Bite Cafe *Eclectic* | ▽ 23 | 13 | 18 | $18 |

Ukrainian Village | 1039 N. Western Ave. (Cortez St.) | 773-395-2483
Ukrainian Villagers tout the "tasty regular dishes" (including weekend brunch) plus "fancy specials" of Eclectic eats at this "out-of-
the-way" outpost with "a grunge setting" and a staff that just might
sport "the most body piercings per server in Chicago" – and all at a
cost that "doesn't take a bite out of your wallet"; N.B. you can BYO
from The Empty Bottle music club next door.

☑ Blackbird ☒ *American* | 27 | 20 | 23 | $57 |

West Loop | 619 W. Randolph St. (bet. Desplaines & Jefferson Sts.) |
312-715-0708 | www.blackbirdrestaurant.com

Make sure this "fabulously polished" West Loop "classic" is on your
list for "pure tastes in a pure space", featuring "local, organic and
unique ingredients" in "exquisite" New American cuisine that
"makes you proud to be from Chicago"; the setting may be "stark"
("the whole white on white thing"), the "tables cramped" and the
"din" "astonishing", but there's "plenty of eye candy", plus "consum-
mately professional" service and "one of the highest-quality wine
selections in the city, at all price ranges"; N.B. the Food rating may
not reflect the addition of Mike Sheerin (ex NYC's WD-50) as chef
de cuisine, taking over the kitchen reins from owner Paul Kahan.

Blind Faith Café *Vegetarian* | 19 | 14 | 17 | $19 |

Evanston | 525 Dempster St. (Chicago Ave.) | 847-328-6875 |
www.blindfaithcafe.com

A "vegetarian's delight" with "vegan choices too" (they serve eggs
but no meat) in an "arty section of Evanston", this "homey" "'70s
throwback" is "accommodating to additions/substitutions for a
given diet", and loyalists "love the baked goods" from the in-house
bakery and the "fresh smoothies"; still, some slam the "erratic service" and suggest it's "slightly overpriced" "for health food";
P.S. "for self-service, sit in the front cafe area."

NEW Blu Coral *Japanese* | - | - | - | M |

Wicker Park | 1265 N. Milwaukee Ave. (bet. Ashland Ave. & Paulina St.) |
773-252-2020
Woodridge | 6320 S. Rte. 53 (Mulligan Dr.) | 630-719-8808
www.blucoralsushi.com

Wicker Park and Woodridge are the latest locales to benefit from the
urban sushi sensibilities of the Starfish/Swordfish/Wildfish crowd,

whose formula mixing fresh, raw fish and contemporary Japanese creations, generous sake and martini lists, and loungey environs played a large role in sexing up suburban supping; these sleek twins are dressed in a cool red, white and blue color scheme, with cozy booths and banquettes, and clubby background music; N.B. an Evanston branch is in the works.

Bluefin *Japanese* | 21 | 18 | 16 | $32

Bucktown | 1952 W. North Ave. (Milwaukee Ave.) | 773-394-7373 | www.bluefinsushibar.com

A "head-turning crowd" gathers for "always-good sushi" "with some inventive rolls" and "great lunch specials" at this "dark" Bucktown Japanese that some swear by as a "date spot"; other fin-atics disagree, though, declaring they've "had better for the price" and sinking the service as "spotty" – perhaps accounting for its rating plunge.

Blue Water Grill *American* | 22 | 23 | 20 | $48

River North | 520 N. Dearborn St. (Grand Ave.) | 312-777-1400 | www.brguestrestaurants.com

This "trendy" New American "East Coast transplant" and "sophisticated watering hole" in River North's "old Spago space" is a "New York–style" "scene" where "the focus is on unique seafood preparations" (special mention for the "sushi and raw oyster bars"); "cool drinks", an "amazing Sunday brunch" and an upstairs lounge with a DJ (on Friday and Saturday nights) also win praise from the "hip yet diverse crowd", though sticklers would still "throw this one back" for a "contrived" concept, "disjointed" service and "expense-account prices."

Z Bob Chinn's Crab House *Seafood* | 23 | 13 | 19 | $36

Wheeling | 393 S. Milwaukee Ave. (Dundee Rd.) | 847-520-3633 | www.bobchinns.com

"They crank it out" at this "fun" North Suburban "fresh-fish" "factory" and mai tai "madhouse", which serves "seafood by the ton" in a "tacky", "cavernous" "picnic setting"; "crab lovers" who "survive the wait" to savor its 100-plus options and "monster salad bar" maintain it's "a mind-blower for out-of-towners" (with an "awesome children's menu" too), but grumps grade it "greasy, pricey" and "noisy", noting they "don't like getting the bum's rush" – though if you "go at lunch, [they're] not as crazy to get you out the door."

Bob San ◑ *Japanese* | 23 | 18 | 20 | $34

Wicker Park | 1805 W. Division St. (Wood St.) | 773-235-8888 | www.bob-san.com

Bob Bee's "hip but relaxed" sister to Sushi Naniwa scores with "excellent", "creative" Japanese "cooked and raw fish" and generally "good service" offered amid a "real", "funky" Wicker Park "neighborhood vibe"; it's peopled with "singles, couples and young families", many of who enjoy the outdoor dining option, even if buzzkills bet there are "some better values out there."

	FOOD	DECOR	SERVICE	COST

Bogart's Charhouse *Steak* | 21 | 18 | 19 | $35 |

Homewood | 18225 Dixie Hwy. (183rd St.) | 708-798-2000
Tinley Park | 17344 Oak Park Ave. (bet. North & 171st Sts.) | 708-532-5592
"The first thing you see is the meat cooler and BBQs flaring" at these
similar but separately owned South and Southwest Suburban steakhouses praised by "Humphrey Bogart fans" for purveying "great
steaks for the price" and "free table salads" within an "atmosphere
that puts you right in the middle of Casablanca"; pickier eaters pronounce the pair "pleasant" and "a good choice if you're in the neighborhood", but "not worth a special trip."

BOKA *American* | 23 | 22 | 22 | $46 |

Lincoln Park | 1729 N. Halsted St. (North Ave.) | 312-337-6070 |
www.bokachicago.com
"Finally, a good pre-theater spot that you'd actually visit even when
you don't have Steppenwolf tickets" fawn flatterers of this Lincoln
Parker's "creative" small and large plates (from a seasonal New
American "menu that changes all the time"), "attractive staff" and
"sophisticated", "high-energy" "date" environment; hecklers, however, hiss about "hype for not a lot of substance", noting it "can be
noisy" and "prices are a little steep", but all agree it has "one of the
best outdoor seating areas"; N.B. the arrival of chef Giuseppe
Tentori (ex Charlie Trotter's) is not reflected in the Food score.

Bongo Room *American* | 24 | 17 | 17 | $18 |

Wicker Park | 1470 N. Milwaukee Ave. (Honore St.) | 773-489-0690
South Loop | 1152 S. Wabash Ave. (Roosevelt Rd.) | 312-291-0100
www.bongoroom.com
Delighted drummers who "dream about" the "interesting pancake
options" arrive "early to get a seat" for the "indulgent" weekend
brunch (they don't serve dinner) at this "Wicker Park standard" with
a "varied and delicious" Traditional American menu that's "worth
every penny and calorie", adding "if you don't want to wait an hour"
try the "great" South Loop location; that said, jaded jurists wonder
"what are all of those people waiting for?"

Boston Blackie's *Hamburgers* | 19 | 13 | 16 | $18 |

Loop | 120 S. Riverside Plaza (bet. Adams & Monroe Sts.) |
312-382-0700 🗲
Streeterville | 164 E. Grand Ave. (St. Clair St.) | 312-938-8700
Deerfield | 405 Lake Cook Rd. (Rte. 43) | 847-418-3400
Glencoe | Hubbard Woods Plaza | 73 Green Bay Rd. (Scott Ave.) |
847-242-9400
Arlington Heights | 222 E. Algonquin Rd. (Tonne Dr.) | 847-952-4700
www.bostonblackies.com
You "need a big mouth" for the "juicy, delicious", "gut-stuffing burgers" at these "classic" Traditional American city and suburban
"joints" that loyalists laud as "dependable stops" for "good, cheap
eats" in a "no-frills", "retro" "sports-bar" atmosphere; still, bummed
beef eaters aren't lining up for what they call "serviceable food",
"variable" service and an annoying "à la carte" price structure –
"with surcharges for basic extras that should be included."

	FOOD	DECOR	SERVICE	COST

🆕 Bourbon ◑ *Southern*   - | - | - | M

Lakeview | 3244 N. Lincoln Ave. (Melrose St.) | 773-880-9520 | www.bourbononlincoln.com

This Lakeview Southern specialist takes its namesake tipple seriously – there are thirtysomething bourbons behind the bar (reinforced by a slew of Irish whiskeys) and bourbon in most of the moderately priced menu items; the dark, easygoing front bar is neighborhood casual, while the back dining room has a rumpus room feel with bare wood tables and padded orange walls.

☑ Brasserie Jo *French*   22 | 21 | 20 | $40

River North | 59 W. Hubbard St. (bet. Clark & Dearborn Sts.) | 312-595-0800 | www.brasseriejo.com

As its steady scoring since last Survey suggests, this Lettuce Entertain You River North 11-year-old remains a "favorite" for fans of its "nicely presented", "delicious" brasserie "comfort food", "extensive beer and wine list" and locale that's "like walking into a 1940s-era Paris" boîte ("large and noisy, as it ought to be"); still, contrarians contend "there are better" examples with "better prices" and "wish the service were as good as the food"; P.S. the sidewalk cafe is "dog-friendly."

🆕 Bravo Tapas & Lounge ◑ *Spanish*   - | - | - | M

Wicker Park | 2047 W. Division St. (Damen Ave.) | 773-278-2727

Situated on three levels, this Spanish sizzler in Wicker Park packs plenty of sex appeal with chile pepper pendulum lights, pulsating music and a water wall; swanksters sip sangria and munch from a big menu of hot and cold tapas or head to the lower-level lounge for DJs, flamenco dancers and occasional live music; N.B. the entire facade opens to a fountain and sidewalk seating on bustling Division Street.

Brazzaz *Brazilian/Steak*   23 | 21 | 24 | $57

River North | 539 N. Dearborn St. (Grand Ave.) | 312-595-9000 | www.brazzaz.com

"Go hungry" but "pace yourself" at this "modern", "elegant" "carnivores' heaven" serving 20-ish varieties of unlimited "grilled protein" with an "unbelievable salad bar" of "warm and cold foods"; eaters enthuse it's an "expense-account outing" that "should be called 'pizzazz' for the sharp and fun experience it delivers", making it a "nice addition to the Brazilian steakhouses that have proliferated in the River North area"; N.B. lunch is less than half the cost of dinner.

Breakfast Club, The *American*   19 | 12 | 18 | $14

West Town | 1381 W. Hubbard St. (Noble St.) | 312-666-2372 | www.chicagobreakfastclub.com

"The 'morning after' crowd" makes its way to this "breakfast nook" "hidden down by the rail tracks" in West Town for "tasty diner-style food" served amid "homey" "pink decor" that reminds some of "eating at grandma's" – especially if the old gal was known for giving "brusque service"; N.B. name notwithstanding, lunch is also served.

	FOOD	DECOR	SERVICE	COST

Bricks *Pizza* — 21 | 14 | 17 | $19

Lincoln Park | 1909 N. Lincoln Ave. (Wisconsin St.) | 312-255-0851 | www.brickspetaluma.com

"As underground as its underground location", this Lincoln Park parlor serves "gourmet" "thin-crust pizzas" in a "groovy" atmosphere with "fun servers", "reasonable pricing" and a "strong beer" list – though the "cavernous" confines are "cozy" and "relaxed" to some raters, "dark" and "dank" to others.

Brioso Ⓜ *Mexican* — 19 | 14 | 18 | $27

Lincoln Square | 4603 N. Lincoln Ave. (Wilson Ave.) | 773-989-9000

Touters of this "trendy" Lincoln Square taqueria appreciate its "fun", "friendly" feel and "hearty" fare, saying its "interesting" "Nuevo-Mexican" meals are "Americanized, but in a good way"; detractors declare the fare "not authentic", though, and decry the "minimal decor", but all agree the drinks are "highly recommended" – as is the outdoor cafe.

NEW Broadway Cellars Ⓜ *American* — - | - | - | M

Edgewater | 5900 N. Broadway (Rosedale Ave.) | 773-944-1208 | www.broadwaycellars.net

Replacing the former South in an underserved strip of Edgewater, this New American entry has a cozy wine-cellar setting, with racks and racks of vino serving as both decor and not-so-subliminal advertising for the flights that can be customized to your taste and meal; the affordable bistro-like menu boasts creative, casual cuisine with Italian and other global influences.

NEW Brockway Chophouse *Steak* — - | - | - | E

Palatine | 110 N. Brockway St. (Slade St.) | 847-963-0600 | www.brockwaychophouse.com

Prime aged steaks, more than a half-dozen house microbrews and a 200-bottle wine list lure Northwest Suburbanites to this spiffy chophouse handsomely done in dark wood and outfitted with terra-cotta walls, a cigar case and a giant buffalo head; live cabaret entertainment (stylings of Sinatra, Billy Joel, big band) is showcased Wednesday through Saturday nights.

Bruna's Ristorante *Italian* — ▽ 23 | 13 | 19 | $31

Southwest Side | 2424 S. Oakley Ave. (24th Pl.) | 773-254-5550

Heart of Italy habitués get a "warm" reception at this "old-world Italian" "throwback to a great old neighborhood"; there's "nothing innovative or new here" but it's "a reliable red-sauce house" that's like a "walk down memory lane" to "grandma's in Palermo" – especially if her place "needs a face-lift."

Buona Terra Ristorante Ⓜ *Italian* — 24 | 20 | 24 | $28

Logan Square | 2535 N. California Ave. (Logan Blvd.) | 773-289-3800 | www.buona-terra.com

This "lovely little storefront" in Logan Square "welcomes" with "delicious and unpretentious [Northern] Italian food" (a "combination of specialty dishes and old favorites"), "thoughtful service" and

"good wine at reasonable prices", all "in a comfortable environment" with murals, "exposed-brick walls" and a garden; P.S. the "Thursday night prix fixe is an amazing bargain."

Butter ⏢ *American*

22 | 21 | 21 | $53

Greektown | 130 S. Green St. (Adams St.) | 312-666-9813 | www.butterchicago.com

Butter lovers melt for the "innovative" New American cuisine that reveals a "commitment to sustainable ingredients" at this "sleek" and "trendy" Greektowner that's "fast becoming an 'in' spot" ("positive energy" and "pretty things abound"); foes, though, fret it's "all over the map" and "tries a little too hard to be hip", adding that the "small portions do not justify the high price tag"; N.B. the Food rating was compiled before the departure of chef Ryan Poli.

Cab's Wine Bar Bistro *American*

22 | 19 | 23 | $38

Glen Ellyn | 430 N. Main St. (Duane St.) | 630-942-9463 | www.cabsbistro.com

"Solid" New American cuisine "well-prepared" by a chef "with an eye for taste and beauty" and served within an "elegant yet cozy" setting by an "unpretentious staff" that "makes great wine picks" has confreres calling a cab and heading for this "welcoming" West Suburban "find"; N.B. periodic wine dinners are an added draw.

Café Absinthe *American*

23 | 21 | 22 | $42

Bucktown | 1954 W. North Ave. (Damen Ave.) | 773-278-4488

"Creative", "diverse" seasonal New American fare and a "very good wine selection" make the heart grow fonder for aficionados of this "old favorite", who aver it's "aging gracefully" in its "secret" ("entrance through the alley") Bucktown digs; "decadence meets urban chic" within the "minimalist setting" replete with "rustic brick walls" and an "open kitchen", but even converts caution it can be "loud" and the seating "a little crowded."

Cafe Ba-Ba-Reeba! *Spanish*

22 | 19 | 19 | $30

Lincoln Park | 2024 N. Halsted St. (Armitage Ave.) | 773-935-5000 | www.cafebabareeba.com

It's "always" a "lively" "party" at this longtime Lincoln Park "crowd-pleaser" that "preceded the [small-plates] craze by years", where pleased *patróns* "share" "super choices" from a "huge menu" of "delish" Spanish snacks – not to mention the "hearty" weekend brunch and "addictive sangria"; still, tart tipsters testify it's a "tapas tourist trap" that's "resting on its laurels", adding it's "not cheap" when you tally the total; P.S. "in the summer, try to get a table on" the "great patio."

Café Bernard *French*

21 | 17 | 20 | $36

Lincoln Park | 2100 N. Halsted St. (Dickens Ave.) | 773-871-2100 | www.cafebernard.com

It "feels like home" but "tastes like Paris" at this "friendly" French bistro, a "best-kept secret" in Lincoln Park for more than three decades, where the "honest", "hearty" cooking is "reasonably priced", paired with a "thoughtful, value-oriented wine list" and served in

"quaint", "comfortable" digs that are especially appealing "if you're not interested in hype"; P.S. "you can get the same menu around back at the [Red] Rooster [wine bar] for less cash."

NEW Café Bionda *Italian*   - | - | - | M

South Loop | 1924 S. State St. (Archer Ave.) | 312-326-9800
Rosebud vet Joe Farina brings old-school Italian abundance to the South Loop with this white-tablecloth restaurant issuing moderately priced *cucina classico* – including fresh pasta, salumi and 'mama's homemade meatballs' – from an open kitchen; the comfy, masculine decor is an interesting blend of old and new; N.B. a Wicker Park branch is in the works.

Cafe Bolero *Cuban*   21 | 17 | 17 | $25

Bucktown | 2252 N. Western Ave. (bet. Belden Ave. & Lyndale St.) | 773-227-9000 | www.cafebolero.com
"Down-to-earth Cuban cooking" and 110 varieties of rum delight denizens of this "cozy", "no-frills" Bucktown *cucina*; "what it lacks in decor it makes up for" with its "inexpensive", "homestyle staples" and "friendly staff", plus "there's often live music to give you a flavor of [island] life"; P.S. "nice outdoor seating" too.

Cafe Central M *French*   23 | 18 | 21 | $36

Highland Park | 455 Central Ave. (bet. Linden & St. Johns Aves.) | 847-266-7878 | www.cafecentral.net
Make for this "small, intimate" "medium-priced Carlos'" spin-off if you crave "creative", "hearty [French] bistro fare" complemented by a "colorful room and staff" (owner "Debbie [Nieto] makes you feel right at home"); most cafe-goers consider it a "top-notch choice for semi-elegant" North Shore "neighborhood" dining, though a contingent claims it can be "crowded, noisy, uncomfortable" and "a bit pricey for what you get"; P.S. "summertime means south-facing tables under umbrellas" on the sidewalk.

Café des Architectes *French/Mediterranean*   22 | 23 | 20 | $42

Gold Coast | Sofitel Chicago Water Tower | 20 E. Chestnut St. (Wabash Ave.) | 312-324-4063 | www.sofitel.com
Wayfarers say "*oui oui*" to this "chichi" "gem" in the Gold Coast's Sofitel Chicago Water Tower, where the "sharp", "stunning" interior is "one of the finest environments" extant, and dining "outdoors is almost like eating in a park"; the "creative", seasonal New French–Med "food is as good as many restaurants costing much more", and is available for breakfast, weekend brunch, lunch and dinner – plus the attendants are "attentive"; N.B. free valet parking is provided at night.

Z Café Iberico ◑ *Spanish*   23 | 15 | 16 | $26

River North | 739 N. LaSalle St. (bet. Chicago Ave. & Superior St.) | 312-573-1510 | www.cafe-iberico.com
It gets "as crowded and noisy as Pamplona's running of the bulls" at this River North small-plates arena resembling a "huge Spanish university cafeteria", where a "mostly young crowd" willingly weathers "long waits" (no reservations Friday–Saturday) to "drink addictive

	FOOD	DECOR	SERVICE	COST

sangria, feast on" "great-tasting", "authentic" dishes and "make friends with surrounding tables"; critics concede it's "cheap" but complain "you get what you pay for", adding "service could be better" and the "no-frills decor" is "bland."

Café la Cave *Continental*

24 | 23 | 24 | $51

Des Plaines | 2777 Mannheim Rd. (bet. Higgins Rd. & Touhy Ave.) | 847-827-7818 | www.cafelacaverestaurant.com

"Old-fashioned Continental" "fine dining" with "waiters in tuxedos" makes this "one of the better" "special-occasion" "bets for the [O'Hare] area"; it's "right out of the '60s" (it "will remind you of a Sinatra movie set, baby!") but stalwarts who find "romance" in the "room with the cozy fireplace" or "the original cave" swear it "stands the test of time" – though less nostalgic New Agers negate it as "a bit stuffy for the 21st century."

Café le Coq Ⓜ *French*

23 | 22 | 20 | $38

Oak Park | 734 Lake St. (Oak Park Ave.) | 708-848-2233

"Coq a doodle doo!" announce adherents of this "upscale French bistro", a "classy place" proffering "traditional" dinners and a "very good Sunday brunch" with "a fun wine list" in a "charming" Oak Park "storefront space"; fence-sitters, though, feel they're "still waiting for [their] first great dish", find the coop "cramped" and say service is "indifferent" on occasion, quipping "perhaps that gives it an air of authenticity"; N.B. the ratings don't reflect a recent chef change.

Cafe Matou Ⓜ *French*

22 | 19 | 21 | $40

Bucktown | 1846 N. Milwaukee Ave. (bet. Leavitt St. & Oakley Ave.) | 773-384-8911 | www.cafematou.com

Feline friends of this "funky", "out-of-the-way" Bucktown "neighborhood winner", whose name translates as 'tom cat', "purr" over chef-owner Charlie Socher's "consistently interesting and well-prepared" "classic French" food with "sublime sauces" from a "menu that changes often" (plus "exceptional specials"), not to mention the "lovely wine selection"; even so, a litter of catty commenters contends service goes "south" on "off nights."

Cafe Pyrenees Ⓜ *French*

21 | 19 | 19 | $36

Libertyville | Adler Square Shopping Plaza | 1762 N. Milwaukee Ave. (Buckley Rd./Rte. 137) | 847-362-2233 | www.cafepyrenees.com

Satisfied scribes see "solid" "simple everyday French" bistro eats at "reasonable prices", especially the "good lunch deals", and an "attentive staff" at this Libertyville "diamond in the rough"; optimists opine it "hasn't lost any of the charm" since it moved from Vernon Hills (plus now it "has a bar"), but pessimists purport that it "seems like just a regular restaurant" now, judging it just "not as good as it used to be."

Café Selmarie *American*

21 | 16 | 18 | $21

Lincoln Square | 4729 N. Lincoln Ave. (Lawrence Ave.) | 773-989-5595 | www.cafeselmarie.com

The "European mood" is "so authentic you want to pay in euros" at this "kid-friendly" "neighborhood treasure" and "dessert oasis"

FOOD | DECOR | SERVICE | COST

table-ing "tasty meals" of New American "comfort foods" (eager eaters "get up early" for its "champion of breakfasts"); the location "on the fountain park in Lincoln Square" provides "perfect people-watching", and "summer nights are magic" on the "charming" patio.

☑ Café Spiaggia *Italian*

24 | 22 | 23 | $48

Gold Coast | 980 N. Michigan Ave., 2nd fl. (Oak St.) | 312-280-2750 | www.cafespiaggia.com

"If you don't want to wear a tie or go bankrupt, but do want great Italian comfort food" with a "well-chosen wine list to match", head to this Gold Coast "oldie but goldie" ("Spiaggia's little sister") that's "ideal" "for a quick bite" for "business" folk, "super shoppers" or even "when eating solo"; it's a "fun, relaxed place", even if the "eclectic setting" has an "awkward" layout and service is either "pretentious" or has "personality", depending on your point of view.

Café Suron Ⓜ *Mediterranean/Persian*

- | - | - | I

Rogers Park | 1146 W. Pratt Blvd. (Sheridan Rd.) | 773-465-6500 | www.cafesuron.com

Nestled inside a historic building (once a hotel), Rogers Park's Persian-Mediterranean oasis serves both staples and creative dishes in a romantic, modern milieu boasting glass block walls, a sky-blue ceiling, bright artwork and a burbling fountain – made even more pleasant by the bargain prices; N.B. there's a small corkage fee for BYO.

Cafe 28 *Cuban/Mexican*

23 | 19 | 20 | $29

Lakeview | 1800-1806 W. Irving Park Rd. (Ravenswood Ave.) | 773-528-2883 | www.cafe28.org

For a "first date" or "gathering" "with a group", this "classy" Lakeview "favorite" yields "yummy Cuban" and Mexican meals (including an "amazing brunch") made from "the freshest ingredients" and accompanied by "fabulous mojitos"; "on quiet nights, it's a symphony", but it's "a cacophony on busy weekends" when "crowds pack the place" – and the sometimes "slow service" combined with a "no-reservations" policy means you should "expect long waits."

Caliterra Bar & Grille *American/Italian*

23 | 19 | 21 | $49

Streeterville | Wyndham Chicago | 633 N. St. Clair St. (Erie St.) | 312-274-4444 | www.wyndhamchicago.com

A "pleasant surprise" awaits voyagers who venture to this Streeterville venue with a "refined, distinctive menu" of "spot-on", "wine-friendly" New American–Italian cuisine and one of "Chicago's best cheese carts"; supporters surmise "some of the locals think it's just a 'hotel dining room' and miss out on a great experience", asserting "if it weren't hidden on the second floor [of the Wyndham Chicago] it would be packed every night."

Campagnola *Italian*

23 | 20 | 22 | $39

Evanston | 815 Chicago Ave. (Washington St.) | 847-475-6100 | www.campagnolarestaurant.com

"Combinations of organic and wholesome ingredients" make for "creative, interesting" fare at this "friendly" "outpost for unique Italian dining", an "upscale" "North Shore treasure" where a "thought-

FOOD DECOR SERVICE COST

ful wine selection" and "service with a delicate touch" are also offered in a "cozy", "understated atmosphere"; P.S. its "outdoor dining is a welcome treat in warmer months."

Canoe Club *American*
19 | 25 | 17 | $35

Orland Park | 15200 S. 94th Ave. (151st St.) | 708-460-9611 | www.thecanoeclubrestaurant.com

It's "like a high-budget beach movie" – complete with "palm trees" and "live sharks" – at this "island-friendly" New American installation serving what swayed surveyors say is "some of the freshest seafood in the South Suburbs", all washed down with "great tropical drinks"; the tide is out, however, for voters who veto the vittles as "variable", say the service is "so-so" and judge the "gymnasium"-sized Hawaiian setting "cute" "until you try to hold a conversation."

Cape Cod Room *Seafood*
21 | 21 | 21 | $52

Streeterville | Drake Hotel | 140 E. Walton Pl. (Michigan Ave.) | 312-787-2200 | www.thedrakehotel.com

The seas part for this "clubby" Streeterville seafood "standby" "with a maritime theme", "a welcome anachronism in food and service style" if you're a "sucker for red-check tablecloths", "Bookbinder soup" "served with a side of sherry" and "Dover sole deboned as it should be"; critics, however, crab that this "classic" is "coasting", snapping "service is not their strong point" and quipping "the only thing that has changed in [74] years is the prices."

Capital Grille, The *Steak*
24 | 23 | 24 | $55

Streeterville | 633 N. Saint Clair St. (Ontario St.) | 312-337-9400
NEW **Lombard** | 87 Yorktown Shopping Ctr. (Highland Ave.) | 630-627-9800
www.thecapitalgrille.com

Lobbyists laud this "loud, lively" Streeterville meatery as an "excellent chain steakhouse" where you can order a "juicy, tender" "dry-aged steak" (though purists would prefer it "if they served prime beef" rather than choice) and "more than a few fish options", backed by an "oenophile's dream wine list" and "out-of-this-world" pineapple martinis; with "polished service" from a staff that does "plenty of sucking up, which is needed given the high prices", it has all "the trappings of a fine power-dinner locale"; N.B. the Lombard offshoot opened post-Survey.

◪ Carlos' *French*
29 | 25 | 28 | $89

Highland Park | 429 Temple Ave. (Waukegan Ave.) | 847-432-0770 | www.carlos-restaurant.com

A "memorable evening" awaits visitors to this 25-year-old North Shore "treasure", a "fine-dining" "temple on Temple Avenue" that's ranked No. 1 for Food among Chicagoland restaurants on the strength of its "superb", "very creative" New French fare, which is accompanied by a "fantastic wine list" and served by a "staff that knows when to be friendly and when to be reserved"; the feel is "formal yet extremely comfortable, with cozy booths and soft lighting", making it a "great celebration place" – "if you can afford it"; N.B. jackets required.

	FOOD	DECOR	SERVICE	COST

NEW Carlos & Carlos M *Italian* — | — | — | M

Arlington Heights | 115 W. Campbell St. (Vail Ave.) | 847-259-5227 | www.carlosandcarlosinc.com

Longtime locals will recall the Carlos & Carlos name from the defunct Bucktown fave, now resurrected in the Northwest 'burbs in Arlington Heights' Metropolis Performing Arts Center; a lovely, wallet-friendly Northern Italian menu of fresh preparations (e.g. duck carpaccio with raspberry vinaigrette), homemade pastas/risotti and classics like chicken Vesuvio and their beloved house salad is offered amid an upscale bistro setting with Mediterranean-blue tablecloths, bay windows and high-tech light fixtures.

Carlucci *Italian* 19 | 18 | 18 | $36

Rosemont | Riverway Complex | 6111 N. River Rd. (Higgins Rd.) | 847-518-0990
Downers Grove | 1801 Butterfield Rd. (I-355) | 630-512-0990
www.carluccirestaurant.com

These fraternal twins with separate owners fare solidly for "straightforward and satisfying" Northern Italian and "imaginative, well-seasoned specials" (though "lunch is where the real bargains are"); still, testy tipsters testify that the Rosemont and Downers Grove "transplants" "will never measure up to the [bygone] original" "in Lincoln Park", observing the output is "ordinary" and the "service uneven" (plus "busy" can mean "noisy").

Carmichael's
Chicago Steak House ● *Steak* 22 | 18 | 21 | $41

West Loop | 1052 W. Monroe St. (bet. Morgan St. & S. Aberdeen St.) | 312-433-0025 | www.carmichaelsteakhouse.com

West Loop surveyors peg this as "primarily a neighborhood place" for "great steaks" "prepared exactly to your liking", as well as other "tasty" "standard steakhouse fare" and a "reasonably priced wine list", served in an "open, casual atmosphere" with a "fabulous outdoor patio"; moderates maintain it has "nothing distinctive" to offer, though, except its "proximity to the United Center."

Carmine's ● *Italian* 21 | 18 | 20 | $39

Gold Coast | 1043 N. Rush St. (bet. Bellevue Pl. & Cedar St.) | 312-988-7676 | www.rosebudrestaurants.com

To allies, this gregarious Gold Coast offshoot of the Rosebud family tree is a "hot spot" for "gargantuan" heaps of "honest-to-goodness Italian" "pasta and other delights" delivered in a "hopping" house where nightly "entertainment is a plus" – enjoying "brilliant live piano" within or "eating outside to watch all the action" on Rush Street; even antis who argue that the food is "not fabulous" and the prices are "above average" grant it's "good for tourists."

Z Carnivale *Nuevo Latino* 22 | 25 | 19 | $40

West Loop | 702 W. Fulton St. (Halsted St.) | 312-850-5005 | www.carnivalechicago.com

"Fun, loud and colorful describe the room, clientele and staff" at this wild West Loop "warehouse" where "exciting" Nuevo Latino menu

FOOD | DECOR | SERVICE | COST

items meet "enormous", "eye-popping" environs, "another amazing visual masterpiece" from Jerry Kleiner (Marché, Red Light); it's "the best party in town", even if it's "expensive for what it is", "service could use a little work" and the noise level can be "almost painful."

Carson's Ribs BBQ
20 | 13 | 17 | $30

River North | 612 N. Wells St. (Ontario St.) | 312-280-9200
Deerfield | 200 N. Waukegan Rd. (bet. Deerfield & Lake Cook Rds.) | 847-374-8500
www.ribs.com

"Finger-licking" loyalists love these City and North Suburban bastions of BBQ for "great messy ribs" with the "zesty" "special house sauce" (and "don't neglect" the "two-inch pork chops" or "au gratin potatoes that are worth a trip on their own"); still, others are unimpressed by what they call the "kitchen's uneven results"; N.B. ratings may not reflect the "aging" Downtown location's remodeling and menu updates.

Catch 35 Seafood
23 | 21 | 21 | $43

Loop | Leo Burnett Bldg. | 35 W. Wacker Dr. (bet. Dearborn & State Sts.) | 312-346-3500
Naperville | 35 S. Washington St. (bet. Benton & Van Buren Aves.) | 630-717-3500
www.catch35.com

One catchword for these "inventive" Asian-inspired seafood and steak sisters is "keeper" claim converts "hooked on" their "oh-so-fresh fish and the various ways it's prepared" (and an "interesting wine list"); the "pre-theater" and "expense-account business crowd" can afford the "power prices" at the Loop original (if the "'80s decor" feels too "corporate", try the "congenial, crowded piano bar"), and the West Suburban site attracts a "trendy Naperville scene" – that said, doubters dub them "not exceptional."

Cereality Cereal Bar & Cafe American
16 | 16 | 18 | $8

Loop | 100 S. Wacker Dr. (Monroe St.) | 312-506-0010 🏢
NEW Evanston | 1622 Sherman Ave. (bet. Church & Davis Sts.) | 847-864-4400
www.cereality.com

The "faddish" "fun" makes "you feel like a kid" at this "clever" "fave" where "efficient" counter staffers in "pajamas (that's right, folks: pajamas)" bowl over surveyors with a "unique" menu of "fabulous cereal concoctions" served in a "zippy" space with "great outdoor river seating"; some soggy skeptics "want to scream 'oh, grow up already'", but it's still Chicagoland's Best Bang for the Buck – after all, "you can afford it even if you're still on an allowance"; N.B. the older Loop location is closed on Sunday.

NEW Chalkboard American
– | – | – | M

Lincoln Square | 4343 N. Lincoln Ave. (bet. Montrose & Pensacola Aves.) | 773-477-7144

A giant chalkboard menu listing seasonal New American creations and updated comfort-food classics is one of the design elements of this Lincoln Square redo of the former Tournesol, along with striped banquettes, framed mirrors and chandeliers, all of which create a

quaint cafe feel; prices – including the wine list with chef's tasting notes – are moderate, while Sunday brunch is an added attraction.

☑ Charlie Trotter's ⑤ *American* | 27 | 25 | 27 | VE |

Lincoln Park | 816 W. Armitage Ave. (Halsted St.) | 773-248-6228 | www.charlietrotters.com

"A religious experience" "worth a mortgage payment" awaits at this Lincoln Parker, the "epitome of [New] American gastronomy" and Chicagoland's Most Popular restaurant, where customers are "dazzled" by "brilliant" chef Charlie Trotter's daily changing menu (with "fantastic pairings" from an "exceptional wine cellar") and "cosseted" by a "masterfully courteous and knowledgeable" staff; a few find the "formal" feel "churchlike" and the whole experience a bit "precious", but most maintain it's "absolutely sublime", especially if you "get a reservation at the kitchen table"; N.B. jackets required, and be aware that it's only open on some Mondays.

☑ Cheesecake Factory *American* | 19 | 19 | 17 | $25 |

Streeterville | John Hancock Ctr. | 875 N. Michigan Ave. (bet. Chestnut St. & Delaware Pl.) | 312-337-1101 ●

Lincolnshire | Lincolnshire Commons | 930 Milwaukee Ave. (W. Aptakisic Rd.) | 847-955-2350

Skokie | Westfield Shoppingtown | 374 Old Orchard Ctr. (Skokie Blvd.) | 847-329-8077

Schaumburg | Woodfield Mall | 53 Woodfield Rd. (Golf Rd.) | 847-619-1090

Oak Brook | Oakbrook Center Mall | 2020 Spring Rd. (bet. Harger Rd. & 22nd St.) | 630-573-1800

www.thecheesecakefactory.com

The "cheesecake lives up to the hype" at these "kid-friendly" city and suburban "crowd-pleasers" that are "remarkably consistent" for their "ridiculously large" Traditional American menus, "absurd waits" and "portions for giants", though some chide them as "cheesy", "cookie-cutter" "contributors to America's expanding waistline" that are "oversized", "overwhelming" and "overrun with tourists"; P.S. "lucky" Streeterville diners can "snag an outdoor table" on Michigan Avenue.

Chef's Station *American* | 23 | 18 | 21 | $42 |

Evanston | Davis Street Metro Station | 915 Davis St. (Church St) | 847-570-9821 | www.chefs-station.com

Commenters commute to this haute hideaway "at the intersection of creative and casual" in Evanston for "great quality" New American dining with an "excellent wine list" (the "prix fixe meal with wine flight is a terrific value"); less enthusiastic eaters equivocate over "uneven service" and "quirky", "un-hip decor", but all agree you can "have a lovely summer" meal on the patio.

Chens *Chinese* | 23 | 20 | 20 | $23 |

Wrigleyville | 3506 N. Clark St. (Addison St.) | 773-549-9100 | www.chenschicago.com

Fans appreciate the "new twists on Chinese" and Japanese fare – including "low-fat options" and "excellent sushi" – made with "high-quality ingredients" at this "fun place" with a "hip", "modern setting"

that makes it "look more expensive than it is" ("it's hard to believe you're eating just a block from Wrigley Field"); P.S. the "delivery guys" are so "quick" they seem to "arrive before you hang up the phone."

Chez Joël *French*

| 22 | 18 | 19 | $37 |

Little Italy | 1119 W. Taylor St. (Racine Ave.) | 312-226-6479 | www.chezjoelbistro.com

"France comes to Little Italy and triumphs" testify touters of this "surprise" French find featuring "fresh", "quality bistro dining" "in the middle of the spaghetti belt"; expansive eaters say the "cute" space is "sometimes a little *too* cozy" (i.e. "very cramped"), but those who find it "comfortable" – especially the "beautiful backyard patio" – are "thankful" that "it's not that well known."

☑ Chicago Chop House *Steak*

| 25 | 20 | 22 | $54 |

River North | 60 W. Ontario St. (bet. Clark & Dearborn Sts.) | 312-787-7100 | www.chicagochophouse.com

A "heavy hitter" "in a city that knows meat", this "quintessential Chicago steak joint" and "ol' boys club" in River North "is rich in tradition – and you can taste it in the food" (including "wonderful prime rib") not to mention see it in the "historical" setting with "tin ceilings", "old Chicago photos" and other "memorabilia", as well as a "great bar area with old-time drinks made the way they should be made"; P.S. "men with white collars" like to "expense this one."

Chicago Diner *Diner*

| 19 | 14 | 18 | $18 |

Lakeview | 3411 N. Halsted St. (Roscoe St.) | 773-935-6696 | www.veggiediner.com

"Homemade goodness without the flesh" sustains supporters of this "earthy" Lakeview "institution" with a "diner feel" that serves both "unique and traditional" vegetarian "comfort food" ("breakfast like mom used to make"), "bakery items", "vegan shakes" and organic wines and beers – though faulting feeders feel the "food sounds better on the menu than it tastes in real life"; P.S. the "outdoor garden is a nice place to sit in the summer."

Chicago Firehouse *American*

| 18 | 21 | 19 | $40 |

South Loop | 1401 S. Michigan Ave. (14th St.) | 312-786-1401 | www.chicagofirehouse.com

First responders rush into this "nifty" setting "in a converted old South [Loop] Chicago firehouse" for "upscale" yet "homestyle" Traditional American fare and "one of the best patios in the city"; a few alarmists, however, feel the "overpriced" "food doesn't live up to the decor"; P.S. it's a "great pre-game place for Bears night games."

Chicago Pizza & Oven Grinder Co. ⊄ *Pizza*

| 22 | 15 | 17 | $21 |

Lincoln Park | 2121 N. Clark St. (bet. Dickens & Webster Aves.) | 773-248-2570 | www.chicagopizzaandovengrinder.com

"There are long lines for a reason" at this Lincoln Park "landmark" and "great old family place", "a true Chicago original" to pie-sanos who praise its "awesome pizza pot pies", "gigantic salads", "out-of-this-world grinders" and a host who "never forgets where you are in

the wait order"; even fans, though, "wish they'd take reservations" and find the "cash-only policy" "slightly irritating", while idealists insist the "unique" signature dish "is not pizza" and "claustro-phobes" criticize its "catacombs"-like setting.

NEW Chicago Pizza Company *Pizza*

— | — | — | I

Rolling Meadows | 1655 E. Algonquin Rd. (Golf Rd.) | 847-258-6036 | www.chicagopizzacompany.com

Northwest Suburbanites who crave the 'pizza bowl' – think deep dish taken to the extreme – from Chicago Pizza & Oven Grinder will find a similar version at this unaffiliated spin-off opened by a former princi-pal; inexpensive thin-crust pies, baked sandwiches and a vast salad selection are also served in the family-friendly setting with cozy wood booths and a massive stone fireplace.

CHIC Cafe *Eclectic/French*

▽ 20 | 12 | 19 | $25

River North | Cooking & Hospitality Institute of Chicago | 361 W. Chestnut St. (Orleans St.) | 312-873-2032

It's a split decision over this student-staffed New French–Eclectic "fine-dining" BYO in a River North culinary college: gourmands gush that there must be "great teachers" at this "unknown gem" with a "lovely view" and "excellent brunch", adding it's "very cheap for what you get" (prix fixe or à la carte lunch, prix fixe–only dinner), but stricter standardists "expected better from aspiring chefs"; N.B. its schedule synchs with the school's season, so phone ahead.

Chief O'Neill's *Pub Food*

▽ 18 | 22 | 20 | $22

Northwest Side | 3471 N. Elston Ave. (Addison St.) | 773-583-3066 | www.chiefoneillspub.com

Neighbors of this "casual Irish pub/restaurant" on the Northwest Side call it "cozy", with "unique decor highlighting Chief O'Neill", a "nice fireplace in winter and outdoor dining in warm weather" (though the "bar atmosphere" can be "a little loud on weekends"); add the somewhat "ambitious" food, "good beer specials" and weekend entertainment and natives label it "like Ireland."

China Grill *Asian*

20 | 22 | 19 | $49

Loop | Hard Rock Hotel | 230 N. Michigan Ave. (Lake St.) | 312-334-6700 | www.hardrockhotelchicago.com

"It's a scene" at this "splashy", "high-class chain" outpost in the Loop's Hard Rock Hotel, where the "big portions" of "trendy, tasty" Asian dishes are "meant for sharing"; still, some supporters who "love the food" think it's "overpriced" (though better bargains may be had with the pre-theater and fixed-price lunch menus), while those who fault the fare as "fake Chinese" and the servers for "up-selling" sug-gest you "have a drink at the bar and then take a cab to Chinatown."

Chinn's 34th St. Fishery *Seafood*

22 | 11 | 19 | $30

Lisle | 3011 W. Ogden Ave. (bet. Fender Ave. & Naper Blvd.) | 630-637-1777 | www.chinns-fishery.com

"Cousin of the famous Bob Chinn's" ("but without the long waits"), this "low-key family seafood spot" in Lisle is "still serving up tasty", "incredibly fresh" fish – and displaying "documentation of today's-

catch flights in the foyer" – along with notorious mai tais that "take the edge off the subpar", "cafeteria-style" ambiance.

Chinoiserie 🚭 Asian
20 | 10 | 16 | $26

Wilmette | 509 Fourth St. (Linden Ave.) | 847-256-0306
"Not your typical Chinese restaurant", this "quaint" Wilmette Asian BYO features a "great blend of cultures" in its "inventive food", which helps backers "be tolerant of service foibles" and the "bizarre" "bed-and-breakfast decor" ("it would be lovely if all the fake flowers would disappear, along with the wallpaper").

Chiyo Japanese
- | - | - | M

Albany Park | 3800 W. Lawrence Ave. (Hamlin Ave.) | 773-267-1555 | www.chiyorestaurant.com
This off-the-beaten-path Albany Park storefront is done up in soothing neutrals and features moderately priced Japanese fare including sushi and sashimi, teriyaki and tempura and shabu-shabu (available with Kobe or prime beef), plus 30 varieties of sake; N.B. the restaurant serves Wagyu beef flown in from Japan.

Cité American
17 | 24 | 18 | $57

Streeterville | Lake Point Tower | 505 N. Lake Shore Dr., 70th fl. (Navy Pier) | 312-644-4050 | www.citechicago.com
After an aborted name/concept change and chef switch, this "romantic" dinner-only New American "special-occasion spot" in Streeterville carries on with its "matchless view" from high atop Lake Point Tower and, some say unfortunately, "tired food" that's "not memorable."

Clubhouse, The American
21 | 22 | 20 | $35

Oak Brook | Oakbrook Center Mall | 298 Oakbrook Ctr. (Rte. 83) | 630-472-0600 | www.theclubhouse.com
Fans figure this "hip but dignified" Traditional American clubhouse in Oak Brook's mall is "a fun place to meet for martinis" "after work", a "power lunch", a "fine Sunday brunch" or a "special meal" of "fantastic sandwiches, sizzling steaks" and desserts "bigger than your head" – but duffers dis it as an "overpriced", "noisy" "suburban" "pickup place"; P.S. there's a "large outdoor dining area."

Club Lago 🅱 Italian
17 | 11 | 20 | $24

River North | 331 W. Superior St. (Orleans St.) | 312-951-2849 | www.clublago.com
"Friendly owners" welcome River North "locals" to this "checkered-tablecloth" "time machine" back to the 1950s, "a great place to have simple traditional [Northern] Italian fare" with a "minimalist wine list" and "without the fuss of trendier venues"; despite this, disenchanted doubters declare it a "dumpy" "throwback to old-school red-sauce joints", adding "if only the red sauce lived up to the memories."

Club Lucky Italian
20 | 17 | 19 | $29

Bucktown | 1824 W. Wabansia Ave. (bet. Honore & Wood Sts.) | 773-227-2300 | www.clubluckychicago.com
Boasters for this "lively" Bucktown "local favorite" "smack dab in a residential neighborhood" swear its "large servings" of Southern

Italian "comfort food", "romantic" "retro atmosphere", "all-ages clientele", "great" "hefty martinis" and "attentive service" amount to "an offer you can't refuse"; P.S. "outdoor dining is a plus in nice weather."

NEW Coalfire Pizza 🅼 *Pizza* — | — | — | I

Near West | 1321 W. Grand Ave. (bet. Ada & Elizabeth Sts.) | 312-226-2625

The showpiece pizza oven at this casual, wood-and-brick Near West pizzeria turns out pies that are a blend of Neapolitan (classic crust, Vesuvian tomatoes) and East Coast (coal-fired) styles; its limited, inexpensive menu also includes calzones and salads, and a few non-alcoholic beverages – it's BYO for now.

Coast Sushi Bar ● *Japanese* 23 | 21 | 20 | $28

Bucktown | 2045 N. Damen Ave. (bet. Dickens & McLean Aves.) | 773-235-5775 | www.coastsushibar.com

Surf's up says the "hot crowd" that haunts this "hipster" Bucktown Japanese BYO for its "creative, tasty" sushi served in environs that exude a "sexy, minimalist vibe"; still, cooler heads consider the experience "hit-or-miss" and note that the "no liquor license" thing "is a real bummer."

Coco Pazzo *Italian* 24 | 22 | 22 | $49

River North | 300 W. Hubbard St. (Franklin St.) | 312-836-0900 | www.cocopazzochicago.com

Firmly "in the first tier of upscale Italian restaurants", this "understated", "reliable" River North "mainstay" is "innovative without being trendy", featuring "fresh, fresh, fresh" "contemporary" Tuscan fare served by a "well-trained staff" in "a lofty, open atmosphere" with "high-beamed ceilings" – all the ingredients for "haute", some say "haughty", dining; yes, it's "pricey" – but fans find it "worth every penny" just "to get away from classic 'Chicago Italian' (aka piles of bad pasta)."

Coco Pazzo Cafe *Italian* 22 | 19 | 20 | $38

Streeterville | Red Roof Inn | 636 N. St. Clair St. (Ontario St.) | 312-664-2777

"One block off the Mag Mile" in Streeterville, this "great city neighborhood restaurant" is "ever-popular" for its "high-quality" Northern Italian output at a "better value" than its "fancier" parent in River North; there's also a "good midpriced wine list", and alfresco addicts appreciate the "nice outdoor seating for people-watching"; P.S. "who would have thought – in a Red Roof Inn?"

Cold Comfort Cafe & Deli 🅼 *Sandwiches* 22 | 13 | 17 | $12

Bucktown | 2211 W. North Ave. (Leavitt St.) | 773-772-4552

Stop into this "casual" Bucktown BYO for "some of the most creative", "quality deli sandwiches" – with "the meat piled high" – amid "modern" digs decorated with "works by local artists", but be warned that the "friendly" folks "can be overwhelmed by the lunchtime rush"; P.S. it's "a fun brunch/breakfast spot" too (they close mid-afternoon).

	FOOD	DECOR	SERVICE	COST

NEW Convito Café & Market *French/Italian*

| - | - | - | M |

Wilmette | Plaza del Lago | 1515 Sheridan Rd. (bet. 10th St. & Westerfield Dr.) | 847-251-3654 | www.convitocafeandmarket.com

Two longtime North Shore siblings, Convito Italiano and Bêtise, have merged into this casual Italian–French country dining destination with a midpriced menu of favorite dishes from both its progenitors; it's set in the former Bêtise space, which has been expanded and re-modeled in earth tones for an upscale rustic feel; N.B. it also houses a gourmet retail area of prepared foods, wine and coffee.

Coobah ● *Filipino/Nuevo Latino*

| 19 | 20 | 16 | $29 |

Lakeview | 3423 N. Southport Ave. (bet. Newport Ave. & Roscoe St.) | 773-528-2220 | www.coobah.com

"Swank and exotic", this Lakeview "date spot" is considered "a full-flavored experience" by "the mid- to late-twentysomething" crowd, which frequents it for "tasty" Nuevo Latino–Filipino fusion fare, "fun drinks" and "loud music" – but more staid surveyors say "the atmosphere is better than the food" and cite "service issues"; P.S. "the outdoor seating is great for people-watching."

NEW Cooper's *American*

| - | - | - | I |

Lakeview | 1232 W. Belmont Ave. (bet. Racine & Southport Aves.) | 773-929-2667

The former Menagerie has been transformed by its owners into this hangout-friendly Lakeview gastropub with modest prices and earthy ambiance; the upscale spins on pub grub include duck confit–pesto pizza and a Reuben panini with housemade corned beef and kraut (plus a few favorites from the old menu), all paired with 50 global brews; N.B. there's occasional live music on the patio.

copperblue M *French/Mediterranean*

| - | - | - | E |

Streeterville | Lake Point Tower | 580 E. Illinois St. (Navy Pier) | 312-527-1200 | www.copperbluechicago.com

Whimsically named after a Bob Mould album, this stylish French-Med on the ground floor of Streeterville's Lake Point Tower showcases an intriguing menu of unusual ingredients and preparations by chef Michael Tsonton (ex Tizi Melloul, Courtright's) and an affordable all-Euro wine list; the cozy, warmly lit dining room features bright murals themed 'work, rest and play' on yellow and orange walls.

NEW Cordis Brothers Supper Club ⑤ *American*

| - | - | - | M |

Lakeview | 1625 W. Irving Park Rd. (Paulina St.) | 773-935-1000 | www.cordisbrothers.com

Serving midpriced Traditional American fare, this classic supper club in Lakeview looks like it's been around for years, complete with cozy booths, nailhead-trim chairs and lots of wood (including a huge bar); N.B. DJs spin nightly entertainment.

Costa's *Greek*

| 21 | 19 | 20 | $30 |

Greektown | 340 S. Halsted St. (Van Buren St.) | 312-263-9700

(continued)

Costa's

Oakbrook Terrace | 1 S. 130 Summit Ave. (Roosevelt Rd.) | 630-620-1100
www.costasdining.com

"Zorba would be proud" of the "great, authentic" "traditional Greek dishes", "old-world service" and "comfortable" milieu at these Greektown and West Suburban "standbys", even if they're "pricier" and "more formal" than most in the genre; N.B. Oakbrook Terrace has piano entertainment on most Wednesdays and weekends, and a roaring fireplace in winter.

NEW Côtes du Rhône *French*

-	-	-	M

Edgewater | 5424 N. Broadway (bet. Balmoral & Catalpa Aves.) | 773-293-2683

Edgewater gets a romantic hideaway with the arrival of this new French bistro serving moderately priced hearty classics; the quaint, cozy setting features paper-covered cafe tables, tin ceilings and tile walls bathed in rendezvous-worthy low lighting.

☑ Courtright's Ⓜ *American*

26	25	26	$58

Willow Springs | 8989 S. Archer Ave. (Willow Springs Rd.) | 708-839-8000 | www.courtrights.com

Excursionists to the Southwest Surburbs eagerly enthuse about this "excellent out-of-the-way" "destination restaurant" where "marvelous", "creative seasonal" New American "meals are carefully planned, expertly prepared and exquisitely presented" in a "classic atmosphere" with "beautiful gardens" ("grazing deer appear magically as if on cue outside the [nearly] floor-to-ceiling windows"); P.S. "the wine alone is worth the trip."

Cousin's Incredible Vitality *Mediterranean*

-	-	-	I

Northwest Side | 3038 W. Irving Park Rd. (Whipple St.) | 773-478-6868 | www.cousinsiv.com

This moderately priced Northwest Side raw vegan (meat-free) mecca pairs Mediterranean vittles (pistachio falafel, collard greens wraps, raw cacao desserts) with smoothies, 'elixirs' and organic wines (including pomegranate), all served in a vibrant jungle-inspired setting; there's also a take-out market, as well as classes in detox, food preparation and yoga; N.B. this cousin is no relation to Cousin's Turkish Dining in Lakeview.

☑ Crofton on Wells Ⓢ *American*

26	19	23	$56

River North | 535 N. Wells St. (bet. Grand Ave. & Ohio St.) | 312-755-1790 | www.croftononwells.com

Surveyors sweet on Suzy Crofton swoon for her "seasonal" New American fare that's "inventive without being over-intellectualized", "wonderfully matched" by a "wine list with plenty of midpriced selections" and served in a River North setting of "spare elegance"; a recent remodeling should please scribes who've taken issue with the "stark" and "clinical" decor, but it will do little to please those who call the experience a pinch "pricey."

	FOOD	DECOR	SERVICE	COST

NEW Cru Cafe & Wine Bar ◐ *American* | - | - | - | M |

Gold Coast | 25 E. Delaware Pl. (bet. N. State St. & N. Wabash Ave.) | 312-337-4001 | www.cruwinebar.com

Debbie Sharpe's Gold Coast wine bar has reopened and expanded with a New American menu of noshes (charcuterie, caviar), light fare and full-blown entrees to complement the big vino selection; the elegant, chandeliered space offers multiple environments including a cushy lounge and an outpost of her Goddess and Grocer gourmet market with seating.

NEW Crust *Pizza* | - | - | - | I |

Wicker Park | 2056 W. Division St. (Hoyne Ave.) | 773-235-5511 | www.crusteatreal.org

Michael Altenberg's breakthrough organic 'pizza lounge' specializes in inexpensive ciabatta-style flatbreads from a woodburning oven, and showcases everything organic, from the food to the wines, beers and infused vodkas; set in Wicker Park's former Settimana Cafe space, the feel is hipster-retro, with exposed brick, bamboo, fabric ceiling panels and recycled aluminum tables, plus an outdoor cafe that seats over 100.

Cuatro ◐ *Nuevo Latino* | 23 | 18 | 18 | $38 |

South Loop | 2030 S. Wabash Ave. (20th St.) | 312-842-8856 | www.cuatro-chicago.com

"*Muy delicioso!*" maintains a majority optimistic about this "terrific addition to" the "up-and-coming" South Loop, an "outpost of coolness" cooking up "wonderful" "creative" Nuevo Latino fare "for a reasonable price" and pouring "great drinks at the bar" – even if a minority isn't raving about the room; N.B. live Latin jazz is presented nightly.

Z Custom House *American* | 24 | 26 | 22 | $61 |

Printer's Row | Hotel Blake | 500 S. Dearborn St. (Congress Pkwy.) | 312-523-0200 | www.customhouse.cc

"One of the city's best chefs", Shawn McClain (who won the 2006 James Beard Award for Best Chef-Midwest) "gives meat and potatoes a whole new meaning" at this Printer's Row "carnivore's delight" that's "worth a field trip to the south side" for its "tremendous menu" of "top-notch" New American fare and "extensive wine list" offered in "lush", "retro-metrochic surroundings"; most maintain it has "the makings of an instant classic" – once management addresses the chorus of "service kinks" comments; P.S. professionals are pleased "it's open for [breakfast and] lunch."

Cyrano's Bistrot & Wine Bar *French* | 20 | 19 | 19 | $38 |

River North | 546 N. Wells St. (Ohio St.) | 312-467-0546 | www.cyranosbistrot.com

"Personable" chef-owner Didier Durand "takes a great deal of pride in this restaurant and it shows" in the "fine", "authentic" bistro fare, "good wine recommendations", "romantic atmosphere" and "reasonable prices" (the "prix fixe is always a great deal") – all aspects of a "French country experience" right in River North; P.S. music mavens maintain the Café Simone Parisian Cabaret downstairs "is a bo-

nus", with live entertainment Wednesday–Saturday, and pet people "love" the "dog-friendly" sidewalk cafe.

D & J Bistro M *French*
25 | 19 | 23 | $39

Lake Zurich | First Bank Plaza Ctr. | 466 S. Rand Rd./Rte. 12 (Rte. 22) | 847-438-8001 | www.dj-bistro.com

A preponderance of respondents prizes this Northwest Suburban "find" that "continues to impress" with the "Gallic charm" of its "excellent" (and "fairly priced") "classic bistro cooking", its "well-chosen wine list" and the "friendly French decor" of its "lovely interior", which stands "in stark contrast to" its "strip-plaza setting."

Dave's Italian Kitchen *Italian*
17 | 11 | 16 | $18

Evanston | 1635 Chicago Ave., downstairs (bet. Church & Davis Sts.) | 847-864-6000 | www.davesik.com

Despite "long waiting times", diehards submit this is "still one of the [Evanston] area's best bargains" for "large portions" of Southern "Italian just like mom used to make" and "tremendous wine bargains" in a "loud", "crowded" "basement" "zoo"; others who "don't understand why this place is so popular" opine that the "ordinary-to-bland" offerings are only for "impoverished" "NU students" or those "too lazy to boil water at home."

David Burke's Primehouse *Steak*
▽ 22 | 22 | 22 | $66

River North | The James Chicago Hotel | 616 N. Rush St. (Ontario St.) | 312-660-6000 | www.brguestrestaurants.com

"Refreshingly innovative", the B.R. Guest gang's ultramodern New American steakhouse in The James Hotel rises "head and shoulders above" others of its ilk, serving up "excellent quality" beef dry-aged on-premises, plus David Burke's signature dishes from his Park Avenue Café days; there's "not only great meat" – Caesar salads made tableside add a "nice bit of entertainment" while the "well-executed supporting dishes" offer "enough of a twist to make us come again"; still, a bull-igerent few deem the "experience uneven."

David's Bistro ⊠M *American*
▽ 24 | 20 | 22 | $36

Des Plaines | Wolf Plaza | 623 N. Wolf Rd. (Central Ave.) | 847-803-3233 | www.davidsbistro.com

The name says 'bistro' but the cuisine is more "creative" than you'd think thanks to "offbeat and interesting" seasonal New American-French fare (with an "excellent wine selection") at this "quaint", "quiet" Northwest Suburban "gem" situated in a "nondescript", "out-of-the-way" "strip shopping center"; P.S. chef-owner David Maish also gives "great cooking classes" and is preparing to open a Schaumburg location.

Davis Street Fishmarket *Seafood*
19 | 15 | 18 | $30

Evanston | 501 Davis St. (Hinman Ave.) | 847-869-3474 | www.davisstreetfishmarket.com

"There are no mysteries" at this "straightforward" and "satisfying" "fresh seafooder" in Evanston pen pragmatists pleased with its "variety of fish" dishes, "prepared without frills" ("you'll find daily choices on the wall menu"), plus some "decent Cajun" cookin' and a

FOOD DECOR SERVICE COST

"raw bar" offered amid "funky" "New England-ish decor" with "fish-nets hanging from the ceiling"; moderates maintain it's "always good, never great", though, and call the service simply "competent"; N.B. a new location is planned for Schaumburg.

de cero 🅕 Mexican
21 | 16 | 17 | $31

Market District | 814 W. Randolph St. (bet. Green & Halsted Sts.) | 312-455-8114 | www.decerotaqueria.com

Muchachos meet at this "tapas-style" Market District taqueria for a "fun alternative to traditional Mexican fare", with "many inventive fillings" of "fresh ingredients" for the "tasty tacos" and "delicious drinks" served in a "hip" yet "rustic environment" with a side of "loud music"; iffier inputters indicate "indifferent service", though, adding that their "appreciation for the novelty idea wanes a little more with every visit"; N.B. DJs spin on weekends.

Dee's Asian
19 | 17 | 18 | $29

Lincoln Park | 1114 W. Armitage Ave. (Seminary Ave.) | 773-477-1500 | www.deesrestaurant.com

Loyalists love this Lincoln Parker for its "wide selection of Asian fa-vorites" (Mandarin, Szechuan, sushi) served in a "cozy" "neighbor-hood" atmosphere with a "great garden for outside dining" – not to mention "hands-on, ever-present owner Dee" Kang, who always "sees to customers' needs"; still, querulous quills question the qual-ity and value of what they call "inconsistent" output that's "consid-erably more expensive" than in Chinatown.

NEW DeLaCosta Nuevo Latino
- | - | - | E

River North | 465 E. Illinois St. (bet. Lake Shore Dr. & McClurg Ct.) | 312-464-1700 | www.delacostachicago.com

Hot Miami chef Douglas Rodriguez (OLA on Ocean, OLA Steak) makes his Midwestern debut with a Nuevo Latino supper-club sizzler on the river serving creative cuisine paired with six styles of sangria and licentious libations including 'poptails' (cocktail popsi-cles); the 12,000-sq.-ft. venue showcases multiple high-style envi-ronments including lounges, a ceviche bar and a 'solarium' overlooking Ogden Slip.

Deleece Eclectic
21 | 17 | 18 | $30

Wrigleyville | 4004 N. Southport Ave. (Irving Park Rd.) | 773-325-1710 | www.deleece.com

Regulars rank this Wrigleyville Eclectic a "neighborhood gem" for its "scrumptious", "interesting global menu", "fantastic [weekend] brunch" and a "cozy feel" abetted by "exposed brick and candles on each table", as well as touting the Monday–Tuesday prix fixe as a "great deal"; P.S. "summer on the sidewalk patio is a treat."

Del Rio 🅕 Italian
18 | 14 | 19 | $35

Highwood | 228 Green Bay Rd. (Rte. 22) | 847-432-4608

Either way, it's "déjà vu all over again" for diners at this "North Shore classic": one Del-egation finds it a "comfortable" "neighborhood" "standby" for "old-fashioned [Northern] Italian food" and the fruits

of a "vast" wine cellar, whereas the other tells of a "tired" time warp where "not much has changed – although it should have."

NEW Depot American Diner, The _Diner_ | – | – | – | I |

Far West | 5840 W. Roosevelt Rd. (S. Austin Blvd.) | 773-261-8422 | www.thedepotamericandiner.com

Retro home cooking and old-fashioned prices draw fans to Austin's friendly Edward Hopper–esque greasy spoon without the grease; behind its unassuming exterior awaits Traditional American fare – complete with blue-plate specials and soda-fountain creations – served in a blast-from-the-past diner setting.

Devon Seafood Grill _Seafood_ | – | – | – | M |

River North | 39 E. Chicago Ave. (Wabash Ave.) | 312-440-8660 | www.devonseafood.com

Fresh seafood is flown in daily from both coasts for lunch and dinner at this casually upscale chowhouse (sibling of a Philadelphia original) with global menu accents as well as classics, a few surf 'n' turf options and a moderately priced wine list; the comfy, clubby bi-level space boasts a visible kitchen, cozy booths in the dining room and a big, convivial bar upstairs.

Dine _American_ | – | – | – | M |

West Loop | Crowne Plaza Chicago Metro Hotel | 733 W. Madison St. (Halsted St.) | 312-602-2100 | www.dinerestaurant.com

Located in the new Crowne Plaza Chicago Metro Hotel, this retro American with a '40s feel woos West Loopers with classic cocktails and upscale, updated comfort food from an exposed kitchen; multiple dining areas on various levels break up the 7,000-sq.-ft. setting done up in rich earth tones and outfitted with comfy leather banquettes; N.B. it now offers a Sunday jazz brunch.

Dining Room at Kendall College, The 🅂 _French_ | 23 | 20 | 21 | $37 |

Near West | Kendall College | 900 N. North Branch St. (Halsted St.) | 312-752-2328 | www.kendall.edu

"Expect a quality meal" "with a bent toward the unusual" – and "without shelling out big bucks" – at this "culinary college" venue where the New French fare is "cooked by the future stars of the Chicago restaurant scene"; ok, so "service by the students can be spotty", but the "swish" space with its "third-floor perch" offers "killer views of the Loop"; N.B. it's closed during school breaks and holidays.

Dinotto Ristorante _Italian_ | 20 | 17 | 19 | $31 |

Old Town | 215 W. North Ave. (Wells St.) | 312-202-0302 | www.dinotto.com

"Tasty" "everyday" eats greet goers to this "great neighborhood Italian", an Old Town "standby" with "reliably good service"; it's a "convenient" stop "before catching a movie across the street", and the "romantic setting" is "nice" for a "date night" – especially the prime "courtyard" patio (with its own bar) that's "like eating in a piazza in Italy"; a minority of _mangia_-ers, however, marks it "middle of the pack."

	FOOD	DECOR	SERVICE	COST

Di Pescara *Eclectic/Italian*
| - | - | - | M |

Northbrook | Northbrook Court Shopping Ctr. | 2124 Northbrook Ct. (Lake Cook Rd.) | 847-498-4321 | www.leye.com

Though the name conjures images of seafood from The Boot, the something-for-everyone menu goes much farther afield at this Lettuce Entertain You Italian-Eclectic (named for a fishing village on the Adriatic coast) in the former Bice space in Northbrook Court; celeb sommelier Alpana Singh's smart wine list is also on offer in the dark, swanky casual-contemporary setting, and a separate take-out area provides convenient curbside parking.

Dixie Kitchen & Bait Shop *Cajun/Southern*
| 19 | 17 | 17 | $19 |

Hyde Park | 5225 S. Harper Ave. (53rd St.) | 773-363-4943
Evanston | 825 Church St. (Benson Ave.) | 847-733-9030
Lansing | 2352 E. 172 St. (Torrence Ave.) | 708-474-1378

"Put some south in your mouth" at this "charming", "fun-as-cow-tipping" city and suburban trio "serving" "solid", "stick-to-your-ribs" Southern-Cajun cooking ("staples like fried green tomatoes, po' boys, étouffée and gumbo") to "a diverse clientele" of Dixie chicks and Dicks; the "rustic decor" is "contrived but cute", and the vittles are a "value."

NEW Dodo ⊘ *American*
| - | - | - | I |

Ukrainian Village | 935 N. Damen Ave. (Walton St.) | 773-772-3636

A small, inexpensive menu of creatively updated American comfort foods (including vegan specials) is served for breakfast, brunch and lunch (but no dinner) at this bustling, friendly Ukrainian Village hangout with a modern beatnik feel; expect a funky vintage setting, complete with an exposed kitchen and whimsical art on the walls.

Don Juan's *Mexican*
| 21 | 16 | 21 | $30 |

Edison Park | 6730 N. Northwest Hwy. (bet. Devon & Ozark Aves.) | 773-775-6438 | www.donjuanschicago.com

Gringos go for this "great mix-and-match" Mex 'cause there are "lots of options for the gourmet, and the rest can get tacos"; co-owner "Maria Concannon is the quintessential hostess with the mostess", and her staffers "make a mean margarita" – cementing this "upbeat", "family-run" Northwest Sider's status as "Number Juan in Edison Park."

Don Roth's Blackhawk *Seafood/Steak*
| 20 | 17 | 21 | $37 |

Wheeling | 61 N. Milwaukee Ave. (Dundee Rd.) | 847-537-5800 | www.donroths.com

Vintagists vouch for this Northwest Suburban surf 'n' turfer, a "quiet", "friendly" "golden oldie" that "retains its glory" with "great" fare like "to-die-for prime rib", "scrod with a ton of tartar sauce" and "the re-creation of the spinning salad bowl from the original Blackhawk", all served amid nostalgic Chicago photography – but modernists who eschew "food the way it used to be back in the '70s" title it "tired."

	FOOD	DECOR	SERVICE	COST

Dorado ⓜ *French/Mexican* ▽ 23 | 15 | 22 | $29

Lincoln Square | 2301 W. Foster Ave. (bet. Claremont & Oakley Aves.) | 773-561-3780 | www.doradorestaurant.com

Though next to "nobody knows it" yet, this "welcome addition" to Lincoln Square boasts an "innovative" kitchen "churning out some serious Mexican"-French fusion fare "at bargain prices", with "bold flavors that jump off the plate"; it's a bit of a "hole-in-the-wall", but at least it's "bright and cheerful", and the BYO policy is an "added bonus"; P.S. "have you tried those duck nachos?"

Dover Straits *Seafood* 18 | 16 | 19 | $34

Mundelein | 890 E. US Hwy. 45 (Butterfield Rd.) | 847-949-1550
Hoffman Estates | 1149 W. Golf Rd. (Gannon Dr.) | 847-884-3900
www.doverstraits.com

Strait-shooters swear by the "quality and variety" of fish fare (starring "great Dover sole"), "nice service" and "old-style setting" that's a "throwback to supper clubs of yesteryear" at these "reliable" suburban seafood sibs; perhaps raters "just a few years away from AARP membership" feel "young" here, but even greenhorns grade it a "righteous value" for "good food – if you don't mind the 1960s look"; P.S. "for a real deal", "catch the early-bird."

Dragonfly Mandarin *Chinese* 14 | 18 | 14 | $33

Market District | 832 W. Randolph St. (Green St.) | 312-787-7600 | www.dragonflymandarin.com

This "swanky", "upscale" "Chinese transplant from the Gold Coast" to the Market District draws defenders of its "delicious" dining amid decor that's "a delight to the senses" (including "a cool lounge" and "great outside seating"), but disenchanted diners give it demerits as "dark, dull and pricey" for the category, suggesting "the neighborhood has so many good restaurants" that you "can get better elsewhere."

Drake Bros.' Steakhouse *Seafood/Steak* 17 | 18 | 19 | $59

Streeterville | Drake Hotel | 140 E. Walton St. (Michigan Ave.) | 312-932-4626 | www.drakebros.com

"Below the radar of most", this Traditional American meat 'n' seafooder in Streeterville's Drake Hotel has boosters who believe it's a "quiet" place for a "good", "old-fashioned" dinner; unfortunately, the "unimpressed" pronounce the food "boring" and complain that the "killer view is not worth the killer price", adding "it was better when it was" the Oak Terrace; N.B. breakfast, Sunday brunch and lunch are also served.

Duke of Perth *Pub Food* 18 | 17 | 18 | $18

Lakeview | 2913 N. Clark St. (Oakdale Ave.) | 773-477-1741
Lakeview's "friendly" "Scottish pub seems transported from the old country", with "solid" "grub" "at a good price" including burgers, shepherd's pie and "some of the city's best [all-you-can-eat] fish 'n' chips on Wednesdays and Fridays" ("this greasy food is just what the doctor ordered"); there's also a "great choice of ales on tap" and "the best scotch list around", plus it's "one of the few bars in Chicago without TVs"; P.S. the patio's "fantastic."

	FOOD	DECOR	SERVICE	COST

Eatzi's *Eclectic*

	18	13	16	$19

Lincoln Park | Century Shopping Ctr. | 2828 N. Clark St. (bet. B'way & Surf St.) | 773-832-9310 | www.eatzis.com

Lincoln Parker's who "love" having "so many choices under one roof" drop into this Eclectic "gourmet-to-go" "in the basement of an indoor shopping mall" "to get takeout" "when they have no time to cook", or to grab "a fast bite" in a "dining area that's like a fast-food court or cafeteria"; conversely, some contrary consumers claim "confusion reigns", everything "looks better than it tastes" and "the novelty and expense wear thin."

Ed Debevic's *Diner*

	14	19	16	$18

River North | 640 N. Wells St. (Ontario St.) | 312-664-1707
Lombard | 157 Yorktown Shopping Ctr. (bet. Butterfield Rd. & 22nd St.) | 630-495-1700
www.eddebevics.com

Diners who are "feeling snarky", "trade insults" with the "smart-aleck staff" at this "campy" River North and South Suburban diner duo, "fun places" for a "'50s" "drive-in type experience" of "fair to good" burgers and milkshakes and a side of "obnoxious-by-design service"; more staid surveyors sidestep the "sass" and "so-so" sustenance, though, hinting it's "had its moment" and wondering "why would anyone" "line up to be treated" "like a private in the army"?

Edelweiss *German*

	▽ 21	18	21	$31

Norridge | 7650 W. Irving Park Rd. (bet. Cumberland & Harlem Aves.) | 708-452-6040 | www.edelweissdining.com

If you "have a hearty appetite and low cholesterol", head to this "friendly" "neighborhood" 35-year-old in the near Suburban Northwest for the "best authentic German[-American] food left in Chicago" – not only is it "tasty" and "reasonably priced" but you also get "the real deal with the beer", plus you can "oompah" the night away to German bands (Friday–Sunday).

Edwardo's Natural Pizza *Pizza*

	20	10	15	$17

Lincoln Park | 2662 N. Halsted St. (bet. Schubert & Wrightwood Aves.) | 773-871-3400
Gold Coast | 1212 N. Dearborn St. (Division St.) | 312-337-4490
Hyde Park | 1321 E. 57th St. (Kimbark Ave.) | 773-241-7960
Printer's Row | 521 S. Dearborn St. (bet. Congress Pkwy. & Harrison St.) | 312-939-3366
Skokie | 9300 Skokie Blvd. (Gross Point Rd.) | 847-674-0008
Wheeling | 401 E. Dundee Rd. (Milwaukee Ave.) | 847-520-0666
Oak Park | 6831 W. North Ave. (Grove Ave.) | 708-524-2400
www.edwardos.com

"Man, what a great pie" moan memoirists about this widespread chain whose "natural" pizzas, "whether stuffed or thin", are topped with "fresh-tasting sauce" and ingredients such as "ambrosial spinach" and "great pesto"; the locations may "not be much in the way of decor or service" but they "still deliver the box of pizza some people dream of" (though others opine they're "good but not the best"); P.S. the lunch specials are perfect "for people on the go."

	FOOD	DECOR	SERVICE	COST

EJ's Place *Italian/Steak*

| 19 | 15 | 18 | $47 |

Skokie | 10027 Skokie Blvd. (Old Orchard Rd.) | 847-933-9800 | www.ejsplaceskokie.com

Earning enthusiasm for its "expensive, quality [prime] meat" and other more "reasonably priced" Northern Italian dishes, this North Suburban steakhouse "relative of Gene and Georgetti" features "uniformly above average" food in a "faux Wisconsin lodge" locale that's "great if you like real wood-burning fireplaces"; knockers note the "knowledgeable service" can "seem stretched", though, adding that for the cost you "might as well make the trek" Downtown.

Eleven City Diner *Diner*

| - | - | - | I |

South Loop | 1112 S. Wabash Ave. (11th St.) | 312-212-1112 | www.elevencitydiner.com

Filling a niche in the South Loop, this retro-inspired revisit of Jewish diner/delicatessens from decades past purveys comforting classics amid cozy dark-wood-and-leather-booth environs with a vintage soda fountain and a lunch counter manned by old-school countermen; modern touches include a barista, the use of local/sustainable produce and phone-ahead curbside takeout; N.B. breakfast is served all day, and late-nighters can nosh till 3 AM on weekends.

El Nandu *Argentinean*

| ∇ 21 | 15 | 20 | $22 |

Logan Square | 2731 W. Fullerton Ave. (California Ave.) | 773-278-0900

This "hidden treasure" in Logan Square is "fun" for "wonderful Argentinean fare" including "huge steaks", "empanadas that burst with flavor" and "tasty sangria" served in "authentic, cozy" environs with "live entertainment on weekends"; N.B. the Decor score may not reflect the restaurant's renovation and expansion.

El Presidente ● *Mexican*

| ∇ 14 | 9 | 12 | $16 |

Lincoln Park | 2558 N. Ashland Ave. (Wrightwood Ave.) | 773-525-7938

Seems there's always "at least one cop present" at this Far West Lincoln Park "late-night must" serving "a good, hot, greasy meal" of "basic Mexican" "anti-hangover food" around the clock; true, there's "no fuss, no fancy" in the "shabby", "dive" setting, but most still find it "fun"; N.B. be sure to BYO.

Emilio's Sunflower Bistro Ⓜ *American*

| - | - | - | M |

La Grange | 30 S. La Grange Rd. (Harris Ave.) | 708-588-9890 | www.sunflowerbistro.com

Named both for partner/executive chef (and local tapas legend) Emilio Gervilla and for its decorative motif (many examples of which were painted by Christopher Spagnola, co-chef with wife Mary), this "cozy" West Suburban offers "well-put-together plates" of "fresh, organic" New American fare, "a clever wine list" and an "eclectic" "bistro feel"; P.S. there's a "tiny martini bar in back with an alley entrance."

Emilio's Tapas *Spanish*

| 21 | 17 | 19 | $31 |

Lincoln Park | 444 W. Fullerton Pkwy. (Clark St.) | 773-327-5100
Hillside | 4100 W. Roosevelt Rd. (Mannheim Rd.) | 708-547-7177

(continued)

FOOD · DECOR · SERVICE · COST

(continued)

Emilio's Tapas La Rioja *Spanish*
Wheaton | 230 W. Front St. (Wheaton Ave.) | 630-653-7177
Emilio's Tapas Sol y Nieve *Spanish*
Streeterville | 215 E. Ohio St. (St. Clair St.) | 312-467-7177
www.emiliostapas.com

"True tapas fans" tout Emilio Gervilla's "tapalicious" tribe for an "elegant experience", "whether you are looking for a bite", "a full dinner" or just to "share some sangria with friends"; its Spanish small plates feature "interesting combinations and flavors" – "three words: bacon, wrapped, dates; three more: garlic, potato, salad" – though a few feel it all adds up to an evening that's "pricey for what you get."

Emperor's Choice ◗ *Chinese* | 23 | 12 | 18 | $23 |
Chinatown | 2238 S. Wentworth Ave. (Cermak Rd.) | 312-225-8800

The "excellent Chinese food" is "fit for royalty" and can be "authentic if desired" – including some "dishes that can be frightening for the casual newcomer" – or "cooked more for the American taste" at this "seafood heaven" that serves until midnight six nights a week, 11 PM on Sundays; it's not every emperor's choice, though, with some despots decrying the "indifferent service" and "ho-hum decor" (though the saltwater tank of "live fish is cool").

Enoteca Piattini Ⓜ *Italian* | 21 | 20 | 21 | $31 |
Lincoln Park | 934 W. Webster Ave. (bet. Bissell St. & Sheffield Ave.) | 773-935-8466 | www.enotecapiattini.net

"For groups or an intimate date", surveyors savor "a satisfying menu" of "quality" Southern "Italian small plates" and a "huge wine list" with "great" "reasonably priced flights" at this "romantic" Lincoln Parker where the "generous portions" are "truly a bargain"; the outdoor dining "is pleasant if you don't mind the noise from the el train", and if you "get a table by the fireplace in winter you'll never want to leave."

Entourage on American Lane *American* | – | – | – | E |
Schaumburg | 1301 American Ln. (bet. Meacham Rd. & National Pkwy.) | 847-995-9400 | www.entourageventures.com

Whether you're a VIP or just a wannabe, check out this sprawling spot for upscale indulgence in the Northwest Suburbs, where Traditional American fare (prime steaks, chops, seafood, salads) is served amid 22,000 sq. ft. of swank; a 48-ft.-tall illuminated martini shaker stands sentry outside, while inside there's a winding staircase, 40-ft.-tall waterfalls, fireplaces, plasma TVs, a baby grand piano, a cigar humidor and a 2,000-bottle wine cellar (plus a private wine locker program).

NEW Erba Ⓜ *Italian* | – | – | – | M |
Lincoln Square | 4520 N. Lincoln Ave. (Sunnyside Ave.) | 773-989-4200

Brioso's owners have expanded their repertoire to include Northern Italian cuisine while staying close by in Lincoln Square; all of the herbaceous seasonal offerings are made from scratch (including the

	FOOD	DECOR	SERVICE	COST

grappa and limoncello), moderately priced and served in an intimate, modern setting of dark woods, fiery hues and chocolate browns, with a spacious outdoor patio that doubles as an herb garden.

Erie Cafe *Italian/Steak*
| 23 | 19 | 22 | $48 |

River North | 536 W. Erie St. (Kingsbury St.) | 312-266-2300 | www.eriecafe.com

"Take the boys for a power lunch" or dinner at this "real Italian steakhouse", a Gene & Georgetti descendent in River North, where "meat and fish in the best Chicago tradition" (including "elephantine prime rib") is delivered with "no-nonsense service" amid "good old-fashioned-joint" atmo complete with a "great river location" (the terrace seating is a "hidden treasure"); still, some offput outsiders opine that the output is "overpriced."

NEW Erik's Restaurant *Eclectic*
| - | - | - | M |

Highwood | Ft. Sheridan Plaza | 752 Sheridan Rd. (bet. Old Elm & Sheridan Rds.) | 847-433-3434

Chef Erik Wicklund (ex Whitehall Hotel) mixes it up at this Eclectic establishment, blending Italian, Asian and American dishes on the midpriced comfort-food menu; the strip-mall setting north of Highwood's main dining district feels like an urban loft thanks to walls of windows, black ductwork and white tablecloths; N.B. the marble bar serves modern martinis and a separate light-bites menu.

erwin, an american cafe & bar ⓜ *American*
| 23 | 19 | 22 | $37 |

Lakeview | 2925 N. Halsted St. (Oakdale Ave.) | 773-528-7200 | www.erwincafe.com

Aficionados of Erwin Drechsler's "homey" yet "urban" Lakeview "neighborhood standby" affirm it's "always a good choice" for a monthly changing menu of New American dishes ("some unusual, some standard, all well prepared"), an "out-of-the-ordinary brunch menu" and an "extensive, excellent wine list"; the "relaxed", "intimate" room is "conversation-friendly" and decorated with a "whimsical mural that makes great Chicago references"; P.S. wallet-watchers appreciate that it's a "good value."

Essence of India *Indian*
| 21 | 15 | 18 | $24 |

Lincoln Square | 4601 N. Lincoln Ave. (Wilson Ave.) | 773-506-0002 | www.essenceofindiachicago.com

Gourmands go to this "good place to experiment with Indian cuisine" that's "convenient to all that Lincoln Square has to offer" and harbors "helpful servers" (and a liquor license); a portion of Punjab proponents purports that "portions tend to be small for the price", though, and opts for the "drive to Devon" instead; N.B. lunch buffet is served on Fridays and Saturdays.

Ethiopian Diamond *Ethiopian*
| 24 | 11 | 15 | $19 |

Edgewater | 6120 N. Broadway (Glenlake Ave.) | 773-338-6100 | www.ethiopiandiamond.com

An "excellent variety for vegetarians and carnivores alike" keeps 'em coming back to this Edgewater Ethiopian, a "fun place to go with

a group" and eat "non-greasy, healthy, yummy food" "with your fingers" – so yummy, in fact, that it makes it "worth missing out on the other fronts", namely decor and service; N.B. a one-man band performs on Friday nights.

☑ Everest 🖾 Ⓜ *French*　27 | 26 | 27 | $91

Loop | One Financial Pl. | 440 S. LaSalle St., 40th fl. (Congress Pkwy.) | 312-663-8920 | www.everestrestaurant.com

Financiers feel an affinity for this "romantic", "formal" "expense-account haven", "still at its peak" thanks to Jean Joho's "delectable" New French–Alsatian cuisine, an "exemplary wine list", "totally professional service" and "a breathtaking view" from "the top of the [Loop] Financial District"; a recent face-lift may appease fans who felt that the "nouveau riche" decor was "stuck in the '80s", though it may do little for those more concerned that the "attitude" "is loftier than the location."

Evergreen ⏺ *Chinese*　22 | 12 | 17 | $23

Chinatown | 2411 S. Wentworth Ave. (24th St.) | 312-225-8898

The "interesting", "authentic" Cantonese-Mandarin cooking is "always good" at this "comfort-food" classic "at a quiet end of Chinatown", so most munchers overlook that it boasts some of the area's "worst ambiance"; P.S. night owls love that it's "open late" (midnight nightly).

Extra Virgin 🖾 *Italian/Mediterranean*　▽ 19 | 20 | 18 | $32

Market District | 741 W. Randolph St. (Halsted St.) | 312-474-0700 | www.restaurants-america.com

Find your way to this "friendly addition" to the Market District, a good "fit in the area" with "interesting and tasty" Italian-Mediterranean small plates and "great drinks" offered in a "lovely space" with an "open feel" – plus patio dining in season.

Fattoush *Lebanese*　▽ 23 | 8 | 21 | $19

Lincoln Park | 2652 N. Halsted St. (bet. Deversey Pkwy. & Wrightwood Ave.) | 773-327-2652 | www.fattoushrestaurant.com

"Very authentic" Lebanese food made "with fresh ingredients" ("just like homemade") and offered at a "friendly price point" lures Lincoln Parkers to this "small, family-run" BYO – so "don't let the" "simple", "cafeterialike decor scare you away" declare "delighted" diners; N.B. bargains include prix fixe deals for lunch and dinner.

☑ Fat Willy's Rib Shack *BBQ/Southern*　23 | 12 | 18 | $21

Logan Square | 2416 W. Schubert Ave. (Western Ave.) | 773-782-1800 | www.fatwillysribshack.com

"Everything is homemade and tasty" at this "family-friendly" Logan Square Southern setup serving "sweet and smoky" "BBQ the way it should be", with "lots of meat choices", including "tender ribs" with "tangy sauce", plus "heart attack–worthy macaroni and cheese", "more soups and salads than you'd think" and "awesome desserts" – all at "reasonable prices"; true, its decor is merely "decent", but at least it's "comfortable (and convenient for takeout)."

	FOOD	DECOR	SERVICE	COST

Feast *American*
| 18 | 17 | 16 | $28 |

Bucktown | 1616 N. Damen Ave. (North Ave.) | 773-772-7100 |
www.feastrestaurant.com

Debbie Sharpe's "dependable" Bucktown New American pairs a
"tasty, varied menu" of "good comfort food" incorporating "a dash
of contemporary" with a "very nice wine selection" – and "romantics" rave about the "beautiful alfresco dining"; some surveyors see
the service as "spotty", though, and those who deem dinner "hit-or-
miss" write the weekend "brunch is the best meal they offer";
N.B. drinkers can opt to BYO on Monday and Tuesday nights.

NEW Feed the Beast ◐ *American*
| - | - | - | I |

Lincoln Square | 4300 N. Lincoln Ave. (Cullom Ave.) | 773-478-9666 |
www.feedthebeastrestaurant.com

Lincoln Square's gastropub serves budget-conscious New American
bar food in a funky brown-orange-tan setting with exposed brick,
cafe tables and wild art (the side room has a more rustic feel left
over from its last occupant, a German bar); dishes come in both
their classic forms and in twists (ostrich burgers, lobster BLT,
cheeseburger pizza), and there's a late-night menu as well as a 'little
monsters' menu for baby barflies.

NEW Fiddlehead Café *American*
| - | - | - | M |

Lincoln Square | 4600 N. Lincoln Ave. (Wilson Ave.) | 773-751-1500 |
www.fiddleheadcafe.com

Seasonal New American fare at moderate prices takes over at the
remodeled Square Kitchen in Lincoln Square, complemented by a long
list of ports and wines by the glass/flight; the mood is modern yet
cozy, with comfy booths, funky light fixtures and a cool marble bar.

Filippo's *Italian*
| 20 | 14 | 19 | $30 |

Lincoln Park | 2211 N. Clybourn Ave. (Webster Ave.) | 773-528-2211 |
www.filipporistorante.com

"Not flashy" "but consistently good", this Lincoln Park Italian "neighborhood standby" serves "big plates" of "unique pastas that never
miss" and a "wide variety of seafood dishes" – all of which "make up
for the sometimes spotty service and average ambiance."

Finley's Grill Room ◐ *American*
| - | - | - | M |

Downers Grove | 3131 Finley Rd. (Branding Ln.) | 630-964-3131 |
www.finleysgrillroom.com

This spacious West Suburban crowd-pleaser serves substantial
American vittles such as a one-pound meatloaf – as well as lighter-
weight alternatives – in an exposed-brick-and-hardwood-floor setting;
there's also a lounge outfitted with big-screen TVs and a fireplace,
befitting a spot from nightclub veterans the Gatziolis brothers.

NEW Fiorentino's Cucina Italiana *Italian*
| - | - | - | M |

Lakeview | 2901 N. Ashland Ave. (George St.) | 773-244-3026 |
www.fiorentinoscucina.com

The Sicilian soul of this Lakeview storefront (previously Prego) extends
to the mostly Southern Italian menu, the hearty hospitality and the

warm, earthy environs with worn wood floors, pottery and rustic art including old black-and-white portraits of the owner's famiglia; alfresco fans can cool their heels in the lush garden patio with ivied walls, hanging plants, strings of lights and fresh herbs for the kitchen.

NEW 545 North *American* `-` `-` `-` `M`
Libertyville | 545 N. Milwaukee Ave. (Lake St.) | 847-247-8700
Quaint Downtown Libertyville plays host to this New American hot spot serving a moderately priced menu of simply styled sustenance (steaks, entree salads), as well as more adventurous fare like Moroccan braised beef short ribs; the former music store has a hip feel with exposed brick, a busy bar and seasonal patio dining.

Z Five O'Clock Steakhouse M *Steak* `26` `12` `22` `$46`
NEW Fox River Grove | 1050 E. Northwest Hwy. (Kelsey Rd.) | 847-516-2900 | www.fiveoclocksteakhouse.com
See review in the Milwaukee Directory.

Fixture ● *American* `-` `-` `-` `M`
Lincoln Park | 2706 N. Ashland Ave. (Diversey Pkwy.) | 773-248-3331 | www.fixturechicago.com
The Meritage folks have expanded their horizons with this New American small-plates spot in a made-over version of the old Burgundy Inn space on the fringe of Lincoln Park; the hot and cold dishes are creative enough to require a chef's glossary, and the cozy, updated space in warm browns and cool blue is also home to a moderately priced wine list with flights and a couple dozen glass pours.

Flat Top Grill *Asian* `19` `14` `16` `$20`
Lakeview | 3200 N. Southport Ave. (Belmont Ave.) | 773-665-8100
Old Town | 319 W. North Ave. (Orleans St.) | 312-787-7676
Market District | 1000 W. Washington Blvd. (Carpenter St.) | 312-829-4800
Evanston | 707 Church St. (bet. Orrington & Sherman Aves.) | 847-570-0100
Oak Park | 726 Lake St. (Oak Park Ave.) | 708-358-8200
www.flattopgrill.com
"If you're not full and happy when you leave it's your own fault" say fans of this "young, fun" chain of "do-it-yourself" all-you-can-eat Asian stir-fries, "solid cheap eateries" where "you choose your own ingredients" from a "great variety of fresh" provender; then again, those lacking "culinary can-do" may end up with "not the best outcome", and certain staffers who "tend to overcook" leave weary wokkers wondering "is the 15 minutes over for these types of restaurants?" N.B. the Lakeview, Old Town and Oak Park outposts have added an all-you-can-eat breakfast on weekends.

NEW Flatwater ● *Eclectic* `-` `-` `-` `M`
River North | 321 N. Clark St. (bet. Kinzie St. & Wacker Dr.) | 312-644-0283 | www.flatwater.us
From the owners of chichi Narcisse comes this extreme makeover of the old Blandino's Sorriso space on the edge of the Chicago River

that's luring a crowd of loungers and Loopers with tropical drinks and three squares of funky Eclectic comfort food; transporting touches include a landscaped terrace, fireplace, massive indoor-outdoor bar and boat dock for the fortunate few; N.B. late-night service runs till 2 AM on weekends.

Fleming's Prime Steakhouse & Wine Bar *Steak*

- | - | - | E

Lincolnshire | Lincolnshire Commons | 930 Milwaukee Ave. (Rte. 33) | 847-793-0333 | www.flemingssteakhouse.com

North Suburban Lincolnshire now has an outpost of the upscale national chophouse chain popular for its prime beef cuts ranging from eight to 40 ounces and 100 wines by the glass; purists will be pleased by the traditional preparations as well as the clubby steakhouse decor of the swanky, 8,000-sq.-ft. space, which includes an open kitchen and outdoor seating; N.B. a River North branch is set to open in 2008.

Flight ● *Eclectic*

19 | 20 | 18 | $36

Glenview | 1820 Tower Dr. (Patriot Blvd.) | 847-729-9463 | www.flightwinebar.com

Frequent fliers land at this "hip", "friendly" North Suburban "quickie" for a "fun place to nosh and drink with friends" on Eclectic "Asian-influenced" small-plate eats in a "sophisticated wine bar" setting that also features an "interesting selection of wines and presentation of flights"; grumps ground it as a "noisy" "mall stop", though, adding that the "concept fails more than it succeeds."

Flo Ⓜ *American*

22 | 17 | 18 | $19

West Town | 1434 W. Chicago Ave. (bet. Bishop & Noble Sts.) | 312-243-0477 | www.eatatflo.com

A flo-tilla of fans favors this "arty", "off-the-beaten-track" West Towner that "caters to the twentysomething pierced crowd" with American "cheap eats", including "great Southwestern" fare (the "Frito pie is a must"), and a "standing-room-only" Sunday brunch – "go midweek to avoid the crowds."

⛝ Fogo de Chão *Brazilian/Steak*

24 | 20 | 24 | $55

River North | 661 N. LaSalle St. (Erie St.) | 312-932-9330 | www.fogodechao.com

"Come hungry" to this River North Brazilian-style "never-ending" "orgy" of "spit-roasted" flesh, an outpost of an "all-you-can-eat South American" steakhouse chain, for a milieu of "meat, men and macho gauchos" bringing "a beef ballet" to your table "on traveling swords" ("food on a weapon always rocks!"), "boosted by a bountiful hot and cold buffet"; dainty eaters demur it's only "for the real meatasaurus", though, and belt-tighteners who eschew an "expensive night out" advise you to go for weekday-only lunch "instead of dinner."

Follia *Italian*

22 | 19 | 19 | $46

Market District | 953 W. Fulton St. (Morgan St.) | 312-243-2888 | www.folliachicago.com

Though "you wouldn't expect to find" it "amongst the 18-wheelers" and warehouses, this "hip" "jewel" makes its home in the Market

District, where its "very tasty" Northern Italian cooking includes "marvelous" "little pizzas" from a "wood-fired oven"; you can also choose from a "good selection of wines", and a "beautiful staff" enhances the "minimalist" "Milano decor" – even if opponents peg it as "pricey"; a sequel, called Tocco, is in the works.

Fonda del Mar *Mexican/Seafood* | - | - | - | M |

Logan Square | 3749 W. Fullerton Ave. (Ridgeway Ave.) | 773-489-3748

At this affordable Logan Square Mexican 'marisqueria' created by veterans of Frontera Grill and Mia Francesca, coastal artwork adorns a sunny yellow dining room where finatics tuck into authentic ceviche, soups, shellfish cocktails and seafood entries from the open kitchen; landlubbers can also choose from a limited selection of meat options.

foodlife *Eclectic* | 16 | 13 | 12 | $16 |

Streeterville | Water Tower Pl. | 835 N. Michigan Ave. (bet. Chestnut & Pearson Sts.) | 312-335-3663 | www.leye.com

Thirteen kitchens issue an Eclectic mix of eats that includes "every kind of ethnic and comfort food" "for the health nut to the trencherman" at this food court in Streeterville's Water Tower Place that's a "notch above" the norm; it's "fast" for when you need to "drop while you shop" (especially "for families of picky eaters"), though snarky shoppers say this "glorified cafeteria" is "overpriced" for a "self-serve concept" and can be as "frenetic as *MTV News*."

NEW Fornetto & Mei's Kitchen *Chinese/Italian* | - | - | - | I |

South Loop | Best Western Grant Park Hotel | 1108 S. Michigan Ave. (11th St.) | 312-294-2488 | www.bestwesternillinois.com

A quick, inexpensive South Loop option near a bevy of tourist attractions, this upscale food court and wine bar in back of the Best Western Grant Park Hotel offers a something-for-everyone station setup that renders the Italian-Chinese culinary combo less incongruous than at its progenitor, Fornetto Mei; Italian choices include a salad bar, wood-fired-oven pizza, panini and pasta, while Asian offerings include dumplings and duck; the thirsty will enjoy its Lavazza coffee bar, smart vino selection and adjacent wine retail shop.

Fornetto Mei *Chinese/Italian* | ▽ 19 | 17 | 20 | $39 |

Gold Coast | The Whitehall Hotel | 107 E. Delaware Pl. (bet. Michigan Ave. & Rush St.) | 312-573-6300 | www.thewhitehallhotel.com

Named for its "wood-burning pizza oven", this "friendly", "intimate" Gold Coast "boutique hotel" restaurant delivers a hybrid of Northern Italian and Chinese chow with a "generous selection of wines by the glass" in "an elegant but not stuffy dining room" – plus "a glassed-in porch with views of a pretty street scene"; adventurers affirm the "fusion" fare is a "neat surprise" but confused contributors complain the "strange menu makes it difficult to decide what to eat"; N.B. low-key live musicians entertain on weekend nights.

	FOOD	DECOR	SERVICE	COST

1492 Tapas Bar *Spanish* | 19 | 18 | 17 | $30

River North | 42 E. Superior St. (Wabash Ave.) | 312-867-1492 | www.1492tapasbar.com

Some explorers find this Spanish small-plates purveyor "tucked" away in a "quaint" River North "brownstone" with "lots of levels" to be a "sophisticated", "romantic" destination for "quality" tapas and "yummy sangria" – minus the "loud post-college crowd" of some competitors; still, others chart a course elsewhere, citing "slow service" and an "unimaginative", "overpriced" menu; N.B. the occasional Flamenco dancers on weekend nights are "a lot of fun."

☒ Francesca's Amici *Italian* | 23 | 19 | 20 | $32

Elmhurst | 174 N. York Rd. (2nd St.) | 630-279-7970

☒ Francesca's Bryn Mawr *Italian*

Edgewater | 1039 W. Bryn Mawr Ave. (Kenmore Ave.) | 773-506-9261

☒ Francesca's by the River *Italian*

St. Charles | 200 S. Second St. (Illinois St.) | 630-587-8221

☒ Francesca's Campagna *Italian*

West Dundee | 127 W. Main St. (2nd St.) | 847-844-7099

☒ Francesca's Famiglia *Italian*

NEW **Barrington** | Cook Street Plaza | 100 E. Station St. (Hough St.) | 847-277-1027

☒ Francesca's Fiore *Italian*

Forest Park | 7407 Madison St. (Harlem Ave.) | 708-771-3063

☒ Francesca's Forno *Italian*

Wicker Park | 1576 N. Milwaukee Ave. (North Ave.) | 773-770-0184

☒ Francesca's Intimo *Italian*

Lake Forest | 293 E. Illinois Rd. (Western Ave.) | 847-735-9235

☒ Francesca's on Taylor *Italian*

Little Italy | 1400 W. Taylor St. (Loomis St.) | 312-829-2828

☒ La Sorella di Francesca *Italian*

Naperville | 18 W. Jefferson Ave. (bet. Main & Washington Sts.) | 630-961-2706
www.miafrancesca.com
Additional locations throughout the Chicago area

"Consistently" "scrumptious" Italian "with an upscale touch", and "at reasonable prices", is the hallmark of this ever-extending family of "rustic, homey" city and suburban eateries, where the frequently "changing menu" makes "everything a special"; peripatetic patrons purport "service can vary" "across locations", however, and ambiance ranges from "romantic" to "ear-splitting", as some branches make "great use of space" whereas others have "tables on top of each other."

Francesco's Hole in the Wall ☞ *Italian* | 24 | 13 | 20 | $33

Northbrook | 254 Skokie Blvd. (bet. Dundee & Lake Cook Rds.) | 847-272-0155

"If you can get into" this "quaint", "tiny" North Suburban old-timer "with a huge following", you'll find "outstanding" "old-world [Southern] Italian" fare; "regulars" who rave about the "handwritten menu filled with delectable offerings" – including "fresh fish and"

"great pastas" – resolutely "put up with long waits, crowded tables, lots of noise" and a "cash-only" policy.

NEW Frasca Pizzeria & Wine Bar *Pizza* | - | - | - | I |

Lakeview | 3358 N. Paulina St. (Lincoln Ave.) | 773-248-5222 | www.frascapizzeria.com

The new go-to for Lakeview locals, this rustic, casual pizzeria issues great aromas and generously topped thin-crust pies from the open kitchen's monolithic pizza oven; a handful of starters, salads and entrees round out the menu, served with a wallet-friendly wine list in bustling environs anchored by a big river-rock bar that's suitable for dining; N.B. there's sidewalk seating too.

NEW fRedhots & Fries 🅂 *Hot Dogs* | - | - | - | I |

Glenview | 1707 Chestnut Ave. (bet. Monroe Ave. & Waukegan Rd.) | 847-657-9200

The North Suburban fast-food scene gets a boost with this casual, ketchup-and-mustard-colored hangout serving Chicago-style dogs, Angus burgers, Belgian frites with dipping sauces, gourmet sausages and, for the health-conscious, salads; like the menu, the service is a cut above hot-dog-stand standards with servers that ferry the food to Formica tables; N.B. expect picnic seating in the warm weather.

Froggy's French Cafe 🅂 *French* | 22 | 18 | 23 | $42 |

Highwood | 306 Green Bay Rd. (Highwood Ave.) | 847-433-7080 | www.froggyscatering.com

A "casual" favorite for "high-quality" Classic "French country food" with a seafood focus, this "North Shore standby" with a "personable staff" is a "popular" "gathering spot for the older group" and also "welcomes families, including kids"; that said, revivalists report that "redecorating and revamping the menu wouldn't hurt"; P.S. "the prix fixe meal has to be one of the best deals out there."

⚎ Frontera Grill 🅂 Ⓜ *Mexican* | 26 | 21 | 22 | $39 |

River North | 445 N. Clark St. (bet. Hubbard & Illinois Sts.) | 312-661-1434 | www.fronterakitchens.com

"Top-of-the-line Mexican [food] with a focus on fresh ingredients" comes courtesy of "culinary hero Rick Bayless" at this River North "treasure" with a "national reputation"; "bold, bright" and "somewhat raucous", it's "less expensive and more casual" than its "refined big brother", Topolobampo, with the same "superb wine selections" and "great margarita-tequila menu", but some say "service can be spotty when it's busy – which is always."

Fulton's on the River *Seafood/Steak* | 20 | 21 | 19 | $51 |

River North | 315 N. LaSalle St. (Wacker Dr.) | 312-822-0100 | www.fultonsontheriver.com

Cousin to Fulton's Crab House at Florida's Disney World, this "huge", "contemporary" "expense-account seafooder" and steakhouse is a "great new find for on-the-river dining" in River North; hooked honchos hail the "big", "diverse menu" of "fresh fish" and "prime steaks" and the "magnificent view", while holdouts who hint at early "kinks" hope "in time it might be a great restaurant."

	FOOD	DECOR	SERVICE	COST

☑ Gabriel's 🅱Ⓜ French/Italian | 26 | 22 | 26 | $62 |

Highwood | 310 Green Bay Rd. (Highwood Ave.) | 847-433-0031 | www.egabriels.com

It's "heaven in Highwood" say habitués of Gabe Viti's French-Italian, a "favorite" for "fantastic", "timeless food" that's "expensive but worth it", plus a "complete, commanding and comforting wine list", "effortless service with impeccable timing" and "elegant" environs; a few who feel it's getting "stale" object that the owner seems less in evidence at "his first creation" now that he has "opened more restaurants" (Miramar, Pancho Viti's).

NEW Gage, The American | - | - | - | M |

South Loop | 24 S. Michigan Ave. (Madison St.) | 312-372-4243 | www.thegagechicago.com

A welcome addition to the South Loop near Millennium Park and the Art Institute, this classy New American restaurant/tavern in a grand old Louis Sullivan building exudes an upscale, vintage feeling with its tin ceiling, green subway tile and massive bar; Dirk Flanigan (ex Blue Water Grill) puts a foodie spin on his midpriced pub fare; N.B. for parking, try the nearby north Grant Park garage.

NEW Gale's Coffee Bar Coffeehouse | - | - | - | I |

Wheeling | Westin Chicago North Shore | 601 N. Milwaukee Ave. (Apple Dr.) | 847-777-6590 | www.cenitare.com

Gale Gand (Tru, The Food Network's *Sweet Dreams*) brings her trademark sweet touch to her namesake sit-down/take-out coffee bar off the lobby at Northwest Suburban Wheeling's new Westin Hotel; the inexpensive menu, served from 6 AM–7 PM in a bright Euro cafe setting, features pastries and baked goods along with simple, fresh salads and sandwiches, Gale's root beer, champagne splits and half- and quarter-bottles of wine.

Gale Street Inn American | 20 | 15 | 19 | $28 |

Jefferson Park | 4914 N. Milwaukee Ave. (Lawrence Ave.) | 773-725-1300 | www.galestreet.com
Mundelein | 935 Diamond Lake Rd. (Rte. 45) | 847-566-1090 | www.galest.com Ⓜ

"The supper clubs of old" live on in these "comfy" "neighborhood institutions" – a "perennial Northwest Side establishment across from the Jefferson Park el stop" and a younger Mundelein location – that are separately owned but serving a similar, "fairly priced" Traditional American menu of "rocking ribs" and other "plain, simple" offerings; the "uninspired", though, report "uneventful meals", advising "do not go out of your way."

Gaylord Fine Indian Cuisine Indian | 22 | 14 | 19 | $28 |

River North | 678 N. Clark St. (Huron St.) | 312-664-1700
Schaumburg | 555 Mall Dr. (Higgins Rd.) | 847-619-3300
www.gaylordindia.net

Two "pleasant" city and Northwest Suburban sites, these "Indian comfort-food" stations "consistently" serve sustenance "that isn't too spicy" as well as "authentic options"; lauders who "love the tandoor

dishes, wonderful naan" and "terrific" lunch buffets write "who goes for the ambiance?" – though the Decor score may not reflect that the River North original "finally received a makeover."

Geja's Cafe *Fondue* 21 | 21 | 21 | $45

Lincoln Park | 340 W. Armitage Ave. (bet. Clark St. & Lincoln Ave.) | 773-281-9101 | www.gejascafe.com

"Classic fondue done right" is the calling card of this "can't-miss date location" in Lincoln Park, where the "kitschy" "'70s" "fun" "will leave you feeling warm and satisfied" – with help from the "excellent wine selection"; cuddlers coo that the nightly classical or "flamenco guitarist" "adds a touch of mystery" to the "catacomblike underground environment" ("secure a booth"), but "splattered" surveyors say it's only "romantic" "if you like sterno with your sweet nothings", warning "don't wear anything you care about."

Gene & Georgetti ●⊠ *Steak* 23 | 14 | 19 | $54

River North | 500 N. Franklin St. (Illinois St.) | 312-527-3718 | www.geneandgeorgetti.com

A "local landmark" "under the el tracks" in River North, this "classic Chicago beefatorium" and "boys' club" provides a "complete cholesterol transplant" via "decadent" *Flintstones*-sized portions" of prime steaks with "good Italian thrown in", all served by "old-fashioned waiters"; fed-up feeders feel that "regulars get preferred treatment" from the otherwise "grumpy" staffers and say the "tired interior" (like something "from a movie set") is "badly in need of an update."

☑ Gibsons Bar & Steakhouse ● *Steak* 25 | 19 | 23 | $56

Gold Coast | 1028 N. Rush St. (Bellevue Pl.) | 312-266-8999
Rosemont | Doubletree Hotel | 5464 N. River Rd. (bet. Balmoral & Bryn Mawr Aves.) | 847-928-9900
www.gibsonssteakhouse.com

"Aggressive carnivores" take an "authentic Chicago power trip" at this Gold Coast "high-roller" haven "where everything is big", including the "excellent cuts of [prime] meat cooked to perfection", "lampshade-sized martinis", the personalities of the "outgoing staff" – and "big check"; there's a "fantastic" "cigar-friendly" bar scene for those "long, crowded waits", so "make a reservation, arrive early and hope for your table before the seasons change"; P.S. "the Rosemont location is as good – and easier" to navigate.

NEW Ginger Asian Bistro ⓜ *Asian/Eclectic* - | - | - | M

Orland Park | 15700 S. Harlem Ave. (157th St.) | 708-633-1818 | www.gingerasianbistroweb.com

This ambitious South Suburban upstart transcends its mall location with imaginative, moderately priced Asian fusion–Eclectic cuisine (daikon ravioli, coffee-braised ribs, cookie dough rolls) artfully plated and served in a swank, intimate setting with warm lighting and multicolored walls meant to represent the different seasons; its limited wine list is supplemented by exotic libations including ginger, cherry blossom and Key-lime-pie martinis.

	FOOD	DECOR	SERVICE	COST

Gio *Italian*
19 | 19 | 20 | $29

Evanston | 1631 Chicago Ave. (bet. Church & Davis Sts.) | 847-869-3900 | www.giorestaurant.com

"Excellent wood-fired pizza" from the brick oven behind the bar plus "good salads" (even a "salad pizza" that's "a winner"), daily pasta and "fish specials", and an "above-average, affordable wine selection" lure Evanston locals to this "unpretentious" Northern Italian charmer "where you can actually talk" most times – though it "can get loud when near capacity"; P.S. it's also "priced very well."

Gioco *Italian*
21 | 20 | 18 | $39

South Loop | 1312 S. Wabash Ave. (13th St.) | 312-939-3870 | www.gioco-chicago.com

"Always hip and always reliable" for "fresh, well-made" "upscale [Northern] Italian" in the "hot new South Loop" neighborhood, this "warm and inviting" "former speakeasy" also serves up "lots of character", along with "loud", "clubby music" and – unfortunately – sometimes "spotty service"; N.B. Fred Ramos (ex Pili.Pili) is now the chef.

Ⓩ Giordano's *Pizza*
21 | 12 | 15 | $19

Loop | 135 E. Lake St. (Upper Michigan Ave.) | 312-616-1200
Loop | 223 W. Jackson Blvd. (Franklin St.) | 312-583-9400
Loop | 310 W. Randolph St. (Franklin St.) | 312-201-1441
River North | 730 N. Rush St. (Superior St.) | 312-951-0747 ◑
Lakeview | 1040 W. Belmont Ave. (Kenmore Ave.) | 773-327-1200
Edison Park | 5927 W. Irving Park Rd. (Austin Ave.) | 773-736-5553
Northwest Side | 2855 N. Milwaukee Ave. (Wolfram St.) | 773-862-4200
Southwest Side | 5159 S. Pulaski Rd. (Archer Ave.) | 773-582-7676 ◑
Southwest Side | 6314 S. Cicero Ave. (63rd St.) | 773-585-6100
Greektown | 815 W. Van Buren St. (Halsted St.) | 312-421-1221
www.giordanos.com
Additional locations throughout the Chicago area

A passel of pie-faces prefers the signature "knife-and-fork" stuffed 'za, "thick, juicy and cheesy" with "sinful" "pastrylike crust", though there are those who "particularly love the thin-crust" at this "chain" contender; fans feel the "slow, unfriendly service" and "lacking decor" "don't even matter" since "the focus is on the pie", but a faction of foes finds the "famous" pizza "pedestrian" and reckons "the rest of the menu needs work"; N.B. the "homey" River North flagship does not accept reservations.

Glenn's Diner Ⓜ *Diner*
– | – | – | M

Ravenswood | 1820 W. Montrose Ave. (Honore St.) | 773-506-1720 | www.glennsdiner.com

Ravenswood diners fishing for moderately priced, creative seafood can opt for the fresh specials scrawled on this spot's giant blackboards while those hankering for the likes of secret-recipe meatloaf, tuna melts, big salads and breakfast anytime can choose from the menu's more Traditional American faves; local artwork, marble counters and a wall of cereal boxes enliven the modern diner surroundings, while all-you-can-eat specials on Tuesday–Thursday nights appeal to big eaters.

	FOOD	DECOR	SERVICE	COST

Glunz Bavarian Haus Ⓜ *Austrian/German* | 19 | 15 | 19 | $30 |

Lincoln Square | 4128 N. Lincoln Ave. (bet. Belle Plaine & Warner Aves.) | 773-472-4287 | www.glunzbavarianhaus.com

Lately a "favorite among the Teutonic taverns", this "updated" German-Austrian venue in Lincoln Square offers Bavarian renditions that are "more modern" than most, but still "hearty" (and "not everything is brown"), along with a "fantastic beer selection on tap" and a location that "looks like a movie set for *The Sound of Music*"; add in garden seating and seasonal entertainment and you get an experience that's "nothing to schnitzel at."

Gold Coast Dogs *Hot Dogs* | 19 | 6 | 13 | $8 |

Loop | 159 N. Wabash Ave. (bet. Lake & Randolph Sts.) | 312-917-1677
Loop | 17 S. Wabash Ave. (Monroe St.) | 312-578-1133 ⊄
Uptown | 1429 W. Montrose Ave. (Clark St.) | 773-472-3600 ⊄
Rogers Park | 2349 W. Howard St. (Western Ave.) | 773-338-0900 ⊄
O'Hare Area | O'Hare Int'l Airport | Terminal 3 | 773-462-9942
O'Hare Area | O'Hare Int'l Airport | Terminal 5 | 773-462-0125 ●⊄
Southwest Side | Midway Int'l Airport | 5700 S. Cicero Ave. (55th St.) | 773-735-6789 ●
West Loop | Union Station | 225 S. Canal St. (Jackson Blvd.) | 312-258-8585 ⊄
Glenview | Glen Town Center | 1845 Tower Dr. (Patriot Blvd.) | 847-724-0123
www.goldcoastdogs.net
Additional locations throughout the Chicago area

"Drunk or sober", supporters say "arf!" to this litter of hot dog stands supplying "one helluva" "quintessential Chicago dog" ("tell 'em to 'drag it through the garden!'") plus "awesome cheese fries"; naysayers neuter this pack, though, vaunting "better versions" of these vittles elsewhere, and suggest some of these doghouses could use a visit from a housekeeper.

Goose Island Brewing Co. *Pub Food* | 16 | 16 | 17 | $20 |

Lincoln Park | 1800 N. Clybourn Ave. (Sheffield Ave.) | 312-915-0071
Wrigleyville | 3535 N. Clark St. (Addison St.) | 773-832-9040
www.gooseisland.com

"You won't find better microbreweries in Chicago" than this "fun", "family-friendly" Lincoln Park–Wrigleyville pair pouring "delicious beers", available in "flights" and "growlers to go"; the "upscale" Traditional American "pub food" ("with some beer in it") comes in second to the suds, though the "Stilton burger is an awesome choice", but "let's be honest – you didn't really come here for the food, did you?"

NEW Gordon Biersch Brewery Restaurant *American* | - | - | - | M |

Bolingbrook | Promenade Bolingbrook | 639 E. Boughton Rd. (Preston Dr.) | 630-739-6036 | www.gordonbiersch.com

West Suburban Bolingbrook is home to the first Illinois location of this microbrewery chain serving casual New American fare –

	FOOD	DECOR	SERVICE	COST

plus lots of salad and pizza options – in posh-for-a-pub environs warmed by eclectic upholstery and architectural lighting; there's also great glassware from which to guzzle the half-dozen beers brewed on the premises.

Grace O'Malley's *Pub Food*

17	16	17	$23

South Loop | 1416 S. Michigan Ave. (14th St.) | 312-588-1800 | www.graceomalleychicago.com

A "casual", "comfortable destination in the area" of the South Loop, this sophomore Irish-American pub is "a great addition to the neighborhood" for the "young, professional crowd", and a "Bears hot spot during football season", with "friendly service"; while a majority vindicates the "good", "varied" offerings, which include a "great" "buffet brunch" and "wine and beer specials", a collection of critics considers it of "inconsistent quality."

Grand Lux Cafe *Eclectic*

20	21	19	$26

River North | 600 N. Michigan Ave. (Ontario St.) | 312-276-2500 | www.grandluxcafe.com

"Basically an upscale Cheesecake Factory" "with many of the same items" – and "just as crammed as its sister" spot – this "boisterous" River North pack-'em-in purveyor proffers an "insanely diverse" Eclectic menu ("fabulous Asian nachos") with an emphasis on "oversized everything" amid "opulent", "over-the-top" surroundings (the "rotunda" "room" provides a "sensational view" of Boul Mich); bashers, though, brand it as "big hype on Michigan Avenue" that's "not bad if you don't mind" "formula" feeding, "crowds with lots of children and strollers", and "medium lux service."

NEW Graze *American*

-	-	-	M

River North | 35 W. Ontario St. (N. Dearborn St.) | 312-255-1234 | www.grazechicago.com

Alums of X/O take the creative New American small-plates concept – including scaled-down entrees – plus a retro-revival cocktail list to River North with high-style presentations at moderate prices for lunch and dinner; the sizable setting has a funky pastoral feel and features rustic reclaimed barn wood and a whimsical wall mural of golden fields and blue sky.

Greek Islands *Greek*

21	18	20	$27

Far South Side | 200 S. Halsted St. (Adams St.) | 312-782-9855 ◐

Lombard | 300 E. 22nd St. (Highland Ave.) | 630-932-4545 www.greekislands.net

Though it probably "hasn't changed since the last time you were there", this "huge, busy" Far South Side "standby" is "beyond criticism" to fans of its "lively", "family-style" "comfort-food" "classics", "fun staff" ("love the '*opa*' cries") and "homey", "Mediterranean-decorated" setting – plus "you can't beat the price"; Trojans take issue, though, saying its "steam-table" sustenance is "for the masses", not the "adventurous"; P.S. to Lombard locals it's "great to have good" Greek cuisine "in the [Western] 'burbs."

	FOOD	DECOR	SERVICE	COST

Green Dolphin Street ⓜ *American* — 19 | 20 | 18 | $46

Lincoln Park | 2200 N. Ashland Ave. (Webster Ave.) | 773-395-0066 |
www.jazzitup.com

"Dinner comes with free entrance to the adjoining jazz club/bar" at
this fringe-dwelling Lincoln Park "date place" "on the riverfront" (with
the "perfect patio" and boat docking in summer); "you could drive by
this place a million times and never realize" what a "cool environment"
is inside, though opinions on the New American cuisine range from
"solid" and "creative" to "overpriced" and "somewhat forgettable."

Green Door Tavern *American* — 14 | 18 | 18 | $21

River North | 678 N. Orleans St. (Chicago Ave.) | 312-664-5496

"You'll be walking crooked before your first drink" at this River North
"haunt", a "landmark" with "leaning walls", "local charisma" and a
circa-1921 speakeasy in the basement; it represents a "fast-
disappearing Chicago-type bar/restaurant" (it's "now surrounded
by million-dollar condos"), with "fun decor" that will "keep your
eyes busy for hours" and help you overlook the "simple" – some say
"so-so" – Traditional American "grub."

ⓩ Green Zebra *Vegetarian* — 25 | 23 | 23 | $51

West Town | 1460 W. Chicago Ave. (Greenview Ave.) | 312-243-7100 |
www.greenzebrachicago.com

"You don't have to be a tree-hugger to love" this West Town "winner"
where Shawn McClain (Spring, Custom House) "makes you want to
eat your vegetables" with his "phenomenal", "complex" "seasonal"
"small plates" ("converts" crow "you'll never miss the meat" –
though a few "chicken and fish dishes" are also offered); add
"knowledgeable service" and "smart" "Zen" surroundings and you
have a "haute" "heaven" – though catty carnivores contend "nothing
impresses as much as the prices."

Grill on the Alley, The *American* — 18 | 18 | 18 | $42

Streeterville | Westin Hotel | 909 N. Michigan Ave. (Delaware Pl.) |
312-255-9009 | www.thegrill.com

A "varied menu" of "very good" Traditional American vittles in an
"old-fashioned", "formal bar-and-grill" setting satisfies Streeterville
steakhouse seekers, especially given that it's "superior for a hotel"
venue and "always a safe bet for getting a table"; still, critical corre-
spondents "who have been to the real Grill on the Alley in Beverly
Hills" are "not thrilled" by what they consider "average" meals at
"Michigan Avenue prices."

Grillroom, The *Steak* — 17 | 18 | 18 | $35

Loop | 33 W. Monroe St. (bet. Dearborn & State Sts.) | 312-960-0000
NEW **Westmont** | 200 W. Ogden Ave. (Washington St.) | 630-824-4090
www.restaurants-america.com

"When you're looking to take lunch up a notch", or for a "pre-show,
pre-symphony spot", supporters suggest this "well-located" Loop
venue where the "reliable" if "nothing-fancy" "steakhouse fare"
comes with an "excellent variety of salads" and "specials showing
more of a seasonal flair", all in a "classic wood-finish" locale; despite

this, diners who deem it "decidedly average" yawn "you sit in a room, and apparently the food is grilled, and there's not much more to it than that"; N.B. the Westmont branch opened post-Survey.

Grotto ⑤ *Italian/Steak* | 18 | 17 | 17 | $40 |
Gold Coast | 1030 N. State St. (Rush St.) | 312-280-1005 | www.grottoonstate.com
Gold Coasters who go for "good dining just off Rush Street" (including "great chicken Vesuvio") frequent this Italian steakhouse for its "romantic setting" with an "awesome bar" and "great tables overlooking the atrium"; worriers "wonder if it can compete with the heavyweights", though, believing it's best suited to "a slightly older crowd looking for drinks."

NEW Gruppo di Amici ◑ Ⓜ *Pizza* | - | - | - | M |
Rogers Park | 1508 W. Jarvis Ave. (Greenview Ave.) | 773-508-5565 | www.gruppodiamici.com
A floor-to-ceiling pizza oven is the centerpiece of the open kitchen at this Rogers Park Roman-style pie palace, home to nine or so crusty, wood-fired creations and an Italian menu featuring calzone and fresh pastas consulted on by Donatella Majore de Vette (La Cucina di Donatella); the family-friendly space has a bustling neighborhood vibe and sidewalk seating.

Gulliver's Pizzeria & Restaurant *Pizza* | 17 | 22 | 18 | $19 |
Rogers Park | 2727 W. Howard St. (California Ave.) | 773-338-2166
A Rogers Park "staple" "for a zillion years" (since 1965), this "extremely kid-friendly" Eclectic eatery serves up "not just pizza but a whole experience" amid "wonderful, weird decor" with a "huge collection of collections", including "antiques", "statuary and chandeliers", plus a "great outdoor beer garden"; still, some Lilliputians who lament the "huge menu" of "bland" fare "wish the food was as interesting" as the interior, adding "stay away from the Mexican and Asian entrees."

NEW Habana Libre *Cuban* | - | - | - | I |
West Town | 1440 W. Chicago Ave. (bet. Bishop St. & Greenview Ave.) | 312-243-3303
Vibrant Cuban flavors at bargain prices have lunch and dinner crowds packing into this West Town BYO, where dim lighting, peachy walls and enticing aromas render the storefront interior much cozier than it appears from the mundane strip-mall exterior; friendly servers, coffee drinks and *batidas* (shakes) add to the authenticity of its neighborhood-y ambiance.

Hachi's Kitchen *Japanese* | - | - | - | M |
Logan Square | 2521 N. California Ave. (Altgeld St.) | 773-276-8080 | www.hachiskitchen.com
The name sounds quaint, but this sexy Logan Square spot – with its sunken lounge area, curving sushi bar and clubby music – is anything but; an omakase offering (chef's choice) and a dozen premium sakes add spark to the Japanese menu featuring all the moderately priced standards you'd expect from a Sai Café sister.

Hacienda Tecalitlan 🗲Ⓜ *Mexican* ▽ 20 | 22 | 21 | $21

Ukrainian Village | 820 N. Ashland Ave. (Chicago Ave.) | 312-243-6667
Supporters say the eats at this "two-story" Ukrainian Village
"Mexican colonial fantasy palace" are "a bit more authentic than the
more trendy spots", plus the "cozy adjoining bar serves big
margaritas" – and if that isn't enough to "love", the "festive" mood
comes "complete with mariachis" and dancing on weekends.

Hackney's *American* 18 | 13 | 17 | $20

Printer's Row | 733 S. Dearborn St. (bet. Harrison & Polk Sts.) |
312-461-1116
Glenview | 1241 Harms Rd. (Lake Ave.) | 847-724-5577
Glenview | 1514 E. Lake Ave. (bet. Sunset Ridge & Waukegan Rds.) |
847-724-7171
Wheeling | 241 S. Milwaukee Ave. (Dundee Rd.) | 847-537-2100
Lake Zurich | 880 N. Old Rand Rd. (Rand Rd.) | 847-438-2103
Palos Park | 9550 W. 123rd St. (La Grange Rd.) | 708-448-8300
www.hackneys.net

For "a great big heaping helping of nostalgia", surveyors say these
suburban American "time warps" (or the newer Printer's Row location) are "still the place to go" thanks to "great greasy burgers" on
"black bread soaked by the juice" plus "that onion loaf thing" that's
"to die for – probably literally"; unsentimental sorts surmise the
"service can be iffy", though, and hint these "hackneyed" hamburger haunts are "living on past laurels."

Hai Yen *Chinese/Vietnamese* 22 | 13 | 17 | $17

🆕 **Lincoln Park** | 2723 N. Clark St. (Diversey Pkwy.) | 773-868-4888
Uptown | 1055 W. Argyle St. (bet. Kenmore & Winthrop Aves.) |
773-561-4077
www.haiyenrestaurant.com

Though "the entire Asian restaurant scene on Argyle is getting more
competitive", this "fancier" find "still stands out" as "one of the best of
its class" to savorers of its "lovely" "fresh" Mandarin-"Vietnamese"
victuals ("their seven courses of beef make life complete"), which
"don't intimidate neophytes" and are accompanied by "great bubble
tea"; a few faultfinders, however, feel it doesn't deliver overall "authenticity"; N.B. the Lincoln Park branch opened post-Survey.

Half Shell 🚫 *Seafood* 22 | 9 | 12 | $29

Lakeview | 676 W. Diversey Pkwy. (bet. Clark & Orchard Sts.) |
773-549-1773

"Lovers" of "outstanding, fresh seafood" insist you "can't go wrong" at
this longtime Lakeview lair, despite its "infamous reputation" of being
a "seedy" "hole-in-the-wall" with "crotchety" "personnel", a "cash-
only" collection policy and sometimes "killer waits" that can make
some claw-craving customers "crabby" (they don't take reservations).

🆕 Hamburger Mary's *Hamburgers* – | – | – | I

Andersonville | 5400 N. Clark St. (Balmoral Ave.) | 773-784-6969 |
www.hamburgermaryschicago.com

A wacky purple awning heralds this Andersonville outpost of the
gay-friendly hamburger chain, a retro-kitsch room serving an

	FOOD	DECOR	SERVICE	COST

Eclectic menu with sassy descriptions and cocktails like the 'zipper ripper'; pumping music and live entertainment lend to the late-night vibe, though a 'little lambs' menu means it's also kid-friendly; N.B. munchies can be had till 2 AM.

Hannah's Bretzel ⑤ *Sandwiches* | - | - | - | I |

Loop | 180 W. Washington St. (bet. N. La Salle & Wells Sts.) | 312-621-1111
NEW **Loop** | Illinois Center | 233 N. Michigan Ave. (S. Water St.) | 312-621-1111
www.hannahsbretzel.com
Pretzel-bread from a 15th century German recipe and organic fillings upgrade the Euro-style sandwiches at this green-chic, counter-service Loop duo, which also sells salads, soups and a dazzling selection of all-natural chocolate bars; an environmentally friendly operation, it uses a low-emission MINI Cooper for deliveries; N.B. visit the Michigan Avenue location if you're looking to eat in.

Happy Chef Dim Sum House ❶ *Chinese* | 23 | 9 | 14 | $16 |

Chinatown | 2164 S. Archer Ave. (Cermak Rd.) | 312-808-3689
"Highly recommended" dim sum is served "à la carte" – but with "no carts" – from 9 AM to 4 PM, while "authentic" and "crazy-cheap" Cantonese fare is offered throughout the day and into the "late night" (2 AM) at this Chinatown chowhouse; "don't expect great service", though, and do expect "minimal decor" that really "needs a kick in the pants."

Harbour House Ⓜ *Seafood* | - | - | - | E |

Winnetka | Laundry Mall | 566 Chestnut St. (Spruce St.) | 847-441-4600
Set in the former Fio space in Winnetka's Laundry Mall, this "sophisticated, yet unpretentious" spot fills a niche with "truly delicious", "innovative seafood dishes" offered along with "outstanding air and land selections", making for one of "the best combined food and atmosphere" experiences in the Northern Suburbs; P.S. other assets include "live music" on Fridays, summer patio seating and weekend brunch.

Hard Rock Cafe ❶ *American* | 13 | 20 | 13 | $25 |

River North | 63 W. Ontario St. (bet. Clark & Dearborn Sts.) | 312-943-2252 | www.hardrock.com
The "awesome" "memorabilia on the walls" is "why you go" to this 21-year-old "chain" member that's "full of spirit" (and "loud music") and serves up "average" American eats that appeal to "kids" and "tourists"; rock critics call it a "T-shirt factory" where the "bland food" is "a sideline" and the "service is always close to bad", quipping that they'll "just drop off the out-of-town relatives next time."

Haro ⑤Ⓜ *Spanish* | - | - | - | M |

Southwest Side | 2436 S. Oakley Ave. (24th Pl.) | 773-847-2400 | www.harotapas.com
This budget-friendly Basque specialist brings tapas, *pintxos* (open-face sandwiches) and entrees to the Heart of Italy, as well as regional wines and three types of sangria served in *porrons*, ceramic pitchers from which you pour the drink directly into your mouth; it's

	FOOD	DECOR	SERVICE	COST

housed in a former antiques shop with ochre walls, warm wood and exposed brick, where live bands and flamenco guitarists perform.

Harry Caray's *Italian/Steak* | 19 | 20 | 19 | $37 |

River North | 33 W. Kinzie St. (Dearborn St.) | 312-828-0966
Rosemont | O'Hare International Ctr. | 10233 W. Higgins Rd. (Mannheim Rd.) | 847-699-1200

Harry Caray's Seventh Inning Stretch *Italian/Steak*

Southwest Side | Midway Int'l Airport | 5757 S. Cicero Ave. (55th St.) | 773-948-6300
www.harrycarays.com

"Named after the beloved former Cubs announcer", these slices of "baseball junkie heaven" where "you could spend hours looking at all the memorabilia on the walls" serve "plentiful plates of flavorful" Italian steakhouse food ("they don't serve steaks here – they serve cows") in an "upscale sports bar" setting; unimpressed umpires, though, flag them as "average" "for the money"; N.B. a Lombard location was set to open post-Survey.

Harvest *American* | - | - | - | E |

St. Charles | Pheasant Run Resort | 4051 E. Main St. (Pheasant Run) | 630-524-5080 | www.pheasantrun.com

A West Suburban getaway in the historic dairy barn of the Pheasant Run Resort, this New American showcases Midwestern ingredients – including pan-roasted Wisconsin pheasant, fresh produce in season and artisanal cheeses – along with hearty steak, seafood and game classics paired with California and regional wines, microbrews and fruit-infused martinis in a warm, retro lodge setting.

Hashalom Ⓜ☞ *Israeli/Moroccan* | - | - | - | I |

Northwest Side | 2905 W. Devon Ave. (Francisco Ave.) | 773-465-5675

"Known mostly by regulars", this Northwest Side "storefront" BYO is noteworthy for its Moroccan-"Israeli fusion cuisine", including what some say are the "best falafel" and lamb shish kebab going; the "staff tries to please", and partialists "wish the place were open more hours" (it serves from noon to 9 PM, Wednesday through Sunday).

HB Ⓜ *American* | 22 | 18 | 19 | $32 |

Lakeview | 3404 N. Halsted St. (Roscoe St.) | 773-661-0299 | www.homebistrochicago.com

"Creative, cheeky [New] American eats" courtesy of executive chef–owner JonCarl Lachman (his new menu and decor aren't reflected in the ratings) beckon a "beautiful straight/gay crowd" to this "quaint" "keeper" in a "petite" "storefront", where "BYO helps keep the tab down"; holdouts hedge, though, saying "when service catches up to the food quality, we may have a Boys Town hit"; P.S. the "tasty" weekend brunch boasts "amazing beignets."

Heartland Cafe *Eclectic/Vegetarian* | 16 | 15 | 16 | $17 |

Rogers Park | Heartland Bldg. | 7000 N. Glenwood Ave. (Lunt Ave.) | 773-465-8005 | www.heartlandcafe.com

For 30 years, this "earthy-crunchy" Rogers Park "health-food" "haven" has been "where the hippies go" for "great beer", "live bands"

and poetry, and "good, hearty" Eclectic and vegetarian eats served with "optimism" (plus some of "the best outdoor seating" in town) – but eaters with images of "everyone wearing tye-dye and putting daisies in soldiers' gun barrels" say the "slacker" staff is too "laid-back" and "wish the food were better"; P.S. there's a "fabulous general store" on-site.

Heat *Japanese* | 25 | 21 | 23 | $85 |

Old Town | 1507 N. Sedgwick St. (North Ave.) | 312-397-9818 | www.heatsushi.com

Sushi is a life and death matter at this "unique" Old Town Japanese omakase-only outpost offering the "most amazing selections of imported seafoods and sake"; the "live-kill" candidates "swim by your feet at the bar", making for plates of "food so fresh it's still moving" – in other words, it's "not for the faint of heart", or the light of wallet, given that it's "very expensive"; N.B. bringing children is discouraged.

☑ Heaven on Seven *Cajun/Creole* | 21 | 16 | 18 | $24 |

Loop | Garland Bldg. | 111 N. Wabash Ave., 7th fl. (Washington Blvd.) | 312-263-6443 ☒ ⌨

River North | 600 N. Michigan Ave., 2nd fl. (bet. Ohio & Ontario Sts.) | 312-280-7774

Naperville | 224 S. Main St. (bet. Jackson & Jefferson Aves.) | 630-717-0777

www.heavenonseven.com

"Tourists" and regulars relish the "reliable" "rajun Cajun" and Creole food served "in good portions" at this "Mardi Gras-ish" trio, home of "spicy" "done right", "more hot sauces than Imelda Marcos had shoes" and a "nonstop party"; some suggest it's "the best you can get in Chicago", though purists purport it "can't compete with real New Orleans food", say "service can be hit-or-miss" and contend it's "coasting on its rep"; N.B. the Loop location still doesn't take credit cards.

Hecky's Barbecue *BBQ* | 21 | 5 | 13 | $17 |

Evanston | 1902 Green Bay Rd. (Emerson St.) | 847-492-1182

Hecky's of Chicago *BBQ*

Near West | 1234 N. Halsted St. (Division St.) | 312-377-7427

www.heckys.com

"Leave the fancy duds at home" and head for this Evanston "institution" earning "thumbs-up" for "cheap eats" with "true BBQ flavor", including "some of the best ribs" around, with "tangy, tasty sauce" – not to mention "authentic, mouthwatering Southern-style fried chicken"; tipsters tell us "takeout is better", though, due to "nonexistent ambiance", and traditionalists tout the original as "better than the [Near West] Chicago" sequel.

Hema's Kitchen *Indian* | 20 | 10 | 13 | $20 |

Lincoln Park | 2411 N. Clark St. (Fullerton Pkwy.) | 773-529-1705

West Rogers Park | 6406 N. Oakley Ave. (W. Devon Ave.) | 773-338-1627

"Wonderful", "offbeat dishes" of "succulent" Indian cuisine made from "fresh ingredients" and "available at all spice levels" appeal to

allegiants of this "favorite" "Devon-area choice", who sometimes "miss seeing Mama Hema around since she now divides her time between two restaurants" (and is planning a third); Lincoln Park locals sense their spin-off is "not as cheap or as good as its sister" spot – but "very little ambiance" and "crazy-slow" service seem to be constants; P.S. both are BYO and "good for vegetarians."

Hemmingway's Bistro *American/French* ▽ | 21 | 21 | 21 | $33
Oak Park | The Write Inn | 211 N. Oak Park Ave. (Ontario St.) | 708-524-0806 | www.hemmingwaysbistro.com
"Left Bank dining" from a "really nice" menu of "creative" French "bistro fare" and Traditional American classics – all fashioned from predominantly organic ingredients and accompanied by a "great wine list" – make this "very relaxed" and "beautiful" "undiscovered jewel" in the "quaint" Write Inn a "great couples' night out" in Oak Park.

NEW Honey 1 BBQ Ⓜ *BBQ* - | - | - | I
Bucktown | 2241 N. Western Ave. (Lyndale St.) | 773-227-5130 | www.honey1bbq.com
The South Side isn't the only spot for barbecue: this family-operated Bucktown BYO bastion slow-cooks Arkansas-style pork (ribs, links, tips and pulled) and chicken in its huge aquarium-style wood smoker, and serves it up with mild or hot house sauces in a friendly if spartan space decorated with photos, sports memorabilia and a plasma TV; prices are as modest as the setting.

NEW Hop Häus ● *Hamburgers* - | - | - | I
River North | 646 N. Franklin St. (Erie St.) | 312-467-4287
A gourmet burger tavern and sports lounge takes over the former Leona's River North, offering 20-plus patty treatments from relatively classic to 'worldly' (global influences), 'pseudo' (non-meat) and 'wildish' (game), served in a casual setting of checkered tablecloths, stained-glass lamps and lots of TVs; craft beers, cocktails and a limited but well-chosen wine list help "keep 'em comin' till 4 in da mornin'."

Hot Chocolate Ⓜ *American* 23 | 22 | 21 | $33
Bucktown | 1747 N. Damen Ave. (Wabansia Ave.) | 773-489-1747 | www.hotchocolatechicago.com
"Chocoholics" will "go here in a heartbeat" for the "scrumptious" sweets from dessert diva Mindy Segal (ex mk), "definitely the high point" of this "trendy", "crowded" Bucktowner ("the pastry work station front and center is proof"); that said, "the savory side" of its "limited but interesting" Traditional American "comfort-food" menu "is no slouch either", and even the "chocolaty decor" is rich – but wallet-watchers warn so are the comestibles' "high prices."

Ⓩ Hot Doug's Ⓩ✄ *Hot Dogs* 25 | 13 | 19 | $9
Northwest Side | 3324 N. California Ave. (Roscoe St.) | 773-279-9550 | www.hotdougs.com
Carnivores "wait in line" at Doug Sohn's "legendary encased-meats emporium", where there's "more seating" and better parking than at

his original haunt but the same "lousy hours" (the kitchen closes at 4 PM); rest assured, though, that "it's worth" it for his "outrageously decadent sausage sandwiches", including more than a dozen "gourmet hot dogs" – no, it's "not an oxymoron" – ranging from "rabbit" to "rattlesnake"; P.S. he "puts the fry in Friday with his duck-fat fries" (available on Saturday too).

Hot Tamales *Mexican*   21 | 12 | 18 | $21

Highland Park | 493 Central Ave. (St. John Ave.) | 847-433-4070 | www.hottamales4u.com

"The atmosphere is loud but the cuisine is louder" at this "crowded" North Shore family "favorite" for "delicious", "creative" (some say "inauthentic") "made-to-order" Mexican such as "duck tacos from heaven" and a "wonderful salmon burrito"; the "non-romantic atmosphere" – and sometimes the staff – "will hurry your meal along", especially "if there's a wait" (no reservations); P.S. "the summer outdoor dining is the hottest seat in town."

House of Blues Back Porch *Southern*   16 | 23 | 17 | $29

River North | 329 N. Dearborn St. (Kinzie St.) | 312-923-2007 | www.hob.com

"Known more for fun" and for "strong drinks" than for its "chainlike" American food "with a Southern slant", this River North haunt harbors "cool" "theme" decor, "especially for music fans"; it's "a little pricey for casual dining", but "eating here lets you skip the line for that night's show" – and the "Sunday gospel brunch" will "cleanse your sins away."

☑ Hugo's Frog Bar & Fish House ● *Seafood*   24 | 19 | 22 | $48

Gold Coast | 1024 N. Rush St. (bet. Bellevue Pl. & Oak St.) | 312-640-0999

Naperville | Main Street Promenade Bldg. | 55 S. Main St. (bet. Benton & Van Buren Aves.) | 630-548-3764
www.hugosfrogbar.com

"Always a hoppin' scene", this "Gold Coast favorite" for "fresh fish" ("unreal crab cakes") shares a kitchen and has some menu crossover with its sib, Gibsons Steakhouse, as well as a "similarly authentic Chicago power trip", "Rush Street prices" and "noise" level; still, waverers "wish the service was as consistent as the food", and penny-wise patrons posit the "portions and prices could both be reduced"; P.S. the Naperville outpost makes locals "feel as if [they're] in on all the action."

NEW Hunter's *Eclectic*   - | - | - | M

St. Charles | 305 W. Main St. (3rd St.) | 630-444-1835

A moderately priced Eclectic menu at this white-tablecloth entry in West Suburban St. Charles includes everything from straightforward Americana to a melting pot of Italian and Thai dishes; the renovated historic building (formerly an antiques store) features exposed brick and Tuscan-inspired faux finishes; N.B. it shares a kitchen with – and cooks lunch for – the unaffiliated tavern next door.

	FOOD	DECOR	SERVICE	COST

NEW Icosium Kafe *African* — | — | — | I

Andersonville | 5200 N. Clark St. (Foster Ave.) | 773-271-5233 | www.icosiumkafe.com

Andersonville's casual Algerian cafe presents an assortment of sweet and savory crêpes, plus a build-your-own option, in a bazaar-like setting that blends Corner Grille hand-me-downs (black-and-white tiled floor, orange booths) with exotic beaded light fixtures and tapestry fabrics; N.B. you can BYO or sip from its selection of fresh juices, organic teas and coffees.

NEW Il Covo *Italian* — | — | — | M

Bucktown | 2152 N. Damen Ave. (Webster Ave.) | 773-862-5555 | www.ilcovochicago.com

A gut rehab of Bucktown's old Babaluci space brings updated urban style and Italian cooking (housemade pastas and gelati, quail saltimbocca, zucchini blossoms with limoncello risotto) to what's now a bi-level hipster haven of exposed brick, honeyed wood and funky, colorful furnishings; the second-floor lounge combines dining with cocktail/smoking seating including a semiprivate arc of banquettes.

Il Mulino New York *Italian* — | — | — | E

Gold Coast | 1150 N. Dearborn St. (bet. Division & Elm Sts.) | 312-440-8888 | www.ilmulinonewyork.com

New York's old-guard Italian has settled into the Gold Coast mansion once home to Biggs; a showy antipasto display graces the foyer, which leads to multiple posh dining rooms (all with fireplaces) where tuxedoed servers present well-heeled diners with high-tariff traditional fare – including many dishes prepared tableside – and a list of 200 Italian wines.

Ina's *American* 19 | 15 | 19 | $22

West Loop | 1235 W. Randolph St. (Elizabeth St.) | 312-226-8227 | www.breakfastqueen.com

"Innovative and delicious" New American "home cooking" "is made from scratch with care" at this "cozy" West Loop "winner" where owner Ina Pinkney is the "great hostess" and diners "delight in" a "funky" feel, "friendly staff", "free parking" and "charming salt and pepper sets"; some surveyors say "stick to breakfast" (if you don't mind a "long wait"), but boosters brag "everything is good here, including dinner."

Z India House *Indian* 23 | 17 | 19 | $25

River North | 59 W. Grand Ave. (bet. Clark & Dearborn Sts.) | 312-645-9500

Buffalo Grove | Buffalo Grove Town Ctr. | 228-230 McHenry Rd. (Lake Cook Rd.) | 847-520-5569

Schaumburg | 1521 W. Schaumburg Rd. (Springinsguth Rd.) | 847-895-5501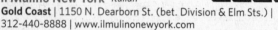

Chicago's "best Indian" fare can be found at this threesome that thrives thanks to "generous portions" of "fantastic", "fresh, authentic" "standards" for both "those who like spicy" and "novices" too; even contributors who consider it "a bit pricey" think the "extensive"

lunch buffets are "an affordable delight", and raters out of River North range are grateful for the "convenient suburban locations."

Indian Garden, The *Indian* | 22 | 13 | 17 | $25 |

Streeterville | 247 E. Ontario St., 2nd fl. (Fairbanks Ct.) | 312-280-4910
West Rogers Park | 2546 W. Devon Ave. (Rockwell St.) | 773-338-2929
Schaumburg | 855 E. Schaumburg Rd. (Plum Grove Rd.) | 847-524-3007
Westmont | 6020 S. Cass Ave. (60th St.) | 630-769-9662
www.indiangardenchicago.com

"Excellent" curries, tikka dishes and vegetarian choices are on the "large" menu at this quartet of Indian installations favored as places "for the entire family to have a great meal" "at a sensible price" (especially via the "bargain lunch buffets"); few mind that they're "not much to look at", though some say "service varies from cordial and attentive to brusque" and slow.

Indie Cafe *Japanese/Thai* ▽ | 19 | 13 | 18 | $22 |

Edgewater | 5951 N. Broadway (bet. Elmdale & Thorndale Aves.) | 773-561-5577 | www.indiecafe.us

"Creative sushi" meets "spice-authentic" Siamese at this "microscopic" BYO "hipster" in Edgewater with "a large, innovative menu" that's "perfect for the bipolar eater" – or for anyone "squeamish" about raw Japanese fare "since their Thai food is equally delicious" (and "the plate presentation is even better"); P.S. when the "cramped" space is "crowded", one can "wait at the bar across the street" and they'll "call you via your cell when your table's ready."

Irazu 🗷🗷 *Costa Rican* | 22 | 8 | 17 | $13 |

Bucktown | 1865 N. Milwaukee Ave. (Western Ave.) | 773-252-5687 | www.irazuchicago.com

"Nice", "earnest" people run this "still-relatively hidden gem", a "small" BYO "with big food" in the form of "consistently fresh", "genuine" Costa Rican cuisine (and some Mex) with "lots of vegetarian choices" – and "don't miss the tropical-fruit-and-oatmeal shakes"; it's "a hole-in-the-wall for sure" ("so basic it's hip"), but there's a "busy, Latin vibe", and "bargain"-hunters bask in "prices that make you think they don't know Bucktown has gentrified."

Irish Oak Restaurant & Pub *Pub Food* ▽ | 19 | 19 | 20 | $18 |

Wrigleyville | 3511 N. Clark St. (Addison St.) | 773-935-6669 | www.irishoak.com

"More than just a cheap imitation", this Wrigleyville watering hole with "true Irish character" is like "a visit to the Emerald Isle without leaving the city", delighting denizens with "pub-style" "comfort food" including "great burgers" and "fantastic fish 'n' chips" paired with "a perfect pour of Guinness" "at the correct temperature"; P.S. the "decor was actually imported from Erin" in crates.

☑ Isabella's Estiatorio 🗷 *Mediterranean* | 26 | 23 | 25 | $45 |

Geneva | 330 W. State St. (4th St.) | 630-845-8624 | www.isabellasgeneva.com

Expect "excellent, innovative Mediterranean" fare that's "full of flavor" (and mostly organic ingredients), accompanied by a "limited" but

"very nice wine list" and served by a "staff committed to delivering an exceptional meal" will "make you feel like you're at the best restaurant Downtown" – "without the attitude" – at this "elegant" new favorite in the Western Suburbs, complete with patio seating; N.B. keep an eye out for their planned outpost in the Market District.

Itto Sushi ● 🅢 *Japanese* | 22 | 12 | 20 | $31 |

Lincoln Park | 2616 N. Halsted St. (Wrightwood Ave.) | 773-871-1800 | www.ittosushi.com

"Basic" "no-frills sushi" and other "authentic Japanese fare" bring loyalists to this longtime Lincoln Park neighborhood "favorite"; it's "friendly" and "family-owned", with "attentive service", making it "great for the price – even if the decor won't win any awards."

Izumi Sushi Bar & Restaurant *Japanese* | ▽ 23 | 18 | 19 | $33 |

Market District | 731 W. Randolph St. (Halsted St.) | 312-207-5299 | www.izumisushi.com

A "hidden" contemporary Japanese "jewel" and sake bar in the Market District, this "quiet alternative" to some of its noisier neighbors harbors "terrific" "innovative sushi" in a "fun" setting with "great background music"; raters reckon it's "worth a return visit", and owls hoot that it's "open late" (1 AM on Fridays and Saturdays, 11 PM otherwise).

Jack's on Halsted *American* | 21 | 17 | 19 | $36 |

Lakeview | 3201 N. Halsted St. (Belmont Ave.) | 773-244-9191 | www.jackjonesrestaurants.com

The menu is "daring" and the "diverse" crowd includes daters "of the same sex" at this seasonal New American "on the edge of Boys Town", where the "casual" "fine dining" has its constituents, as does the "nice brunch" on Sundays and "perfectly twinkly" "upscale atmosphere" afforded by the "great attached wine bar"; doubters have decided it's "dependable but not extraordinary", though theatergoers think it might be the "best of the pre–Briar Street options."

Jacky's Bistro *American/French* | 23 | 20 | 23 | $44 |

Evanston | 2545 Prairie Ave. (Central St.) | 847-733-0899 | www.jackysbistro.com

New American meets "hearty French" in the near North Suburbs at this "cozy place to linger over a good meal" "in a bistro setting" with an "impressive wine list" and "excellent service"; those who judge that "Jacky's departure hasn't hurt" call it "a sure bet", but other jurists are jaded by his "absence from the kitchen" – not to mention the "city prices."

NEW Jai Yen *Japanese* | - | - | - | I |

Lakeview | 3736 N. Broadway (bet. Grace St. & Waveland Ave.) | 773-404-0555 | www.jai-yen.com

At this affordable Lakeview BYO, a big menu of mostly Japanese eats – including sushi plus a few Pan-Asian favorites like fried rice and pad Thai – is served in a small space brightened by fresh green accents and a pair of aquariums; fruity bubble teas, Thai iced coffee and virgin piña coladas are among the nonalcoholic drink options.

	FOOD	DECOR	SERVICE	COST

J. Alexander's *American*

| 20 | 19 | 20 | $31 |

Lincoln Park | 1832 N. Clybourn Ave. (bet. Willow & Wisconsin Sts.) | 773-435-1018
Northbrook | 4077 Lake Cook Rd. (bet. I-294 & Sanders Rd.) | 847-564-3093
Oak Brook | 1410 16th St. (bet. Castle Dr. & Spring Rd.) | 630-573-8180
www.jalexanders.com

Chums of this Traditional American chain champion its "hearty" "grown-up" "comfort food" offered in a "spacious", "conversation-friendly" "steakhouse atmosphere" with consistently "solid service", "comfortable seating" and "no hype", cheering "your dollar is well spent" for a "date" or a "family meal – without going over the top"; still, some dissatisfied chowhounds are "unimpressed" with what they find to be "formula" fare, especially "in a city of excellent independent dining" options.

Jane's *American/Eclectic*

| 21 | 19 | 21 | $30 |

Bucktown | 1655 W. Cortland St. (Paulina St.) | 773-862-5263 | www.janesrestaurant.com

It's "cozy but alive" "with good vibes" at this "adorable", "crowded" "place for a date", "for girls to catch up or for a family brunch" that's "tucked away" on a Bucktown "residential street"; the New American–Eclectic edibles include "some unique takes on comfort food" and "plenty of grazing for vegetarians", and "now that they've expanded, the waits aren't so bad" – and, as always, it's "nice to enjoy dining outside in warm weather."

☒ Japonais *Japanese*

| 24 | 26 | 20 | $58 |

Near West | 600 W. Chicago Ave. (Larrabee St.) | 312-822-9600 | www.japonaischicago.com

"Toward the top of the list for sushi", this Near West "upmarket [Japanese] fusion" "hot" spot dishes out a "remarkable menu" of "innovative cuisine" and "dazzling decor" enhanced by a "very attractive crowd of twenty- to fiftysomething" "eye candy"; ok, it's a "budget buster", "but you're paying for" the "chic, happening ambiance" (and folks "love" the "hoppin' lounge" "on the river"), though classicists who call it "too trendy for its own good" also aren't savoring the "serious attitude."

Jay's Amore
Ristorante & Lounge ☒ *Italian*

| - | - | - | M |

West Loop | 1330 W. Madison St. (bet. Ashland & Racine Aves.) | 312-829-3333 | www.jaysamorechicago.com

Habitués of the West Loop's former Amore who "hope the new owners kept the cooks" will be happy to hear they've been retained, as well as the extensive menu of "solid", "predictable" Northern Italian classics "at reasonable prices", though the cozy exposed-brick-and-wood interior has been dressed up with tablecloths, mirrors and artwork, art deco light fixtures and plasma TVs playing sports in the bar; P.S. it's a "great place to go before a Bulls or Blackhawks game."

	FOOD	DECOR	SERVICE	COST

Jilly's Cafe Ⓜ *American/French* | 23 | 17 | 23 | $40

Evanston | 2614 Green Bay Rd. (Central St.) | 847-869-7636 |
www.jillyscafe.com

"Romantics" frequent this "tiny" New American–New French "treasure" in the near North Suburbs for "consistently high-quality food and service" amid "charming" country inn surroundings that feel "cozy and familiar, even if it's your first visit"; claustrophobes caution "go on a slow night", though, or you'll find yourself "listening to three conversations at once" in the "crowded" setting; P.S. "Sunday brunch is a great buy."

Jin Ju Ⓜ *Korean* | 22 | 20 | 20 | $31

Andersonville | 5203 N. Clark St. (Foster Ave.) | 773-334-6377
The "fresh and creative" "upscale Korean food with a twist" at this Andersonville spot may be "a bit pricey" for the genre, but it comes with "great style" and "hip, dark" ambiance that "makes even a bad date tolerable"; even those who generally "eschew trendy ethnic-tini drinks" swear that "their soju concoctions hit the spot" – which is part of why it's "noisy" and "packed on weekends" with "pretty people."

Ⓩ Joe's Seafood, | 26 | 21 | 25 | $57
Prime Steak & Stone Crab *Seafood/Steak*

River North | 60 E. Grand Ave. (Rush St.) | 312-379-5637 |
www.joesstonecrabchicago.com
Some sated surveyors swear this River Norther, a "great Midwestern version of Joe's Stone Crab" in Florida, is "better than the Miami original" thanks to "wonderful seafood feasting", "terrific" prime steaks and "to-die-for sides and Key lime pie", all "professionally served" in a "classic", "clubby", sometimes "raucous" setting; still, waverers who wither during the "long waits (even with reservations)" figure "for this kind of money" you could "head south to SoBe for the real thing."

Joey's Brickhouse *American* | 18 | 17 | 16 | $25

Lakeview | 1258 W. Belmont Ave. (Racine Ave.) | 773-296-1300 |
www.enterthechef.com
Lakeview locals are glad to have this "interesting take on" seasonal Traditional American "home cooking" – including a "great [jazz] brunch" – in the neighborhood, especially since it's "very kid-friendly" and "fits any budget"; supporters say it "should be more popular", but critics call out "sporadic service" and "hit-or-miss" cooking as hindrances.

John's Place Ⓜ *American* | 18 | 13 | 17 | $20

Lincoln Park | 1200 W. Webster Ave. (Racine Ave.) | 773-525-6670 |
www.johnsplace.com
"Homey-hip" and "family-friendly", this Lincoln Park "neighborhood haunt" is regarded as "reliable" for "solid, basic American food" with an "excellent kids' menu"; while some commenters veto it as a "veritable babypalooza", moderates maintain it's "much more enjoyable now that one room is for adults" and the other for families

with kids – except at "crowded weekend brunch"; N.B. the Food and Decor ratings don't reflect the largely revamped space and menu.

Joy Yee's Noodle Shop *Asian* 21 | 11 | 15 | $16
Chinatown | 2159 S. China Pl. (Archer Ave.) | 312-328-0001
Evanston | 521 Davis St. (Chicago Ave.) | 847-733-1900
Naperville | 1163 E. Ogden Ave. (Iroquois Ave.) | 630-579-6800
www.joyyee.com

"Gargantuan portions" at "modest prices" draw "noisy" "crowds" to this Asian noodle network wielding "a wide variety of unusual dishes" – "the menu has a picture of every" item – and about "a billion choices" of "awesome bubble teas" and "excellent fruit drinks" ("with blenders whirring above the din"); though they're "extremely popular", a faction feels the meals "lack authentic taste."

Julius Meinl Café *Austrian* 21 | 21 | 19 | $14
Lakeview | 3601 N. Southport Ave. (Addison St.) | 773-868-1857 | www.meinl.com

"Attention is paid to every last detail" at this "civilized" Lakeview coffeehouse, a "truly Austrian cafe experience" where patrons polish off "pastries to die for", "crave"-worthy salads and soups, "the best coffee in this country" and a "ridiculous selection of teas" "served on silver platters" in a "fancy European dining room" with occasional "live classical music" – small wonder "it's become a favorite spot (if you can get a seat)."

Kabul House Ⓜ *Afghan* 20 | 13 | 20 | $18
Skokie | 3320 Dempster St. (McCormick Blvd.) | 847-763-9930 | www.kabulhouse.com

For "an excellent intro to an unusual cuisine", try this North Suburban "gem" where "authentic" Afghani fare (including "mouthwatering vegetarian entrees") is "humbly prepared and served" in "modest surroundings" by a staff that "values your business"; it's also a "good place to take kids with an adventurous palate", even if the "limited menu" "never changes", and though there's "no alcohol", you can BYO.

Kamehachi *Japanese* 22 | 18 | 19 | $32
River North | Westin River North | 320 N. Dearborn St. (Kinzie St.) | 312-744-1900
Streeterville | 240 E. Ontario St. (bet. Fairbanks Ct. & St. Clair St.) | 312-587-0600
Old Town | 1400 N. Wells St. (Schiller St.) | 312-664-3663 ◑
Lincolnshire | City Park Complex @ BIN 36 | 275 Parkway Dr. (Aptakisic Rd.) | 847-541-8800
Northbrook | Village Green Shopping Ctr. | 1320 Shermer Rd. (Waukegan Rd.) | 847-562-0064
www.kamehachi.com

Raters rely on this "traditional Japanese" clan for "fresh sushi", as well as "really good non-sushi" sustenance, in settings that vary by venue (the Old Town location has a "nice garden in the summer"); perhaps it's "not innovative", but it's certainly dependable" – though hedgers who hint it "has not kept up" in the raw-fish race bemoan "bite-sized portions" and "hit-or-miss" help.

	FOOD	DECOR	SERVICE	COST

NEW Kanok *Japanese*

| - | - | - | I |

Lakeview | 3422 N. Broadway (bet. Cornelia Ave. & Roscoe St.) | 773-529-2525 | www.ka-nok.com

This funky little Boys Town BYO serves inexpensive Japanese and Pan-Asian fare, including some intriguing daily specials and brunch on weekends; housing a small sushi bar, the casual storefront has a real bare-bones feel with its white walls and concrete floor.

NEW Kansaku *Japanese*

| - | - | - | M |

Evanston | 1514 Sherman Ave. (Grove St.) | 847-864-4386

Ooodles of makis and sakes join a gargantuan, moderately priced Japanese menu at this chic Evanston eatery with an angular sauna feel thanks to wood, wood and more wood; some interesting cocktails, dim lighting and the requisite loungey music help qualify it for membership in the current group of clubby sushi bars.

Kan Zaman *Lebanese*

| ∇ 21 | 16 | 18 | $25 |

River North | 617 N. Wells St. (Ontario St.) | 312-751-9600

"Yummy", "interesting" Lebanese food (including a "great veggie platter"), as well as comfortable "booths" and "coveted pillow couches" – plus "the sounds and sights of belly dancing [on weekends] while you smoke" hookahs – combine to make this River North BYO an exotic "good time."

Karma *Asian*

| ∇ 24 | 28 | 20 | $42 |

Mundelein | Crowne Plaza Hotel | 510 E. Rte. 83 (Rte. 45) | 847-970-6900 | www.karmachicago.com

With a "room that feels more like a trendy Downtown hot spot than a [North] Suburban hotel restaurant", this "beautiful" "surprise" "in an unexpected location" – Mundelein's Crowne Plaza Hotel – serves "elegant", "genuinely good" Asian fusion fare amid "cool" "postmodern rice paddy" decor (careful: "don't step into the reflecting pool").

Karyn's Cooked *Vegetarian*

| ∇ 19 | 17 | 19 | $22 |

River North | 738 N. Wells St. (Superior St.) | 312-587-1050 | www.karynraw.com

"For those who like to eat healthy or vegan, but still want good, tasty food", this "small", "très chic" River North "gem" with a "copper-accented" interior fills the bill with "vegetarian gourmet" fare (including Sunday brunch), "high levels of comfort and class", and organic beers and wines; still, some carnivores call it a "weird trip", yawping "you gotta wanna eat this stuff before you come."

Karyn's Fresh Corner *Vegetarian*

| ∇ 17 | 14 | 15 | $27 |

Lincoln Park | 1901 N. Halsted St. (Armitage Ave.) | 312-255-1590 | www.karynraw.com

If you like it raw, consider this casual cafe/market and fine-dining BYO combo in Lincoln Park offering all-day dining (including Sunday brunch) on 'raw vegan living foods'; the casual side, affiliated with a holistic health center, offers an all-you-can-eat buffet plus ice cream and sandwich bars, while the restaurant has a serene spa-like setting with outdoor seating.

Katsu Japanese *Japanese* ▽ 26 | 18 | 21 | $45

Northwest Side | 2651 W. Peterson Ave. (California Ave.) | 773-784-3383
Seekers of "sublime sushi" say it's "well worth the detour" to this
"off-the-beaten-path" Northwest Sider filleting the "freshest fish
around", including "noteworthy items from the market in Tokyo",
and serving "some Japanese dishes not commonly found in other
restaurants"; "Katsu and his wife make every guest feel like longtime friends" – or "like royalty" if you opt for "the omakase meal, ordered in advance" for larger parties.

Kaze Sushi *Japanese* 24 | 20 | 19 | $45

Roscoe Village | 2032 W. Roscoe St. (Seeley Ave.) | 773-327-4860 |
www.kazesushi.com
Disciples of this "elegant", "upscale" Roscoe Village Japanese
"standout" devour its "inspired", "innovative sushi" "with amazing
seasonal toppings", urging others to "just do the chef's choice
menu – you won't regret it" ("you pick from a price range"); passers
perceive the personnel as "pretentious", though, and the eats "too
experimental" ("I don't like my sushi oiled and 'shroomed") and
"overpriced for the serving size"; P.S. "excellent outdoor seating"
entices in warm weather.

Keefer's ⓩ *Steak* 23 | 22 | 22 | $51

River North | 20 W. Kinzie St. (Dearborn St.) | 312-467-9525 |
www.keefersrestaurant.com
"Known for its excellent steaks but offering great food in all categories", including "wonderful seafood", River North's "Keefer's is a
keeper" to coveters of its "contemporary American" "urban"-"chic"
setting ("more stylish" "than the typical steakhouse"), "attentive
staff" and "great happy-hour grown-up bar scene" with "fish bowl-
sized martinis"; challengers who lack "expense accounts" complain
about the "steep prices", though, suggesting you "try it for lunch",
as the tariff is "easier to handle."

ⓩ Kevin ⓩ *Asian/French* 26 | 22 | 23 | $58

River North | 9 W. Hubbard St. (State St.) | 312-595-0055 |
www.kevinrestaurant.com
Kevin Shikami's "passion for food shows" in his "excellent" and "vi-
sually stunning" "haute" New French–Asian fusion fare at this "refined" River Norther with "beautiful, calming decor" that's "equally
good for business or romance"; still, contributors concerned about
"uneven" experiences cite an "elitist attitude", saying they'd more
easily tolerate the price tag "if only the service lived up to the food";
N.B. a new Loop location, named Shikago, is planned.

KiKi's Bistro ⓩ *French* 23 | 19 | 22 | $44

River North | 900 N. Franklin St. (Locust St.) | 312-335-5454 |
www.kikisbistro.com
"There's a reason the classics are classic" crow confreres of this
"real bistro" that "looks like it belongs in the French countryside",
despite its River North setting; the "mature crowd" that calls it a
"cozy" and "affordable" "delight" with "consistent preparations" of

FOOD | DECOR | SERVICE | COST

"traditional fare" says it "never changes, thank goodness", though some "underwhelmed" upstarts find "nothing memorable" about this "old-fashioned" offering.

Kinzie Chophouse *Steak*

20 | 17 | 20 | $45

River North | 400 N. Wells St. (Kinzie St.) | 312-822-0191 | www.kinziechophouse.com

"Under the radar" in River North, this "red-blooded steakhouse" is a "cozy little corner place with lots of regulars" who tout is as "tried-and-true", with "very tasty" steaks and chops served in a "friendly" setting that's not as "glitzy" or "plastic" as some competitors' (and "a good choice for lunch if you're near the Mart"); still, wallet-watchers might consider it more often if they "cut the portions and prices in half."

Kit Kat Lounge & Supper Club ● M *Eclectic*

15 | 19 | 19 | $33

Wrigleyville | 3700 N. Halsted St. (Waveland Ave.) | 773-525-1111 | www.kitkatchicago.com

"Nothing like being serenaded with torch songs by a drag queen while you're eating a steak" say supporters who go for the "amazingly fun" entertainment and "expansive list" of "cleverly named cocktails" – not the "merely average food" – at this Eclectic Boys Town eatery that's "popular for bachelorette parties"; P.S. there's also "great outdoor seating."

Kitsch'n on Roscoe *Eclectic*

17 | 19 | 18 | $18

Roscoe Village | 2005 W. Roscoe St. (Damen Ave.) | 773-248-7372

Kitsch'n River North *Eclectic*

River North | 600 W. Chicago Ave. (Larrabee St.) | 312-644-1500 www.kitschn.com

"Kitschy, kooky" and "kid-friendly", this "groovy" couple of "retro" "trips" are "just plain fun" "for fans of '60s/'70s TV and memorabilia", with a "surprisingly creative menu" of Eclectic "comfort food" at "reasonable prices"; still, bummed buzzkills bag the "weird concoctions" and "seriously cheesy" concept, and some raters regard the River North branch as "much less cozy than the Roscoe Village" original (which is "even better when the back garden is open"); N.B. hours vary by location and season.

Kizoku Sushi & K Lounge *Japanese*

▽ 25 | 22 | 21 | $47

River North | 358 W. Ontario St. (Orleans St.) | 312-335-9888 | www.kizokusushi.com

"Inventive presentations" of "stellar sushi" and "innovative drinks" impress indulgers in the "enjoyable" (if "pricey") experience at this "lovely, tranquil" River North Japanese "beautifully done up in a lounge style" – plus "people are talking about" its "bold", "buzz-generating" 'body sushi' offering, wherein raw-fish fare is served atop a scantily clad woman (starting at $500 for a party of four); N.B. the ratings may not reflect the post-Survey owner change and the addition of French-Vietnamese dishes.

Klay Oven *Indian*

| | 20 | 15 | 17 | $33 |

River North | 414 N. Orleans St. (Hubbard St.) | 312-527-3999 |
www.klayovenrestaurant.com

"Good, basic Indian" fare that's "fresh" and "beautifully served"
makes this "serene" River Norther a "solid" choice for city dwellers;
it may not be "as authentic as the places on Devon", and the decidedly "typical" decor adds up to rather "bland ambiance", but its
"buffet lunch is a deal" – and it's "great for pickup" too.

NEW Koda Bistro Ⓜ *French*

| | - | - | - | M |

Far South Side | 10352 S. Western Ave. (bet. 103rd & 104th Sts.) |
773-445-5632 | www.kodabistro.com

This South Side bistro offers loose interpretations of classic French
fare (including stalwarts like steak frites and escargots bourguignon)
and a nice little affordable wine list; the setting eschews tradition for a
more modern mood, with a glowing LED light show built into the bar.

Kohan Japanese *Japanese*

| | - | - | - | M |

South Loop | University Village Mktpl. | 730 W. Maxwell St. (Halsted St.) |
312-421-6254

The South Loop's down-and-dirty Maxwell Street Market now boasts
a string of spiffy storefronts, including this Japanese steak-and-sushi
setup where the dining-room grilling lacks the circus factor typical of
the old-guard chains; the casual space – done up in wood and slate,
ceramic tiles and backlit paper panels – is similarly gimmick-free.

Koi *Asian*

| | 19 | 22 | 18 | $30 |

Evanston | 624 Davis St. (bet. Chicago & Orrington Aves.) | 847-866-6969 |
www.koievanston.com

To gourmands who get this "upscale Chinese-sushi" hybrid as "a
great addition to the Evanston dining scene", there's gold in the
"Pan-Asian fare", "excellent drink list including rare and delicious teas"
and "hip" "yet elegant" environs with a "welcoming fireplace"; on
the flip side, disheartened diners "wish" the "expensive", "inconsistent food" and sometimes "inattentive staff" "lived up to the style."

Koryo Ⓜ *Korean*

| | ▽ 19 | 16 | 20 | $23 |

Lakeview | 2936 N. Broadway St. (bet. Oakdale & Wellington Aves.) |
773-477-8510

Surveyors split over whether this "trendy" "upscale" Lakeview
Korean is "authentic" and "interesting" (with "real kimchi" that "would
make a statue sweat") or overly "Americanized" and "bland", with
some moderates maintaining the "menu offers a variety of choices
for both the timid and adventurous"; eaters agree, however, on the
"helpful" nature of the staff.

Kroll's *American*

| | - | - | - | M |

South Loop | 1736 S. Michigan Ave. (18th St.) | 312-235-1400 |
www.krolls-chicago.com

Green Bay's Lambeau Field neighbor and butterburger stalwart (the
patties arrive on buttered, toasted buns, hence the name) encroaches
into Bears territory – the South Loop near Soldier Field, no less –

with this American oupost whose menu features items both traditional (deep-fried cheese curds, chili with spaghetti, milkshakes) and contemporary (salads, wraps); the casual, upscale space, with booths, high-top tables, sports memorabilia and a vast bar/lounge, though, bears little resemblance to the retro diner–style original.

NEW KS Seafood *Chinese/Seafood*

| - | - | - | I |

Chinatown | Chinatown Mall | 2163 S. China Pl. (Cermak Rd.) | 312-842-1238

Within weeks of opening, this Chinatown Mall budget-friendly Taiwanese was forced by public demand to translate its seafood-centric, Chinese-only menu since its American menu is a comparative yawn of standards; for a chance to try exotic specialties like stinky tofu and fried baby eels, foodies forgive the glaringly bright decor of lime-sherbet walls and a handful of bare tables (including a few big communal rounds).

Kuma's Corner ◐ *American*

| - | - | - | I |

Logan Square | 2900 W. Belmont Ave. (Francisco Ave.) | 773-604-8769 | www.kumascorner.com

"Gaining in popularity", this "wonderful addition" to Logan Square is a "cozy" spot with "great service" and "excellent" American fare, from Kobe beef sliders to "the world's best macaroni and cheese" to 16 burger varieties; "don't let the tattoos and piercings fool you": the "nice staff" is "extremely knowledgeable about food, wine and beer pairings" – and "the patio is terrific."

Kuni's *Japanese*

| 25 | 14 | 19 | $31 |

Evanston | 511-A Main St. (bet. Chicago & Hinman Aves.) | 847-328-2004

For 20 years, faithful fish fans have flocked to this "consistently excellent" North Suburbaner, the "best in a wide, wide radius" for sushi and sashimi that "can't be beat for flavor or freshness", "beautifully carved by Kuni-san", "a traditional sushi master", as well as "a full range of other Japanese dishes"; N.B. impatient sorts are advised to go early, as they only take reservations for parties of six or more.

Kyoto *Japanese*

| ∇ 22 | 16 | 20 | $28 |

Lincoln Park | 2534 N. Lincoln Ave. (Altgeld St.) | 773-477-2788 | www.kyotochicago.com **M**
Winnetka | 1062 Gage St. (Green Bay Rd.) | 847-784-9388 **M**
Downers Grove | Best Buy Shopping Ctr. | 1408 Butterfield Rd. (bet. Finley Rd. & Highland Ave.) | 630-627-8588 **⑤**

Raters who regard the raw fish at this "friendly" trio of Japanese town and country outposts as "excellent" also hail the "combination plate that fills you up for a very reasonable price"; still, some who deem the experience merely "decent" recommend takeout; N.B. the ratings may not reflect the Lincoln Park branch's menu and decor changes.

La Bocca della Verità **M** *Italian*

| 18 | 15 | 19 | $30 |

Lincoln Square | 4618 N. Lincoln Ave. (bet. Lawrence & Wilson Aves.) | 773-784-6222 | www.laboccachicago.com

A "quaint" "neighborhood Italian" with "family character", this Lincoln Square spot has adherents who admire its "simple,

delicious" fare and "homey atmosphere", saying it "will bring you back to that last Roman holiday"; a chorus of antis, though, claims that it's "nothing special" and the output is "overpriced for what it is" – though the "outdoor dining is comfortable."

La Cantina 🅱 *Italian/Seafood* | 19 | 18 | 22 | $32

Loop | 71 W. Monroe St. (bet. Clark & Dearborn Sts.) | 312-332-7005 | www.italianvillage-chicago.com

"Part of the Italian Village" complex (and of "Chicago history"), this Northern "Italian seafood" "classic" has been serving it up in a "straightforward" manner for 50 years in a "quaint, dark basement" setting that regulars find "comfortable and familiar" – "get a booth near the fish tanks" "for romance or privacy" – and "excellent for pre-theater or Symphony Center dining" due to its central Loop locale.

NEW La Cantina Grill *Mexican* | - | - | - | I

South Loop | 1911 S. Michigan Ave. (bet. Cullerton & 18th Sts.) | 312-842-1911

A welcome addition to the South Loop, this casual, cheap Mexican cantina proffers the usual south-of-the-border suspects along with a smattering of more serious entrees like tilapia basted with garlic butter; the small, dimly lit terra-cotta and deep-blue room has vintage black-and-white photography and a hodgepodge of artifacts, which help set a fun, funky mood – as do the fruit-flavored margaritas.

La Cazuela Mariscos *Mexican/Seafood* | - | - | - | I

Rogers Park | 6922 N. Clark St. (bet. Farwell & Morse Aves.) | 773-338-5425

"Amazing", "inexpensive" "fresh fish served Mex-style" is the draw at this "fun", "friendly" Rogers Park BYO taqueria where the "brightly lit" "coffee-shop ambiance" comes complete with "Formica tables" and outdoor seating in season; P.S. "it helps to know Spanish."

La Crêperie 🅼 *French* | 20 | 17 | 16 | $22

Lakeview | 2845 N. Clark St. (bet. Diversey Pkwy. & Surf St.) | 773-528-9050 | www.lacreperieusa.com

Devotees declaim "don't mess with anything" at this Lakeview lair that "seems like it should be located off a cobblestone side street" – from the "wonderful", "huge" "crêpes and other traditional French [bistro] dishes" to the "well-worn", "old-world" "dive" digs that may make you "want to smoke long, thin cigarettes and feverishly scribble manifestos"; demimondaines also dig the "easy-on-the-wallet" prices, "excellent brunch" and "romantic, bohemian garden area."

La Cucina di Donatella *Italian* | ∇ 22 | 15 | 16 | $31

Rogers Park | 2221 W. Howard St. (Ridge Blvd.) | 773-262-6533

The namesake owner's "personal touch" and "European zest for life" are evident at this Rogers Park "favorite", where "everything is cooked to order" from a menu of "sophisticated, super-fresh" seasonal Italian cuisine ("diners can stuff themselves and never touch a tomato"); expect "genuine trattoria atmosphere" with an "open kitchen" and "small outdoor dining area", and remember "to bring your own wine."

	FOOD	DECOR	SERVICE	COST

La Donna *Italian*

19 | 16 | 19 | $29

Andersonville | 5146 N. Clark St. (Foster Ave.) | 773-561-9400 | www.ladonnarestaurantchicago.com

Amici announce it's "always crowded and for good reason" at this Andersonville "neighborhood" ristorante cooking a "combination of authentic Italian dishes" and some "with creative touches" ("oh, the pumpkin ravioli!") in a "casual-romantic" setting "with floor-to-ceiling windows"; conflicted consumers mark it "middle of the pack", though, and note that it's "not comfortable."

La Fette Ⓜ *American/French*

- | - | - | E

Old Town | 163 W. North Ave. (bet. LaSalle & Wells Sts.) | 312-397-6300 | www.lafette.net

Its "balanced" New American–French "bistro cooking" appeals to champions of this "small" and "friendly" "undiscovered gem" in Old Town, home to an "unassuming, ever-changing menu" served with "personal attention" in a "quaint", "romantic" room; N.B. the global grape list spotlights Illinois wines.

La Fonda Latino Ⓜ *Colombian*

19 | 15 | 17 | $26

Andersonville | 5350 N. Broadway St. (Balmoral Ave.) | 773-271-3935

"Authentic Colombian", including "awesome arepas" and "great empanadas", plus other South American table treats are the call at this "cozy" "plantain paradise", a "great little place to try something different" set behind an "unassuming facade" in Andersonville; well-wishers also write about the "wonderful lunch buffet" and "tropical fruit juices", and there are those who "would kill for the sangria recipe."

La Gondola *Italian*

Lincoln Park | Wellington Plaza | 2914 N. Ashland Ave. (Wellington Ave.) | 773-248-4433 | www.lagondolachicago.com

"Extremely reliable old-school" "bargain Italian" such as "homemade pastas", "terrific pizza" and "kick-ass eggplant Parmesan" is still being served in this "small" Lincoln Park longtimer in a "strip mall" with a lot of "parking spots"; fans who feel it's "better for takeout" or delivery may be pleased by a post-Survey renovation.

Lake Side Café *Vegetarian*

Rogers Park | 1418 W. Howard St. (Sheridan Rd.) | 773-262-9503 | www.lake-side-cafe.com

Value-conscious vegetarian specialists have set up shop in this smart, casual Rogers Park storefront with about a dozen bamboo tables and a 95 percent organic menu offering lots of vegan options and ever-changing specials; place your order with the cooks at the counter and they'll bring it to you (the same multitaskers also make a broad range of beverages, including smoothies, freshly squeezed juices, tea and coffee drinks).

Lalo's *Mexican*

16 | 16 | 17 | $23

River North | 500 N. LaSalle St. (Illinois St.) | 312-329-0030

(continued)

Lalo's

Lincoln Park | 1960 N. Clybourn Ave. (bet. Clifton Ave. & Cortland St.) | 773-880-5256

NEW Des Plaines | 1535 Ellinwood Ave. (bet. Lee & Pearson Sts.) | 847-296-1535

Near South Side | 3515 W. 26th St. (bet. Drake & St. Louis Aves.) | 773-522-0345

Near South Side | 4126 W. 26th St. (Kedvale Ave.) | 773-762-1505

Southwest Side | Midway Int'l Airport | 5757 S. Cicero Ave. (55th St.) | 773-838-1604

Glenview | 1432 Waukegan Rd. (Lake Ave.) | 847-832-1388

Schaumburg | 425 S. Roselle Rd. (bet. Schaumburg Rd. & Weathersfield Way) | 847-891-0911

Berwyn | 3011 S. Harlem Ave. (31st St.) | 708-484-9311

Oak Park | 804 S. Oak Park Ave. (Rte. 290) | 708-386-3386

www.lalos.com

Additional locations throughout the Chicago area

A "good variety" of "solid", "Americanized Mexican food served in a fun party atmosphere" with "powerful" "fish-bowl" "margaritas" and "mariachi" music (at some sites) is enough for frequenters of this family of "kid-friendly" cantinas; still, some say "skip it" due to "subpar" sustenance without "much flair or flavor", while other "disappointed" diners deem them "not authentic."

Landmark ● *American*
21 | 22 | 22 | $43

Lincoln Park | 1633 N. Halsted St. (North Ave.) | 312-587-1600 | www.landmarkgrill.net

"The BOKA boys [Kevin Boehm and Rob Katz] did it again" at this Lincoln Park "see-and-be-seen" "hit in the making", where a "trendy, thirtysomething crowd" indulges in "quality" New American offerings from an exhibition kitchen presented in a "chic" setting whose "various levels and nooks" – including a "noisy", "funky lounge" – feature "different feels"; P.S. it's "convenient to the theaters" nearby.

L'anne 🖼 Ⓜ *Vietnamese*
∇ 20 | 19 | 15 | $48

Wheaton | 221 W. Front St. (bet. Hale St. & Wheaton Ave.) | 630-260-1234 | www.lannerestaurant.com

This spot's "unique", "inventive menu" of Vietnamese-focused French-Asian fusion fans the flames for followers of the "quaint" West Suburban supplier of a "city dining experience", which for critics can include "portions" that "are small in comparison to the prices" and "spotty service"; N.B. a pianist tickles the ivories on weekend nights.

🝫 Lao Sze Chuan House *Chinese*
24 | 10 | 16 | $19

Westmont | 1331 West Ogden Ave (Main St.) | 630-663-0303

🝫 Lao Sze Chuan Spicy City ● *Chinese*

Chinatown | 2172 S. Archer Ave. (Princeton Ave.) | 312-326-5040

🝫 Szechuan House *Chinese*

Palatine | 321 E. Northwest Hwy. (Hicks Rd.) | 847-991-0888

www.laoszechuan.com

Those who "like it spicy" say "chef Tony" Hu delivers "the real thing" with his "fresh, well-seasoned, authentic dishes" at these Szechuan-

	FOOD	DECOR	SERVICE	COST

Mandarin mainstays; of the service voters say "some days it's good, some days it's not", but they still swear the "Chinatown establishment sets the standard" (it's "worth the occasional line-out-the-door wait") and the suburban sites are the "best around" of their kind; N.B. the Decor rating may not reflect the Westmont branch's relocation.

La Peña 🅜 *S American*   ▽ 20 | 13 | 16 | $24

Northwest Side | 4212 N. Milwaukee Ave. (Montrose Ave.) | 773-545-7022 | www.lapenachicago.com

Expect a "great evening" at this "fun", "bustling" Northwest Sider serving "good portions" of "innovative Ecuadorian preparations", including "lots of fish and seafood dishes", plus "some of the best cocktails" like its signature tropical-fruit margarita; this place "pumps with energy" (i.e. "can be noisy") since there's live music or DJ entertainment and a dance floor – perhaps the sidewalk seating is quieter.

NEW La Petite Amelia *French*   - | - | - | M

Evanston | 618 Church St. (bet. Chicago & Orrington Aves.) | 847-328-3333 | www.lapetiteamelia.com

French bistro favorites from pâté to profiteroles are the bill of fare at this wallet-friendly North Suburban Gallic outpost with classic, cozy ambiance created by warm yellow walls, wood floors and white tablecloths; quaffs include French beers, plenty of wines by the glass and house carafes by the half liter or liter.

la petite folie 🅜 *French*   24 | 19 | 19 | $44

Hyde Park | Hyde Park Shopping Ctr. | 1504 E. 55th St. (Lake Park Blvd.) | 773-493-1394 | www.lapetitefolie.com

"Hyde Park's sole claim to fine dining" rests with this "fancy" Classic French "surprise" "hidden" "in a strip mall", serving "top-notch traditional" cuisine with a "criminally cheap wine collection" in its "lush Parisian rooms"; even surveyors who sense the "service is not as professional as the food" and find the whole affair "behind the times" agree it's of "generally high quality", and the "early-bird prix fixe" dinner and "lunches are a fantastic value."

La Piazza 🅢 *Italian*   ▽ 25 | 21 | 24 | $35

Forest Park | 410 Circle Ave. (Madison St.) | 708-366-4010 | www.piazzacafe.com

Effusive eaters enthuse about this "excellent find" in the Western suburbs for "simply outstanding" regional Italian that's "authentic, freshly prepared" and "elegantly presented" with "attentive service", "usually with a visit from chef-owner" Gaetano di Benedetto; look for "lots of" "strong" choices among the "fresh, creative daily specials and traditional favorites on the menu", as well as a "great wine list", "unique decor" and live jazz on Wednesday–Saturday nights; N.B. no relation to the Naperville spot of the same name.

La Piazza 🅢🅜 *Italian*   - | - | - | M

Naperville | Naperville Plaza | 192 W. Gartner Rd. (Catalpa Ln.) | 630-305-9280 | www.lapiazzanaperville.com

This "great little" independent Naperville Italian-Eclectic is "better than it looks from the outside", with an "interesting menu" of "imag-

inative cuisine" and a "cozy", "understated" "cafe feel" that "adds to its appeal" – plus free weekly wine tastings are offered on Wednesdays; N.B. no relation to the Forest Park spot of the same name.

La Sardine ⑤ French — 23 | 20 | 22 | $41

West Loop | 111 N. Carpenter St. (bet. Randolph St. & Washington Blvd.) | 312-421-2800 | www.lasardine.com

"Well-executed *classique* French" bistro fare packs 'em into this "delightful" West Looper that's "perfect for a Paris-style lunch or dinner" but with "better service" – plus it's "not as frenetic as" its tiny sister, Le Bouchon (though it can be just as "noisy when busy"); P.S. the penny-wise praise the "half-price wine nights on Mondays" and "Tuesday night prix fixe (a steal)."

La Scarola Italian — 23 | 12 | 17 | $32

Near West | 721 W. Grand Ave. (bet. Halsted St. & Milwaukee Ave.) | 312-243-1740 | www.lascarola.com

"Consistently one of the best medium-range" Italian *ristoranti* around, this "crowded", "bustling" "Near Wester" features "excellent", "no-nonsense" "comfort food" (kudos for the heaps of "fresh pastas"); enthusiasts insist that if you "eat there more than once they treat you like family", even if some critics don't dig being "crushed into the little storefront" space.

Las Palmas Mexican — - | - | - | M

Bucktown | 1835 W. North Ave. (Honore St.) | 773-289-4991 | www.laspalmaschicago.net

Buffalo Grove | 86 W. Dundee Rd. (Old Buffalo Grove Rd.) | 847-520-8222

The newer Buffalo Grove location of this longtime Mexican mini-chain follows in the steps of the Bucktown flagship, serving a chef-driven, creative take on traditional cuisine in an upscale rustic setting decorated with colorful paintings; the prices are higher – though still moderate – than at its handful of casual suburban siblings.

Las Tablas Colombian/Steak — 21 | 13 | 16 | $24

Lincoln Park | 2965 N. Lincoln Ave. (Wellington Ave.) | 773-871-2414
Northwest Side | 4920 W. Irving Park Rd. (Cicero Ave.) | 773-202-0999

It's "always hopping" at these "warm and friendly" Colombian steakhouses serving "different and tasty" "meat, meat and more meat" "on wooden tablas" – with, some say, "uncomfortable benches" – that add up to "great value for the money" (plus "BYO helps you save" even more); locationwise, the Lincoln Park branch is "more authentic" while the Northwest Side spot is more "family-friendly", but both are "especially busy on weekends."

La Strada Ristorante Italian — 19 | 17 | 19 | $38

Loop | 155 N. Michigan Ave. (Randolph St.) | 312-565-2200 ⑤
NEW Hoffman Estates | 2380 Lakewood Blvd. (Barrington Rd.) | 847-765-1700
www.lastradaristorante.com

Raters who rely on this quarter-centarian for "consistently good", "real Italian" fare also like its "lively bar", "windows overlooking

Michigan Avenue" and setting "near Millennium Park and the Art Institute"; "other than its convenient location" in the Loop, though, "nothing sets it apart" according to detractors who decry the decor as "dark" and "dated", bemoan the food as "bland" and condemn the service as "cavalier"; N.B. the Hoffman Estates branch opened post-Survey.

La Taberna Tapatia ● *Mexican* ▽ 21 | 10 | 15 | $21

Roscoe Village | 3358 N. Ashland Ave. (Roscoe St.) | 773-248-5475

"Interesting selections" of "not-the-basic Mexican" served in a small-plates format make friends for this "hip" haunt in Roscoe Village, where "yummy margaritas, a nice outdoor area" and DJ entertainment Wednesday–Sunday augment the appeal; it's "small" and popular with "celebrating groups", though, so be warned that a "shortage of tables" can "lead to lines."

La Tache *French* 21 | 20 | 19 | $39

Andersonville | 1475 W. Balmoral Ave. (bet. Clark St. & Glenwood Ave.) | 773-334-7168

Andersonville has adopted this "popular hideout" for "solid" "traditional French" bistro plates – as well as some featuring "creative twists"; it's "a great deal for Sunday brunch", especially "outside when summer finally finds Chicago", but a few gourmets grade it "good but not spectacular", while motivational experts maintain that the "service could be better."

La Tasca *Spanish* 23 | 21 | 21 | $32

Arlington Heights | 25 W. Davis St. (Vail Ave.) | 847-398-2400 | www.latascatapas.com

Respondents pick this Spanish purveyor in the Northwest Suburbs for its "great variety of options" in the small-plates department (though "full entrees are available" as well), plus "killer sangrias"; the "fun", "friendly" setting makes it a "great place to go with friends" or "kids" – or even "to have a romantic evening" with that special someone.

La Vita *Italian* ▽ 20 | 21 | 23 | $34

Little Italy | 1359 W. Taylor St. (Loomis St.) | 312-491-1414 | www.lavitarestaurant.com

For surveyors who flag this "real [Northern] Italian" as a Little Italy "favorite", the authentic cuisine is "a cut above the average", as are the "excellent service and wine list"; it's "not one of the most famous", but partialists praise the "pretty" place with "great atmosphere" as "well worth a visit"; N.B. you can catch rays on the rooftop in warm weather.

Lawry's The Prime Rib *Steak* 24 | 21 | 23 | $49

River North | 100 E. Ontario St. (Rush St.) | 312-787-5000 | www.lawrysonline.com

"There's still something exciting about seeing them roll a cart up and carve off a caveman-size piece of prime rib" "with all the trimmings" ("love the spinning salad bowl" and the "good Yorkshire pud-

	FOOD	DECOR	SERVICE	COST

ding") for fans of this "old-school" Traditional American "meatery" in River North's "historic", "ornate" McCormick mansion; it's "getting long in the tooth but is still a classic", and while not everyone agrees it's "worth the price", the "delicious sandwiches" at lunch are certainly "a value."

Le Bouchon 🗷 *French*   22 | 17 | 19 | $39

Bucktown | 1958 N. Damen Ave. (Armitage Ave.) | 773-862-6600 | www.lebouchonofchicago.com

Bistro junkies "just can't get enough of" this "lively, authentic" Bucktown "institution" that "attracts well-mannered diners" looking for "solid" "country French" "favorites" – "some of the best" around – from Jean-Claude Poilevey's kitchen; no wonder so many put up with "interminable waits for a table" in "noisy", "closetlike" confines, and service that swings from "wonderful" to "grumpy."

🗷 Le Colonial *Vietnamese*   23 | 24 | 21 | $46

Gold Coast | 937 N. Rush St. (bet. Oak & Walton Sts.) | 312-255-0088 | www.lecolonialchicago.com

"Beautiful people" consume "beautiful food" – "high-quality", "traditional" "French-influenced Vietnamese" preparations "you long for later" – at this Gold Coast "semi-chain" outpost "blending romantic and trendy" within an "ethereal" environment that fairly "oozes Saigon" (plus a "sexy, sultry" "world-class bar upstairs"); there's nothing like "a private balcony table overlooking Rush Street for a romantic evening", but even so, quibblers question "sky-high prices" for "sparse portions."

🗷 Le Français 🗷 *French*   28 | 25 | 28 | $93

Wheeling | 269 S. Milwaukee Ave. (Dundee Rd.) | 847-541-7470 | www.lefrancaisrestaurant.com

"Thank you for coming back to us" say surveyors about the return of "masterful" chef Roland Liccioni, who has "re-created the magic" at this "delightful, upscale special-occasion" North Suburban spot after "many ownership changes" with his New French cooking featuring "bold, delicious flavors" and "incredible sauces"; serving the "select clientele" are "helpful" staffers who are "professional" but "not afraid to be human", and the wine list is similarly "outstanding", so few fault it for being "fully priced" – especially given the "reasonable prix fixe lunch" on Tuesday–Friday; N.B. the restaurant closed temporarily in May 2007, with no firm re-opening date.

🗷 Le Lan 🗷 *French/Vietnamese*   26 | 22 | 24 | $56

River North | 749 N. Clark St. (Chicago Ave.) | 312-280-9100 | www.lelanrestaurant.com

"Elegant" New French–Vietnamese fusion fare featuring a "quiet innovation in flavors" and "outstanding presentations" lures a "lively" crowd to this "dark, stylish" den in River North that sports "spare", "tasteful decor" and a "service-oriented" staff; while a coterie of critics "expected more", they're pleased with the "gems" on its "terrific wine list"; N.B. the recent addition of new chef Bill Kim (ex Charlie Trotter's, Susanna Foo) may outdate the above Food score.

Lem's BBQ ●⇗ *BBQ* ▽ 24 | 4 | 13 | $16

Far South Side | 311 E. 75th St. (bet. Calumet & Prairie Aves.) | 773-994-2428

It's all about "great" "BBQ at an unbeatable price" at this "takeout-only" spot that's "worth the journey" to the Far South Side for what cohorts crow "could be the best ribs" in Chicago ("get extra sauce" for the "lean, tender smoky meat"); N.B. they're open till 2 AM nightly, closed Tuesdays.

Leonardo's Ristorante Ⓜ *Italian* ▽ 23 | 19 | 25 | $37

Andersonville | 5657 N. Clark St. (Hollywood Ave.) | 773-561-5028

Discoverers of this Northern Italian, an "unexpected gem in an up-coming area of town", salute its "great food and value" that's "definitely worth checking out"; "really nice waiters", "widely spaced tables" and "modest wine prices" also help to make it a "nice" (if sometimes "noisy") addition to Andersonville.

Le P'tit Paris *Continental/French* ▽ 22 | 18 | 23 | $51

Streeterville | 260 E. Chestnut St. (Dewitt Pl.) | 312-787-8260

Camarades of candlelit Continental-Gallic dining appreciate this "gem" in the Streeterville site of the former Zaven's, where "retro selections" of "very good, rich food" are "professionally" served in an atmosphere "friendly" enough to call "a French version of *Cheers* after your first visit"; N.B. the Food rating may not reflect the post-Survey appointment of Michael Foley (ex Printer's Row) as consulting chef.

Ⓩ Les Nomades 🅂Ⓜ *French* 28 | 26 | 28 | $90

Streeterville | 222 E. Ontario St. (bet. Fairbanks Ct. & St. Clair St.) | 312-649-9010 | www.lesnomades.net

This "refined" former private club in Streeterville "still satisfies" thanks to chef Chris Nugent, who uses "generous quantities of luxury ingredients" in his "excellent" New French cuisine, which is backed by a "fine" wine list and "superb service"; the "formal" (some say "stuffy") setting has an "understated", "hushed" tone that befits "a romantic rendezvous" or "an important business dinner" for a "cut-above" clientele that can afford "top-of-the-line prices."

Ⓩ Le Titi de Paris Ⓜ *French* 26 | 24 | 25 | $63

Arlington Heights | 1015 W. Dundee Rd. (Kennicott Ave.) | 847-506-0222 | www.letitideparis.com

"Still a superb spot" under longtime chef and now owner Michael Maddox, this "island of culinary excellence among the strip malls and highways" of the Northwest Suburbs issues "modern French cuisine" along with an "encyclopedic wine list"; a "fresh service perspective" contributes to a "fine-dining value" "without the pretense" – though some consider the style too "friendly" "for a fancy restaurant."

Le Vichyssois Ⓜ *French* ▽ 24 | 21 | 22 | $53

Lakemoor | 220 W. Rte. 120 (2 mi. west of Rte. 12) | 815-385-8221 | www.levichyssois.com

Traditionalists who "miss real French cuisine the way it was meant to be done" "wish they lived closer" to Bernard Cretier's "out-of-the-

way" Northwest Suburban "bastion" of "authentic", "old-school" Franco fare that's been "very consistent over" the past 30 years; stalwarts suggest you "get the prix fixe menu and relax in the gracious atmosphere", even if "the service is sometimes not up to the cuisine."

☒ Lobby, The *Continental/Seafood*   23 | 26 | 23 | $49

River North | Peninsula Hotel | 108 E. Superior St., 5th fl. (bet. Michigan Ave. & Rush St.) | 312-573-6760 | www.peninsula.com

Lobby loiterers revel in the rarefied air of this "understated but extremely elegant" River North hotel retreat with "gorgeous floor-to-ceiling windows" (that "high ceiling matches the prices") and an "excellent", "light" seafood-centric Continental menu supplemented by "wonderful afternoon tea", a "decadent" "chocolate buffet" and jazz band on Friday and Saturday evenings, and a "fabulous Sunday brunch"; the jury is still out, though, on whether the service is up to "the standards of the Peninsula."

☒ Lou Malnati's Pizzeria *Pizza*   24 | 13 | 17 | $18

River North | 439 N. Wells St. (Hubbard St.) | 312-828-9800
Lincoln Park | 958 W. Wrightwood Ave. (Lincoln Ave.) | 773-832-4030
Southwest Side | 3859 W. Ogden Ave. (Cermak Rd.) | 773-762-0800
Evanston | 1850 Sherman Ave. (University Pl.) | 847-328-5400
Lincolnwood | 6649 N. Lincoln Ave. (bet. Devon & Pratt Aves.) | 847-673-0800
Buffalo Grove | 85 S. Buffalo Grove Rd. (Lake Cook Rd.) | 847-215-7100
Elk Grove Village | 1050 E. Higgins Rd. (bet. Arlington Heights & Busse Rds.) | 847-439-2000
Schaumburg | 1 S. Roselle Rd. (Schaumburg Rd.) | 847-985-1525
Naperville | 131 W. Jefferson Ave. (Washington St.) | 630-717-0700
Naperville | Shops of 95th | 2879 W. 95th St. (Rte. 59) | 630-904-4222
www.loumalnatis.com
Additional locations throughout the Chicago area

Standing "supreme", this "local chain" boasts a "cult following" of "addicts" who relish its "ridiculously good", "real Chicago pizza" – both the "decadent deep-dish" and the "even-better thin-crust" version – and "love the butter crust", "pure, simple sauce" with "chunks of tomato" and "thick cheese"; still, its reign at the top of the pie charts "of the known world" (and the local competition) is "not undisputed", with some citing "inconsistent service" and "cookie-cutter decor" as drawbacks.

Lou Mitchell's *Diner*   22 | 11 | 19 | $15

O'Hare Area | O'Hare Int'l Airport | Terminal 5 | 773-601-8989 ◗
West Loop | 565 W. Jackson Blvd. (Jefferson St.) | 312-939-3111 ⊟

"Welcome to the City of Big Shoulders" at this "landmark" West Loop coffee shop, a "piece of old Chicago" serving a "great" American breakfast still "in the skillet" as well as other "honest diner food" from the crack of dawn to mid-afternoon; the retro setting's "kitschy", the "veteran servers can be insulting" and the "cash-only [policy] is a pain" – and "prepare to wait in line" (with free "doughnut holes and Milk Duds to nosh on"); N.B. the airport outpost is a quick take-out station.

Lovell's of Lake Forest *American*

20 | 23 | 22 | $53

Lake Forest | 915 S. Waukegan Rd. (Everett Rd.) | 847-234-8013 |
www.lovellsoflakeforest.com

Boosters believe this "classy" capsule "belongs in the top flight of
Chicago suburban choices" thanks to its "lovely" "North Shore decor"
done up with "NASA mementos" and "Apollo 13 artifacts", chef-
owner Jay Lovell's "imaginative-without-being-cute" "gourmet"
New American cooking and the chance to meet his father, "real hero
and astronaut" Jim Lovell – though others fault the "pseudo-formal-
ity", "uneven service" and food that "fails to please for the price";
P.S. "check out the basement bar and grill for a less expensive visit."

Lucca's M *American/Mediterranean*

19 | 22 | 20 | $35

Lakeview | 2834 N. Southport Ave. (Wolfram St.) | 773-477-2565 |
www.iloveluccas.com

This "lovely little corner restaurant" in Lakeview is a "neighborhood
favorite" to locals who like its "quaint atmosphere" ("love to see the
latest artwork for sale on the walls") and "surprisingly private" "alfresco dining in the summer", as well as its "carefully crafted plates"
featuring "a delicious blend" of Mediterranean and Traditional
American flavors; still, some who "wouldn't rush back" submit "if only
they put more effort into execution, this would be a terrific spot."

Lucia Ristorante *Italian*

▽ 22 | 14 | 19 | $22

Wicker Park | 1825 W. North Ave. (Honore St.) | 773-292-9700

An "interesting combination of deli and eatery", this Wicker Park
BYO is a "fun place to go with friends" for "delicious" Italian fare; the
"friendly" service includes attention from the "hands-on owner",
and it's "great for a quick lunch" as the counter "up front makes the
best sandwiches in the neighborhood."

Lula *Eclectic*

25 | 17 | 19 | $29

Logan Square | 2537-41 N. Kedzie Blvd. (bet. Fullerton Ave. & Logan Blvd.) |
773-489-9554 | www.lulacafe.com

"The official cool spot of Logan Square", Jason Hammel and Amalea
Tshilds' "arty" "cafe" with "high (organic) ideals and reasonable
prices" "stakes out a territory midway between trendy and comfort
food" with an "Eclectic" "vegetarian- and vegan-friendly" menu
"marrying complex flavors"; the "funky" setting with "rotating art"
is home to a "hip crowd and servers" – in fact, the only "bad news"
is that "the no-reservations policy leads to long waits every night
of the week."

LuLu's Dim Sum & Then Sum *Asian*

19 | 14 | 17 | $20

Evanston | 804 Davis St. (Sherman Ave.) | 847-869-4343 |
www.lulusdimsum.com

For a fix of "very good Americanized" Pan-Asian small plates, "soups
and noodle dishes that never disappoint", "Northwestern students"
and others "who don't want a big bill" descend upon this Evanston
"hangout" offering a "fantastic array" of foods amid "fun decor using
everything from wild colors to funky art to Godzilla figurines"; purists,
however, pan the provender as a "pale imitation" of the original fare.

	FOOD	DECOR	SERVICE	COST

Luna Caprese ⓜ *Italian* ▽ 25 | 15 | 20 | $34

Lincoln Park | 2239 N. Clybourn Ave. (Greenview Ave.) | 773-281-4825 | www.lunacaprese.com

A "sweet, cozy date spot" in Lincoln Park, this "undiscovered gem" serves a "diverse menu" of "wonderful" Southern Italian sustenance, including "housemade pastas", along with "well-priced wines"; adding to the warm "welcome" of its "hospitable chef-owner" is the "wonderful aroma" of its "quaint" setting, which just might make "you feel like you're in an Italian home."

Lupita's ⓜ *Mexican* 21 | 15 | 19 | $20

Evanston | 700 Main St. (Custer Ave.) | 847-328-2255 | www.lupitasmexicanrestaurant.com

Regulars rate this "pleasant and bright" North Suburban "neighborhood place" as "better than a typical Mexican restaurant has to be" thanks to "very good food" featuring "homemade sauces" and "extra-special menu specials"; of course, "dynamite margaritas" also add to the festivities, as does the "daily entertainment of people-watching" and "live guitar music on weekends."

Lutnia ⓜ *Polish* - | - | - | E

Northwest Side | 5532 W. Belmont Ave. (Central Ave.) | 773-282-5335

"People wanting to explore the world via their meals" promote this "elegant Polish venue" on the Northwest Side that makes you "feel you have gone to Warsaw", "with true old style you don't find often anymore" – including "some things cooked at your intimate and carefully decorated table" by "people [who] try very hard to give you a pleasant, satisfying experience"; N.B. live piano music is offered Friday-Sunday.

LuxBar ● *American* 17 | 19 | 18 | $30

Gold Coast | 18 E. Bellevue Pl. (State St.) | 312-642-3400 | www.luxbar.com

"For the young, successful" "super-tight jeans" and "busy power-lunch crowds", this casual Gold Coaster (a spin-off of Gibsons, "without the wallet-breaking cost") is a "swanky little cocktail" "hot spot" where "tasty staffers" serve "pretty decent", even "upscale" Traditional American "bar food" in a "fun, noisy", "upbeat city atmosphere"; conversely, some contributors criticize it as conceptually confused, i.e. "trying to be down-home, trendy and a neighborhood spot all in one."

L. Woods Tap & Pine Lodge *American* 19 | 18 | 19 | $29

Lincolnwood | 7110 N. Lincoln Ave. (Kostner Ave.) | 847-677-3350 | www.leye.com

"Consistently good, standard" Traditional "Americana fare" feeds fans of this "comfy" "rib, steak, burger and bar joint" with a "woodsy" "Wisconsin"-esque "cabin look" located "halfway between the North 'burbs and the city"; unhappy campers, however, size it up as "spectacularly ordinary"; P.S. when faced with the "sometimes long wait", regulars report "the take-out [store] is a viable alternative."

	FOOD	DECOR	SERVICE	COST

☑ Maggiano's Little Italy *Italian*   20 | 19 | 20 | $31

River North | 516 N. Clark St. (Grand Ave.) | 312-644-7700
Skokie | Westfield Shoppingtown | 175 Old Orchard Ctr. (bet. Golf & Old Orchard Rds.) | 847-933-9555
Schaumburg | 1901 E. Woodfield Rd. (Rte. 53) | 847-240-5600
Oak Brook | Oakbrook Center Mall | 240 Oakbrook Ctr. (Rte. 83) | 630-368-0300
www.maggianos.com

Regulars "rely" on these "red-sauce" "Italiano" chain joints for their "can't-lose formula" of "affordable", "hearty" "standards" served "family-style" in a "boisterous" "retro" atmosphere where "everyone always seems to be having a great time" – but some dissenters who knock what they call a "faux" vibe and "obscenely large portions" of "blah", "cookie-cutter" cuisine believe it's better to "bring the kids [than] the Italian food lovers."

Magnolia Cafe Ⓜ *American*   25 | 21 | 22 | $36

Uptown | 1224 W. Wilson Ave. (Magnolia Ave.) | 773-728-8785
"Uptown needs a place like this" "sophisticated yet approachable" New American "neighborhood gem" serving "succulent" "gourmet" fare, "with regular changes to the [seasonal] menu" and "without the pretentious surroundings"; in fact, this "petite" place is "warm and inviting" enough to make you "feel like you're dining at your best friend's house" – even if "the seating is a bit tight."

Magnum's Prime Steakhouse *Steak*   23 | 19 | 20 | $50

Rolling Meadows | 1701 W. Golf Rd. (New Wilke Rd.) | 847-952-8555 ☒
Lombard | 777 E. Butterfield Rd. (bet. Highland Ave. & Meyers Rd.) | 630-573-1010
www.magnumsprimesteakhouse.com

"Consistently good" prime "steaks as they should be" continue to please patrons ("more of a business crowd") of these suburban beeferies boasting "intimate" settings that smack of "city sophistication", with live piano music nightly and "nice people" on staff; skeptics, however, submit that "service varies widely" and the "enormous portions" are "pricey" but "not exceptional."

Maiz Ⓜ⏤ *Mexican*   ▽ 25 | 19 | 23 | $24

Humboldt Park | 1041 N. California Ave. (Cortez St.) | 773-276-3149
"Absolutely delicious Mexican street treats" "based on corn products" and "made by hand" using "authentic everything" "speak of the culture of Mexico City" at this "unassuming" "Humboldt Park" "winner" (now in its third location) from chef-owner/head waiter Carlos Reyna; it's a "foodies' haven" "when you consider the quality", "unusual menu items" and "low prices"; N.B. it's cash only, and no reservations.

Mama Desta's Red Sea *Ethiopian*   ▽ 18 | 9 | 13 | $19

Lakeview | 3216 N. Clark St. (Belmont Ave.) | 773-935-7561
"A solid choice" for "really tasty, filling, Ethiopian finger food" with a "good amount of spice and flavor" ("vegetarians can't go wrong here"), this Lakeview longtimer remains a "fun" "place

	FOOD	DECOR	SERVICE	COST

to share" an "inexpensive" "meal" and some "honey wine" "with a group of people" – as long as you don't mind the "ugly room" and "disappointing service."

Mambo Grill ☒ *Nuevo Latino* 19 | 15 | 16 | $30

River North | 412 N. Clark St. (bet. Hubbard & Kinzie Sts.) | 312-467-9797 | www.mambogrill.com

Fans fandango to this "loud, upbeat" River North "nightspot" for "flavorful" Nuevo Latino cuisine and "bargain" drink specials; picky eaters "prefer the interesting" cocktails to what they consider to be "forgettable food" – and some even prefer "the people-watching to the cocktails", especially now that the outdoor mojito bar is open (after 5 PM); P.S. it's also "good for lunch", with sidewalk seating in summer.

⊠ Manny's *Deli* 23 | 8 | 15 | $15

South Loop | 1141 S. Jefferson St. (Roosevelt Rd.) | 312-939-2855 ☒

Southwest Side | Midway Int'l Airport | 5700 S. Cicero Ave. (55th St.) | 773-948-6300

www.mannysdeli.com

"The local color is laid on as thick as the corned beef" at this beloved South Loop breakfast-and-lunch "institution", an "anachronistic" "steam-table cafeteria, with sandwiches made to order", peopled "by old-timers, new wavers, tourists and politicians" enjoying a taste of "true Chicago" – so go ahead and "just yell out what you want" to the "countermen, who are caricatures of themselves" (and now you can pay by credit card); N.B. the airport site serves dinner and alcohol.

Marché *French* 20 | 22 | 19 | $44

Market District | 833 W. Randolph St. (Green St.) | 312-226-8399 | www.marche-chicago.com

"Still going strong" as a "be-seen" boîte, this onetime Market District "pioneer" has evolved to "standby" status for its "boisterous" brasserie setting with "bizarre", "dramatic decor", "solid, classic [French] bistro fare" and "hipster staff"; ok, so it's "not as wild as it once was, but it still knocks the socks off out-of-towners, and it's fun even for locals", though its legacy of "lots of turnover" in the kitchen has some saying that "inconsistency is the downfall."

Margie's Candies *American* 23 | 16 | 17 | $11

Bucktown | 1960 N. Western Ave. (Armitage Ave.) | 773-384-1035 ◗
Ravenswood | 1813 W. Montrose Ave. (Ravenswood Ave.) | 773-348-0400

Though "you can eat lunch or dinner" here, "it's really about the ice cream" at this Bucktown American "classic" "with an old-fashioned parlor feel", "disabled table jukeboxes" and "staffers in bow ties and vests", where "sundaes as big as your head" topped "with homemade caramel and fudge sauce" are served in "giant seashell bowls" (and don't forget to take home some "hand-dipped chocolates"); P.S. sweet-toothers who gripe that "they haven't updated" the original in years may want to check out the Ravenswood location, which is only two years old.

	FOOD	DECOR	SERVICE	COST

NEW Marigold M Indian
- - - M

Uptown | 4832 N. Broadway (W. Lawrence Ave.) | 773-293-4653 | www.marigoldrestaurant.com

Modern, romantic and dimly lit, this Uptown Indian restaurant offers fresh, multiregional cuisine that's moderately priced (though somewhat expensive relative to its more traditional counterparts); the hip vibe is bolstered by bright jewel-toned walls, lounge-style low seating and exotic elixirs you won't find on Devon Avenue.

Mas Nuevo Latino
22 19 20 $37

Wicker Park | 1670 W. Division St. (Paulina St.) | 773-276-8700 | www.masrestaurant.com

Still "trendy" and "entertaining", this Wicker Park "date-night place" issues "inventive" and "delicious" Nuevo Latino food, along with "wonderful cocktail choices", "attentive service" and a "great vibe" that have raters requesting *mas, por favor* – though budgeters balk, saying prices are "high" "for what you get"; N.B. sidewalk seating adds to the summer scene.

NEW Matsuri M Japanese
- - - M

Geneva | Dodson Pl. | 507 S. Third St., Ste. B (South St.) | 630-208-9222

This sophisticated yet midpriced Japanese newcomer has settled into a serene taupe-toned dining room with chic cylinder lighting in West Suburban Geneva; its lunch and dinner menus of classic cooked fare and sushi are joined by a long roster of creative rolls, as well as a selection of wine and beer, but alas no sake.

Matsuya ● Japanese
21 12 17 $23

Wrigleyville | 3469 N. Clark St. (Sheffield Ave.) | 773-248-2677

Before the raw-fish frenzy, this "traditional" Wrigleyville Japanese "with a long history" was serving "solid and simple sushi" – along with "excellent chicken and steak teriyaki" and "really good udon" – in a "casual, family-friendly atmosphere" staffed by "competent" servers; devotees have decided it "deserves a spot on anyone's midweek list", but some saddened veterans swear it's gone "downhill."

Matsu Yama Japanese
▽ 22 13 19 $27

Lakeview | 1059 W. Belmont Ave. (bet. Kenmore & Seminary Aves.) | 773-327-8838 | www.matsuyamasushi.com

"Tasty, inventive rolls" and "numerous traditional" Japanese selections, all "at a fair price", rack up a roster of regulars for this "unsnooty" Lakeview "sushi joint"; some say the "cooked dishes are not as good", and most agree there's "no atmosphere to speak of", but "BYO is a huge plus" and the Wednesday–Sunday "lunch specials are a buy."

May Street Market ⊠ American
- - - M

Near West | 1132 W. Grand Ave. (May St.) | 312-421-5547

New American fare with German-Austrian and other global influences comes to the Near West neighborhood via this chic, moderately priced eatery; the neutral dining room is accented with open ductwork and a flowing vine mural while a separate lounge with plush aqua furniture is anchored by a massive flagstone wall with a

candle-filled alcove; N.B. the value-oriented wine list was created in conjunction with a retailer to reduce the usual markup.

Maza *Mideastern* | 23 | 16 | 19 | $28 |

Lincoln Park | 2748 N. Lincoln Ave. (Diversey Pkwy.) | 773-929-9600
This "dreamy" Lincoln Park place for Middle Eastern meze ("a million little plates" of "excellent appetizers", including lots of veggie options) is "family-owned and -operated with Lebanese graciousness" and is blessed with a "homey", "old-world feel" and an "eager-to-please staff"; in short, it's "just what you want in a neighborhood restaurant" – no wonder regulars "would eat here every night."

McCormick & Schmick's *Seafood* | 21 | 19 | 20 | $43 |

NEW Loop | 1 E. Wacker Dr. (bet. State St. & Wabash Ave.) | 312-923-7226
Gold Coast | 41 E. Chestnut St. (Rush St.) | 312-397-9500
www.mccormickandschmicks.com
Teeming with a "tremendous variety of" "good, fresh fish, simply prepared", this "clubby", "masculine" Gold Coast seafooder cheers chums with "a constantly changing menu", "private booths", a "nice summer patio" and a "happy hour that couldn't be happier", considering the "great specials"; raters who don't take the bait, however, rank the repasts as "run-of-the-mill, high-end chain food" "for expense-accounters" and say service swims between "delightful" and "uninterested"; N.B. the Loop location opened post-Survey, and an Oakbrook branch will open up in October 2007.

Medici on 57th ◑ *American* | 18 | 16 | 13 | $15 |

Hyde Park | 1327 E. 57th St. (bet. Kenwood & Kimbark Aves.) | 773-667-7394
A sentimental "favorite" of South-Siders, this "classic Hyde Park" "college hangout" and BYO comforts colleagues with "consistent" Traditional American fare, including "juicy burgers", "very good pizza" and "nice" "breads baked next door", all dished up in a "dark", "traditional grunge" "coffeehouse atmosphere" where it's "fun to read the writing on the walls" and "famous carvable wood tables"; P.S. "the patio garden is an oasis."

Meiji *Japanese* | 24 | 23 | 21 | $42 |

West Loop | 623 W. Randolph St. (bet. Desplaines & Jefferson Sts.) | 312-887-9999 | www.meijirestaurant.com
"Impress your date" at this West Loop "entrant in a crowded field" where the "upscale sushi" is "creative and novel" and the "other authentic Japanese dishes" include some "not found elsewhere"; the "attentive staff", "specialty martinis with Asian and American influences", and the "dark", "minimalist" ambiance also "shine."

Melting Pot, The *Fondue* | 21 | 18 | 20 | $41 |

River North | Millennium Center Towers | 609 N. Dearborn St. (bet. Ohio & Ontario Sts.) | 312-573-0011 ◑
Buffalo Grove | 1205 W. Dundee Rd. (Arlington Heights Rd.) | 847-342-6022

(continued)

FOOD DECOR SERVICE COST

(continued)

Melting Pot, The

Schaumburg | 255 W. Golf Rd. (bet. Higgins & Roselle Rds.) |
847-843-8970

Oakbrook Terrace | 17 W. 633 Roosevelt Rd. (Summit Rd.) | 630-495-5778
www.meltingpot.com

If you relish a "long, leisurely" "interactive dining experience", this
"enjoyable" city and suburban fondue family makes for a "unique
night" of "dunkin' fun" – whether on "business", with "the whole
family" or for a "romantic date"; still, authenticists assess the execution as "Americanized" and "too expensive" considering you're
"cooking your own meal"; P.S. decor varies by location, but the River
North branch has "one of the coolest bars in Chicago, where you can
play chess, backgammon or shuffleboard."

Meritage Cafe & Wine Bar *American*   22 20 20 $43

Bucktown | 2118 N. Damen Ave. (bet. Armitage & Webster Aves.) |
773-235-6434 | www.meritagecafe.com

With a focus on "delicious" Pacific Northwest preparations and a
"special affinity for fish and game", an "always-innovative" seasonal
New American menu is paired with an "extensive list" of regional
wines at this "trendy, romantic" Bucktown "date spot" that also offers
"upscale brunch"; there are those who find the service "uneven",
though, and the fare "overpriced for what you get"; P.S. "the patio offers amazing calm and charm in an otherwise bustling neighborhood."

Merle's Smokehouse *BBQ*   21 17 19 $24

Evanston | 1727 Benson Ave. (Church St.) | 847-475-7766 |
www.merlesbbq.com

Gluttons go for a "great meaty gnaw" at this "funky" North Suburban
"palace of BBQ" that "delivers" "very good" "saliva-inducing" eats
"with lots of options on the ribs preparation, sauces and sides", all
served by a "friendly staff" in a "relaxed" "barnlike" atmosphere
"that the college students love and adults enjoy" (or you can opt for
delivery or carryout); a rack of "unimpressed" raters, though, judges
it "just an average experience."

Merlo *Italian*   23 20 21 $44

Lincoln Park | 2638 N. Lincoln Ave. (Wrightwood Ave.) |
773-529-0747

Gold Coast | 16 W. Maple St. (bet. Dearborn & State Sts.) | 312-335-8200
www.merlochicago.com

An "ever-changing menu" showcasing "sophisticated preparations"
of "totally authentic" Bolognese fare – "you can tell [the pasta] was
just handmade" – with "authentic sauces" and "a quality wine list"
are served in "charming, staid" settings to the tune of "opera music", making for "a special evening out" at this Northern Italian twosome (a Wrightwood Avenue original and a Gold Coast offshoot);
"disappointed" diners who "were expecting more", however, point
out that "prices have increased" and the "vibe is a little pretentious";
N.B. Lincoln Park's front room has morphed into a wine bar with a
separate light fare menu.

	FOOD	DECOR	SERVICE	COST

☑ Mesón Sabika *Spanish* → 23 | 21 | 19 | $35

Naperville | 1025 Aurora Ave. (east of West St.) | 630-983-3000

☑ Tapas Gitana *Spanish*

Northfield | Northfield Village Ctr. | 310 Happ Rd. (bet. Willow Rd. & Winnetka Ave.) | 847-784-9300
www.mesonsabika.com

☑ Tapas Valencia *Spanish*

Bloomingdale | 241 E. Lake St. (Lakeview Dr.) | 630-582-1500 |
www.tapasvalencia.com

"Good choices for suburban tapas", this Spanish trio under the Mesón Sabika roof serves similar "strong" slates of "delicious" small plates plus "especially good desserts", "refreshing sangria" and "excellent Sunday brunch" – though those who nag it as "not all that inspired" also snark about "slow service"; "set in an old mansion", the Naperville original "makes you feel like a guest at a millionaire's estate" with a "most inviting patio"; N.B. the jury's still out on the newest locale in Bloomingdale.

M. Henry 🅜 *American* → 24 | 18 | 19 | $18

Andersonville | 5707 N. Clark St. (Hollywood Ave.) |
773-561-1600

"You can't get naughtier pancakes anywhere" than at this "imaginative, upscale" Andersonville BYO hosting New American breakfasts, brunches and lunches that are "always packed – and for good reason"; the "egg dishes hold surprise hot/sweet/tart tastes", the "vegetarian dishes are the bomb", the service is "friendly" and the "charming", "cozy" confines include "old windows suspended between tables to act as dividers"; sensitive sorts can't stand the "extreme noise level" and "lengthy waits", but hank-erers "wish they were open for dinner."

Mia Francesca *Italian* → 23 | 17 | 19 | $32

Lakeview | 3311 N. Clark St. (School St.) | 773-281-3310 |
www.miafrancesca.com

"For a reasonably priced meal" from a "daily changing menu" of "high-quality and creative but approachable Italian food", "you "can't go wrong" at this "elbow-to-elbow" Lakeview "staple", progenitor of the prolific Francesca famiglia (live wires like "all the energy on the first floor" while refuge-seekers who "can't stand the noise" "ask for a table upstairs or in the carriage house"); meanwhile, weary wags wonder why there's "always a wait even with reservations", and a quorum of quibblers query "why is this place so busy?"

Michael 🌑🅜 *French* → 25 | 18 | 17 | $50

Winnetka | 64 Green Bay Rd. (Winnetka Ave.) | 847-441-3100

Winnetkans "welcome" this "upscale" addition from chef-owner Michael Lachowicz (ex Le Français, Les Deux Gros), whose "well-crafted" New French fare with "brilliantly reduced sauces" is consumed in a "comfortable", "conversation-friendly" space; still, some fence-sitters feel its "food is better than the overall experience", saying it "needs time to perfect" the "somewhat bland" setting and

	FOOD	DECOR	SERVICE	COST

"questionable service", while trenchermen suggest the "smallish" servings are "overpriced"; N.B. lunch is served on Fridays only.

NEW Midtown Kitchen & Bar 🗷 *American*

	–	–	–	M

Loop | 203 N. LaSalle St. (bet. W. Haddock Pl. & W. Lake St.) | 312-379-5086 | www.restaurants-america.com

From the group that brought us the Loop's One North and Townhouse, this vast, midpriced New American offers business folk and theater district denizens bi-level dining for lunch and dinner, plus a chic lounge with plasma TVs and a separate bar menu, all in a modern, mahogany-accented metropolitan setting; for those in a hurry, there's a convenient grab-and-go area.

Mike Ditka's *Steak*

	20	19	19	$43

Gold Coast | Tremont Hotel | 100 E. Chestnut St. (Rush St.) | 312-587-8989 | www.mikeditkaschicago.com

"If you like big leather chairs, cigars and giant beers", you may want to intercept this "relaxed", "upscale Chicago-style" American steakhouse "adorned with sports memorabilia" and "testosterone", where you can dine on "succulent" meat ("gotta try 'da pork chop'"), "watch sporting events" with other "party animals" and perhaps even "shake hands with da coach"; fair-weather fans take a "pass", though, postulating the "food is not the important thing here" and designating it primarily for "dedicated Bears fans, dedicated smokers and dedicated tourists", though the smokers will have to find somewhere else to puff in 2008, when the city's restaurants go smoke-free.

Milk & Honey *American*

	21	16	15	$14

Wicker Park | 1920 W. Division St. (bet. Damen & Wolcott Aves.) | 773-395-9434 | www.milkandhoneycafe.com

The New American "food is particularly fresh" at this "cutie" of a Wicker Parker, where the morning meal is "better than breakfast in bed" (they mix "amazing" "granola you might dream about") and the "fantastic sandwiches" and "interesting salads" make for a "lovely lunch" – "whether you sit indoors or out"; "only counter orders are taken", and the "lines on weekends are out the door", but boosters who believe it's "worth it" ("if you can stand the cell phone and stroller" crowd) lament that "they're not open late enough."

Miller's Pub ☽ *Pub Food*

	17	15	18	$23

Loop | 134 S. Wabash Ave. (bet. Adams & Monroe Sts.) | 312-263-4988 | www.millerspub.com

A "time-tested" Loop "landmark", this "true Old Chicago" "holdout" is a "classic watering hole" "with celebrity pictures on the walls" and customers representing "a cross-section of humanity"; the "old-fashioned" American eats are "not haute cuisine", but they're "plain, good food" at a "bargain" price, and the "rough-around-the-edges but real" space is "bustling with activity at all hours" (the bar only closes between 4 and 10 AM); still, sterner surveyors deem it "dreary" and think "the menu, staff and decor all need an upgrade."

	FOOD	DECOR	SERVICE	COST

Mimosa 🅜 *French/Italian* | 23 | 17 | 22 | $39

Highland Park | 1849 Second St. (bet. Central Ave. & Elm Pl.) | 847-432-9770 | www.mimosacafe.com

"Nice to have in Highland Park", this "pleasant" "hideaway" cooks up "carefully prepared" New French–Italian cuisine (including "seasonal specials") along with "interesting wine pairings", all "reliably served" by a "very good staff"; compatriots are also "comfortable" with the "quiet", candlelit confines, calling them more than "adequate for an in-town storefront restaurant."

NEW Minnies ◑ *American* | - | - | - | I

Lincoln Park | 1969 N. Halsted St. (Armitage Ave.) | 312-943-9900 | www.minnies.com

Smaller-than-small plates served in multiples of three lure Lincoln Parkers to this bastion of downsized dining; Minnies' minis include classic American burgers, sandwiches and salads, served in a grown-up diner setting with a huge take-out area up front (takeout is 24-hours on Thursday–Saturday nights) as well as a bar stocked with miniature booze bottles and pony beers (there's a lively selection of nonalcoholic drinks and coffees too).

Mirabell 🅢 *German* | ▽ 20 | 18 | 22 | $26

Northwest Side | 3454 W. Addison St. (bet. Kimball & St. Louis Aves.) | 773-463-1962

For a schnitzel "fix", Bavaria-boosters bear toward the Northwest Side for "good, hearty" "old-style" "German food and drinks in one of the few such places left" – one where the "rustic" setting rife with steins, figurines, murals and staff in traditional costume is as heartwarming as the "reasonable prices"; N.B. there's outdoor garden seating.

🆉 Mirai Sushi 🅢 *Japanese* | 26 | 20 | 20 | $46

Wicker Park | 2020 W. Division St. (Damen Ave.) | 773-862-8500

"In the face of a Chicago sushi explosion", this "hip" Wicker Park Japanese "remains the best" per raters who prefer its "pricey" but "pristine fish" – the "unusual" "maki don't disappoint but the quality of the straight-up sashimi sets this place apart" – or "put themselves in the chef's hands for a sublime omakase dinner"; add the "divine sake" (over 30 varieties) and the "scene", especially "upstairs", where it's "definitely darker and more swank", and it's no surprise satisfied surveyors make this their "go-to" for raw fin fare.

Miramar *French* | 19 | 19 | 20 | $39

Highwood | 301 Waukegan Ave. (Highwood Ave.) | 847-433-1078 | www.miramarbistro.com

Fans of Gabriel Viti (Gabriel's, Pancho Viti's) say "Highwood is hotter than ever" thanks to this "hopping" French-ster "with a Cuban accent" and its "very good" "take on bistro fare", "nice wine list (for a casual restaurant)", "well-made mojitos" and "great people-watching" amid ambiance that's "quiet midweek" and a "hectic" "meet/meat market scene" on the weekends (when DJ entertainment adds to the "ridiculous noise level"); some say they "expected

more" and hint that "service can be a little overbearing", but all agree the "outdoor seating is wonderful."

Mitchell's Fish Market *Seafood*

| - | - | - | E |

Glenview | Glenview Town Ctr. | 2601 Navy Blvd. (bet. Eastlake Ave. & Willow Rd.) | 847-729-3663 | www.mitchellsfishmarket.com

It's no fish tale: this upscale-casual Michigan-based chain member in North Suburban Glenview's booming shopping-dining enclave specializes in a vast variety of fresh-daily seafood (from simple to internationally influenced) and a few landlubber items as well, amid nautical decor with model boats, an exhibition display room and oyster-bar accents; N.B. there's outdoor dining and a literal fish market too.

Mity Nice Grill *American*

| 18 | 15 | 18 | $27 |

Streeterville | Water Tower Pl. | 835 N. Michigan Ave., Mezzanine Level (bet. Chestnut & Pearson Sts.) | 312-335-4745 | www.leye.com

"Nicer than a diner but still affordable", this "oasis" "in the hubbub of Water Tower Place" dishes out "dependable" Traditional American "comfort food" and "tiny desserts" that "just hit the spot" "for only one dollar"; the "welcoming staff" and "cozy" "supper-club atmosphere" make it a "great place to relax" (if you can "find" it "hidden away" "in back of [the] food court"), though a share of shoppers takes its measure as "mighty average."

Mizu Yakitori & Sushi Lounge *Japanese*

| - | - | - | M |

Old Town | 315 W. North Ave. (Park Ave.) | 312-951-8880

Yakitori is the specialty of this chic Old Town Japanese offering a menu of 20-plus skewered items charcoal-flamed on an open grill, as well as traditional dishes such as tempura or tonkatsu, and the usual raw-fish suspects; you can dine at the granite-topped sushi bar or in the adjacent dining room, where warm lighting and monochrome paintings soften the stark black-and-white decor.

Mj2 Bistro 🅰 *Eclectic*

| - | - | - | M |

Park Ridge | 800 W. Devon Ave. (Brophy Ave.) | 847-698-7020 | www.mj2bistro.com

"Nicely executed" Eclectic "cooking with Asian and South American flair" has visitors to this Park Ridge bistro saying "finally – creative food in the [Northwest] Suburbs"; "friendly service", a global wine list and "ok prices" are other reasons it's a "great find in an unexpected locale."

🆉 mk *American*

| 26 | 24 | 25 | $62 |

River North | 868 N. Franklin St. (bet. Chestnut & Locust Sts.) | 312-482-9179 | www.mkchicago.com

Chef Eric Simmons (ex Bradley Ogden in Las Vegas) has come aboard Michael Kornick's "suave", still-"humming" River North "hot spot" that's managed to "endure and reinvent itself" time and again, offering New American cooking that's "outstanding without being fussy or pretentious"; the "bi-level" "loft" interior is "sleek" and the "attentive, accommodating" staffers know the "masterful wine list" and cheeses "like it's their business", so even if some raters report "rushed service" and "dreadfully noisy" digs, more maintain it's a "favorite."

	FOOD	DECOR	SERVICE	COST

☑ Mon Ami Gabi *French* | 22 | 22 | 21 | $41 |

Lincoln Park | Belden-Stratford Hotel | 2300 N. Lincoln Park W.
(Belden Ave.) | 773-348-8886
Oak Brook | Oakbrook Center Mall | 260 Oakbrook Ctr. (Rte. 83) |
630-472-1900
www.monamigabi.com

There's "always a happy hubbub" at these "fun Frenchie bistros",
"solid Lettuce" Entertain You city-and-suburban "standbys" serving
"great, reasonably priced French standards", including "unbeatable
onion soup" and "classic steak frites" with *magnifique* sauces"
(plus *loyalistes* "love the wines on the cart offered for tasting");
some purists purport that "the proliferation of locations makes even
the original seem a little bit plastic", but friends insist "if you have to
eat at a chain restaurant, this is the one."

Montarra *American* | ▽ 22 | 25 | 21 | $45 |

Algonquin | 1491 Randall Rd. (County Line Rd.) | 847-458-0505 |
www.montarra.com

A "Chicago-like experience" "for the Northwest Suburbs", this "up-
and-coming" New American's "excellent" if "expensive" entrees –
including steakhouse favorites and "creative salads" – are served
amid the "special ambiance" of an "extraordinary" space "dressed
up" with genuine Dale "Chihuly glass sculptures"; some surveyors
suggest it's "less unusual" than it was "when it opened", but many
graders gauge it a "good choice for a celebration meal."

Moon Palace *Chinese* | ▽ 21 | 13 | 20 | $21 |

Chinatown | 216 W. Cermak Rd. (Wentworth Ave.) | 312-225-4081
"Surprisingly good Shanghainese dishes" – some "not really avail-
able elsewhere" in the area – join a roster of "reliable", "popular
Chinese classics" and "a full bar" at this "cheap" Chinatown
"standby" with "friendly service" and, sadly, some "shabby decor";
N.B. they offer validated parking.

☑ Morton's, The Steakhouse *Steak* | 26 | 21 | 24 | $59 |

Loop | 65 E. Wacker Pl. (bet. Michigan & Wabash Aves.) |
312-201-0410
Gold Coast | Newberry Plaza | 1050 N. State St. (Maple St.) | 312-266-4820
Rosemont | 9525 W. Bryn Mawr Ave. (River Rd.) | 847-678-5155
NEW Northbrook | 699 Skokie Blvd. (Dundee Rd.) | 847-205-5111
Schaumburg | 1470 McConnor Pkwy. (Meacham Rd.) | 847-413-8771
Westchester | 1 Westbrook Corporate Ctr. (22nd St.) | 708-562-7000
www.mortons.com

"Still the standard" for "scrumptious slabs of the best [prime] beef
known to man", this "granddaddy" (tops among Chicago steakhouses) is a "candy store for carnivores" complete with the "show-
and-tell" presentation cart, "huge sides" and "soufflés meant to be
shared", a "great wine list" and a "professional staff"; decor at various locations may stray from the "quintessential", "manly" Gold
Coast "mother ship", and some raters reckon it's "resting on its laurels", but a well-fed majority insists this "class act" is "worth" its
"break-the-bank prices."

	FOOD	DECOR	SERVICE	COST

☑ Moto 🅱🅼 *Eclectic* — 25 | 23 | 26 | $116

Market District | 945 W. Fulton Mkt. (Sangamon St.) | 312-491-0058 |
www.motorestaurant.com

"Sophisticated palates who appreciate playfulness in cuisine" say "be prepared to be shocked and awed" at this "minimalist" Market District "marriage of science and food", where Homaro Cantu "does deconstructing wonders" with his five- to 18-course Eclectic tasting menus delivered by "knowledgeable" "staffers"; to some "food geeks" its "amazing techniques" amount to "theatrical" postmodern "alchemy" that actually "tastes amazing", but some obdurate observers are "over the chef–mad scientist" thing; N.B. Otom, a New American comfort food spin-off, is set to open on the same block.

Mr. Beef 🅱🄯 *Sandwiches* — 23 | 6 | 14 | $9

River North | 666 N. Orleans St. (bet. Erie & Huron Sts.) | 312-337-8500

"Digging in" to the "hot, delicious Italian beef" at this cash-only River North sandwich "dive" is "a Chicago tradition" for a big slice of stalwarts, as are the "surly guys behind the counter" and the "picnic tables" peopled by "cops, workers and execs"; as for "decor – who needs it?" ask insiders, considering you can just "close [your] eyes and feel the juice dripping down [your] arm"; P.S. rumor has it it's "Jay Leno's must-stop when in" town.

Mrs. Murphy & Sons Irish Bistro 🅼 *Irish* — ▽ 21 | 25 | 19 | $29

Lakeview | 3905 N. Lincoln Ave. (Byron St.) | 773-248-3905 |
www.irishbistro.com

Set "in a converted funeral home" in Lakeview, this surprisingly "lovely" contemporary Irish eatery boasts a "beautiful" interior with bars handmade in Ireland and three fireplaces; lauders love the "great" menu featuring upscale "twists on pub fare", which is paired with tap pours of Gaelic and Belgian brews plus a big native whiskey selection, though voting vacillates on the service.

Mrs. Park's Tavern ⬤ *American* — 17 | 15 | 17 | $33

Streeterville | Doubletree Guest Suites Hotel | 198 E. Delaware Pl. (Michigan Ave.) | 312-280-8882

A "good Streeterville option" for "comforting" Traditional American eats (as well as offerings that are more "creative, but not bizarre"), this "hotel eatery [in the Doubletree Guest Suites] is actually popular with locals as well as conventioneers" and a "pleasant" "spot to eat outside in the summer", though faultfinders feel the "fair food" "fails to wow."

Mt. Everest Restaurant *Indian* — 21 | 14 | 18 | $22

Evanston | 630 Church St. (bet. Chicago & Orrington Aves.) | 847-491-1069 | www.mteverestrestaurant.com

"Excellent" "Indian standards and some interesting Nepalese home-style dishes" "at reasonable prices" (including a "bargain" of a daily lunch buffet) please patrons of this "popular", "comfortable" North Suburbanite with "warm service"; holdouts, however, hedge by hinting that the "Himalayan fare" is "great for Evanston" but "not as good as on Devon Avenue."

	FOOD	DECOR	SERVICE	COST

NEW Mulan *Asian* — | — | — | M

Chinatown | Chinatown Sq. | 2017 S. Wells St., 2nd fl. (China Pl.) |
312-842-8282 | www.mulanrestaurant.com

At this ultrachic but moderately priced Chinatown entrant from chef-owner Kee Chan (Heat), each of the avant-garde Asian dishes combines meat and seafood, e.g. duck breast with sea horse; regulars recommend entering by the East Gate and warn that it's hard to know where to look first (the inverted wine decanters on the tables, the plush ultrasuede booths, the aqua wave in the floor), or which vino to order from an extensive list of New World selections; N.B. there's now a full bar.

NEW Mundial Cocina Mestiza *Mexican* — | — | — | I

Near South Side | 1640 W. 18th St. (bet. S. Marshfield Ave. &
S. Paulina St.) | 312-491-9908

The gentrification of the Near South Side's heavily Hispanic Pilsen has ushered in this unassuming, pumpkin-hued Mexican BYO with a casual cafe feel (traditional tiles, knickknacks); the open kitchen issues fresh, affordable fare like homemade tamales, tortillas and crepas, smart salads, oyster shooters (bring tequila) and chef-quality entrees – all of which can be washed down with rotating agua frescas.

My Pie Pizza *Pizza* 21 | 12 | 17 | $15

Lincoln Park | 2010 N. Damen Ave. (Armitage Ave.) | 773-394-6900
Bucktown | 2417 N. Clark St. (Fullerton Pkwy.) | 773-929-3380

"Classic, crispy, gooey thin-crust" and "great deep-dish" "pizza is served in the pan so it stays hot at the table" at this pair of "old-school" parlors where you can indulge in "different pastas", "little sandwiches" and a "very good" salad bar; the "dark", "kitschy, comfy '70s decor" at the Bucktown original "hasn't changed in [almost] 30 years" (though "the fireplace is a grand thing on a cold night"), while the Lincoln Parker is BYO with limited seating.

Myron & Phil's Steakhouse Ⓜ *Steak* 21 | 13 | 21 | $37

Lincolnwood | 3900 W. Devon Ave. (bet. Crawford & Lincoln Aves.) |
847-677-6663 | www.myronandphils.com

A "venerable North Side steakhouse", this "traditional" Lincolnwood spot is a "reliable" "relic", "delivering a great meal" – from "fish to steaks, with everything else in between" – amid a "Rat Pack" "supper-club" setting for 35 years; "if you're under 75, you immediately drop the average age, but where else can you get a [complimentary] relish tray anymore?" ("chopped liver . . . mmm"); N.B. there's piano music Thursday–Saturday nights, and in a nod to the mod, the re-modeled bar now sports plasma TVs.

Mysore Woodland *Indian* ▽ 17 | 9 | 13 | $18

West Rogers Park | 2548 W. Devon Ave. (Rockwell St.) |
773-338-8160
Westmont | 6020 S. Cass Ave. (60th St.) | 630-769-9663

Followers of this West Rogers Park BYO and its alcohol-serving Westmont sibling say both are "hard to beat" for "meatless dining" from an all-"vegetarian" menu of subcontinental standards; perhaps

it's "not the Indian cuisine most folks are used to", but supporters swear "you'll leave very full, but be craving more very soon."

Nacional 27 ⓩ *Nuevo Latino*   22 | 24 | 20 | $42

River North | 325 W. Huron St. (Orleans St.) | 312-664-2727 | www.nacional27.net

It's "a carnival for the palate" at this River North "hot spot" with "breathtaking decor" that serves "Latin libations" and a Nuevo Latino "smorgasbord" of chef Randy Zweiban's "inventive", "well-prepared" fare, including "creative tapas", "from every country south of the Rio Grande"; P.S. sedate sorts "beware": its usually "quiet", "cool vibe" gives way "later in the evening" Thursdays-Saturdays "as the main floor turns into a dance floor", with "salsa that doesn't come in a bowl."

☑ Naha ⓩ *American*   26 | 23 | 24 | $59

River North | 500 N. Clark St. (Illinois St.) | 312-321-6242 | www.naha-chicago.com

Expect "unfussy", "innovative fine dining" at this River North "favorite" that's considered "consistently among the best"; Carrie Nahabedian's "exciting menu" of "fresh" New American fare with "Mediterranean" flair is paired with a "thoughtful wine list", "seductively served" by a "cool staff" and "shown off" in a "clean-lined", "minimalist" space that "feels like a spa" – in fact, the "excellent" experience is "only marred by the high decibel level" "when it's crowded"; P.S. don't miss "one of the city's best burgers (lunch only)."

Nancy's Original Stuffed Pizza *Pizza*   21 | 10 | 16 | $18

Lakeview | 2930 N. Broadway (Wellington Ave.) | 773-883-1977 ◖

Northwest Side | 3970 N. Elston Ave. (Irving Park Rd.) | 773-267-8182 ⇱

Niles | 8706 W. Golf Rd. (Milwaukee Ave.) | 847-824-8183

Elmhurst | 940 N. York Rd. (Grand Ave.) | 630-834-4374
www.nancyspizza.com

"Zesty sauce is slathered on top of gooey cheese and loads of top-pings" to create the "delicious" stuffed pizza at this pie panoply, which also garners zealots for its "filling pasta entrees" and "good antipasto salad" – plus you can "feed your late-night cravings" at the Lakeview location; of course, since this is Chicago 'za we're talkin' about, not everyone agrees "you can't beat it."

Narcisse ◐ *Eclectic*   ▽ 20 | 25 | 22 | $46

River North | 710 N. Clark St. (bet. Huron & Superior Sts.) | 312-787-2675 | www.narcisse.us

Hungry "hip"-sters feel it's "fun to eat" at this "dark, swanky, roman-tic and Euro" River North "champagne bar", a "trendy", "unique" place to "nosh on [Eclectic] vittles while nibbling your significant other" amid "velvety decor" and lots of "eye candy" – though some lounge lizards insist it's "more for the bubbles than the food" ("a secondary issue"); N.B. there's an extensive cigar menu, as well as DJ entertainment most nights.

	FOOD	DECOR	SERVICE	COST

New Three Happiness *Chinese*

| 19 | 11 | 17 | $21 |

Chinatown | 2130 S. Wentworth Ave. (Cermak Rd.) | 312-791-1228
"The carts move fast and the staff talks faster" at this "busy" Chinatown mainstay serving "great dim sum" daily, as well as traditional Cantonese cooking; it's a "good place to bring large groups and families with kids or elderly relatives", even if "the atmosphere is lacking and the service is spotty"; N.B. no relation to the similarly named Three Happiness nearby.

Next Door Bistro ⓜ⌿ *American*

| 21 | 13 | 19 | $34 |

Northbrook | 250 Skokie Blvd. (bet. Dundee & Lake Cook Rds.) | 847-272-1491
An "interesting mixture" of "very good" American (including "great roast chicken") and Italian favorites "for a remarkably low price" is the draw at this "fun but always crowded" North Shore "neighborhood" eatery that's "still good after all these years" – but patrons who "prefer [Francesco's] Hole in the Wall", its co-owned next-door neighbor, mark this as merely its "waiting room", while hurt habitués heckle that "the host is only nice to his friends"; P.S. "it's about time to start taking credit cards – we're in a new millennium!"

NEW Niche ⓢ ⓜ *American*

| - | - | - | E |

Geneva | 14 S. Third St. (State St.) | 630-262-1000 | www.nichegeneva.com
Chef Jeremy Lycan and more than a dozen staffers of the late 302 West have regrouped to once again offer quality New American cooking priced just above midrange to West Suburban Geneva; the intimate space (formerly Chez Francois) has a clean feel in white and wood with a granite bar and walk-in wine room housing the well-thought-out selections.

Nick's Fishmarket *Seafood*

| 24 | 21 | 23 | $56 |

Loop | Bank One Plaza | 51 S. Clark St. (Monroe St.) | 312-621-0200 ⓢ
Rosemont | O'Hare Int'l Ctr. | 10275 W. Higgins Rd. (Mannheim Rd.) | 847-298-8200
NEW Deerfield | 483 Lake Cook Rd. (bet. S. Pfingsten & Waukegan Rds.)
www.nicksfishmarketchicago.com
One school of surveyors sees these "somewhat formal", "upscale" Loop and O'Hare area fisheries as "solid" choices for an "extensive selection" of "fine seafood" served by a "tuxedoed staff" in a "quiet" "supper-club setting" that's "good for business dinners" or a "date"; opposing forces feel these "stodgy" "throwbacks" with "unremarkable" underwater fare and "hit-or-miss service" "need to be revamped from decor to menu", and wallet-watchers wager "for these prices, you could buy oceanfront somewhere"; N.B. the Deerfield branch opened post-Survey.

Ⓩ Nine ⓢ *Seafood/Steak*

| 22 | 24 | 20 | $55 |

West Loop | 440 W. Randolph St. (Canal St.) | 312-575-9900 | www.n9ne.com
"To see or be seen, that is the question" at this "chic", "sleek", "slick" and "sexy" West Loop surf 'n' turfer where even those not into the "trendoid bar scene" admit the "inventive and beautifully

FOOD | DECOR | SERVICE | COST

served food" and "dramatic, architecturally stunning facility" (with a central champagne and caviar bar on weekends) make the "pageantry", "glitz factor" and "high prices" "worth the trip"; it's also a "great power-lunch spot" and "convenient to the Civic Opera House", though grudging graders say it doesn't quite "live up to the hype"; N.B. the post-Survey return of original chef Michael Shrader may outdate the above Food score.

NEW Ninefish *Japanese* — | — | — | M

Evanston | 2438 Main St. (McDaniel Ave.) | 847-328-9177
Midpriced Japanese dishes are served in this serene, strip-mall spot with a steel-and-glass sushi bar just west of central Evanston; a low-lit waiting lounge displaying a collection of cast-iron teapots (used in serving its tea selection) and the jazz background music steer sedately away from the trend of sushi spots that feel like nightclubs.

NEW 9 Muses ● *Greek* — | — | — | I

Greektown | 315 S. Halsted St. (Jackson Blvd.) | 312-902-9922
Trendier than the Greektown classics, this clubby, high-style Hellenic hot spot a-muses with an inexpensive mix of traditional Greek fare, newer noshes and a hefty helping of pastas, salads and sandwiches; dressed up with wood and ochre tones, it includes a big bar and an open-air patio with lush greenery; N.B. DJs spin on Saturdays, and food is served nightly till midnight.

Z NoMI *French* 26 | 27 | 26 | $71

Gold Coast | Park Hyatt Chicago | 800 N. Michigan Ave. (Chicago Ave.) | 312-239-4030 | www.nomirestaurant.com
"Ethereal" "Zen" environs including "Chihuly chandeliers" and an "unbeatable view" of the Water Tower earn the No. 1 Chicagoland Decor score for this Gold Coast "lap-of-luxury" lair where the "intriguing flavor combinations" of chef Christophe David's "exquisite" New French cuisine pair with "quality sushi" and an "excellent wine list" to warrant the "special-occasion" "splurge"; additional assets are the "discreet service", "killer Sunday brunch", "lovely outdoor terrace" and "very swishy bar", though you still have a segment that finds the service "stuffy" and doesn't relish "paying for the view."

Nookies ⊄ *Diner* 19 | 11 | 19 | $15

Old Town | 1746 N. Wells St. (bet. Lincoln & North Aves.) | 312-337-2454
Nookies Too *Diner*
Lincoln Park | 2114 N. Halsted St. (bet. Dickens & Webster Aves.) | 773-327-1400
Nookies Tree ●⊄ *Diner*
Lakeview | 3334 N. Halsted St. (Buckingham Pl.) | 773-248-9888
"Tried-and-true", this trio (with a fourth outpost planned for Edgewater) of Traditional Americans slings "simply great breakfasts" ("wonderful pancakes", "large omelets") "any time of the day", and "diner" lunches and dinners, all at a "good value"; despite "mixed service", they're a "favorite" "for families", and "you can always find the boys out" at the Boys Town "gayborhood staple", "especially during the late night" (Too and Tree are open 24 hours on

	FOOD	DECOR	SERVICE	COST

Friday and Saturday) – after which "the 'hangover helper' does not disappoint"; P.S. "get up early because the lines get long."

Noon-O-Kabab *Persian* ▽ 20 | 11 | 14 | $21

Northwest Side | 4661 N. Kedzie Ave. (Leland Ave.) | 773-279-8899 | www.noonokabab.com

"Noon or night", this Northwest Side seller of sustenance on a stick and "excellent baba ghanoush" is a safe bet for people with a penchant for Persian, who prate that "the food's so good you can't resist – and since it's so inexpensive, you won't need to"; some locals laud it as "something good in the 'hood", while others who see it as "not the best Middle Eastern" suggest you "stick with the kebabs."

Z North Pond M *American* 25 | 27 | 23 | $59

Lincoln Park | 2610 N. Cannon Dr. (bet. Diversey & Fullerton Pkwys.) | 773-477-5845 | www.northpondrestaurant.com

The "uncommon combination" of Bruce Sherman's "wonderfully crafted" "seasonal" cuisine, a "tranquil", "idyllic setting" of "lovely Arts and Crafts rooms" with "great skyline views" and an "excellent wine list" make this New American "on the pond in [Lincoln] Park" "one of Chicago's finest and most unique" places for a "romantic meal or special occasion"; most surveyors "feel transported a million miles away", but others are earthbound by "inconsistent food and service" and "prices that have crept up"; P.S. they serve summer lunch and "delightful Sunday brunch" year-round.

NEW Nosh *Eclectic* - | - | - | I

Geneva | 211 James St. (2nd St.) | 630-845-1570

This funky, family-friendly Eclectic set in a former auto-parts store brings urban-style brunching to quaint Geneva with its affordable menu of creative comfort food; it features a colorful interior of duct-work, space-age lighting and a retro diner counter.

Oak Tree *American* 17 | 15 | 15 | $21

Gold Coast | Bloomingdale's Bldg. | 900 N. Michigan Ave., 6th fl. (bet. Delaware Pl. & Walton St.) | 312-751-1988

"Standard" Traditional American fare "at ok prices" has its place, such as when you're looking for a "good" all-day breakfast with "fresh-squeezed OJ", "a quick bite" "before a hard day of shopping" or an early "pre-movie" dinner, and that's what you'll find at this "diner" "oasis" in the Bloomie's building, a "hangout for [Gold Coast] locals"; there's also a "nice view if you are near the windows", though some power-shoppers predict "inconsistent" service and "lots of waiting"; N.B. alcohol is not served.

Z Oceanique ⓈFrench 27 | 21 | 24 | $52

Evanston | 505 Main St. (bet. Chicago & Hinman Aves.) | 847-864-3435 | www.oceanique.com

"Unpretentious" "fine dining" is the house special at this North Suburban New French "treasure" where chef-owner Mark Grosz creates "a flawless assortment of beautifully prepared dishes" featuring the "best seafood in the Chicago area", plus "plenty of alter-

nate choices for meat people"; expect an "excellent wine list" and "well-educated staff" in a "pleasant" setting where you can "enjoy the food and your companions without being dressed to the nines" (though luxe-lovers would "upgrade" the atmosphere); P.S. try "the $39 three-course dinner Monday–Friday."

O'Famé *Pizza*   17 | 12 | 16 | $22
Lincoln Park | 750 W. Webster Ave. (Halsted St.) | 773-929-5111 | www.ofame.com

"Both the thick and thin pizza", as well as "their signature salad", are "great" at this "friendly" and "unpretentious" Lincoln Park parlor with "fair prices" and "efficient service"; "everything else is pretty average", though, including the "unassuming decor", but at least the staff knows how to handle "groups and kids", making it a "good-in-'hood choice" – and "delivery is a plus."

Old Jerusalem *Israeli*   19 | 8 | 14 | $14
Old Town | 1411 N. Wells St. (bet. North Ave. & Schiller St.) | 312-944-0459 | www.oldjerusalemrestaurant.com

Some of "the best cheap food" in town is the "great Middle Eastern grub" – such as "yummy falafel" and "melt-in-your-mouth schwarma" – at this "laid-back" Old Town Israeli BYO that's been in business for three decades; the "simple" "small storefront" space is "friendly" and "family-run", but it's "not a date place, dude" (possibly why many consider it "great for delivery").

Olé Olé ● *Nuevo Latino*   - | - | - | M
Andersonville | 5413 N. Clark St. (Balmoral Ave.) | 773-293-2222

An upbeat mood prevails at this Andersonville addition with vibrant, modern decor (a spicy red color scheme, glass doors that open to the street) and a Nuevo Latino menu that updates everything from ceviche to salads; N.B. there's no reserving, but the kitchen serves till 2 AM on weekends.

One North ⊠ *American*   18 | 19 | 17 | $34
Loop | UBS Building | 1 N. Wacker Dr. (Madison St.) | 312-750-9700 | www.rdgchicago.com

"Cozy yet sophisticated decor", a "nice outdoor eating area" and a "convenient" Loop locale make this "bustling" New American a "great location for an after-work" "or pre-theater dinner" (plus there's a happenin' lunch scene); to some, the "consistent eats are "very good", but badgerers believe that "unimaginative" fare, "spotty service" and "horrible acoustics" make this "much more of a watering hole than a dining destination."

⊠ one sixtyblue ⊠ *French*   25 | 24 | 23 | $56
Market District | 1400 W. Randolph St. (Ogden Ave.) | 312-850-0303 | www.onesixtyblue.com

"Exciting and adventurous meals" await at this "stylish" New French establishment co-owned by basketball icon Michael Jordan that's "worth the detour" to the fringe of the Market District for "terrific" cuisine "balancing creativity and simplicity" from Martial Noguier,

"a chef who cares", plus "a good selection of reasonably priced wines" and a "beautifully designed" room by Adam Tihany; it's a package that leads satisfied respondents to describe it as a "perfect place" "for a romantic dinner" or "before a concert at the United Center."

OPA Estiatorio Greek | ▽ 19 | 19 | 19 | $30 |

Vernon Hills | 950 Lakeview Pkwy. (Hawthorn Pkwy.) | 847-968-4300 | www.oparestaurant.com

"Very good Greek cuisine" "at a value", including plentiful seafood, with "wine prices" reminiscent of "what Greektown charged decades ago", lures Hellen-ophiles to this "pleasant" room in North Suburban Vernon Hills boasting "a nice patio overlooking" Bear Lake; P.S. it "can be noisy and crowded, especially on the weekends – lunch is much more sedate and comfortable."

Opera Asian | 23 | 23 | 20 | $42 |

South Loop | 1301 S. Wabash Ave. (13th St.) | 312-461-0161 | www.opera-chicago.com

Chef Paul Wildermuth "reinvents Chinese food" with his "brilliant, modern Pan-Asian cuisine" – including "gourmet vegan" options – at this "funky", "showy" South Looper with an "open", "exotic" atmosphere filled with a "bizarre mix of people"; it's "expensive", the "main room is noisy" at times and "the service could be more attentive", but the staff's "colorful", the "private" "little vault rooms" are "romantic" and the "huge sharing portions help control costs", as do the "great tasting menus" at various price points.

Orange Eclectic | 23 | 16 | 17 | $17 |

Lakeview | 3231 N. Clark St. (Belmont Ave.) | 773-549-4400
South Loop | 75 W. Harrison St. (bet. Clark & Federal Sts.) | 312-447-1000
www.orangebrunch.com

The Eclectic eats for breakfast, lunch and brunch (no dinner) are "totally tasty" at this "quirky" Lakeview and South Loop duo where the "creative spins on Traditional [American] reliables" include "inventive pancake recipes", "green eggs and ham", "fantastic coffee" and "your own combinations" of "fresh-squeezed juices"; the "kicky" orange-themed settings can resemble "a madhouse on weekends" (especially Clark Street) with "long waits" and no reservations, and holdouts harangue the "hit-or-miss" experience is "not worth the hype and high prices"; N.B. a Roscoe Village location is in the works.

Original Gino's East, The Pizza | 22 | 13 | 15 | $19 |

River North | 633 N. Wells St. (Ontario St.) | 312-943-1124
NEW **Streeterville** | 162 E. Superior St. (Michigan Ave.) | 312-266-3337
Lincoln Park | 2801 N. Lincoln Ave. (Diversey Pkwy.) | 773-327-3737
O'Hare Area | 8725 W. Higgins Rd. (bet. Cumberland & River Rds.) | 773-444-2244
Rolling Meadows | 1321 W. Golf Rd. (Algonquin Rd.) | 847-364-6644
Orland Park | 15840 S. Harlem Ave. (159th St.) | 708-633-1300
Naperville | 1807 S. Washington St. (bet. Foxcroft & Redstart Rds.) | 630-548-9555

(continued)

(continued)

Original Gino's East, The

St. Charles | Tin Cup Pass Shopping Ctr. | 1590 E. Main St. (Tyler Rd.) | 630-513-1311

Wheaton | 315 W. Front St. (West St.) | 630-588-1010
www.ginoseast.com

While none is the original 'Original' (despite the re-acquisition of the space that once housed the original), "the legend lives on" at these chain outposts for lovers of "scrumptious" "traditional Chicago deep-dish" pie with "cornmeal crust" ("nice thin-crust" too) and salads that are "just as good"; contributors call the rendition in the River North "tourist area" a "good place to take out-of-towners" to "write on" the "graffiti-laden walls" (they "were moved" from the "character-filled former" flagship), but doubters demand that management "take 'Original' the hell off the sign"; N.B. some sites are privately owned.

☑ Original Pancake House, The *American*   23 | 14 | 18 | $15

Streeterville | 22 E. Bellevue Pl. (bet. Michigan Ave. & Rush St.) | 312-642-7917 ⊡

Lincoln Park | 2020 N. Lincoln Park W. (Clark St.) | 773-929-8130 ⊡

Hyde Park | Village Ctr. | 1517 E. Hyde Park Blvd. (bet. 51st St. & Lake Park Blvd.) | 773-288-2323 ⊡

Oak Forest | 5148 W. 159th St. (bet. Laramie & Le Claire Aves.) | 708-687-8282 ⊡

Oak Park | 954 Lake St. (Forest St.) | 708-524-0955
www.originalpancakehouse.com

☑ Walker Bros. Original
Pancake House *American*

Lincolnshire | 200 Marriott Dr. (Milwaukee Ave.) | 847-634-2220

Highland Park | 620 Central Ave. (bet. Green Bay Rd. & 2nd St.) | 847-432-0660

Wilmette | 153 Green Bay Rd. (bet. Central & Lake Aves.) | 847-251-6000

Arlington Heights | 825 W. Dundee Rd. (bet. Arlington Heights Rd. & Rte. 53) | 847-392-6600

Lake Zurich | Lake Zurich Theatre Development | 767 S. Rand Rd. (Rte. 22) | 847-550-0006
www.walkerbrosoph.com

"Loosen the belt a notch" before a visit to this chain of "quintessential" American pancake "joints" that's "exactly what it's supposed to be" – namely, "the standard-bearer" for "gimongous", "coma-inducing breakfasts" most "any time of day"; like the hours and credit-card policy, the settings vary by location, ranging from "worn-out" "diner" to "stained glass and wood", but the "long lines don't lie" about the "high-quality" and "reasonable prices"; P.S. though all are considered "eggcellent", the Walker Bros. sites appear to have the edge decorwise.

NEW Osteria di Tramonto *Italian*   - | - | - | M

Wheeling | Westin Chicago North Shore | 601 N. Milwaukee Ave. (Apple Dr.) | 847-777-6570 | www.cenitare.com

Tru's Rick Tramonto cooks classic and thinking-man's multiregional Italian with wine selections to match at Northwest Suburban Wheeling's new Westin hotel; the moderately priced, seasonal

menu is at once rustic and modern – a philosophy carried through in the decor with its exposed brick, glass wine-wall and open kitchen with dining counter; N.B. breakfast includes goodies from partner Gale Gand's on-site coffee bar.

Osteria Via Stato *Italian*

21 | 19 | 21 | $47

River North | 620 N. State St. (Ontario St.) | 312-642-8450 | www.leye.com

A "boffo" "family-style" Italian dining experience is on the table at this Lettuce Entertain You "all-you-can-eat free-for-all" in River North, where "you pick the main dish" from "just a few choices" and "the food just keeps coming"; the "stone-and-dark-wood decor provides a warm atmosphere", made even more "cozy" by "some communal seating", but respondents who feel "rushed" gripe that the "gimmick" is "too much circus" and say "service is a work-in-progress"; P.S. if the fare seems "overpriced", "eat at the much-cheaper enoteca in front."

NEW Over Easy Café *American*

- | - | - | I

Ravenswood | 4943 N. Damen Ave. (bet. Ainslie & Argyle Sts.) | 773-506-2605

Closed after a fire last summer, this inexpensive breakfast-lunch BYO has reopened, serving its Traditional American fare in a small Ravenswood space decked out with retro Formica tables, exposed-brick walls and wooden eggs dangling from the ceiling; N.B. it's boisterous when busy, with sidewalk waits – and free coffee – at peak hours.

Oysy *Japanese*

21 | 17 | 18 | $31

River North | 50 E. Grand Ave. (bet. Rush St. & Wabash Ave.) | 312-670-6750

South Loop | 888 S. Michigan Ave. (9th St.) | 312-922-1127

Northbrook | 315 Skokie Blvd. (Dundee Rd.) | 847-714-1188
www.oysysushi.com

Enthusiasts explain that "everything's fresh and tasty" at these "stylish and hip" South Loop, River North and North Shore spots with "succulent sushi" and a "good selection" of cooked Japanese fare, including "nice small plates", served in a "beautifully minimal" "space-age environment"; lauders also love the "lunch specials", but some suggest that the "pleasant but not very knowledgeable servers" could provide "much better service."

Pacific Blue *Seafood*

▽ 25 | 19 | 20 | $35

Glen Ellyn | 536C Crescent Blvd. (Main St.) | 630-469-1080 | www.pacificbluerestaurant.com

"Succulent", "sophisticated and fresh seafood" appeals to West Suburbanites who reel in the "reasonably priced menu and wine list" and "conversation-friendly" beach-house atmosphere (complete with "great" "live jazz on the weekends") at this "nice neighborhood place" in Glen Ellyn; N.B. a children's menu is available.

Palm, The *Steak*

23 | 19 | 22 | $56

Loop | Swissôtel | 323 E. Wacker Dr. (bet. Lake Shore Dr. & Michigan Ave.) | 312-616-1000

(continued)

(continued)

Palm, The

Northbrook | Northbrook Court Shopping Ctr. | 2000 Northbrook Ct. (Lake Cook Rd.) | 847-239-7256
www.thepalm.com

"Filled with celebs and wannabes", these "venerable" Loop and North Suburban "meat-palace" "classics" are known for "excessive portions (at excessive prices)" of "prime steaks" and "huge lobsters", plus "excellent service" and "clubby, dark" decor "with nostalgia dripping from the walls"; nonetheless, a contingent of contentious carnivores concludes there are "better options" "in a town with a surplus of great steakhouses"; P.S. wallet-watchers "love the family-style menu" special that feeds three, available Sunday–Thursday (Northbrook only).

NEW Palmito ⓈⓂ *Costa Rican*   - | - | - | I

Lakeview | 3605 N. Ashland Ave. (Addison St.) | 773-248-3087 | www.palmitochicago.com

A shoebox-sized BYO with mango walls and about a dozen tables, this authentic Costa Rican spot serves comfort and contemporary dishes (including a grilled pork chop with a cumin-ginger spice rub) at bargain prices in a friendly, homey Lakeview setting; beverages include blended fresh fruit drinks and the traditional coffee chorreado.

Pane Caldo *Italian*   24 | 20 | 22 | $57

Gold Coast | 72 E. Walton St. (bet. Michigan Ave. & Rush St.) | 312-649-0055 | www.pane-caldo.com

"Genuinely interesting and well-prepared" Northern Italian cuisine from a constantly changing menu and a "wine list to die for" are presented by a "very good" staff at this "serious", "sophisticated" Gold Coast "find" with an "intimate" (i.e. "elbow-to-elbow") feel; penny-pinchers warn, though, that it's "way overpriced", making it "a luxury to go here."

Pappadeaux Seafood Kitchen *Seafood*   20 | 18 | 19 | $33

Arlington Heights | 798 W. Algonquin Rd. (Golf Rd.) | 847-228-9551
Westmont | 921 Pasquinelli Dr. (Oakmont Ln.) | 630-455-9846
www.pappas.com

These sister suburbanite "chain"-sters lure fin-fans with their "diverse menus" of "delicious", "fresh" fish with a Louisiana "flair" – the "blackened dishes" have many boosters – and "big, fun seafood-shack" interiors that are pretty much "always deafening"; "large portions and fair prices make them winners with families", but faultfinders figure the food is "faux Cajun" and the "service is sometimes shaky"; P.S. "live [Saturday night zydeco] music is an added feature" at the Westmont branch, and Arlington Heights does a Sunday brunch buffet.

Parkers' Ocean Grill *Seafood*   21 | 21 | 21 | $44

Downers Grove | 1000 31st St. (Highland Ave.) | 630-960-5701 | www.selectrestaurants.com

Serving "simple preparations" of "great seafood" in a "lovely" "country-club atmosphere", this "large" West Suburban "fish

	FOOD	DECOR	SERVICE	COST

"house" is "upscale without the snob appeal", though a passel of parsimonious pollsters perceives it as "a bit too pricey" "for the delivered goods"; N.B. there's live music on weekends and a patio in season.

Park Grill *American*

19	20	18	$36

Loop | Millennium Park | 11 N. Michigan Ave. (bet. Madison & Washington Sts.) | 312-521-7275 | www.parkgrillchicago.com

"Amazing Millennium Park" is home to this "awesomely located New American" whose "menu with lots of variety will please upscale tourists and locals alike" (the "great burgers" get the most raves), as will the "fun view of the [ice] skaters" and "nice fireplace" in winter and "fabulous outdoor area in summer"; picky eaters postulate the "pretty good" "but expensive" "food isn't up to the challenge", though, making the "beautiful scenery" "the real star here", and advise that "service is uneven" since the "staff is stretched too thin."

Parlor ●M *American*

19	19	20	$33

Wicker Park | 1745 W. North Ave. (bet. Hermitage Ave. & Wood St.) | 773-782-9000

"An interesting take" on "well-prepared", "down-home" Traditional American "comfort foods" ("e.g. meatloaf and hamburgers") and "a fun", "albeit small, bar" with "good wines by the glass" and retro cocktails make this "classy" "1940s"-inspired "joint" with a "comfy vibe" a "great new" addition to the Wicker Park neighborhood; N.B. since opening they've added a patio.

Parrot Cage, The ⊠M *American*

-	-	-	M

Far South Side | South Shore Cultural Ctr. | 7059 S. Shore Dr. (71st St.) | 773-602-5333

A proving ground for its staff of Washburne Culinary Institute students (their classes are held upstairs), this New American on the Far South Side offers a reasonably priced seasonal menu in a white-tablecloth setting; the parrot theme is carried out in the tropical color scheme, with picture windows providing lake views.

Parthenon ● *Greek*

20	15	18	$26

Greektown | 314 S. Halsted St. (bet. Jackson Blvd. & Van Buren St.) | 312-726-2407 | www.theparthenon.com

"Old-fashioned Greek" goodies are offered at "value" prices at this "unpretentious", "reliable and boisterous" Greektown bastion that "delivers what one expects" – "amazing" flaming saganaki ("watch your eyebrows!"), "homemade gyros" and "lamb, lamb, lamb"; it's "fun" "family-style dining", and there's also "free valet parking", even if more finicky factions figure fans of its "heavy food" and "gruff service" "must be into nostalgia."

Pasta Palazzo ⊅ *Italian*

22	15	18	$17

Lincoln Park | 1966 N. Halsted St. (Armitage Ave.) | 773-248-1400

"Keep it on the down-low" cry coveters of the "cheap, good eats" at this Lincoln Park Italian "hideout", saying you're "guaranteed a tasty meal" from a "simple but complete menu" of "fast-food pasta"; you can dine in the "cool, urban" space ("where you may share a long ta-

ble with strangers") "if you don't mind the cramped" confines – otherwise, avail yourself of the "great takeout"; N.B. cash only.

NEW Patty Burger *Hamburgers*

| – | – | – | I |

Loop | 72 E. Adams St. (bet. Jewelers Row & S. Michigan Ave.) | 312-987-0900 | www.pattyburger.com

The Loop flagship of this quality-conscious, budding fast-food chain serves 100 percent Angus burgers that are hand-formed and cooked to order on fresh-baked buns just like in the good ol' days, which the clean, diner decor is meant to evoke; chili, veggie burgers, fries, shakes and breakfast sandwiches round out the fairly limited menu.

Pegasus ● *Greek*

| 22 | 20 | 20 | $28 |

Greektown | 130 S. Halsted St. (bet. Adams & Monroe Sts.) | 312-226-4666

Pegasus on the Fly *Greek*

Southwest Side | Midway Int'l Airport | 5700 S. Cicero Ave. (55th St.) | 773-581-1522 ●

Lombard | Yorktown Ctr. | 203 Yorktown Shopping Ctr. (Highland Ave.) | 630-424-1441

www.pegasuschicago.com

"More upscale than some Greektown establishments", this "consistent" "favorite" "goes beyond the typical gyros or souvlaki" with "never-ending choices" of "hubcap-sized" Hellenic plates presented with "warm service" in a "bright, decorated room" – or "in summer" you can "sit on the rooftop deck" "overlooking Downtown", either "for drinks" or to order from "a smaller menu"; P.S. the airport stand is "a great quick meal at Midway", and there's a stand in the food court at Lombard's Yorktown Shopping Center too.

Penang ● *Malaysian*

| 19 | 14 | 17 | $22 |

Chinatown | 2201 S. Wentworth Ave. (Cermak Rd.) | 312-326-6888

"A nice break from the mainstream", this "reasonably priced" outpost in the "heart of Chinatown" features a "good mix" of "very tasty" Southeast Asian food on its "exotic menu", which includes "both Chinese Malaysian and ethnic Malay" fare, as well as some Thai and sushi offerings; still, some noshers needle that you "need to order well"; N.B. they've added a karaoke lounge upstairs, and insomniacs appreciate that they're open till 1 AM.

Penny's Noodle Shop *Asian*

| 19 | 12 | 17 | $13 |

Lincoln Park | 950 W. Diversey Pkwy. (Sheffield Ave.) | 773-281-8448

Wrigleyville | 3400 N. Sheffield Ave. (Roscoe St.) | 773-281-8222 Ⓜ
Wicker Park | 1542 N. Damen Ave. (North Ave.) | 773-394-0100 Ⓜ
www.pennysnoodleshop.com

Oak Park | 1130 Chicago Ave. (Harlem Ave.) | 708-660-1300 | www.pennysnoodleshopoakpark.com

Oodles of slurpers support these "no-frills" noodleries as "nice to have in the neighborhood" for their "great selection" of "amazingly affordable" "quickie Asian" eats, which are "tasty" (if "not haute cuisine") and offered in "casual", "packed" digs with "quick service" (for many, the chain's also a "regular on the takeout-restaurant ro-

tation"); skeptics, though, sigh "same old, same old", saying "everything's bland" at these "run-of-the-mill" eateries "for beginners"; N.B. they all serve beer and wine except Wrigleyville, which is BYO.

People Lounge ◑ *Spanish* — | — | — | M

Wicker Park | 1560 N. Milwaukee Ave. (Damen Ave.) | 773-227-9339 | www.peoplechicago.com

The small-plates craze hits Wicker Park with this Spaniard housed in a former liquor store and serving a limited-but-growing menu of seasonal tapas (e.g. an emphasis on cold items in summer); global tunes from live acts and DJs fill the warm, wood-accented room that features massive iron chandeliers, a 30-ft.-long bar and communal tables with bench seating.

Pepper Lounge ◑Ⓜ *American* 22 | 23 | 22 | $33

Wrigleyville | 3441 N. Sheffield Ave. (Clark St.) | 773-665-7377 | www.pepperlounge.com

"A fun little find" for a "night-in-the-city experience", this "sophisticated", "gay-friendly" New American is also "one of the few non-cheesy places in" Wrigleyville, with its "well-presented", "creative and flavorful" fare, some of the "best French and chocolate martinis in town", "great background music" and a "gorgeous patio" (and they do brunch too); a few faultfinders, however, feel the "food can be hit-or-miss."

Pete Miller's Seafood & 21 | 20 | 20 | $45
Prime Steak *Seafood/Steak*

Evanston | 1557 Sherman Ave. (bet. Davis & Grove Sts.) | 847-328-0399 ◑
Wheeling | 412 N. Milwaukee Ave. (Dundee Rd.) | 847-243-3700
www.petemillers.com

"Mouthwatering" "thick steaks" and "great fish" "served up with a healthy portion of live jazz" most nights keep these "solid" North Suburban seafood-steakhouse "joints jumping"; a retinue of raters relies on the "dark and classy" yet "informal atmosphere" (the newer Wheeling location is "more stylish") for a "relaxed meal" or some billiards with a "very good burger", but others' enthusiasm peters out over service "delays" and "overpriced" fare with "low-octane flavor"; N.B. a Schaumburg location is in the works.

Petterino's *American* 19 | 20 | 20 | $38

Loop | Goodman Theatre Bldg. | 150 N. Dearborn St. (Randolph St.) | 312-422-0150 | www.petterinos.com

Loop locals and Goodman Theatre-goers feel "welcome" at this "convenient", "consistent" Traditional American with "old-fashioned, fun" fare (some Italian) and "caricatures of celebs" in a "red-velvet" "'40s" "supper-club" setting (granted, it gets "hectic before a show", but they "really hustle to make sure you make the curtain"); tougher critics, however, lower that curtain on this "cliché" "attempt at Rat Pack" "retro", saying "lackluster food" makes it "one of the least interesting of the Lettuce Entertain You restaurants."

| | FOOD | DECOR | SERVICE | COST |

☑ P.F. Chang's China Bistro *Chinese* — 20 | 20 | 19 | $28
River North | 530 N. Wabash Ave. (Grand Ave.) | 312-828-9977
Northbrook | 1819 Lake Cook Rd. (Northbrook Court Dr.) | 847-509-8844
Schaumburg | Woodfield Mall | 5 Woodfield Mall (bet. Frontage & Golf Rds.) | 847-610-8000
Lombard | 2361 Fountain Square Dr. (bet. Butterfield & Meyers Rds.) | 630-652-9977
www.pfchangs.com

Flatterers of this "friendly" foursome favor its "nontraditional", "varied" Mandarin-style munchables made from "fresh", "identifiable ingredients", plus its "excellent cocktails" and Great Wall of Chocolate dessert ("as big as" the real thing) offered in "upscale-casual" confines with "tasteful decor"; but while adherents assert they "look for" outposts of the "consistent chain" "in every city", foes find the feel "formulaic" and the fare "faux Chinese", saying it's "not for purists."

Philander's Oak Park *American* — ▽ 21 | 23 | 21 | $44
Oak Park | Carleton Hotel | 1110 Pleasant St. (bet. Maple Ave. & Marion St.) | 708-848-4250 | www.carletonhotel.com

"Cozy", "clubby" and "charming", this "intimate" "white-tablecloth" dining experience "in an old hotel in scenic Oak Park" includes "great" New American cuisine, "attentive service" and a "hot middle-aged bar scene" with live "music at the piano" nightly; all told, it's a "great place to hang out."

Phil & Lou's ☑ *American* — ▽ 17 | 19 | 17 | $29
West Loop | 1124 W. Madison St. (bet. Halsted St. & Racine Ave.) | 312-455-0070 | www.philandlous.com

Cohorts of this "comfortable" West Looper purport it's a "perfect match for the neighborhood", saying they like to "kick back and relax" over its "dependable", "down-home" American food or even kick up their heels at the retro DJ dance party on Friday nights; others with "bad experiences" to report berate it as "boring", but most insist it's "a safe place to eat before a game."

Philly G's *Italian* — 22 | 19 | 21 | $35
Vernon Hills | 1252 E. Hwy. 45 (Rte. 21) | 847-634-1811 | www.phillygs.com

Retaining its "proud family" heritage, this Northwest Suburban "casa de garlic" serves "good roadhouse-y Italian" (including "great veal") within the "beautiful, comfortable rooms" of a restored home; the "charming" patio and weekend entertainment help make it "a nice date restaurant", but some judges jot "the jury is still out" since scion Phil Gilardi Jr. took control.

Phil Stefani's 437 Rush ☑ *Italian/Steak* — 21 | 18 | 22 | $44
River North | 437 N. Rush St. (Hubbard St.) | 312-222-0101 | www.stefanirestaurants.com

"Well-prepared" "classic Italian steakhouse" cooking in "grand proportions" is the draw at this "clubby", "comfortable" River Norther "with old-time service" and a "lively", "large bar area" (it's also "great for a business lunch or dinner"); still, raters who rank it "reli-

able but never spectacular" – with prices that are "a bit high" – assign it "secondary" status on their personal lists.

Phoenix *Chinese*   22 | 13 | 16 | $21

Chinatown | 2131 S. Archer Ave., 2nd fl. (Wentworth Ave.) | 312-328-0848
Patrons of this Chinatown chow-palace are pleased by its "great variety, freshness and service", pronouncing it "one of the best places for daily dim sum" (offered from carts until 3 PM) and deeming "dinner a gracious experience" as well, with a "menu that focuses on Mandarin cuisine"; an abundance of "families adds to the cheer" of its "relaxed, open" space, though at peak hours "its popularity can be a bit daunting" due to the resulting "long lines and crowded rooms."

Piazza Bella *Italian*   21 | 18 | 20 | $28

Roscoe Village | 2116 W. Roscoe St. (bet. Damen & Western Aves.) | 773-477-7330 | www.piazzabella.com
"Romantic, candlelit and casual", this Roscoe Village "neighborhood Italian trattoria" is "well-frequented" for its "classic dishes", such as "cracker thin-crusted pizzas and various" "nice pastas", plus "good steak and fish as well" ("the specials are usually impressive" too); a "welcoming staff" and "nice wine list" further enhance the "happy atmosphere"; P.S. "if you want to sit outside", be warned that the patio gets "very crowded in the summer."

Piece *Pizza*   22 | 15 | 15 | $18

Bucktown | 1927 W. North Ave. (bet. Damen & Wolcott Aves.) | 773-772-4422 | www.piecechicago.com
If you believe "beer and pizza [are the] staples of life" and "you're not in the mood for traditional Chicago" pie, check out this "large, industrial" Bucktowner – its "great New Haven–style" thin-crust 'za "with interesting combinations" of toppings, plus "excellent large salads" and "tasty" microbrews, appeal to a "young, hip" crowd, making it a favorite place to "watch a game" or cut loose on the "loud", "wacky karaoke nights" (Thursdays, and with a live band on Saturdays).

Pierrot Gourmet *French*   21 | 20 | 20 | $30

River North | Peninsula Hotel | 108 E. Superior St. (bet. Michigan Ave. & Rush St.) | 312-573-6749 | www.peninsula.com
"Traditional French bistro" fare served in a "quaint" "informal" setting (especially "for a top-level hotel") makes this River Norther a "favorite" "place for a quick, quality bite" – from "great coffee and breakfast pastries" to "a light lunch" with a glass of wine from a "pretty decent list" to "afternoon tea" to "outdoor cafe dining on Rush Street" (and even "for meeting people at the communal tables"); "inconsistent service" is a concern to some, however, and "lower prices would have [others] returning more often."

Pine Yard *Chinese*   20 | 11 | 15 | $20

Evanston | 1033 Davis St. (Oak St.) | 847-475-4940 | www.pineyardrestaurant.com
"Very good", "straightforward" Szechuan and Mandarin "dishes done with careful attention" create converts to the cause of this

North Suburban "standby" ("lunch is a deal", and beer and wine are served); those unwilling to overlook the "prickly" personnel and "cheesy decor", though, say "you may want to take out", while purists take a pass, purporting the provender "puts the American back in Chinese-American cuisine."

pingpong ● Asian
21 | 15 | 16 | $18

Lakeview | 3322 N. Broadway (bet. Aldine Ave. & Buckingham Pl.) | 773-281-7575 | www.pingpongrestaurant.com

This Boys Town BYO plates "quality" Pan-Asian "fusion" fare and dishes it out in an "ultramodern" space, "complete with pulsating beats", that strikes supporters as "cute as a button" (they take no reservations, but the "great crowd-watching in summer makes the wait almost enjoyable"); still, wags wonder "if minimalist white counts as decor", while sensitive sorts suggest that "good food doesn't entirely offset the slow service" from certain "snippy" staffers; N.B. a recent expansion is not reflected in the Decor score.

☑ Pita Inn Mideastern
24 | 10 | 16 | $11

Glenview | 9854 N. Milwaukee Ave. (Golf Rd.) | 847-759-9990
Skokie | 3910 W. Dempster St. (Crawford St.) | 847-677-0211
Wheeling | 122 S. Elmhurst Rd. (Dundee Rd.) | 847-808-7733
www.pitainn.com

The "fabulous", "plentiful", "healthy and tasty Middle-Eastern" and "Med favorites" accompanied by "fresh-out-of-the-oven pita" are a "different", "high-quality" "fast food" at this North Suburban trio with "quick service"; the "unassuming location" ("who needs decor when the food is so great?") is "packed every night of the week" with "every type of person" (it's "great for vegetarians") – after all, who wouldn't want to "eat like a king [on] a pauper's budget"?

Pizza Capri Pizza
19 | 13 | 15 | $18

Lincoln Park | 1733 N. Halsted St. (Willow St.) | 312-280-5700
Lakeview | 962 W. Belmont Ave. (Sheffield Ave.) | 773-296-6000
Hyde Park | 1501 E. 53rd St. (Harper Ave.) | 773-324-7777
www.pizzacapri.com

"Unique pizza" "that is a little more grown-up" thanks to "interesting toppings" (some "love the BBQ chicken" variety, while others say "try the rosemary potato" version), as well as "solid pastas", "great sandwiches" and "terrific salads" have surveyors saying this "unpretentious", "efficiently run" Italian trio "is excellent for what it aims to be"; P.S. the Lincoln Park branch "mostly does takeout and delivery", while the Hyde Park location is separately owned.

Pizza D.O.C. Pizza
22 | 14 | 17 | $24

Lincoln Square | 2251 W. Lawrence Ave. (Oakley Ave.) | 773-784-8777 | www.pizza-doc.com

"Wonderful", "refined" "Italian-style pizzas" with "crackerlike crust" from a "wood-burning oven", plus "always-fresh" pastas, "terrific" antipasto and a "nice wine list" woo lovers of this "casual" Lincoln Square "neighborhood place"; still, emergency meal technicians swear the pie "sometimes comes out more soggy than crisp",

and say both the "lacking service" and "rustic" "interior could use some work" (though "the open kitchen cozies up the space").

Pizzeria Uno ● *Pizza*
22 | 14 | 15 | $20

River North | 29 E. Ohio St. (Wabash Ave.) | 312-321-1000

Pizzeria Due ● *Pizza*

River North | 619 N. Wabash Ave. (bet. Ohio & Ontario Sts.) | 312-943-2400
www.unos.com

"Prepare to be rolled out on a dolly" after dining at either of these Chicago "originals" with lots of "history behind" them, as you'll be "so full" with "one of the better deep-dish pies" around; diehards aren't dissuaded by "workmanlike service", "scrunched-in tables" and "long waits due to heavy tourist traffic", insisting "this is still Chicago's pizza" and advising "accept no substitutes" – these "classics" "bear little or no resemblance to the national chain they spawned."

P.J. Clarke's *American*
17 | 15 | 17 | $24

Streeterville | Embassy Suites Hotel | 302 E. Illinois St. (Columbus Dr.) | 312-670-7500

Gold Coast | 1204 N. State Pkwy. (Division St.) | 312-664-1650
www.pjclarkeschicago.com

"Lively" and "crowded", these Gold Coast and Streeterville "watering holes" serving "standard" Traditional American provender are "popular" "for a casual beer and burger", "watching a game", "good people-watching on weekdays for the after-work crowd" and as "meeting spots" for "over-35 singles"; rueful raters, however, report that the original on State, a "once-great neighborhood haunt", now "reminds [them] of a chain" with "ho-hum" eats – though both branches are unrelated to and "without the history of the NY original."

Platiyo *Mexican*
20 | 20 | 19 | $31

Lakeview | 3313 N. Clark St. (bet. Buckingham Pl. & School St.) | 773-477-6700 | www.platiyo.com

Though now under new ownership, this "friendly", "funky" Lakeview cantina still "does for Mexican what [its former cousin next door] Mia Francesca has done for Italian", serving up "fresh" "modern" fare with a "gourmet touch" (such as "interesting, very tasty moles and sauces" as well as "amazing margaritas") and "vibrant surroundings"; N.B. they also offer Sunday brunch, patio dining and live music some nights.

Poag Mahone's Carvery & Ale House ☒ *Pub Food*
17 | 14 | 14 | $18

Loop | 175 W. Jackson Blvd. (bet. LaSalle & Wells Sts.) | 312-566-9100 | www.poagmahone.com

The "better-than-average" Traditional American "pub grub" at this Loop location includes a "damn good burger", which "you can eat in peace" at lunch – as opposed to "after work", when it's "packed to the gills" with "painfully loud" patrons who perhaps find it funny that the name means 'kiss my ass' in Gaelic; a minority maligns it as "a pseudo pub in an office building", with "mediocre", "cookie-

cutter food and decor", but barflies bellow "after a happy-hour double scotch on the rocks, who really cares?"

Pompei Bakery *Italian*   20 | 14 | 16 | $15

Lincoln Park | 2955 N. Sheffield Ave. (Wellington Ave.) | 773-325-1900
Little Italy | 1531 W. Taylor St. (bet. Ashland Ave. & Laflin St.) | 312-421-5179
Schaumburg | 1261 E. Higgins Rd. (bet. Meacham Rd. & National Pkwy.) | 847-619-5001
Oakbrook Terrace | 17 W. 744 22nd St. (Summit Ave.) | 630-620-0600
River Forest | 7215 W. Lake St. (Harlem Ave.) | 708-488-9800
www.pompeibakery.com

First opened in Little Italy in 1909 (though at a different location from that nabe's current branch, today a rater "favorite"), this "cheap, dependable" chain of "solid" "cafeteria-style Italian" installations issues "very good pizzas" that qualify as "comfort by the slice", plus "unique sandwiches" and "great soups and salads"; it's "not quite fast food – but service is quick", making it an "easy" stop with kids; N.B. the River Forest branch opened post-Survey.

NEW Pops for Champagne ● *American*   – | – | – | E

River North | Tree Studios | 601 N. State St. (Ohio St.) | 312-266-7677 | www.popsforchampagne.com

This pricey bubbly bar has relocated to River North's historic Tree Studios and now qualifies as a bona fide dining option too, with its expanded menu offering raw-bar selections, caviar, New American small plates, desserts and even lunch; its swanky bi-level setup – with a champagne-hued bar/dining aerie upstairs and intimate jazz club downstairs – stays true to its name with an exhaustive list of sparkling selections; N.B. keep the celebration going at home with a trip to its adjacent retail store.

Potbelly Sandwich Works *Sandwiches*   20 | 15 | 18 | $9

Loop | One Illinois Ctr. | 111 E. Wacker Dr. (Michigan Ave.) | 312-861-0013 🅂
Loop | 175 W. Jackson Blvd. (bet. Financial Pl. & Wells St.) | 312-588-1150 🅂
Loop | 190 N. State St. (Lake St.) | 312-683-1234
Loop | 303 W. Madison St. (Franklin St.) | 312-346-1234 🅂
Loop | 55 W. Monroe St. (Dearborn St.) | 312-577-0070 🅂
River North | 508 N. Clark St. (bet. Grand Ave. & Illinois St.) | 312-644-9131
River North | The Shops at North Bridge | 520 N. Michigan Ave., 4th fl. (Grand Ave.) | 312-644-1008
Lincoln Park | 1422 W. Webster Ave. (Clybourn Ave.) | 773-755-1234
Lincoln Park | 2264 N. Lincoln Ave. (bet. Belden & Webster Aves.) | 773-528-1405
Wrigleyville | 3424 N. Southport Ave. (Roscoe St.) | 773-289-1807
www.potbelly.com
Additional locations throughout the Chicago area

"There's a reason the lines are out the door" at this beloved bevy of "fast-food" "favorites" "at the top of their game" with "tasty, toasty sandwiches" that "satisfy" "addicts" from "vegetarians to the big-

gest carnivore"; though some "first-time"-ers complain of a "confusing ordering system", most insist the "unbelievably speedy" counter staff has it "down to a science", ensuring "you'll never waste a lot of time getting your food."

Prairie Grass Cafe Ⓜ American   21 | 18 | 19 | $40
Northbrook | 601 Skokie Blvd. (bet. Dundee & Lake Cook Rds.) | 847-205-4433 | www.prairiegrasscafe.com
"Chefs [Sarah] Stegner and [George] Bumbaris bring their Ritz-Carlton pedigree to everyday family" dining at this North Suburban "neighborhood benchmark", where the "wonderful, upscale" New American "comfort food" showcases "high-quality ingredients" and "straightforward preparations" ("don't miss the shepherd's pie"); ayes also appreciate the "nod to Chicago's history" in the "cavernous", "polished, prairie-style setting", but nays note it's "noisy" – and "disappointed" deserters "expected more from such talented chefs."

P.S. Bangkok Ⓜ Thai   20 | 13 | 17 | $19
Wrigleyville | 3345 N. Clark St. (bet. Aldine Ave. & Roscoe St.) | 773-871-7777 | www.psbangkok.com
P.S. Bangkok 2 Thai
Lincoln Park | 2521 N. Halsted St. (bet. Fullerton Pkwy. & Wrightwood Ave.) | 773-348-0072
Separately owned, these fraternal Siamese twins dish up "delicious", "consistently good" Thai "with great versions of classics as well as regional" treats, plus an "outstanding" Sunday buffet at Wrigleyville (which serves beer and wine – Lincoln Park is BYO); their "casual" settings, however, are marred by what some Thai-rants target as "tired" decor and "inconsistent service", making them take-out and "delivery favorites."

Puck's at the MCA Ⓜ American   20 | 21 | 16 | $23
Streeterville | Museum of Contemporary Art | 220 E. Chicago Ave. (Mies van der Rohe Way) | 312-397-4034 | www.mcachicago.org
"You get to enjoy the Museum of Contemporary Art's atmosphere, plus a fabulous terrace with a lake view", at this "airy", "ultramodern" Wolfgang Puck place "with just the right touch of snob appeal" as well as New American "gourmet sandwiches", "salads and entrees" (plus "you can eat here without paying the museum admission" and now, thanks to the new counter menu, get your meal to go); P.S. it's "only open for lunch", its "great Sunday brunch buffet" and during the 'Tuesdays on the Terrace' live "jazz evenings in summer."

Ⓩ Pump Room, The American   21 | 24 | 23 | $56
Gold Coast | Ambassador East Hotel | 1301 N. State Pkwy. (Goethe St.) | 312-266-0360 | www.pumproom.com
Fans "half expect Sinatra to walk in the door and order a martini" at "this Gold Coast grande dame" in the Ambassador East Hotel, where you can "experience the splendor" of "a bygone era" (it opened in 1938) "via photographs of the day's great celebrities on the walls"; a change in ownership and a series of chef shifts muddied the culinary water a couple of years ago, and while some surveyors

now swear the New American fare "is better again", others insist "the food and service lack what they once had."

Quartino ● *Italian*
- | - | - | M

River North | 626 N. State St. (Ontario St.) | 312-698-5000 | www.quartinochicago.com

From the Gibsons gang comes this River North Italian where chef John Coletta (ex Caliterra, Carlucci) offers an extensive small-plates menu full of intriguing variations on bruschetta, antipasto, risotto and cured meats from the in-house *salumeria*; the earthy, bustling setting boasts a big bar area and an open kitchen, which serves until 1 AM; N.B. the name comes from the quarter-liter *quartinos* in which the 21 house wines are served.

NEW Quince M *American*
- | - | - | M

Evanston | The Homestead Hotel | 1625 Hinman Ave. (Davis St.) | 847-570-8400 | www.quincerestaurant.net

Evanston's former Trio at The Homestead Hotel gives way to this midpriced, sophisticated New American, offering pairings from a well-chosen global wine list; the serene, romantic setting features golden lighting, creamy colors and a dramatic wall inset with a gas fireplace on a marble slab.

NEW Radhuni Indian Kitchen *Indian/Pakistani*
- | - | - | I

Lakeview | 3227 N. Clark St. (bet. Belmont Ave. & School St.) | 773-404-5670

Gracious hospitality warms the casually elegant, curry-hued dining room at this Indian and Pakistani eatery in Lakeview; patrons can BYO or just enjoy its lassi drinks and lime soda.

Raj Darbar *Indian*
20 | 12 | 16 | $23

Lincoln Park | 2660 N. Halsted St. (Wrightwood Ave.) | 773-348-1010

"Quality Indian fare", including "excellent lentil dishes" and "authentic paneer", makes this subcontinental a "popular local choice in the heart of Lincoln Park", especially for those "not feeling up to the trek to Devon"; some assess the food as "not the greatest" of the genre, and others feel the "reasonable prices" are undercut by the "portion size, especially for delivery or carryout", but at least the "good" fixed-price Sunday buffet is all you can eat.

RA Sushi ● *Japanese*
19 | 19 | 19 | $30

Gold Coast | 1139 N. State St. (Elm St.) | 312-274-0011
Glenview | 2601 Aviator Ln. (Patriot Blvd.) | 847-510-1100
www.rasushi.com

"Great choices of creative rolls" plus "many delicious noodle dishes" – and a "good lunch menu as well" – find favor with fans of this "fun" Gold Coast Japanese chain outpost with an "amazing happy hour on weekdays" and an "excellent crowd on Friday/Saturday nights" (some say the "great people-watching", "decor and scene are really the reason to come"); the "outside seating is nice in the summer" and there's a late-night bar menu until 1 AM; N.B. the Glenview location opened post-Survey and a Lombard spot is set to open in July 2007.

CHICAGO

	FOOD	DECOR	SERVICE	COST

Red Light *Pan-Asian*
23 | 23 | 20 | $42

Market District | 820 W. Randolph St. (Green St.) | 312-733-8880 | www.redlight-chicago.com

"Upholding high food standards", "incredible" chef "Jackie Shen works her magic" at this "intoxicating", "hopping" Market District fusion "fantasy" where "Pan-Asian meets the club scene"; "delighted" denizens who "never tire of dining" on her "creative", "high-quality" cuisine, accompanied by "refreshing mango martinis" and served in a "flashy, over-the-top" setting, admit it's "expensive" but insist it's "still a value in the see-and-be-seen category."

Red Lion Pub *Pub Food*
16 | 18 | 18 | $18

Lincoln Park | 2446 N. Lincoln Ave. (Fullerton Pkwy.) | 773-348-2695

"More authentic than many", this "classic British pub" in Lincoln Park possesses an "intimate" "dive" atmosphere that matches its "good draughts", "cider on tap" and "traditional English fare at a reasonable price" (seems "every patron in the place is eating the fish 'n' chips"); there's also the promise of "fun, intelligent conversation with the bartender and patrons", plus the "friendly" "servers are always willing to tell of their experiences with the ghosts" that "supposedly" inhabit the premises.

NEW Republic Pan-Asian Restaurant & Lounge *Asian*
- | - | - | M

River North | 58 E. Ontario St. (Rush St.) | 312-440-1818

Modern Asian dining on a grand scale hits River North with this hip, architectural spot divided into a swanky main-floor bar/lounge, upstairs dining room and separate sake bar; the kitchen explores various regions, from maki to Chinese standards, hot pots to curries, with two levels of omakase (three- or seven-course) taking a tour of the whole menu; N.B. the ladies' room, tiled to the nines and outfitted with a shell-shaped sink, is worth a peek.

Retro Bistro ⑤ *French*
25 | 18 | 23 | $42

Mt. Prospect | Mt. Prospect Commons | 1746 W. Golf Rd. (Busse Rd.) | 847-439-2424 | www.retrobistro.com

A "favorite among in-the-know" Northwest suburbanites, this French bistro confers a touch of "old Paris" via "consistently" "exceptional, top-quality food" accompanied by a "very good wine selection" ("ask for the reserve list") at prices that make it a "really nice value" – especially the "prix fixe bargain"; "welcoming" staffers who really "know the menu" are another asset, and while the setting says "strip mall" in both "location and decor", the "food will make you think you're somewhere else."

Reza's *Mideastern*
19 | 15 | 18 | $24

River North | 432 W. Ontario St. (Orleans St.) | 312-664-4500 ◑
Andersonville | 5255 N. Clark St. (Berwyn Ave.) | 773-561-1898 ◑
Oak Brook | 40 N. Tower Rd. (Butterfield Rd.) | 630-424-9900
www.rezasrestaurants.com

"Relaxed" and "reliable", these sister "best buys" harbor a "huge selection" of "delicious Middle-Eastern cuisine" to "satisfy carnivores

and vegheads" alike, making them "perfect for large groups with differing tastes on a moderate budget"; the "plentiful servings" include "enough dill rice to feed all of Persia" plus "free-flowing tea", but that's not enough for naysayers who negate it as "not a gourmet experience" (merely "a cut above a buffet") and suggest that "service can be lackluster."

Rhapsody *American*   21 | 22 | 20 | $45

Loop | Symphony Ctr. | 65 E. Adams St. (bet. Michigan & Wabash Aves.) | 312-786-9911 | www.rhapsodychicago.com

The "seasonal offerings" of "innovative but restrained" New American cuisine are "music to the taste buds" at this Loop "lovely" in the Symphony Center with a "tranquil", "staid" dining room, "lively bar" and "gorgeous patio"; proponents pick it as "the perfect overture" to a concert or Art Institute visit (and recommend it as a "power-lunch" spot too), though dissidents detect dissonance in the form of "unpolished" service; N.B. hours are per the concert schedule, and performance-night "reservations are a necessity."

Ribs 'n' Bibs ● *BBQ*   22 | 6 | 13 | $15

Hyde Park | 5300 S. Dorchester Ave. (53rd St.) | 773-493-0400

You'll be "planning another pilgrimage" after your first visit to this Hyde Park "carry-out place" where the "aroma of barbecue" makes for "great advertising" ("walk downwind and savor the smell"); "you get an entire bucket" of "real ribs vs. Northside counterparts" "slathered in great sauce", "each one as delicious as the next", but be aware that management "doesn't mess around with decor" ("you really can't sit in the place") – and "don't come for the service, unless you call 'take-a-number' service."

Riccardo Trattoria Ⓜ *Italian*   - | - | - | M

Lincoln Park | 2119 N. Clark St. (bet. Dickens & Webster Aves.) | 773-549-0038 | www.riccardotrattoria.com

Chef-owner Riccardo Michi (ex Bice), a native of Milan, proudly prepares many of his mother's recipes at this casually elegant, affordably priced Tuscan trattoria in Lincoln Park's erstwhile Via Emilia space; N.B. the BYO policy helps keep costs down.

Rinconcito Sudamericano *S American*   ▽ 17 | 6 | 16 | $23

Bucktown | 1954 W. Armitage Ave. (Damen Ave.) | 773-489-3126

Rios d' Sudamerica Ⓜ *S American*

🆕 **Bucktown** | 2010 W. Armitage Ave. (Damen Ave.) | 773-276-0170 | www.riosdesudamerica.com

"Traditional" and "authentic", this Bucktown BYO is home to "huge portions of very comforting and tasty" South American fare, including "Peruvian specialties", that have takers testifying "your taste buds will thank you" – and your wallet as well, as it's "a value"; still, the unsatisfied insinuate the fare is "uninspired", the "atmosphere is so-so" and the "service is not as good" as it once was; N.B. Rios d'Sudamerica, a spin-off, is unrated.

	FOOD	DECOR	SERVICE	COST

Ringo *Japanese*
▽ 22 | 11 | 20 | $23

Lincoln Park | 2507 N. Lincoln Ave. (bet. Fullerton Pkwy. & Wrightwood Ave.) | 773-248-5788 | www.rin-go.us
Raw-fish lovers cheer this Lincoln Park local "treasure" serving "fresh", "tasty rolls", "terrific specials" and "good rice-bowl dishes"; there's "not much atmosphere", and the "food may lack some imagination, but this is a great entry-level sushi house", and you "can't beat the BYO policy, friendly service" and "bargain" prices; N.B. efforts are underway to expand and add a sushi bar.

Riques *Mexican*
21 | 10 | 19 | $18

Uptown | 5004 N. Sheridan Rd. (Argyle St.) | 773-728-6200 | www.riqueschicago.com
"Wonderful, fresh" and "authentic Mexican food" – "not just burritos and tacos" – served "at a great price" in an "out-of-the-way" Uptown location ("don't be put off by the neighborhood") has contributors crowing they "can't get enough of" this "friendly" (and "vegetarian-friendly") BYO; P.S. you can "travel Mexico" without leaving town via chef-owner Enrique Cortes' "regional cuisine on Saturday nights."

Rise *Japanese*
20 | 18 | 14 | $33

Wrigleyville | 3401 N. Southport Ave. (Roscoe St.) | 773-525-3535 | www.risesushi.com
An "outstanding menu" of "beautiful, fresh" fish "and enough non-sushi" Japanese fare for landlubbers is coupled with a "creative drink menu", "cool decor", "good people-watching" and "fun" "open-air dining" at this "clubby" Wrigleyville spot; despite these attributes, though, regulars report it "has fallen off recently" (as have its ratings, across the board), perhaps because those who feel they've "given it too many chances" are "less impressed every time" with "glitz over substance" and "painful service" from an "arrogant", "surly" staff.

ristorante we *Italian*
18 | 20 | 17 | $44

Loop | W Hotel | 172 W. Adams St. (LaSalle St.) | 312-917-5608 | www.ristorantewe.com
Contributors seem conflicted about this Loop Northern Italian that's tempering the steaks 'n' sauces trend with a Tuscan twist – some say it's a "trendy and upbeat" "minimalist's paradise" with an "interesting menu" of "good" eating that's "worth every penny" ("nice service" too), while others opine it's an "uppity" "hotel restaurant" where "the food doesn't quite measure up" and the staff is "confused"; N.B. a DJ entertains nightly except Sunday.

Ritz-Carlton Café *American*
- | - | - | E

Streeterville | Ritz-Carlton Hotel | 160 E. Pearson St., 12th fl. (Michigan Ave.) | 312-573-5160 | www.fourseasons.com
Despite the demise of the formal Dining Room, you won't go hungry for fine dining at Streeterville's Ritz, thanks to the Café's upgraded dinner menu of expensive New American cuisine (breakfast, lunch and brunch remain unchanged) and wine offerings, which now include the hotel's master list of 350 selections; the partitions have

been removed, opening the space entirely onto the vast lobby with its soothing fountain.

Riva *Seafood*   18 | 20 | 17 | $46

Streeterville | Navy Pier | 700 E. Grand Ave. (Lake Shore Dr.) | 312-644-7482
NEW Naperville | 2020 Calamos Ct. (Westings Ave.) | 630-718-1010
www.stefanirestaurants.com

Supporters see "something for everyone on the menu" – from American "fresh-fish" dishes to "Italian seafood" preps to "great steaks" – at this "huge" but "lovely" Streeterville destination where, "from the right tables", the "spectacular" lakefront views are worth braving the "carnival atmosphere" of Navy Pier for; still, antis insist "the locale's the star", the ambiance "depends on how loud the tourists" are and the prices are "ridiculous" "for what you get" – namely "lackluster food" and "nonchalant service"; N.B. a second location opened post-Survey in Naperville.

R.J. Grunts *American*   19 | 16 | 18 | $21

Lincoln Park | 2056 N. Lincoln Park W. (Dickens Ave.) | 773-929-5363 | www.leye.com

"Sentimental" surveyors trust this "loud, crowded" Lincoln Park "classic" – "the first 'Lettuce' restaurant" – known for "hearty" American fare served by "cheeky" staffers in a setting dominated by "groovy music" and "photos of staffers over the years"; it "still feels very '70s", and perhaps it's "not up with the latest things people like to eat", but for every dismisser who dubs it "dated" there's a diehard declaring "try and close it and I'll chain myself to the doors in protest."

Z RL *American*   22 | 26 | 23 | $49

Gold Coast | 115 E. Chicago Ave. (Michigan Ave.) | 312-475-1100 | www.rlrestaurant.com

"Wear something cashmere" to Ralph Lauren's "see-and-be-seen" Gold Coast American that "delivers what it should – straightforward", "old-school" fare "and cold martinis" amid ambiance likened to "an old hunting club" with "portraits on the walls" instead of "dead animals" (or "your grandfather's study, if your grandfather was unbelievably rich"); peopled with "blue blazers", "hungry shoppers", "little old ladies with gloves" and "conceited" "Bitsy and Mitsy types", it's also "loved" for its "especially cozy bar", "pretentious" vibe and "glib waiters"; P.S. "great for people-watching from the patio."

Robinson's No. 1 Ribs *BBQ*   19 | 6 | 14 | $21

Lincoln Park | 655 W. Armitage Ave. (Orchard St.) | 312-337-1399 | www.ribs1.com **M**
West Loop | Union Station | 225 S. Canal St. (bet. Adams St. & Jackson Blvd.) | 312-258-8477
Oak Park | 940 W. Madison St. (Clinton St.) | 708-383-8452 | www.rib1.com

"Falling-off-the-bone ribs", "tender chicken" and "BBQ pork sandwiches (mmmmm)" slathered in "rich, spicy sauce" prompt plenti-

ful "finger lickin'" at this "no-frills" threesome; gourmands are grateful that they're "not as tourist-oriented" as some "chain" competitors and are generally willing to ignore the "nonexistent decor" – though most nevertheless "order delivery or take it home."

Rock Bottom Brewery *American*   16 | 15 | 16 | $22

River North | 1 W. Grand Ave. (State St.) | 312-755-9339
NEW **Lombard** | 94 Yorktown Shopping Ctr. (Highland Ave.) | 630-424-1550
Warrenville | 28256 Diehl Rd. (Winfield Rd.) | 630-836-1380
www.rockbottom.com

For some, "the beers are the reason to stop by" these "crowded, noisy", "comfortable" Traditional American "gathering places", but in addition to the "great microbrews" (including "amusing flights" and "seasonal" choices) there's "a nice variety" of "comfort food"; still, critics wonder "why go for chain conformity in a town with great watering holes?", contending the "run-of-the-mill" "pub fare" and service are "unremarkable"; P.S. River North's rooftop deck "is quite a swinging singles joint."

Rockit Bar & Grill ◐ *American*   19 | 19 | 16 | $28

River North | 22 W. Hubbard St. (bet. Dearborn & State Sts.) | 312-645-6000 | www.rockitbarandgrill.com

A "fun" "30-and-under" crowd of "frat" types and "eye candy in skimpy outfits" convenes at this "rockin'" River North Traditional American "sandwich-and-easy-meal place", a "much-needed happy-hour destination" and "pre-partying" staging area with "above-average bar food" and a Bloody Mary cart that's becoming "one of the great Chicago brunch traditions"; diners who "don't quite understand all the hubbub" are "disappointed by the food" and "overpriced drinks", and say the staff is sometimes "overwhelmed."

⚡ Roditys ◐ *Greek*   22 | 17 | 20 | $25

Greektown | 222 S. Halsted St. (bet. Adams St. & Jackson Blvd.) | 312-454-0800 | www.roditys.com

One of the Greektown "classics", this "authentic" "fave" "holds its own" and "can always be counted on" for "consistently good", "quality" "Greek food" at a "value" served in a "family-style atmosphere" that will have you swilling ouzo and breaking plates (well, almost"); N.B. they're open till midnight, 1 AM on weekends.

Ron of Japan *Japanese/Steak*   18 | 17 | 18 | $37

Streeterville | 230 E. Ontario St. (bet. Fairbanks Ct. & St. Clair St.) | 312-644-6500
Northbrook | 633 Skokie Blvd. (Dundee Rd.) | 847-564-5900

Aficionados of tabletop-cooked Japanese steakhouse sustenance assert these Streeterville and North Suburban "throwbacks" are "as good as always" and "fun for a big group", with "usually personable" "show"-men and "good food"; others advise that these teppanyaki "tourist traps" are "getting tired", with "stale" chefs and "outdated decor", adding "you stink when you leave"; P.S. "prepare to sit with strangers" at the communal tables.

NEW Room 21 *Steak* — | — | — | E
South Loop | 2110 S. Wabash Ave. (bet. Cermac Rd. & 21st St.) | 312-328-1198 | www.room21chicago.com
This fashionable – and expensive – New American grill in the South Loop is set in a former Al Capone brewery that has been transformed by Jerry Kleiner's signature metalwork, furnishings and lighting, surrounded by retro wall patterns on steroids; its classic steakhouse fare is tweaked with modern sauce options for the prime beef and paired with a wide-ranging wine list (in both style and price) that includes premium champagnes by the glass; N.B. French doors and a fanciful gate open to a vast landscaped garden getaway.

RoSal's Italian Kitchen � *Italian* 24 | 16 | 22 | $29
Little Italy | 1154 W. Taylor St. (Racine Ave.) | 312-243-2357 | www.rosals.com
"Excellent", "hearty" Southern Italian and a "staff that makes you feel at home" lure loyalists to this "quaint" Little Italy "storefront space" with "a lot of charm" and "a real family-owned feeling"; P.S. the "Sicilian wine is a wonderful surprise", and they serve a bargain lunch buffet.

Rose Angelis Ⓜ *Italian* 22 | 20 | 21 | $28
Lincoln Park | 1314 W. Wrightwood Ave. (bet. Racine & Southport Aves.) | 773-296-0081 | www.roseangelis.com
Enthusiasm runs high from eaters who enjoy the "hearty portions" of "dependably good" "homemade Italian" (including "veggie-friendly" selections)" and "incredible value" at this "sweet, romantic" Lincoln Park "institution" in a "cozy" townhouse "with tons of character"; it can be "tough to get into as they don't take reservations", and dubious diners "don't know why people tolerate the long waits" (especially "when you can get takeaway") for what they consider "heavy" fare.

🅩 Rosebud, The *Italian* 21 | 18 | 19 | $36
Little Italy | 1500 W. Taylor St. (Laflin St.) | 312-942-1117
🅩 Rosebud of Highland Park *Italian*
Highland Park | 1850 Second St. (Central Ave.) | 847-926-4800
🅩 Rosebud of Naperville *Italian*
Naperville | 48 W. Chicago Ave. (Washington St.) | 630-548-9800
🅩 Rosebud of Schaumburg *Italian*
Schaumburg | 1370 Bank Dr. (Meacham Rd.) | 847-240-1414
🅩 Rosebud on Rush *Italian*
River North | 720 N. Rush St. (Superior St.) | 312-266-6444
🅩 Rosebud Theater District 🅧 *Italian*
Loop | 3 First National Plaza | 70 W. Madison St. (bet. Clark & Dearborn Sts.) | 312-332-9500
www.rosebudrestaurants.com
"Consistently good", "old-fashioned" Italian is served "by the barrel" at these "crowded", "touristy", "high-energy spots" (especially

	FOOD	DECOR	SERVICE	COST

the "classic Chicago" "legend" in Little Italy) that are "a real trip back in time" – complete with "Sinatra playing in the background"; service runs from "pleasant" to "surly", though, and peeved paesani posit "piggy portions don't hide that the food" is a "throwback to the old days before Americans knew what real Italian food is."

Rosebud Steakhouse *Italian/Steak*

23	21	22	$51

Gold Coast | 192 E. Walton St. (Mies van der Rohe Way) | 312-397-1000 | www.rosebudrestaurants.com

Gold Coast locals like to "see and be seen" at this purveyor of "hearty" "Italian specialties along with gargantuan steaks" and one of the "best burgers in the city", all served "in a great location" that's "like going to a" "laid-back" "private club" (albeit one that can be "unbearably noisy"); the "staffers are real pros" who "take good care of you, especially if you are a regular", and "portions are stupidly big" – "but they're good about splitting."

Roy's *Hawaiian*

24	21	23	$50

River North | 720 N. State St. (Superior St.) | 312-787-7599 | www.roysrestaurant.com

"Close your eyes and you'll think you're in Hawaii" enjoying "a fantastic meal" of "innovative" "upscale" regional cuisine at this River North outpost of "one of the best high-end chains out there", where "beautifully presented" "signature dishes" featuring a "unique assortment" of "extremely fresh seafood" are enhanced by an "interesting and good-value wine list" and a "fun cocktail menu"; veterans of the Honolulu original, however, lament "like all branch restaurants with nonresident chefs, the food suffers from the separation."

Ruby of Siam *Thai*

20	13	16	$18

Evanston | 1125 Emerson St. (Ridge Ave.) | 847-492-1008
Skokie | Skokie Fashion Sq. | 9420 Skokie Blvd. (Gross Point Rd.) | 847-675-7008
www.rubyofsiam.com

Insiders insist "if you live near" a branch of this BYO duo, "you don't really have to bother finding any other place for Thai" in the Northern Suburbs, since each offers "a huge menu" of "reliable selections" from a "kitchen willing to substitute", making them "frequent destinations for vegetarians" and "good places to take kids with an adventurous palate"; add in "fabulous value", and you can see why touters tolerate "average atmosphere" and "iffy service."

Rumba 🆑Ⓜ *Nuevo Latino*

18	22	18	$40

River North | 351 W. Hubbard St. (bet. Kingsbury & Orleans Sts.) | 312-222-1226 | www.rumba351.com

"For a fun night of dinner and dancing", this "moderately priced" River North Nuevo Latino offers a "different dining experience", with "true Latin American tastes" and "great drinks" served in an "upbeat", "upscale setting" (though foodies feel the fare "needs to catch up with the decor"); P.S. "the noise level increases greatly as you progress through the evening", especially on weekends when they offer free salsa lessons.

Russell's Barbecue *BBQ*
18 | 10 | 13 | $15

Rolling Meadows | 2885 Algonquin Rd. (bet. Carriageway & Newport Drs.) | 847-259-5710
Elmwood Park | 1621 N. Thatcher Ave. (North Ave.) | 708-453-7065
www.russellsbarbecue.com

This "no-nonsense" West Suburban "institution", a "trusty old BBQ stop" that's "been there forever" (since 1930), is "a favorite for pulled pork and beef sandwiches and fallin'-off-the-bone tender smoked ribs"; even devotees who rave that the fare "is great" admit the "decor and service aren't", while some tepid tasters "think you had to grow up with this food" "to really appreciate" it; N.B. at a mere 27 years of age, the Rolling Meadows location is a relative newcomer.

Russian Tea Time *Russian*
22 | 20 | 21 | $36

Loop | 77 E. Adams St. (bet. Michigan & Wabash Aves.) | 312-360-0000 | www.russianteatime.com

"A real culinary trip" "right in the heart of" the Loop, this "cozy" "hideaway" presents a "menu that reads like a Russian novel, with a story explaining the history of each" "interesting choice" of "trusty" Russian fare; red-heads also revere the "old-world service", "burgundy-and-brass" interior "filled" with "lovely flowers", "samovars and velvet", "nice afternoon tea" and "flights" of "great infused vodkas", calling it "the best choice if you are bound for the symphony or Art Institute."

Z Ruth's Chris Steak House *Steak*
24 | 20 | 23 | $57

River North | 431 N. Dearborn St. (Hubbard St.) | 312-321-2725
Northbrook | Renaissance Hotel | 933 Skokie Blvd. (Dundee Rd.) | 847-498-6889
www.ruthschris.com

These River North and North Suburban steakhouse outposts hew to the "proven formula" of their "reliable chain", offering "always the same great meal" – "sizzling platters" of "scrumptious" prime beef with "lots of butter", plus "seafood options that provide a nice balance to the red meat", amid "comfortable", "classy" "dark-wood" decor; even so, chompers with "sticker shock" state "for what I pay here, I expect something [more] memorable", while the home team harps that they're "not very Chicago."

Sabatino's ● *Italian*
23 | 17 | 22 | $30

Northwest Side | 4441 W. Irving Park Rd. (bet. Cicero & Pulaski Aves.) | 773-283-8331

"A time warp" of "old Chicago Italian" dining, this Northwest Side "classic" does an "excellent job with the standard menu" (plus "great specials") served in "plentiful portions" that "preclude even the contemplation of dessert"; the "warmly bustling" setting is "like stepping into an old-time movie", "with the baby grand piano [played live on weekends], dim lighting, booths tucked into corners and behind pulled curtains" – part of why it "draws crowds" ranging from "families with kids" to "older" folks.

	FOOD	DECOR	SERVICE	COST

Sabor do Brasil Ⓜ *Brazilian* — — — E

Orland Park | 15750 S. Harlem Ave. (157th St.) | 708-444-2770 | www.sabor-do-brasil.com

Churrascaria-style chowhounds head to this Southwest Suburban for all-you-can-eat rotisserie meats, including numerous varieties of beef, pork, lamb, chicken and sausage – just be careful not to fill up on all the heavy sides; it's certainly not cheap, but its menu is priced below the city competition and served in a warmly lit space accented with exposed brick, dark wood, golden walls and an authentic-looking adobe facade.

Sage Grille *American* — — — M

Highwood | 260 Green Bay Rd. (Highwood Ave.) | 847-433-7005 | www.sagegrille.com

Urban dining descends on suburban Highwood with this moderately priced New American offering ingredient-driven culinary creations, plus simple steaks and chops (with the increasingly de rigueur choice of sauce) and desserts by Trotter's/Trio alum Tamara White; the comfortably upscale setting is a hybrid of city chic and bistro ease; N.B. a kids' menu is available.

Sai Café *Japanese* 24 15 21 $33

Lincoln Park | 2010 N. Sheffield Ave. (Armitage Ave.) | 773-472-8080 | www.saicafe.com

"For the love of maki, just go" to this "wonderful neighborhood sushi bar" that's "been around Lincoln Park for [more than 20] years" urge enthusiasts of its "nice, large cuts" of "fresh fish" "and other Japanese preparations" "prepared by super chefs"; with its "homey", "relaxing" feel, it's "not as flashy" "as the trendy places", but most agree it's a "value" – so "plan ahead to get a table" or expect "lengthy waits on weekend nights"; N.B. the Decor score may not reflect the spot's partial remodeling.

NEW **Sakuma's**
Japanese Restaurant *Japanese* — — — M

Streamwood | 43 S. Sutton Rd. (Schaumburg Rd.) | 630-483-0289

This midpriced Suburban Northwest strip-mall spot is on a roll with fanciers of fresh raw fish (from a vast list), creative maki and sashimi preps, and Japanese classics, plus three omakase (chef's choice) menus; the simple setting features a long sushi bar and white walls hung with traditional artifacts.

Ⓩ **Salbute** Ⓢ *Mexican* 26 16 22 $41

Hinsdale | 20 E. First St. (bet. Garfield & Washington Sts.) | 630-920-8077 | www.salbute.com

Scoring highly for its "excellent, authentic regional Mexican cuisine", this "quaint", "modest storefront" in the West Suburbs accompanies its daily menu of "mouthwateringly spectacular" food with "margaritas that will knock your socks off"; even admirers, though, admit it's "expensive" and say the "tiny" space can sometimes feel "cramped" ("better make a reservation").

	FOOD	DECOR	SERVICE	COST

Saloon Steakhouse, The *Steak*
23 | 19 | 23 | $51

Streeterville | Seneca Hotel | 200 E. Chestnut St. (bet. Lake Shore Dr. & Michigan Ave.) | 312-280-5454 | www.saloonsteakhouse.com

A Streeterville "locals'" "secret" that "does just what it should do", this "clubby" steakhouse serves "some of the finest beef", including "succulent Wagyu" (prized by patrons as "on the money") and "fine, fine martinis too" in "classy", "pleasant surroundings" (the "perfect place for a business lunch"); the "nice" "older" clientele values the "friendly", "professional staff" and also likes that this "Chicago meat and potatoes" "standby" is "less crowded and noisy than nearby competitors" – and "without the attitude."

Salpicón *Mexican*
24 | 19 | 22 | $42

Old Town | 1252 N. Wells St. (bet. Goethe & Scott Sts.) | 312-988-7811 | www.salpicon.com

"Every dish seems new and inventive and delicious" at this "colorful" Old Town "gem" showcasing Priscila Satkoff's "haute", "authentic" "Mexican with elegant presentation and savory sauces", plus "tons of tequila options" and a "surprisingly" "great wine list"; surveyor service assessments seesaw from "fabulous" to "snooty", and budgeters believe it's "a bit pricey", but it's a "must for anyone who likes their Mex with a modern twist."

Saltaus ◑⊠ *Eclectic*
▽ 19 | 25 | 16 | $48

Market District | 1350 W. Randolph St. (Ada St.) | 312-455-1919 | www.saltaus.com

The departure of onetime chef-partner Michael Taus (Zealous) shortly after its opening occasioned a kitchen switch to the current Eclectic menu, an "interesting fusion" of modern Mediterranean and Asian, which may explain why this "trendy [Market District] newcomer" is still "finding its way"; positive signs include a "top-notch crowd", an "ample wine collection", "spare" yet "sophisticated decor", "a hip lounge upstairs" and a "warm host-owner"; N.B. a DJ spins on some weekends, and there's Zen garden seating in season.

Salvatore's Ristorante Ⓜ *Italian*
▽ 21 | 20 | 20 | $36

Lincoln Park | 525 W. Arlington Pl. (Clark St.) | 773-528-1200 | www.salvatores-chicago.com

For nearly 30 years, this "hidden" Lincoln Park Northern Italian "tucked away on a side street" has "charmed" chowhounds who favor "old-fashioned, quiet" dining (it's "not the place to see and be seen") on "underpriced" edibles with "good sauces", which are served in a "romantic" "ballroom"-like setting or on the "terrace overlooking a garden" (it's "popular for weddings and special events"); on the other hand, modernists maintain it's "outdated."

Samah ◑ *Mideastern*
- | - | - | M

Wrigleyville | 3330A N. Clark St. (Buckingham Pl.) | 773-248-4606 | www.samahlounge.com

Dreamlike ambiance awaits visitors to this late-night Wrigleyville Middle Eastern lounge whose interior includes multiple seating ar-

	FOOD	DECOR	SERVICE	COST

eas draped and cushioned with luxurious fabrics; classic fare such as falafel and shish kebab is complemented by a range of coffee and tea drinks, belly dancing (Thursdays and Fridays) and optional hookah-puffing, but don't expect a tipple with your toke – no alcohol is served, or allowed in.

NEW Sam & Harry's Steakhouse *Steak* — | — | — | E

Schaumburg | Renaissance Schaumburg Hotel & Convention Ctr. | 1551 N. Thoreau Dr. (Meacham Rd.) | 847-303-4050 | www.samandharrys.com

Classic, expensive steakhouse fare including corn-fed prime beef plus lobsters and seafood (flown in daily) is supplemented by a Cab-heavy wine list offering 51 pours by the glass at this dramatic dining room just off the futuristic lobby of the Renaissance Schaumburg Hotel; the architectural, glassed-in setting boasts a center wine storage room and pairs of butter-yellow settees standing in for booths.

San Gabriel Mexican Cafe *Mexican* 20 | 16 | 18 | $28

Bannockburn | Bannockburn Green Shopping Ctr. | 2535 Waukegan Rd. (Half Day Rd.) | 847-940-0200

"A nicely balanced menu" of "very good, fresh Mexican" fare "with some interesting specials", plus "great tableside guacamole" and a "good tequila selection (especially for the [Northern] Suburbs)" appeal to amigos of this "casual" "strip-mall" spot; some surveyors, though, can't get past certain "ups and downs" they perceive, most notably in relation to the "uneven service"; N.B. a mariachi band makes music on Thursdays.

Sangria Restaurant & Tapas Bar Ⓜ *Nuevo Latino* 16 | 18 | 14 | $29

Lincoln Park | 901 W. Weed St. (Fremont St.) | 312-266-1200 | www.sangriachicago.com

As you'd guess, this "colorful", "happening" Nuevo Latino "hangout" in Lincoln Park has a "great sangria selection", but it also serves "fun" small plates; still, the consensus is that "the point of going here is not the food" (most find the "average" offerings "uninteresting") or service (which many feel "is worse than a coffeehouse"), but rather "the cool atmosphere and beautiful people" – though management and chef changes post-Survey may make a difference.

San Soo Gab San ◐ *Korean* ▽ 21 | 8 | 16 | $24

Northwest Side | 5247 N. Western Ave. (Foster Ave.) | 773-334-1589

This "great" Northwest Side "Korean BBQ joint" "should be on every night person's 'A' list", as it offers an "amazing all-night grilled-meat extravaganza" and "huge assortment of *panch'an*" (the savory, spicy and pickled little extras); it's "always crowded", partly because it's such a "good bargain", and you can have "great fun figuring out what the heck the items are", "but service is choppy" so "go with someone with experience."

	FOOD	DECOR	SERVICE	COST

Santorini ● *Greek/Seafood* | 21 | 19 | 20 | $32

Greektown | 800 W. Adams St. (Halsted St.) | 312-829-8820 |
www.santorinichicago.com

If you "need an evening in the Greek Islands", try this "more upscale"
and "enlightened" "white-tablecloth" Hellenic "specializing in seafood" with "tableside filleting" (they "do the other specialties equally
well"); veterans vow that the "very comfortable, almost elegant" environs are "quieter" and "not so touristy" as "most of its [Greektown]
neighbors", and it's especially "warm and inviting by the fireplace"
"on a cold night", though some say "service is hit-or-miss."

NEW Sapore di Napoli Ⓜ *Pizza* | - | - | - | I

Lakeview | 1406 W. Belmont Ave. (N. Southport Ave.) | 773-935-1212 |
www.saporedinapoli.net

A three-tiered, space-age brick oven bakes pies in less time than it
takes to choose the toppings on the thin, Neapolitan-style 12-
inchers at this Lakeview BYO pizzeria and gelateria, which also
serves the usual-suspect starters, salads and, at lunch, panini; the
teeny, nine-table storefront is as low-key and affordable as, well, a
neighborhood pizza joint.

Sapori Trattoria *Italian* | 22 | 17 | 20 | $30

Lincoln Park | 2701 N. Halsted St. (Schubert Ave.) | 773-832-9999

It's "always packed" at this "charming" Lincoln Park "favorite", so
"reserve for sure" for a "warm and friendly", "authentic" "trattoria
experience" with "fresh Italian food" including "homemade pastas"
(habitués are "hooked" on both the pumpkin and lobster ravioli) and
"delicious specials" that are "so good, you always feel like you're
getting such a deal" (there's also an "extensive list of wines at reasonable prices"); P.S. garden seating helps alleviate the "crowded",
sometimes "noisy" conditions inside.

Sayat Nova *Armenian* | 20 | 14 | 19 | $27

Streeterville | 157 E. Ohio St. (bet. Michigan Ave. & St. Clair St.) |
312-644-9159 | www.sayatnovachicago.com

The "authentic Armenian fare" is a "great value" at this "cozy",
"family-run" Streeterville "treasure tucked away just off Michigan
Avenue", an "offbeat choice for something out of the ordinary", with
"interesting" if "somewhat seedy decor"; most of the time it's a
"quiet hideaway", but DJs (two Saturdays a month) and hookahs
(every night) heat up the scene.

Schwa Ⓩ *American* | ▽ 26 | 14 | 24 | $54

Lincoln Park | 1466 N. Ashland Ave. (LeMoyne St.) | 773-252-1466 |
www.schwarestaurant.com

Prescient patrons predict chef Michael Carlson "will be a star some-
day" as they "dream of [their] next meal" of his "spectacular" "seasonal" New American cuisine, "artfully presented" within the
"minimalist, unpretentious atmosphere" of "the smallest dining
room and kitchen imaginable" (formerly Lovitt and Savoy Truffle) on
Lincoln Park's western edge; bargain-hunters find it "a bit pricey",
but supporters swear this "little-restaurant-that-could" is "a must";

	FOOD	DECOR	SERVICE	COST

P.S. "plan ahead, given the" space limitations, "and inquire about the daily menu, since it's BYO."

Scoozi! *Italian* | 21 | 19 | 20 | $35

River North | 410 W. Huron St. (bet. Kingsbury & Orleans Sts.) | 312-943-5900 | www.leye.com

"Still fun" and "consistent", this River North "crowd-pleaser" "never gets tired" to surveyors supportive of its "solid execution" of "down-to-earth, identifiable" "Americanized Italian" fare served at "fair prices" by a "happy" staff within a "huge", "noisy" and "rustic" warehouse" setting; tarter tongues tell us this "typical Lettuce operation" "is a bit passé" and there's "nothing original" on its "generic" menu, but it's "good" "for the whole family"; P.S. there's a "hopping" "happy-hour scene."

Scylla Ⓜ *Seafood* | 25 | 20 | 24 | $49

Bucktown | 1952 N. Damen Ave. (Armitage Ave.) | 773-227-2995 | www.scyllarestaurant.com

When "craving something from the sea", this "is the place to be" rhyme ravers who relish Stephanie Izard's "terrific" "cutting-edge" "fresh fish" dishes with "unusual" Mediterranean treatments at this Bucktown seafooder (the "savvy servers" also rate a special mention); perhaps its "intimate" setting in a "funky" "little house" is a tad "too cozy" for claustrophobes, but it's nevertheless earning itself a reputation as "a force to be reckoned with"; N.B. the Food and Cost scores do not reflect a newly broadened, lower-priced menu.

Ⓩ Seasons *American* | 26 | 27 | 27 | $78

Gold Coast | Four Seasons Hotel | 120 E. Delaware Pl., 7th fl. (bet. Michigan Ave. & Rush St.) | 312-649-2349 | www.fourseasons.com

A "classic" "for all seasons", this Gold Coast "formal" "fine-dining" destination treats guests "like royalty", with "pampering" service, a "magnificent", "refined" setting seen as "one of Chicago's prettiest rooms" and "excellent" New American cuisine augmented by an "amazing wine selection"; those who suggest "the food is sometimes a little less than expected for the price" may not have visited since chef Kevin Hickey (ex Ritz-Carlton) "came on board"; P.S. for many, the "out-of-this-world" "Sunday brunch is the reason to head here."

Ⓩ Seasons Café ◗ *American* | 25 | 25 | 26 | $45

Gold Coast | Four Seasons Hotel | 120 E. Delaware Pl., 7th fl. (bet. Michigan Ave. & Rush St.) | 312-649-2349 | www.fourseasons.com

Eaters who know to expect most "everything you get at Seasons for [nearly] half the price" – namely "excellent food and service" – savor this Gold Coast "feel-good experience"; you can "check your shopping bags" and "relax" over a "simple menu" of Traditional American fare ("the lobster club is to die for") in a "tasteful", "civilized setting."

NEW Sequel Ⓢ *American* | - | - | - | E

Lombard | 44 Yorktown Convenience Ctr. (bet. Butterfield Rd. & Highland Ave.) | 630-629-6560 | www.sequelb.com

It's part deux for West Suburban Lombard's beloved Bistro Banlieue, whose owners have transformed it from French bistro to more cre-

ative (and expensive) New American fine dining with an expanded global wine list; the change also brings new decor with luxe details like leather-inlaid woodwork.

1776 🗷 *American* 24 | 19 | 22 | $41
Crystal Lake | 397 Virginia St./Rte. 14 (bet. Dole & McHenry Aves.) | 815-356-1776 | www.1776restaurant.com
"A [New] American revolution" in the "far Northwest" suburbs, this "out-of-the-way" Crystal Lake "jewel" proffers "unique", "fine food" (including "wild game"), and owner Andy Andresky "knows his vintages well", making it "a great choice for wine lovers"; "the building used to house a KFC" and is "not long on atmosphere", but it's "comfortable", and the "service will make you feel at home"; P.S. don't forget to check out the "excellent early-birds, theme dinners and tapas nights."

Shallots Bistro *French/Mediterranean* ▽ 21 | 19 | 21 | $46
Skokie | 4741 W. Main St. (Skokie Blvd.) | 847-677-3463 | www.shallotsbistro.com
Laura Frankel's North Suburban French-Med bistro "serves the orthodox community" with "innovative", "high-end" kosher food, including a "nice selection of meats and fish, great desserts" and a "good wine list" (plus "seasonal tasting menus add variety"); "good service", an "intimate setting" and "alfresco dining" add to the appeal; P.S. they keep "short hours" (service ends at 9 PM most nights, and they're closed on Fridays and summer Saturdays).

🗷 Shanghai Terrace 🗷 *Asian* 24 | 26 | 25 | $57
River North | Peninsula Hotel | 108 E. Superior St., 5th fl. (bet. Michigan Ave. & Rush St.) | 312-573-6744 | www.chicago.peninsula.com
"Attention to detail and interesting flavors" are hallmarks of this "exceptional", "marvelously appointed temple of outstanding Pan-Asian cuisine" in the Peninsula that "transports" raters with the "refined elegance" of its "gorgeous" River North setting and its "quality service" – whether "for special occasions" or "expense-account" dining" (fans also praise its rooftop terrace as "the most beautiful Zen garden in the city" and "the ideal summer date venue"); a minority, however, finds it "pricey above its merit."

🗷 Shaw's Crab House *Seafood* 23 | 19 | 21 | $46
River North | 21 E. Hubbard St. (bet. State St. & Wabash Ave.) | 312-527-2722
Schaumburg | 1900 E. Higgins Rd. (Rte. 53) | 847-517-2722 www.shawscrabhouse.com
"Plain, simple fresh fish" and "surprisingly good sushi too" make these River North and Northwest Suburban "standbys" a "Chicago seafood tradition", with "professional" service and "a choice between formal and casual dining rooms" (many patrons "prefer the informality" of the "oyster bars, with their great selection, throwback atmosphere" and "live music"); still, others opine that its somewhat "pedestrian" profferings have "gotten rather pricey."

	FOOD	DECOR	SERVICE	COST

Shine & Morida *Chinese/Japanese* | 20 | 18 | 19 | $30 |

Lincoln Park | 901 W. Armitage Ave. (Fremont St.) | 773-296-0101 | www.shinemorida.com

"One-stop Chinese-Japanese" dining from a "unique, diverse menu" "has earned a loyal following" of "dual"-minded Lincoln Park "locals" for this "upscale" "hybrid" serving "solid" Mandarin meals – some say this is the "better" option – and "very fresh sushi" (it's also "a great spot for takeout or delivery"); a "family crowd dominates" the side-by-side "modern" environments in the "early hours – until the sleeker singles and couples take over later on."

Shiroi Hana *Japanese* | 18 | 8 | 17 | $20 |

Lakeview | 3242 N. Clark St. (Belmont Ave.) | 773-477-1652

A "standby", this 21-year-old Lakeview Japanese "budget-sushi" spot satisfies seekers of a "good variety" of "fresh" "standards" that are "not as expensive as" the raw-fish fare at more "yuppified places"; it's "always full, but [there's] seldom a wait" – though be warned it's "not for romantics" as the "decor is awful."

NEW Shor *American* | – | – | – | E |

South Loop | Hyatt Regency McCormick Pl. | 2233 S. Martin Luther King Dr. (Cermak Rd.) | 312-528-4140 | www.mccormickplace.hyatt.com

Tucked in the back of the South Loop's Hyatt Regency McCormick Place, this Traditional American grill serves a limited, straightforward menu of pricey prime beef plus a few seafood and poultry dishes, juxtaposed against a modern setting with raised banquettes and warm pendant lighting; breakfast and lunch are also offered to hungry conventioneers.

Shula's Steakhouse *Steak* | 20 | 19 | 19 | $62 |

Streeterville | Sheraton Chicago | 301 E. North Water St. (Columbus Dr.) | 312-670-0788

Itasca | Wyndham Northwest Chicago | 400 Park Blvd. (Thorndale Ave.) | 630-775-1499

www.donshula.com

"If you like the 1972 Dolphins, you'll like" these two members of a national team of "upscale" "sports-themed steakhouses celebrating Shula's splendid career"; the defense deems them "well done", with "great service and food" ("huge" "aged steaks" and seafood too), but the offense scores them "too expensive for the quality" (the "black Angus offerings can't stand up to the prime cuts" elsewhere) and thinks "the coach should have stuck with football."

Siam Café *Thai* | – | – | – | I |

Uptown | 4712 N. Sheridan Rd. (bet. Lawrence & Leland Aves.) | 773-769-6602

In Uptown since 1969, before the area's gentrification, this low-key, family-run restaurant is a refreshing return to neighborhood ethnic dining before Thai was trendy; the dated decor (note the aquariums) is beside the point – it's all about solid, traditional Siamese standards at retro-cheap prices, including a bargain lunch buffet; N.B. beer and wine only.

Sidebar Grille ⊠ *Eclectic*

– | **–** | **–** | **M**

Loop | 221 N. LaSalle St. (Wacker Dr.) | 312-739-3900 | www.sidebargrille.com

This Loop Eclectic serves moderately priced American faves (ribs, steaks, Cobb salad, turkey club) and a mix of global goodies (Thai beef salad, quesadilla, fish tacos) in a comfy, carpeted space appointed with leather booths, walnut tables and multiple TVs airing sports or the stock ticker; there's also a big smoke-free bar area and a cafe for morning coffee or a quick lunch.

⊠ Signature Room *American*

18 | **27** | **20** | **$54**

Streeterville | John Hancock Ctr. | 875 N. Michigan Ave., 95th fl. (bet. Chestnut St. & Delaware Pl.) | 312-787-9596 | www.signatureroom.com

With "better views than the [John Hancock Center's] actual observation deck", this Streeterville New American is "the greatest place to bring" "out-of-towners" for a "gargantuan Sunday brunch", a "reasonable lunch buffet" or just "a drink in the bar", but veterans with "vertigo and wallet cramps" advise "go somewhere else" for dinner because this "overpriced" "towering tourist trap" "can afford to under-perform" with its "pedestrian" food and service; N.B. live jazz spices up weekends.

Silver Cloud Bar & Grill *American*

18 | **14** | **17** | **$19**

Bucktown | 1700 N. Damen Ave. (Wabansia Ave.) | 773-489-6212 | www.silvercloudchicago.com

Bucktown's "quintessential neighborhood place" qualifies as a "low-key hangout" and "hangover place" with "homey", "artery-clogging" Traditional American "comfort food" reminiscent of "elementary school" – "go for the sloppy joes or the grilled cheese and tomato soup" – and a "great drink selection"; it "looks like a trashy diner" with "lots of '70s sparkle furniture inside", plus there's "great outdoor seating" ("you can bring your dog", though Fido has to stay outside the fence).

Silver Seafood ● *Chinese/Seafood*

∇ **22** | **7** | **17** | **$23**

Uptown | 4829 N. Broadway St. (Lawrence Ave.) | 773-784-0668

"It almost takes longer to read the menu than to eat" at this "Cantonese-style" Chinese seafood spot where Uptowners turn up for "delicious", "authentic", "fresh" fare (some of the fodder is "live" when you arrive, so "you can watch it swim before you" consume it); still, frustrated fish lovers fault the "horrible" setting and feel that management "needs to have a proficient English speaker on staff."

NEW Simply It *Vietnamese*

– | **–** | **–** | **I**

Lincoln Park | 2269 N. Lincoln Ave. (W. Belden Ave.) | 773-248-0884

Upscale Vietnamese cuisine at downscale prices lures Lincoln Parkers to this trendy-casual storefront BYO with a Pasteur-Le Colonial pedigree; refreshingly different dishes (steamed stuffed escargots, pineapple calamari) and familiar faves are served in a loftlike atmosphere with exposed brick and ductwork, funky art and a wall of fresh fruit for smoothies; N.B. the daily lunch special is a real bargain.

	FOOD	DECOR	SERVICE	COST

Slice of Life/ Hy Life Bistro ⊜ *Eclectic/Vegetarian*

▽ 13	12	13	$25

Skokie | 4120 W. Dempster St. (bet. Crawford Ave. & Keeler St.) | 847-674-2021

Filling a Suburban North niche "for the orthodox" diner, this double-kitchen duo (one mainly vegetarian, the other Eclectic) draws diverse comments for its "wide selection" of fare – some cite "good kosher pizza" in its support, whereas others insist only a "captive audience" "would put up with such poor food"; P.S. hours vary by season.

Smith & Wollensky *Steak*

22	20	20	$55

River North | 318 N. State St. (Wacker Dr.) | 312-670-9900 | www.smithandwollensky.com

"Bone or no bone, that is the question" at this "classic" River North steakhouse that "ranks high for a chain" on the strength of "excellent slabs" of prime dry-aged meat "with the expected accompaniments", "a kick-ass" if "expensive" "wine list" and "fabulous martinis" in a "fantastic" "riverside location"; fans find it "pricey but worth it" and say the cafe "downstairs is a bargain" (and "open late"), though moderates who muse "there are better places" "in the steak race" cite "attitude issues" and "inconsistent" service.

Smoke Daddy *BBQ*

20	12	15	$19

Wicker Park | 1804 W. Division St. (bet. Ashland & Damen Aves.) | 773-772-6656 | www.thesmokedaddy.com

Fans of "good, smoky flavor" "love the great ribs, sweet potato fries" and "yummy pulled pork" at this Wicker Park "local hangout" serving "just plain ol'" "bodacious" BBQ; supporters also like its "barlike" setting decorated with vintage Chicago photos and guitars on the walls and say another "plus" is that there's "a live band every night with no cover", though some suggest "the bands are hit-or-miss" and "service is slow."

NEW Smoque BBQ Ⓜ *BBQ*

-	-	-	I

Northwest Side | 3800 N. Pulaski Rd. (Grace St.) | 773-545-7427 | www.smoquebbq.com

Five guys serious about their BBQ are behind this casual, kid-friendly Northwest Side BYO, with counter service dishing out paper-covered trays of no-nonsense classics like babyback and St. Louis ribs along with a handful of standard sides and a cute little peach cobbler.

socca *French/Italian*

21	18	20	$34

Lakeview | 3301 N. Clark St. (Aldine Ave.) | 773-248-1155 | www.soccachicago.com

"They're happy to have you" at this "elegant" but "unpretentious" "gourmet" "surprise" "amid the hustle and bustle" of Lakeview/Wrigleyville, where the "simple, rustic" French-Italian bistro fare features "high-quality ingredients" (with "a touch of the unexpected thrown in") and the decor includes "amazing windows"; fence-sitters, however, perceive some "odd combinations" that "don't quite work", and purport that the "painfully loud room mars an oth-

erwise friendly and appealing restaurant" (recently installed sound tiles may mute that issue); P.S. the "side patio is nice and relaxing."

sola *American*   - | - | - | M

Lakeview | 3868 N. Lincoln Ave. (Byron St.) | 773-327-3868 | www.sola-restaurant.com

Carol Wallack split from Deleece to launch this Lakeview New American with Asian and Hawaiian accents and reasonable prices that extend to the wine list; the soft, modern space is done in warm yellows and browns and lit by a 'sea' of pendant light fixtures, a wall of windows and a double-sided fireplace set in a stone room divider; those having trouble finding it should keep in mind that the restaurant entrance is on Byron Street; N.B. now serves a weekend brunch.

NEW Sol de Mexico *Mexican*   - | - | - | I

Northwest Side | 3018 N. Cicero Ave. (bet. Nelson St. & Wellington Ave.) | 773-282-4119

Relatives of Geno Bahena are carrying on the family legacy at this Northwest Side storefront BYO that revisits the moles he made famous at the original Ixcapuzalco (cooked here by Geno's mom); the fresh, multiregional Mexican dishes are bargain-priced and served in a casual setting accented with south-of-the-border artifacts and vibrant paintings by famed Chicago artist Oscar Romero, including one of Geno and Rick Bayless in a Mexican market.

South Gate Cafe *American*   18 | 18 | 19 | $34

Lake Forest | 655 Forest Ave. (Deerpath Rd.) | 847-234-8800

Set on Lake Forest's Market Square, this "upscale local hangout" serves a "varied American menu" of "tasty" food; insiders favor the "clubby" interior with fireplace, while fresh-air fiends say "summertime out in the courtyard is how to enjoy this place" – still, some middlers maintain they've "never had a bad meal here, but never a great one either", while foes simply "don't get the attraction."

South Water Kitchen *American*   17 | 17 | 17 | $31

Loop | Hotel Monaco | 225 N. Wabash Ave. (Upper Wacker Dr.) | 312-236-9300 | www.southwaterkitchen.com

Traditional American "home cooking" "with modern twists" and a "cute" "high-ceiling room" have some Loop denizens grading this "great" "for a quick and hearty" lunch, a "drink after work" or a "pretheater" dinner, but "uneven" food and "hit-or-miss service" sour surveyors – though it's "convenient if you're staying at the hotel."

NEW Spacca Napoli Pizzeria Ⓜ *Pizza*   - | - | - | M

Ravenswood | 1769 W. Sunnyside Ave. (bet. Hermitage & Ravenswood Aves.) | 773-878-2420

Lines sometimes stretch out the door at this earthy yet modern Neapolitan pizzeria in Ravenswood thanks to the hearty, rustic pies produced in a 6.5-ton Italian wood-burning pizza oven, the centerpiece of the open kitchen; the setting is upscale-casual, with cafe tables and lots of windows providing natural light; N.B. the bar serves beer, wine and Italian liqueurs like limoncello and grappa.

	FOOD	DECOR	SERVICE	COST

Z Spiaggia *Italian* | 26 | 27 | 25 | $80 |

Gold Coast | One Magnificent Mile Bldg. | 980 N. Michigan Ave., 2nd fl. (Oak St.) | 312-280-2750 | www.spiaggiarestaurant.com

Expect a "peak dining experience" at this "honed-to-perfection", "luxury" Gold Coaster boasting a "sumptuous" setting with "spectacular views" of the Michigans (both Lake and Avenue), chef Tony Mantuano's "sublime", "incomparable Italian" cuisine, an "excellent", "extensive wine list" and "superlative service"; most maintain it's "one of the few places where the high price tag is worth it", though a segment of surveyors submits that the staff's "snooty" and the "small portions" are "overpriced" (served only in the cafe, "lunch is a lot less expensive"); N.B. jackets required, jeans not allowed.

Spoon Thai *Thai* | 22 | 12 | 16 | $17 |

Lincoln Square | 4608 N. Western Ave. (Wilson Ave.) | 773-769-1173 | www.spoonthai.com

"Not at all the usual Thai fare", this Lincoln Square BYO's "interesting", "authentic and aromatic" chow – including "edgy dishes" such as its "unique catfish curry with eggplant" – makes it a "cheap-eats" "favorite" that has devotees declaring the "owners should charge double (but we're glad they don't)"; if you find the decor "a little depressing", remember that it's "great for pickup or delivery."

Z Spring M *American/Seafood* | 27 | 25 | 25 | $59 |

Wicker Park | 2039 W. North Ave. (Damen Ave.) | 773-395-7100 | www.springrestaurant.net

Shawn McClain's "incredible creations" of "perfectly prepared" New American seafood "with a slight Asian slant" inspire acolytes to ask "is it impolite to lick the plate?" at this "hip" Wicker Park place that's "as fresh and exciting as the season it's named after"; the "quietly elegant setting" "in a converted bathhouse" is "beautiful and peaceful", the service is "polished but not overwhelming" and there's an "outstanding wine list", all of which adds up to "a wonderful experience" – so if you don't have a "special occasion, just come up with one."

Stained Glass Wine Bar Bistro *American* | 23 | 20 | 22 | $42 |

Evanston | 1735 Benson Ave. (bet. Church & Clark Sts.) | 847-864-8600 | www.thestainedglass.com

"Fun flights" and an "interesting modern American menu, served well" by a "knowledgeable", "unpretentious" staff, make this "reliable" restaurant "tucked between Evanston storefronts" equally "great for a fancy dinner or just a bite after a movie" – especially given the "inventive wine pairings" from its "wide-ranging list" and its "warm" space.

Stanley's Kitchen & Tap *American* | 19 | 13 | 15 | $19 |

Lincoln Park | 1970 N. Lincoln Ave. (Armitage Ave.) | 312-642-0007 | www.stanleysrestaurant.com

Stanley's on Racine *American*

NEW **West Loop** | 324 S. Racine Ave. (Van Buren St.) | 312-433-0007

"A good neighborhood joint" for "down-home" Traditional American eating, "drinking and hanging out", this "fun" "fake roadhouse" and "family restaurant hidden in a bar" in Lincoln Park slings "classic

mac 'n' cheese", "better meatloaf than mom's" and a "maximum-cholesterol" weekend brunch that gets "very crowded" – especially "during football season"; N.B. the Racine branch opened post-Survey.

Starfish Japanese

23 | 19 | 20 | $41

Market District | 804 W. Randolph St. (Halsted St.) | 312-997-2433 | www.starfishsushi.com

"Delectable sushi" (including "wonderful rolls" that are "artistic and original in preparation and presentation") draws maki-munchers to this "romantic" Market District Japanese serving a "wide variety of sake choices" and "really fun martinis" – plus assessors also appreciate that it's "worth the price."

Star of Siam Thai

20 | 14 | 18 | $18

River North | 11 E. Illinois St. (State St.) | 312-670-0100 | www.starofsiamchicago.com

"Cheap and cheerful", this River North old-timer (opened in 1984) is "a humble choice" serving "reliably delicious" Thai with "no surprises" – "simply good stuff" that "they'll spice up if you request it hot"; in addition to "traditional tables and chairs", the "simple setting" offers "cubby holes to sit in (a fun departure)", and "fast service" makes it a "great" place to "grab a quick lunch" – though some surveyors score it as strictly "serviceable."

State American

- | - | - | M

Lincoln Park | 935 W. Webster Ave. (Bissell St.) | 773-975-8030 | www.statechicago.com

With one of the longest menus in memory, this tech-y Lincoln Park New American offers a vast selection of moderately priced, all-day eats (salads, burgers, wraps, entrees, etc.) in a former grocery store; the electronic amusements include WiFi access, dozens of plasma screens, 20 free-access computer workstations and laptop rentals.

Stetson's Chop House Steak

23 | 19 | 20 | $49

Loop | Hyatt Regency | 151 E. Wacker Dr. (bet. Michigan & Stetson Aves.) | 312-239-4495 | www.hyatt.com

"Impressed" diners declare "don't dismiss" this "solid steakhouse" just "because it's in a tourist-filled [Loop] hotel", as it serves "huge portions" of prime "dry-aged" beef in a "casual" setting with a "nice bar"; holdouts tally it a trifle "typical", though, and call it "a good steakhouse in a great steak town"; N.B. there's live jazz nightly except Sundays.

Stir Crazy Asian

19 | 16 | 17 | $21

Northbrook | Northbrook Court Shopping Ctr. | 1186 Northbrook Ct. (bet. Skokie Blvd. & Waukegan Rd.) | 847-562-4800

Schaumburg | Woodfield Mall | 5 Woodfield Mall (Frontage & Golf Rds.) | 847-330-1200

Oak Brook | Oakbrook Center Mall | 105 Oakbrook Ctr. (Rte. 83) | 630-575-0155

Warrenville | 28252 Diehl Rd. (Windfield Rd.) | 630-393-4700 www.stircrazy.com

Frequent fryers find "nothing more fun than choosing your own ingredients, heaping them as high as possible in a bowl", then "watch-

ing" as they're "cooked fresh in front of you" at this "convenient and friendly" clan of Asian stir-fry stations with "many menu options" (including "prepared dishes"); it's "quick" and "good for kids", though some raters rank the results "run-of-the-mill" and the settings sometimes "hectic" and "noisy enough to drive you stir crazy."

Sullivan's Steakhouse *Steak*

| 23 | 22 | 22 | $50 |

River North | 415 N. Dearborn St. (Hubbard St.) | 312-527-3510
Naperville | 244 S. Main St. (bet. Chicago & Jackson Aves.) | 630-305-0230
www.sullivansteakhouse.com

"They do a really nice job" "for either business or romance" at this "polished", "clubby" duo in River North and the Western Suburbs, where the certified Angus steaks are "excellent" and "the onion rings are as big as doughnuts"; some respondents regard it as "a notch below some of the other places" due to "disappointing service", but others observe "the jazz and the great bar set it apart" – plus it's "a bit less expensive"; P.S. "the pineapple martinis are addictive."

⊠ Superdawg Drive-In *Hot Dogs*

| 22 | 16 | 18 | $9 |

Northwest Side | 6363 N. Milwaukee Ave. (Devon Ave.) | 773-763-0660 ●⊘⊟
Southwest Side | Midway Int'l Airport | 5700 S. Cicero Ave. (55th St.) | 773-948-6300
www.superdawg.com

An "icon" of "Americana" on the Northwest Side, this "true drive-in" "of the 1950s era" delivers "dawgs to die for" in "amusing little boxes" plus "deeelicious" shakes and fries – all the ingredients of "perfect summer evenings" (and travelers can get a taste at the Midway Airport outpost); besides, you "gotta love the two flirting hot dogs on the roof", though smart alecks "don't understand why there isn't a little" cocktail weenie up there too, since the couple's "been standing there for years – perhaps they should lie down!"

NEW Sura *Thai*

| - | - | - | M |

Lakeview | 3124 N. Broadway (Briar Pl.) | 773-248-7872 | www.surachicago.com

Lakeview's futuristic Thai–Asian fusion restaurant (from the folks behind NYC's Spice, Sea and Peep) serves its midpriced fare in a clubby, white-on-white space-station setting accented by splashes of red; adding to the time-travel vibe, servers dial your order into wireless handhelds.

Sushi Ai ⊠ *Japanese*

| - | - | - | M |

Palatine | 710 W. Euclid Ave. (Parkside Dr.) | 847-221-5100

'Sushi love' swoops down on the Northwest 'burbs via this sophisticated Japanese, where a master sushi chef creates unique maki in conjunction with a thorough roster of the raw and the cooked, all served alongside a generous sake selection in an intimate Asianchic setting that belies its strip-mall location; N.B. the lunch boxes are a bargain.

	FOOD	DECOR	SERVICE	COST

Sushi Naniwa *Japanese*

21 | 12 | 20 | $33

River North | 607 N. Wells St. (bet. Ohio & Ontario Sts.) | 312-255-8555 | www.sushinaniwa.com

An "authentic sushi bar" "without all the fluff" of some newer competitors, this River North Japanese from owner Bob Bee (of Bob San fame) is known for "reliable", "very fresh fish" "at a reasonable price"; perhaps the "standard", "no-frills" decor is "not particularly memorable", but the service is "attentive without being annoying" and there's "great outdoor seating in the summer" – plus it's also "good for takeout."

☑ SushiSamba rio *Japanese/S American*

21 | 26 | 17 | $48

River North | 504 N. Wells St. (bet. Grand Ave. & Illinois St.) | 312-595-2300 | www.sushisamba.com

"Super-cool atmosphere" wins the day at this "jumping" "Asian-Latin-themed" River Norther with a "wild" "nightclub feel" ("PartySamba Rio!"), "amazing roof bar" and "lots of pretty people" using "interesting" "coed bathrooms"; surveyors are split on whether the sushi–South American amalgam is "unique and exciting" or "schizophrenic", but those with the "sneaking suspicion" they're "not hip enough to be in the room" posit it "provides that Miami touch that nobody was really asking for", advising "be sure to get glammed up to get the respect of" the "uninformed" staff.

☑ sushi wabi ● *Japanese*

26 | 18 | 19 | $41

Market District | 842 W. Randolph St. (bet. Green & Peoria Sts.) | 312-563-1224 | www.sushiwabi.com

Drawing "a mostly younger crowd", this "swank, trendy" Market District "spot serves a unique blend of new sushi as well as the typical standby" stuff in "cool", "urban-contemporary" confines with "loud music and low lighting"; the "killer" cuts and "creative maki rolls" ("fantastic hot" Japanese fare too) can produce "killer waits", and service strikes critics as "complacent."

Swordfish *Japanese*

▽ 25 | 22 | 23 | $37

Batavia | 207 N. Randall Rd. (McKee St.) | 630-406-6463 | www.swordfishsushi.com

"High-end, innovative sushi finally reaches the far West Suburbs", prompting novices to note "now I know why people like this stuff", at this "trendy" Japanese sister of Wildfish where "incredibly" "fresh fish" – and "much more" – is served in a "subtle, modern" setting that surveyors say will make you "feel like you're in a Downtown restaurant"; P.S. it also offers a "thoughtfully planned wine list."

Tagine *Moroccan*

- | - | - | I

Ravenswood | 4749 N. Rockwell St. (Lawrence Ave.) | 773-989-4340

Though the namesake slow-cooked stews are the specialty of the house, this bargain-priced Moroccan storefront in Ravenswood also dishes up variations on couscous and kebabs, all served in a modern, pillow-strewn space enlivened by juicy shades of mango and grape; N.B. it's BYO.

	FOOD	DECOR	SERVICE	COST

Takkatsu ☒ *Japanese* — — — M

Arlington Heights | 161 W. Wing St. (Vail Ave.) | 847-818-1860
Reincarnating the shuttered Winnetka spot of the same name is this cozy Suburban Northwest hideaway in a new condo building with a serene dining space and a bar proffering Japanese beer, sake and shochu; the moderately priced Japanese menu emphasizes tonkatsu - the traditional breaded-and-fried pork cutlet.

☒ Tallgrass ☒ *French* 28 24 25 $69

Lockport | 1006 S. State St. (10th St.) | 815-838-5566 | www.tallgrassrestaurant.com
"Spectacular", "innovative" New French fare and a "deep wine list" (600 labels strong) fuel this "venerable" "foodie's paradise" "in the middle of nowhere" – aka historic Southwest Suburban Lockport – that's "well worth the drive from anywhere"; gourmets gush they "would go broke if they [lived] nearby", returning for chef-partner Robert Burcenski's "fine haute cuisine" with "wonderful presentation" in a "very private", "romantic" space; N.B. jackets are suggested.

NEW Tamarind *Asian* — — — M

South Loop | 614 S. Wabash Ave. (Harrison St.) | 312-379-0970 | www.tamarindsushi.com
At this South Loop hipster, Pan-Asian eats from potstickers and tamarind duck to stir-fries (chosen from a 'fresh bar') and sushi make up the massive, moderately priced menu, served alongside juicy 'fruitinis', bubble teas and slushies, and unusual sweets like banana-chocolate egg rolls; the cool setting features juicy kiwi, tamarind and bamboo accents.

Tango *Argentinean* ▽ 20 15 19 $33

Naperville | 5 W. Jackson St. (Washington St.) | 630-848-1818 | www.tangogrill.com
It's "lots of fun" to chow on "excellent" steaks or "sample the tapas and sit on the roof" quaffing "homemade sangria" at this Argentinean "addition to Naperville's eclectic choice of eateries."

☒ Tango Sur *Argentinean/Steak* 24 16 18 $27

Wrigleyville | 3763 N. Southport Ave. (Grace St.) | 773-477-5466
Satisfied surveyors say "it's all about" the "obscenely large, delicious cuts" of "succulent, flavorful meat" at this "lively" Wrigleyville BYO Argentinean steakhouse in a "dark, intimate" "storefront"; it's seemingly "always packed" with "locals" who "line up out the door" since it's "an absolute steal", though critics contend the "quality isn't first rate" and the "earnest service" can be "unreliable", adding that management "should improve" the "unassuming" interior – though you can "eat outside on a nice night."

Tank Sushi *Japanese* 21 20 18 $35

Lincoln Square | 4514 N. Lincoln Ave. (Sunnyside Ave.) | 773-769-2600 | www.tanksushi.com
"Sleek" and "spiffy" for Lincoln Square, this "indulgent" Japanese "pleasure" combines "clever maki rolls" made from "fresh

FOOD | DECOR | SERVICE | COST

ingredients" – "if you're looking for traditional sushi, this isn't the place" – with "brilliant drinks, beautiful presentation and surroundings" that "can be very loud" ("ambient club music"); some feel it's "service-challenged", and tight-fisted tipsters say it's "slightly overpriced", so "go before" 6 PM on weekends for the "half-price deal."

NEW Taos ❶ Southwestern — | — | — | M

Roscoe Village | 2114 W. Roscoe St. (bet. Hamilton & Hoyne Aves.) | 773-248-6899

Midpriced Southwestern sustenance and cheaper bar bites are spooned out in this lively, rustic-hip Santa Fe–esque eatery in Roscoe Village; the long narrow space features deep red walls of reclaimed barn wood, golden lighting and a cozy corner area for group dining.

Tapas Barcelona Spanish — 20 | 19 | 17 | $26

Evanston | Northshore Hotel Retirement Home | 1615 Chicago Ave. (bet. Church & Davis Sts.) | 847-866-9900 | www.tapasbarcelona.com

"Eat communally to savor the most sensations" at this "festive" Spaniard serving North Suburbanites "very good" tapas, "great sangria" and the "best sherry selection" in the vicinity; pleased patrons praise it as "perfect in summer for dining in the pretty garden" "but also fun in the noisy exciting dining room" done up in "lots of cool tiles and colors", though some warn of "rough service" and say the food "never really surprises or wows" – "but the price is right."

Tarantino's Ⓜ Italian — 21 | 20 | 20 | $35

Lincoln Park | 1112 W. Armitage Ave. (Seminary Ave.) | 773-871-2929

John Tarantino's "upscale Lincoln Park" establishment is a "cozy place for a simple dinner or a romantic night out" over "quality Italian" fare that's "consistently" "solid and fresh" – "without the high price tag"; some say "service can be on or off" and feel there are "probably better options out there", but more maintain it's "everything one could want in a neighborhood restaurant"; P.S. "have a martini at the bar", as there's a "great list" to choose from.

Tasting Room, The ❶Ⓩ Eclectic — 18 | 20 | 19 | $32

Market District | 1415 W. Randolph St. (Ogden Ave.) | 312-942-1313 | www.tlcwine.com

"A tasting adventure" awaits visitors to this "laid-back" "yet still trendy" Market District "hideaway" boasting "a breadth of [Eclectic] appetizers that many wine bars seem to lack" plus "staffers who know the inventory and can describe with accuracy each" option from the "fantastic selection" ("at good prices"); the "convivial atmosphere" of its "roomy" space lures loungers to the "leather couches" and "chairs in the open loft upstairs", where they're wowed by an "unrivaled" "city-skyline view."

NEW Ta Tong Japanese/Thai — | — | — | I

Lakeview | 2964 N. Lincoln Ave. (bet. George St. & Wellington Ave.) | 773-348-6500

Lakeviewers are lured to this Thai and sushi BYO with a wallet-friendly menu that goes on and on, incorporating touches of other

cuisines in a something-for-everyone smorgasbord; its dining room is all casual-chic Asian simplicity, fronted with doors that open partially to the great outdoors in season.

Tavern ⎇ *American* ▽ | 23 | 25 | 25 | $59 |

Libertyville | 519 N. Milwaukee Ave. (bet. Cook Ave. & Lake St.) | 847-367-5755

North Suburban fans who "feel very lucky" to have this "local" New American "favorite" "so close" swear it serves the "best steaks in" the area, "excellent fresh seafood" and an "ample list of fine wines", all within a setting sporting "extra special and unique" decor – no wonder so few mind that it's "a bit pricey"; P.S. "the dessert list is satisfyingly sweet."

Tavern on Rush ➊ *Steak* | 19 | 19 | 19 | $45 |

Gold Coast | 1031 N. Rush St. (Bellevue Pl.) | 312-664-9600 | www.tavernonrush.com

A "great celeb hot spot", this "consistent", "no-nonsense" Traditional American steakhouse has a "crowded, lively" "bar downstairs" and "dining above", where "you can sit and watch the action on Rush" (it's also a "wonderful place to sit outside for lunch in the summer"); still, some say the "prime people-watching takes your mind off" the "disappointing service" and "high cost", while others see it as a "singles bar" for the "Viagra-triangle crowd" "looking for love in all the wrong places"; N.B. weekend brunch is also served.

Tecalitlan ➊ *Mexican* ▽ | 23 | 16 | 19 | $17 |

West Town | 1814 W. Chicago Ave. (Wood St.) | 773-384-4285

"Holy" "big burrito!" hail honchos who hanker for the "generous portions" of "delicious", "authentic Mexican food" and "great value" at this "laid-back", "retro" West Town "original"; it's "open very late" – until 3 AM on weekends – and it's "always full", plus there's "takeout" available too.

Tempo ➊⇄ *Diner* | 19 | 11 | 17 | $16 |

Gold Coast | 6 E. Chestnut St. (State St.) | 312-943-4373

"Open 24 hours to better serve the late, late crowd", this "nice" Gold Coast "landmark" is a "classic diner" that's "great morning, noon and night" for "wonderful, enormous omelets" and other "tasty" "coffee-shop" fare; there's "pleasant sidewalk dining in season", but "expect to wait for breakfast/brunch on the weekends", when it's "a zoo" – though it can be "dead at dinner"; P.S. yep, it's still "cash only."

NEW Tepatulco *Mexican* | – | – | – | M |

Lincoln Park | 2558 N. Halsted St. (bet. W. Lill & Wrightwood Aves.) | 773-472-7419 | www.tepatulco.com

Mole master Geno Bahena is back at the stove, this time in a Lincoln Park regional Mexican named for his hometown; the well-priced menu focuses on local and organic ingredients in dishes both traditional and modern, served in the former Las Fuentes space, the highlight of which is a back garden perfect for sipping something from its list of quality tequila.

	FOOD	DECOR	SERVICE	COST

Terragusto Italian Café ⓜ *Italian* — — — M

Roscoe Village | 1851 W. Addison St. (bet. Ravenswood & Wolcott Aves.) | 773-248-2777 | www.terragustocafe.com

Theo Gilbert (ex Trattoria No. 10, Spiaggia) created this intimate, reasonably priced Italian BYO to showcase his devotion to organic, sustainable and local ingredients; salads are served with handmade vinegars, pasta is made fresh and the limited entree list is simplicity itself (including a daily fish seared and roasted); the casually elegant, tablecloth-free Roscoe Village setting also serves panini for lunch, and there's a small 'local market' area vending farm-fresh ingredients – from produce, flour and eggs to sauces and cheeses.

Texas de Brazil Churrascaria *Brazilian* — — — E

Schaumburg | Woodfield Mall | 5 Woodfield Mall (Frontage & Golf Rds.) | 847-413-1600 | www.texasdebrazil.com

Southern Brazil comes to the Suburban Northwest via this upscale churrascaria chain with a touch of Texas hospitality (it's a Dallas import); all-you-can-eat meat (just don't fill up on the huge salad bar) is served by a swashbuckling staff wielding skewers like cutlasses in the rugged Southwestern setting.

Thai Classic *Thai* ▽ 23 | 15 | 18 | $20

Lakeview | 3332 N. Clark St. (bet. Belmont Ave. & Roscoe St.) | 773-404-2000 | www.thaiclassicrestaurant.com

It may "look like a standard neighborhood Thai place", but its "extensive menu" of "high-quality", "authentic" preparations and "cheap" prices (aided by a BYO policy) have raters raving over this "excellent spot" in Lakeview with a "friendly and efficient staff" and a "fantastic buffet on Saturday and Sunday"; P.S. some like it "especially for takeout or delivery."

Thai Pastry *Thai* 22 | 10 | 14 | $18

Uptown | 4925 N. Broadway St. (bet. Argyle St. & Lawrence Ave.) | 773-784-5399 | www.thaipastry.com

"If you like Thai, don't miss" the "awesome, cheap" "authentic" eats with "fresh, vibrant flavors" and "some different offerings than most" at this Uptown Siamese where "BYO is a big plus"; most are "forgiving of the atmosphere" (those who feel it "brings the food down" "order for takeout or have it delivered"), others opine that "the only letdown is the service, which can be slow and inattentive" – "but not rude."

Think Café *American/Eclectic* 24 | 18 | 23 | $33

Bucktown | 2235 N. Western Ave. (Lyndale St.) | 773-394-0537 | www.think-cafe.com

The "best secret of Bucktown" may be this Eclectic-American "gem" and "BYO bargain" that's "more sophisticated than you would think", having "grown into a very good restaurant" with "a nice balance of traditional items", "unique creations" and "not-to-be-missed desserts", all at "great prices"; rapt raters have "no second thoughts about returning" to the "quaint", "romantic" space, where "friendly owners" and "charming staffers" who "take what they do very seriously" provide "wonderful service."

	FOOD	DECOR	SERVICE	COST

Three Happiness ● *Chinese*   `22` `10` `17` `$19`

Chinatown | 209 W. Cermak Rd. (20th St.) | 312-842-1964

"A Chinatown classic" that's "been there forever" (since 1971), this "family-run casual Chinese kitchen" with Cantonese "home cooking" and "steam-cart dim sum" is "always packed" with folks who come for the "great food" (especially "late-night eats", as it's open 24 hours on the weekend, and only closed from 6-9 AM on weekdays), not the "lacking atmosphere" or "spotty service"; P.S. it's unrelated to the bigger, more visible New Three Happiness on the corner.

312 Chicago *American/Italian*   `19` `19` `19` `$38`

Loop | Hotel Allegro | 136 N. LaSalle St. (Randolph St.) | 312-696-2420 | www.312chicago.com

Dialers declare this "convenient" "class act" in the Loop's Hotel Allegro a "good spot for breakfast", a "power lunch", or an "after-work or pre-theater bite" thanks to a "nice, varied menu" of "delicious" Italian-American cooking that's "better than typical hotel dining room" fare, plus "great people-watching" – all "without breaking the bank"; still, some skeptical surveyors give it static, nagging about "noise", "pedestrian" provender and "rushed service" "before show."

Tiffin *Indian*   `22` `15` `17` `$25`

West Rogers Park | 2536 W. Devon Ave. (Maplewood Ave.) | 773-338-2143

"Everything's great from soup to dessert" at this "upscale" "jewel among the cheap eateries on Devon Avenue" in West Rogers Park, where the Indian "menu is quite diverse" (with plenty of "vegetarian options"), the interior is "comfortable", the staff is "helpful" and the prices are "very reasonable" (the "weekday lunch buffet is a steal"); P.S. they offer a "good wine selection" – and beer too.

Timo Ⓜ *Italian*   `-` `-` `-` `M`

Near West | 464 N. Halsted St. (Grand Ave.) | 312-226-4300 | www.timochicago.com

After eight years, John Bubala has reconcepted his Near West French-American pioneer, Thyme, and reopened it as this Italian modernist with a well-crafted, midpriced menu, served in a setting that features stained glass–like murals on the windows and contemporary light fixtures both indoors and on the renowned landscaped patio; his existing small-producer wine list will feature an expanded Italian section.

Timpano Chophouse *Italian/Steak*   `-` `-` `-` `M`

Naperville | 22 E. Chicago Ave. (Washington St.) | 630-753-0985 | www.timpanochophouse.net

An Orlando-based chain has stepped into the Western 'burbs space that formerly held Samba Room with this swanky, big-city version of an Italian steakhouse; torch songs and Sinatra-era crooning set a clubby mood amid dark, handsome surroundings with leather booths, white tablecloths and a martini lounge.

	FOOD	DECOR	SERVICE	COST

Tin Fish *Seafood*
22 | 18 | 20 | $36

Tinley Park | Cornerstone Ctr. | 18201 S. Harlem Ave. (183rd St.) | 708-532-0200
Oakbrook Terrace | 17 W. 512 22nd St. (Midwest Rd.) | 630-279-0808
www.tf-tinfish.com

A school of surveyors savors this suburban seafood two-fer for "extremely fresh" "edibles from the deep" "done your way", a "fantastic raw bar" and "well-thought-out, reasonably priced wine list"; the decor strikes some as "classy" and "clever", but a few fin-icky feeders feel both the "chain" ambiance and "'you guys' service" are "more casual than expected, considering the food quality" – also, some note "noise" issues, though boosters believe "the food makes up for it."

☑ Tizi Melloul *Mediterranean/Mideastern*
21 | 25 | 20 | $41

River North | 531 N. Wells St. (Grand Ave.) | 312-670-4338 | www.tizimelloul.com

"Come to the casbah" in River North, where "you can't help but feel cool" amid the "amazingly funky/exotic decor" with "different rooms to choose from" (including the "truly unique", "private" "round room"); to fully appreciate the "innovative flavors", "be adventurous" with the "unusual" and "high-quality" Middle Eastern-Mediterranean cuisine, then soak up the "fun drinks", "sexy vibe" and "occasional belly dancing" (on Sunday nights).

Toast *American*
22 | 16 | 18 | $16

Lincoln Park | 746 W. Webster Ave. (Halsted St.) | 773-935-5600
Bucktown | 2046 N. Damen Ave. (Dickens Ave.) | 773-772-5600

Tasters toast this Traditional American twosome for "imaginative creations" such as "orgasmic stuffed French toast", "fluffy omelets" and "huge pancakes" "piled high with fresh fruit, granola and yogurt", all served within a "homey" "luncheonette" atmosphere; despite reports of "abrupt if not abusive service" and "hellish waits", hordes "still keep going back for the food"; P.S. "the Bucktown location has a nice back patio" but "no Bloody Marys [or other alcohol] . . . be warned!"

NEW Tokyo 21 ● Ⓢ Ⓜ *Asian*
- | - | - | M

Lincoln Park | 901 W. Weed St. (Fremont St.) | 312-337-2001 | www.tokyo21chicago.com

On the fringe of Lincoln Park, the Kamehachi crew is pairing outside-the-box sushi inventions and nontraditional dishes tapping influences from Japan, Thailand, China and Korea with sake flights and sexy shochu cocktails; the clubby 'parlor' setting features trendy Tokyo gaming machines, velvet booths and a red-hot bar with a built-in light show; N.B. it's only open Wednesday–Saturday, but on weekends serves it up till 2 AM.

Tomboy *American*
21 | 19 | 19 | $37

Andersonville | 5402 N. Clark St. (bet. Balmoral Ave. & Clark St.) | 773-907-0636 | www.tomboyrestaurant.com

Andersonville appreciates this "classy"-"casual" "see-and-be-seen spot" where the New American "food and patrons are all yummy",

the "great exposed-brick atmosphere" is "romantic" and "gay"-friendly, and their aquisition of a liquor license hasn't obviated the "welcome BYO policy" (only a "$7 corkage" fee); still, a cadre of contributors considers the food "good but not haute cuisine" and the service "spotty"; N.B. there's live jazz on Thursdays.

Tony Rocco's River North *Italian*   - | - | - | M

River North | 416 W. Ontario St. (bet. Kingsbury & Orleans Sts.) | 312-787-1400 | www.tonyroccosrivernorth.com

River North is home to this affordable rustic Italian ristorante that sounds like a chain but is actually a family-run independent named for the owner's son (her daughters and granddaughters get menu items); think macaroni and meatballs, thin-crust pizzas and a giant antipasto-style salad for two, served in cozy confines with exposed brick and a whimsical mural of Chicago; N.B. delivery within a two-mile radius means the luxury of brunch brought to your door.

Topo Gigio Ristorante *Italian*   20 | 17 | 19 | $34

Old Town | 1516 N. Wells St. (bet. Division St. & North Ave.) | 312-266-9355 | www.topogiogiochicago.com

"Popular in the neighborhood", this "solid" Old Town "traditional Italian" performer "has become a classic" thanks to "delicious comfort food" (including seafood options such as "rich squid ink pasta" on Fridays), a "cute and kitschy atmosphere with images of Topo Gigio – the famous mouse – all over the place", "great outdoor eating" and "people-watching" in summer and "reasonable prices"; catty consumers, however, take a swipe at the bill of fare and staff, branding them "boring" and "bored", respectively.

Ⓩ Topolobampo Ⓢ Ⓜ *Mexican*   27 | 23 | 25 | $57

River North | 445 N. Clark St. (bet. Hubbard & Illinois Sts.) | 312-661-1434 | www.rickbayless.com

"This is what the food in heaven must taste like" posit praisers of this "pinnacle" of Mexican *alta cucina* in River North, where "every bite" of "creative genius" Rick Bayless' cuisine is "utterly swoon-worthy", the tequila list is "to die for" and the "passionate staff" "pampers" patrons; most feel it's "more elegant than its attached sister restaurant, Frontera Grill", with fare that "really is better", even if a handful of heretics wonder "is it worth the price difference?"; P.S. "book well ahead", as getting "weekend reservations can take forever."

NEW Townhouse Restaurant & Wine Bar Ⓢ *American*   - | - | - | M

Loop | DeLoitte Bldg. | 111 S. Wacker Dr. (Monroe St.) | 312-948-8240 | www.restaurants-america.com

Masculine corporate chic imbues this Loop New American (think One North, from the same owners) serving a moderately priced menu that's equal parts small plates, salads, sandwiches and entrees; the upscale-casual setting accented with mosaic tile, a wine display wall and picture windows overlooking the business bustle includes a convenient take-out area; N.B. it's closed on weekends.

	FOOD	DECOR	SERVICE	COST

NEW Tramonto's Steak & Seafood *Seafood/Steak*

| - | - | - | E |

Wheeling | Westin Chicago North Shore | 601 N. Milwaukee Ave. (E. Lake Cook Rd.) | 847-777-6575 | www.cenitare.com

This pricey steak-and-seafood member of the Rick Tramonto–Gale Gand quartet in the Wheeling Westin has settled into a sophisticated, eye-popping setting with an exhibition kitchen and two-story ceilings, accommodating a lofty waterfall wall; the vast menu includes such over-the-top indulgences as a whole foie gras, complemented by a world-class vino selection – housed in a glass wall designed to hold 10,000 bottles – overseen by former Trotter's sommelier Belinda Chang.

Trattoria D.O.C. *Pizza*

| - | - | - | M |

Evanston | 706 Main St. (Custer Ave.) | 847-475-1111 | www.trattoria-doc.com

A scaled-up cousin of Pizza D.O.C., this Evanstonian appeases appetites with an expanded selection of 30-some *pizze* (individual-sized thin crust with vegetarian, seafood and meat options), a full menu of hearty Italian offerings and a bar with a nice selection of wines and beers from The Boot – all in a snazzy storefront setting with a prominent brick wood-burning oven and wall of windows overlooking Main Street.

Trattoria Gianni Ⓜ *Italian*

| 18 | 15 | 20 | $38 |

Lincoln Park | 1711 N. Halsted St. (bet. North Ave. & Willow St.) | 312-266-1976 | www.trattoriagianni.com

Raters regard this "friendly", "traditional trattoria" serving "simple, authentic" Italian fare as a "great neighborhood hangout" and "dependable pasta spot near the theaters" in Lincoln Park ("they always make sure you make your show"); sure, "the decor could be improved", but the "service is consistently very good" – and even those who find the experience "ordinary" admit it's "pleasant."

Trattoria No. 10 Ⓢ *Italian*

| 23 | 20 | 21 | $39 |

Loop | 10 N. Dearborn St. (Madison St.) | 312-984-1718 | www.trattoriaten.com

Considered a "quiet oasis" "in a hectic neighborhood", this "charming" "Loop classic" is a "favorite of the theater" and "business-lunch" crowds, serving up "a slice of real Italy in a sea of Americanized" versions ("homemade ravioli", "jump-at-you fresh fish") within a "dark", "cozy" "underground" setting; some with sizable stomachs growl over "high-ish prices [for] smallish portions", but the "value" "happy-hour buffet runs circles around the competition."

Trattoria Roma *Italian*

| 19 | 15 | 20 | $30 |

Old Town | 1535 N. Wells St. (bet. North Ave. & Schiller St.) | 312-664-7907 | www.trattoriaroma.com

"Authentic [Southern] Italian fare" earns this "wonderful neighborhood spot" a loyal following of Old Town "locals" who like the "great basic" food, "rustic grotto" atmosphere and "outdoor seating in the summer"; service comments conflict, though, with some praising

| | FOOD | DECOR | SERVICE | COST |

the staff for creating a "relaxed" environment "without the attitude" but others quipping that the "speed of service is also authentic to Italy – leisurely."

NEW **Trattoria 31** *Italian* — | — | — | M

Near South Side | 605 W. 31st St. (Wallace St.) | 312-326-3500 | www.trattoria31.com

Sox fans and Bridgeport denizens welcome this intimate neighborhood Italian rustling up rustic favorites in a casual setting suitable for pre- or post-game dining; evocative photos of vintage Chicago set a nostalgic mood befitting this old-guard enclave.

NEW **Treat Restaurant** *Eclectic* — | — | — | I

Humboldt Park | 1616 N. Kedzie Ave. (North Ave.) | 773-772-1201 | www.treatrestaurant.com

As unpretentious as its Humboldt Park neighborhood, this funky cafe offers an inexpensive menu of Eclectic fare (an artichoke Parmesan sandwich, chicken tikka masala); the garish blue-and-yellow-striped building gives way to a woodsy, bohemian interior with local art adorning the walls; N.B. there's occasional live music.

Tre Kronor *Scandinavian* 24 | 16 | 21 | $18

Northwest Side | 3258 W. Foster Ave. (bet. Kedzie & Kimball Aves.) | 773-267-9888 | www.swedishbistro.com

"A taste of Sweden [and Norway] from the food to the trolls on the walls" sums up this "off-the-beaten-path" Scandinavian BYO "treasure" on the Northwest Side proffering "something decidedly different" with its "authentic", "traditional" fare – such as "lots of herring" (at lunch) and "great blueberry soup" for dessert – at "reasonable" prices within a "cozy", "homelike atmosphere"; N.B. Christmas brings live music, an extravagant all-you-can-eat dinner and magicians for the kids (also on weekends in summer).

Z Tru *French* 28 | 27 | 28 | $117

Streeterville | 676 N. St. Clair St. (bet. Erie & Huron Sts.) | 312-202-0001 | www.trurestaurant.com

"Art and food meet and really, really like each other" at this jackets-required Streeterville "temple of excess" that "amazes" with "progressive, daring" New French plates plus sommelier Scott Tyree's "divinely inspired" 1,400-bottle wine selection, all borne by a virtually "flawless" staff within a "stark, simple" setting sporting an "original Andy Warhol" and "a lovely little tuffet for Madame's handbag"; "sticker shock" aside, it's a "magical experience" that "will become a lasting memory"; N.B. the Food score was tallied when founding chefs Rick Tramonto and Gale Gand were still at the helm.

T-Spot Sushi & Tea Bar *Japanese* — | — | — | M

Lakeview | 3925 N. Lincoln Ave. (Larchmont Ave.) | 773-549-4500 | www.tspotsushiandteabar.com

This Japanese newcomer in Lakeview combines creative rolls, raw-fish fare (including a create-your-own-tartare option) and a modicum of cooked seafood (no poultry or meat options) with a serious

FOOD | DECOR | SERVICE | COST

tea program offering about 35 selections by the cup or pot; the hip, nightclubby setting features black-and-yellow brick walls, a sushi bar and bright lounge furniture.

Tsuki ● *Japanese* — 22 | 23 | 19 | $39

Lincoln Park | 1441-45 W. Fullerton Ave. (Janssen Ave.) | 773-883-8722 | www.tsuki.us

"Hip"-sters herald this Lincoln Park "standout in a crowded field" as "a showcase" for "wonderfully prepared Japanese cooked and raw dishes", both "traditional and contemporary", including "novel sushi and interesting small dishes", conveyed in a "clublike but serene space" by a "good" staff; tougher tipsters say it's "too trendy", though, from its clientele to its "techno-chic decor"; P.S. "go early for the kids' bento boxes – Hello Kitty" for girls, a train motif for boys.

Tsunami *Japanese* — 20 | 17 | 17 | $39

Gold Coast | 1160 N. Dearborn St. (Division St.) | 312-642-9911 | www.tsunamichicago.com

A relative old-timer at 10 years of age, this "solid sushi choice" on the Gold Coast slices "delicious basics" of raw-fish fare and other Japanese faves ("stay for the tempura and udon noodles"); some say its offerings seem "less innovative" now, with nothing "unique or off-the-wall", while others assess the "aging" dining room as "nothing special", but "romantics" suggest the sofas "upstairs near the fireplace" "for a relaxed experience", or avail yourself of the "great patio seating."

Tucci Benucch *Italian* — 18 | 17 | 18 | $29

Gold Coast | 900 N. Michigan Ave., 5th fl. (Walton St.) | 312-266-2500 | www.leye.com

The "hearty", "convenient, middle-of-the-road family" Italian fare (including the "best baked spaghetti around") "holds its own" at this Lettuce Entertain You offering in the Gold Coast's Bloomingdale's building; "regulars love it" for a "relatively cheap" "shopping lunch or informal dinner" with "relaxed service" and "cozy", "villa-esque decor", but cranky shoppers who deem it merely "decent" dub it "Disneyland meets Tuscany."

Tufano's Vernon Park Tap Ⓜ⊘ *Italian* — 21 | 12 | 19 | $25

Near South Side | 1073 W. Vernon Park Pl. (bet. Harrison & Racine Sts.) | 312-733-3393

"Run, don't walk" – and "take cash" – to this "old-time" "classic" on the Near South Side known since 1930 for "huge amounts of cheap", "homestyle" Southern Italian dishes (made from recipes handed down from the current owner's grandmother) and a "casual", "fun family atmosphere"; if for no other reason, it's "worth visiting because there are not a lot of places like this left."

Turquoise *Turkish* — 21 | 16 | 17 | $29

Roscoe Village | 2147 W. Roscoe St. (bet. Damon & Western Aves.) | 773-549-3523 | www.turquoisedining.com

"More than just the bar it appears to be", this "nice" entry offers restless Roscoe Villagers a Turkish tour via the "bright Mediterranean

flavors" of its "reasonably priced fare", including "flavorful meats and seafood"; some suggest the "genial" "though unpolished" staff sometimes provides "splintered service", but at least "there's a friendly atmosphere", and "the owners try hard to make you feel welcome."

Tuscany *Italian*   22 | 18 | 19 | $33

Wrigleyville | 3700 N. Clark St. (Waveland Ave.) | 773-404-7700
Little Italy | 1014 W. Taylor St. (Morgan St.) | 312-829-1990
Wheeling | 550 S. Milwaukee Ave. (bet. Dundee & Hintz Rds.) | 847-465-9988
Oak Brook | 1415 W. 22nd St. (Rte. 83) | 630-990-1993
www.stefanirestaurants.com

"Tuscan before Tuscan was cool", these "lively", "dependable Phil Stefani outlets" – the Little Italy *paterfamilias* and its various offspring – dish out "hearty" "traditional" Northern Italian fare plus "original dishes" ("two words: pear ravioli"); each manages to seem "elegant and homey at the same time", though "every location is a little different", and the original has a "cool throwback bar", but assets aside, some type it as "typical" and say "service can be slow."

Tweet Ⓜ🍴 *Eclectic*   21 | 16 | 20 | $28

Uptown | 5020 N. Sheridan Rd. (Foster St.) | 773-728-5576 | www.tweet.biz

This "Uptown gem" features an "arty" vibe, "fab staff" and "Eclectic menu" of "funk-a-licous" breakfast and lunch fare made from "fresh, high-quality", "organic" ingredients; it can be "noisy and crowded", especially at the "outstanding" weekend brunch, while a few birdies tell of "uneven food (some dishes make it but some just don't)" and cheep that "the whole cash-only thing is really inconvenient"; N.B. it has stopped serving dinner and now closes at 3 PM.

Twin Anchors *BBQ*   22 | 13 | 18 | $27

Old Town | 1655 N. Sedgwick St. (bet. Eugenie St. & North Ave.) | 312-266-1616 | www.twinanchorsribs.com

"Delicious but divey (and therefore great)", this "quintessential" BBQ in Old Town (opened in 1932) "should be declared a historical landmark" say supporters who swear by its "succulent", "fall-off-the-bones" "ribs basted in a zesty sauce" – and "good chicken, burgers, chili and salad" too; with a "fun Wisconsin-like" "tavern" feel and "atmosphere to spare", it's constantly "crowded" with "friendly, sometimes rowdy" folk enjoying the "good jukebox" and "TV sports", so expect a "possibly lengthy wait" ("they don't accept reservations").

Twist *Eclectic*   22 | 18 | 18 | $26

Lakeview | 3412 N. Sheffield Ave. (Clark St.) | 773-388-2727 | www.twistinchicago.com

"The most inventive" Eclectic small plates, "good seasonal specials" and "traditional" Spanish tapas all fit in this "little" Lakeview lair with "a lot of character"; add "awesome sangria" and "efficient servers" and it's a "fun place to start the night" and "a great group dining destination" – but it's "small and the tables are cramped" so "get there early to avoid a wait."

	FOOD	DECOR	SERVICE	COST

Twisted Spoke ⬤ *Pub Food*　　18 | 17 | 17 | $17

Wrigleyville | 3369 N. Clark St. (Roscoe St.) | 773-525-5300
Near West | 501 N. Ogden Ave. (Grand Ave.) | 312-666-1500
www.twistedspoke.com

Roar up to these Near West and Wrigleyville "upscale dives" for some "big, big burgers and cold, cold beer" plus other "better-than-average" Traditional American "pub fare" and even some "respectable salads" served in a "pseudo-biker bar" setting with "metal tabletops, motorcycle parts everywhere" and "gruff service"; some say the "food's better with a hangover" – especially at the "great brunch" starring "killer Bloody Marys" – and the weekly "Smut and Eggs [event] at midnight on Saturdays" is "a must-see" for "porn" fanciers.

Udupi Palace *Indian*　　▽ 23 | 11 | 17 | $16

West Rogers Park | 2543 W. Devon Ave. (bet. Maplewood Ave. & Rockwell St.) | 773-338-2152
Schaumburg | Market Sq. | 730 E. Schaumburg Rd. (Plum Grove Rd.) | 847-884-9510
www.udupipalace.com

To Southern Indian seekers, this West Rogers Park "favorite" and its Northwest Suburban sib are "bona fide dosai palaces" supplying "great vegetarian" entrees plus "a few meat dishes for carnivores" in "huge portions" and at "extremely reasonable prices"; perhaps the settings are "not fancy", but some nevertheless find them "interesting"; N.B. the city spot is BYO.

NEW Uncle John's BBQ 🖼🗒 *BBQ*　　- | - | - | I

Far South Side | 337 E. 69th St. (Calumet Ave.) | 773-892-1233

Smokin' slabs, links and tips plus chicken and every combo plate imaginable have loyalists heading to the Far South Side for BBQ basics from the aquarium-style smoker of a beloved local pitmaster; the no-frills, takeout-only space has an air of authenticity and age that belies its 2006 birthday; N.B. they're open till midnight on weekends.

Uncommon Ground *Coffeehouse*　　21 | 20 | 19 | $20

Wrigleyville | 3800 N. Clark St. (Grace St.) | 773-929-3680 | www.uncommonground.com

"In the midst of the Wrigleyville madness", this "coffee shop/bar/restaurant" is a "favorite hangout" for a "diverse clientele", providing "room upon room" of "entertainment options", including "some of the best live acts", plus "yummy" Eclectic eats incorporating some "organic" ingredients (including "excellent brunches" all week long); loungers label the "laid-back atmosphere" "addictive", with some preferring the "front room with fireplace" and others heading for the "nice patio" – "it's the bomb."

Z Va Pensiero *Italian*　　26 | 23 | 25 | $51

Evanston | Margarita Inn | 1566 Oak Ave. (Davis St.) | 847-475-7779 | www.va-p.com

A "long-standing" destination for "distinctive, quality Italian" that's "both satisfying and imaginative", this "upscale" "old-world" North Suburbanite in a "quaint" "residential" hotel "enchants"

	FOOD	DECOR	SERVICE	COST

with "wonderful service" – including "knowledgeable" "wine assistance" with the "fantastic", "handpicked" "all-Italian" list – and a "soothing", "romantic" setting complete with a "lovely" "terrace"; true, it's "not cheap", but it's still "one of Evanston's great special-occasion restaurants."

Venus Greek-Cypriot Cuisine *Greek*   ▽ 19 | 17 | 22 | $33

Greektown | 820 W. Jackson Blvd. (bet. Green & Halsted Sts.) | 312-714-1001 | www.venuschicago.com

Admirers of this "lovely", "adventurous" "addition to Greektown" delight in its "delicious and unique twist" on Hellenic fare, as it serves "not only Greek" cuisine but also dishes with a wider "Mediterranean flair", including "some typically Cypriot dishes"; it's "an interesting variation in a neighborhood where each place [serves] the same food", and there's also a lunch buffet and live weekend entertainment; P.S. "follow the waiter's suggestions" – but don't miss "the slow-cooked lamb."

Vermilion *Indian/Nuevo Latino*   21 | 19 | 19 | $46

River North | 10 W. Hubbard St. (bet. Dearborn & State Sts.) | 312-527-4060 | www.thevermilionrestaurant.com

"An interesting mix of foodies" finds "delicious" "new things to try" on the "intriguing menu" of "cutting-edge" "Indian-Latin fusion" cuisine at this "hip", "intimate" River Norther with "simple but sexy decor"; still, some traditionalists assert that the "unique concept" "doesn't quite work" (and comes with a "steep price tag" to boot), adding that the "stark" setting can be "noisy"; N.B. the ratings may not reflect a post-Survey menu revamp.

Via Carducci *Italian*   20 | 17 | 17 | $30

Lincoln Park | 1419 W. Fullerton Ave. (Southport Ave.) | 773-665-1981 | www.viacarducci.com

Enjoy "quality" Southern Italian (including "wonderfully done traditional offerings" and "authentic specials") "without breaking the bank" at this "very intimate", "bustling" spot "nestled in Lincoln Park"; it's "always packed" with allies who applaud its "casual", "uncomplicated approach", though on the other side of the via, opponents peg it as "uninspired" and wonder if management "could squeeze any more tables into the dining room"; N.B. its adjacent wine bar, Via Due, serves a slightly different menu.

Viand Bar & Kitchen *American*   ▽ 23 | 20 | 21 | $32

Streeterville | 155 E. Ontario St. (St. Clair St.) | 312-255-8505 | www.viandchicago.com

"Hidden in the Marriott Courtyard" in Streeterville, this "little gem" is seen as "funky and cool", from its New American fare (with some organic ingredients) to its "avant-garde decor" ("interesting table settings") and "innovative cocktails"; partakers are also pleased by the "well-priced, thoughtful list" of vino, "half-price Wednesday wine night" and sidewalk seating; N.B. post-Survey, Steve Chiappetti (ex Café le Coq, Grapes and Mango) stepped in as chef and shifted the menu's focus toward comfort food.

	FOOD	DECOR	SERVICE	COST

Viceroy of India *Indian* — 20 | 12 | 17 | $24

West Rogers Park | 2520 W. Devon Ave. (bet. Campbell & Maplewood Aves.) | 773-743-4100
Lombard | 233 E. Roosevelt Rd. (Highland Ave.) | 630-627-4411
www.viceroyofindia.com

"All the basics are covered well" at this "popular" West Rogers Park and West Suburban pair that some reporters rate as a "safe bet" for "tasty" Indian food that's definitely "the real thing" – and "reasonably priced", to boot; still, those who see them as "nothing special" submit that the fare "is adjusted for the hoi polloi", the "banquet setting" is somewhat "cheesy" and the staff is sometimes "unfriendly."

Victory's Banner *Eclectic* — 23 | 13 | 18 | $14

Roscoe Village | 2100 W. Roscoe St. (Hoyne Ave.) | 773-665-0227 | www.victorysbanner.com

This 100 percent "vegetarian hot spot" in Roscoe Village is a "favorite" "retreat" for conscientious consumers craving "unconditionally good" Eclectic fare made from "the freshest" ingredients – including a "wonderful breakfast" that's one of "the best around" – and served by a "devoted" staff; some say the "meditative" setting is "heavenly" and "rejuvenating", while others warn you have to "overlook the odd decor and messages praising the swami", but it's "always crowded" – and "worth the wait"; N.B. no dinner service.

Z Vie ⧗ *American* — 27 | 23 | 23 | $55

Western Springs | 4471 Lawn Ave. (Burlington Ave.) | 708-246-2082 | www.vierestaurant.com

"Wow"-ed West Suburbanites feel "lucky to have" this New American in the "quaint", "sleepy" town of Western Springs, where chef-owner "Paul Virant brings many of his Blackbird sensibilities" to his "haute" "seasonal" "dishes with excellent flavor combinations", paired with a "very interesting wine list"; just "steps from the train station", it's even "worth the reverse commute for adventurous Chicagoans", though some call the "modern, minimalist" decor "cold" and others purport it would be "perfect" "if the service could catch up with the brilliance of the food."

NEW Viet Bistro & Lounge *Vietnamese* — – | – | – | I

Rogers Park | 1346 W. Devon Ave. (bet. Glenwood & Wayne Aves.) | 773-465-5720

Rogers Park is home to this long-awaited spin-off of the late Pasteur, serving inexpensive Vietnamese cuisine tweaked with Eclectic influences; the chic double storefront has a mod lounge on one side and dining on the other, with high-backed tamarind-hued banquettes set against exposed-brick walls.

Village, The ● *Italian* — 19 | 20 | 20 | $32

Loop | Italian Village | 71 W. Monroe St., 2nd fl. (bet. Clark & Dearborn Sts.) | 312-332-7005 | www.italianvillage-chicago.com

The "last of the [Loop] survivors" "from days gone by", this "sentimental favorite" of the Italian Village trio is "filled with old-school"

"nostalgia and charm" and plates "plentiful servings" of "predictable satisfying fare" (including "the best chicken Vesuvio") in a "wonderful interior" where "couples can enjoy private booths" with "twinkling lights" supplying the "stars"; modernists who find it "tired", however, say service swings from "charming" and "efficient" to "rushed" and "indifferent", and foodies find the fare "fancy eatin' for kids and tourists."

Vinci ⓜ Italian   22 20 21 $40

Lincoln Park | 1732 N. Halsted St. (Willow St.) | 312-266-1199 | www.vincichicago.com

Satisfied surveyors say that the "quiet, dignified Italian dining" "never goes out of style" at this "upscale" Lincoln Park "favorite" where "Paul LoDuca continues to create a warm place with excellent food" (props for the "amazing polenta with mushrooms"), a "good wine list and equitable pricing" in a "convenient" location that's "wonderful" for theatergoers; P.S. it's also a "great place for Sunday brunch" and "monthly wine dinners" that represent "a fantastic deal."

Vito & Nick's ⊄ Pizza   - - - I

Far South Side | 8433 S. Pulaski Rd. (84th Pl.) | 773-735-2050 | www.vitoandnick.com

Fans of this family-friendly, family-run classic on the Far South Side have been flocking here since 1965 for cheap, crisp Sicilian thin-crust pies (especially the versions with their special sausage), plus standard Italian faves; the grotto environs are as cheesy as the pizza – which is part of the fun; N.B. no dessert, no credit cards and the owners vow that the pizza will never be delivered.

Vive La Crepe ⓜ Eclectic/French   ▽ 20 14 15 $19

Evanston | 1565 Sherman Ave. (bet. Davis & Grove Sts.) | 847-570-0600 | www.vivelacrepe.com

A "really interesting twist on crêpes" – "not filled" but with "delicious" sauces and ingredients "poured on top" – characterizes the "cheap" Eclectic–New French fare at this "cute little spot" in Evanston; its "nice" savory options and "yummy dessert" varieties are a "taste of France" that's "fun for a change", even if a few feel they're "not fantastic"; N.B. check out the signature hard cider served in a tea cup.

Vivere ⓢ Italian   21 21 21 $47

Loop | Italian Village | 71 W. Monroe St. (bet. Clark & Dearborn Sts.) | 312-332-4040 | www.vivere-chicago.com

Loyal Loopers look for la dolce vita at this "funky-upscale" spot, the "hippest" of the Italian Village triumvirate with "quite good" seasonal contemporary Italian fare (backed by an "extensive wine list") and a "most accommodating" staff, especially to "business-lunch"-ers and "theater- and concertgoers"; still, those for whom the "food just misses the mark" and the "futuristic Italian spaceship" "decor is getting tired" feel "the upscale price isn't warranted considering the value" and "schmaltzy charm" of its siblings in the same complex.

	FOOD	DECOR	SERVICE	COST

Vivo *Italian* — 21 | 20 | 19 | $40

Market District | 838 W. Randolph St. (bet. Green & Peoria Sts.) | 312-733-3379 | www.vivo-chicago.com

"Still a solid player" despite all the "new places in the area", this Market District pioneer continues to please with "excellent Italian cuisine" – including "heavenly gnocchi and fettuccine" and "outstanding fish specials" – served "in a trendy loft setting" that's "crowded, yet cozy"; it's "too loud sometimes but otherwise enjoyable" some surveyors say, adding that "service can be a bit uneven"; P.S. many "love eating in the elevator shaft", whose table seats six.

Volare *Italian* — 23 | 16 | 22 | $34

Streeterville | 201 E. Grand Ave. (St. Clair St.) | 312-410-9900 | www.volarerestaurant.com

A taste of "true *Italiano*" "hidden away off Michigan Avenue" in Streeterville, this "friendly", "bustling" "backstreet trattoria" with "the feel of an old-fashioned neighborhood Italian supper club" and a "wonderful" patio puts out "big portions" of "delicious" "classics", including some of "the best osso buco and risotto" around and "well-prepared fresh seafood selections" – thus a visit here is "very enjoyable", except for the "close tables" and "terrible waits"; N.B. an Oak Brook location is in the works.

Volo Restaurant & Wine Bar ⌧ *American* — 20 | 19 | 21 | $36

Roscoe Village | 2008 W. Roscoe St. (Damen Ave.) | 773-348-4600 | www.volorestaurant.com

Expect a "cool mood" with "fun and creative wine flights to match the creative" and "delectable" New American small plates at this "hip wine bar" in Roscoe Village, where the "welcoming atmosphere" includes "conviviality", "great background music" and a "huge wine list" with "nice descriptions" that help you choose; it can be "packed", but outdoor seating "practically doubles the number of tables"; still, some point out that it's "not vegetarian-friendly", as the non-meat "options are very limited."

Vong's Thai Kitchen *Thai* — 21 | 20 | 19 | $37

River North | 6 W. Hubbard St. (State St.) | 312-644-8664 | www.vongsthaikitchen.com

"Interesting" Thai fare with an "upscale", "metro flair" finds favor at this River North Lettuce Entertain You partnership with famed chef Jean-Georges Vongerichten, a "value" considering the "quality", "good service" and "serene" "Far East" decor; diners who are "disappointed" by "the more casual food and presentation" at "the most down-market Vong there is" would "just as soon go to a neighborhood" Siamese and "save money" (though the "$1 dessert menu [at lunch] is the best concept ever").

NEW Wakamono ☻ *Japanese* — - | - | - | M

Lakeview | 3317 N. Broadway St. (W. Buckingham Pl.) | 773-296-6800 | www.wakamonosushi.com

The owners of pingpong serve up this tiny, no reserving, neighborhood-chic Lakeview BYO offering 'Japas' (yes, folks,

	FOOD	DECOR	SERVICE	COST

Japanese small plates) and 'jet-fresh' sushi including a long list of maki both modern and classic in a saunalike wood interior (with sidewalk seating in summer) enlivened by a tree mural and mosaic tile table-tops; catering to night owls, it serves until 11:30 PM nightly.

Wave *Mediterranean*

20	24	18	$48

Streeterville | W Chicago Lakeshore | 644 N. Lake Shore Dr. (Ontario St.) | 312-255-4460 | www.waverestaurant.com

"Cool, modern decor" complements the "beautiful-people" patrons at this "stylish" Streeterville spot for "innovative and delicious" Mediterranean small plates within the "hipster's paradise" of the W hotel; "the price is a little steep", considering what some call the "lack of 'wow' factor" in the food (and no one's raving about the service), but wave-runners reckon the "movie-set" scene and view "out to the Navy Pier Ferris wheel" make it "perfect for a some-what special occasion."

Weber Grill *BBQ*

19	16	18	$34

River North | Hilton Garden Inn | 539 N. State St. (Grand Ave.) | 312-467-9696
Schaumburg | 1010 N. Meacham Rd. (American Ln.) | 847-413-0800
Lombard | 2331 Fountain Sq. Dr. (Meyers Rd.) | 630-953-8880
www.webergrillrestaurant.com

"Authentic American BBQ" aficionados who "camp out" at these "tourist-friendly" city and suburban sizzlefests – where virtually "everything" is grilled on "huge Weber kettles" – believe they bring "basic meat and potatoes" "to the highest level", making them a "lower-cost alternative to the high-priced steakhouses"; still, "char"-red chewers who chastise them for "generic chain" grub, "weak service" and "noisy atmospheres" brag "my backyard is much better."

Webster Wine Bar ❶ *Eclectic*

17	21	20	$28

Lincoln Park | 1480 W. Webster Ave. (bet. Ashland Ave. & Clybourn St.) | 773-868-0608 | www.websterwinebar.com

"Black-clad patrons pose, chatter and sip their Gigondas appreciatively" at this "casually elegant" Lincoln Park wine-bar "gem" where the "huge, fairly priced wine list" is paired with a "small but well-done menu" of Eclectic seasonal small plates; service is "knowledgeable" (if sometimes "slow") in the "laid-back" "living-room" setting, "a place for a first date or to hang out with friends" "after movies at Webster Place" – plus they have a "late kitchen" (1 AM on weekends), though some gourmets "go for the flights, not the food."

West Town Tavern ⧈ *American*

23	20	21	$41

West Town | 1329 W. Chicago Ave. (Throop St.) | 312-666-6175 | www.westtowntavern.com

Drew and Susan Goss "pay attention to everything" at their "deservedly popular" West Towner that's "more upscale than its name would suggest" considering the "high-quality" Traditional American "comfort food" ("best pot roast this side of my mother's"), "winning wines" and "wonderful beer selection"; a "friendly" staff works the "warm", "hip" "exposed-brick interior", which strikes support-

ers as "low-key" and "carefree" – though some report it can get "crowded and noisy."

White Fence Farm 🅼 *American* | 21 | 18 | 19 | $22

Romeoville | 1376 Joliet Rd. (2 mi. south of I-55) | 630-739-1720 | www.whitefencefarm.com

Born in 1954, this Southwest Suburban American "blast from the past" "beats the cluck out of typical fast-food chicken joints" with its "awesome" "crispy-fried" bird, "unbelievably delicious" corn fritters and "kitschy relish trays", and its "half *Hee Haw,* half elegant plantation house" setting – including a "big museum with old cars and much more" and a petting zoo – "has to be seen to be believed"; P.S. "don't forget to check out your physique in the funny mirrors while you wait."

Wiener's Circle, The ◐⇏ *Hot Dogs* | 20 | 6 | 13 | $7

Lincoln Park | 2622 N. Clark St. (Wrightwood Ave.) | 773-477-7444

"Gimme a charred red hot dammit!" demand "rude"-sters who relish the "funny, filthy-mouthed" "late-night" shtick (engaged in by customers and staff) as much as the "outstanding Chicago dogs", "amazing cheeseburgers" and "great shakes" at this "one-of-a-kind" Lincoln Park "sitcom-in-waiting"; still, be warned that "all the love goes in the bun, not in the decor" and there's "almost nowhere to sit" – plus some say "never go here sober."

🅉 **Wildfire** *Steak* | 23 | 21 | 21 | $40

River North | 159 W. Erie St. (bet. LaSalle & Wells Sts.) | 312-787-9000

Lincolnshire | 235 Parkway Dr. (Milwaukee Ave.) | 847-279-7900

Glenview | 1300 Patriot Blvd. (Lake Ave.) | 847-657-6363

Schaumburg | 1250 E. Higgins Rd. (National Pkwy.) | 847-995-0100

Oak Brook | Oakbrook Center Mall | 232 Oakbrook Ctr. (Rte. 83) | 630-586-9000

www.wildfirerestaurant.com

Spreading like their namesake, this "insanely popular" passel of Traditional American steakhouses from the "Lettuce Entertain You group" keeps carnivores "coming back" with "hearty Midwest-sized portions" from a "crowd-pleasing menu" of "awesome wood-fired" fare ("juicy" steaks and chops), "delicious chopped salad" and "great martini flights" in a "classy", "clubby" "'40s-style" setting; salivating surveyors swear it's "worth the wait" ("even with reservations"), but wet blankets rank these "noisy" "madhouses" "really rather ordinary, just on a grand scale."

Wildfish *Japanese* | ▽ 25 | 22 | 20 | $39

NEW **Deerfield** | Deerfield Commons Shopping Ctr. | 730 Waukegan Rd. (bet. Deerfield Rd. & Osterman Ave.) | 847-317-9453

Arlington Heights | Arlington Town Sq. | 60 S. Arlington Heights Rd. (Northwest Hwy.) | 847-870-8260

"A great selection of traditional and contemporary sushi as well as [other] delicious dishes" delight denizens of this "hip" "city" Japanese

"hidden in a [Northwest] Suburban mall"; maki lovers are also "surprised" by the "minimal", "sleek decor" with "terrific" "private booths" and say the service is "attentive", if "not especially friendly"; N.B. a second location opened in Deerfield in early 2007.

Wishbone *Southern*   21 | 17 | 18 | $20
Roscoe Village | 3300 N. Lincoln Ave. (School St.) | 773-549-2663
West Loop | 1001 W. Washington Blvd. (Morgan St.) | 312-850-2663
NEW **Berwyn** | 6611 Roosevelt Rd. (East Ave.) | 708-749-1295 **M**
www.wishbonechicago.com

"Boisterous" and "family-friendly", this trio dishes up "delicious", "homey" Southern and "sometime-Cajun" cooking with a side of "whimsy" ("note the 'chickeney' decor touches"); a sizable demographic deems it "dependable" for a "great brunch", plus "hearty and filling" lunches and "dinners as well", all at "tolerable prices", even if "sometimes the wait is a little long" and "service is hit-or-miss", but a faction feels the experience is "fair to middling"; N.B. the Berwyn location opened post-Survey.

Wolfgang Puck's Grand Café *American*   18 | 17 | 17 | $28
Evanston | Century Theatre Complex | 1701 Maple Ave. (Church St.) | 847-869-9653 | www.wolfgangpuckevanston.com

"Good for salads" and "satisfying, creative" "wood oven–fired pizzas", this "high-energy" Evanston "local chain site" "attached to the movie complex" tenders its "tasty" New American edibles amid a mix of "futurism and art deco" where "outdoor dining and people-watching are a plus"; puckish pens, however, say "service is spotty" and pronounce the provender "ordinary" and "a bit pricey for the result" – especially "when you expect so much more from the big name."

Woo Lae Oak *Korean*   ▽ 19 | 18 | 17 | $35
Rolling Meadows | 3201 Algonquin Rd. (Newport Dr.) | 847-870-9910
"Very interesting" choices of "good Korean food" beyond the "simple kalbi/bulgoki grill" make this "consistent", "understated" and "entertaining" establishment in the Suburban Northwest "as close as you can get" to the real thing according to raters who "can't wait to go back."

NEW **Xel-Há** *Mexican*   - | - | - | M
River North | 710 N. Wells St. (Superior St.) | 312-274-9500 | www.xel-ha-yucatancuisine.com

Named for the Yucatán region that inspires the cooking of chef Dudley Nieto (ex Adobo Grill, Zapatista), this River North mid-priced Mex offers 60 tequilas and counting, plus a nice little vino list; having changed little from its previous incarnations as Meztiso and SWK, the front room houses a long mahogany bar, while the back is a cozy oasis surrounded by wine storage walls.

Yard House *American*   17 | 16 | 17 | $24
Glenview | The Glen | 1880 Tower Dr. (Patriot Blvd.) | 847-729-9273 | www.yardhouse.com

With well "over 100 on tap", "from all over the world", there may be "too many beers to choose from" – and "what a great problem to have"

swoon suds lovers smitten with this North Suburban "microbrewery-type chain" outpost that also offers a "varied, value-conscious menu" of American eats "for anytime, with or without kids"; the bonanza of brews, however, falls flat with those who perceive the provender as "pedestrian"; P.S. if the "lively" environs seem "loud", adjourn to the "great outside seating."

NEW Yolk *American* `- - - I`

South Loop | 1120 S. Michigan Ave. (11th St.) | 312-789-9655
Breakfast-seekers in the South Loop can wake up to an inexpensive array of decadent French toast, crêpes and frittatas, while lunchers can refuel on sandwiches and salads at this daytime New American eatery that closes at 3 PM; the casual setting is done in an eye-opening yolk-yellow color scheme and features booth and counter seating.

Yoshi's Café M *Asian/French* `23 17 22 $42`

Lakeview | 3257 N. Halsted St. (Belmont Ave.) | 773-248-6160 | www.yoshiscafe.com
Adherents allege this "super-cool" New French–Asian fusion pioneer "in the middle of Boys Town" is "much better than the über-trendy fly-by-nights that surround it" thanks to "imaginative", "high-quality food" (a "gourmet bargain") and "understated" "bistro" atmosphere blessed with a "warm crowd" and "seasoned vet servers" – plus chef-owner Yoshi Katsumura "is always on hand"; divergers detect "one too many ingredients" in his "different" dishes, though, and describe the decor as that of "a diner converted into a 'nice' place."

Zapatista *Mexican* `20 18 18 $29`

South Loop | 1307 S. Wabash Ave. (13th St.) | 312-435-1307 | www.zapatistamexicangrill.com
"Wonderful", "fresh Mexican" with "subtle flavors" is served "south of the border (Roosevelt Street, that is)" at this South Loop "hot spot" where the "funky party atmosphere" "is lively and the volume is loud enough to drown out a bullfight" ("but who cares when you're drinking" "potent", "tasty margaritas"?); deserters are undecided, though, saying the fare's "not revolutionary" and management's "still ironing out kinks with the service"; N.B. the Food rating may not reflect a post-Survey chef change.

Z Zealous 🅂M *American* `24 26 23 $71`

River North | 419 W. Superior St. (Sedgwick St.) | 312-475-9112 | www.zealousrestaurant.com
"Loftlike ceilings", a "bamboo grove" and a "stunning glass wine cellar in the center of the dining room" make for a "minimalist" milieu at this "serene", "sophisticated" spot, a "prime" River North locale for "a quiet meal" or a "special occasion" thanks to "touted chef" Michael Taus' "excellent", "edgy" New American cooking with "daring, unusual combinations" and the "personable" staff's "high standards of service"; still, opponents opine that the "gorgeous decor" "outpaces" the "overpriced" food, which they feel "falls a little short."

	FOOD	DECOR	SERVICE	COST

Zest *American/Eclectic* | 20 | 22 | 19 | $36 |

Streeterville | Hotel InterContinental | 505 N. Michigan Ave. (Illinois St.) | 312-321-8766 | www.chicago.interconti.com

"Great" Eclectic–New American "hotel dining" in "tastefully Euro" environs "looking out at Michigan Avenue" and "great hospitality", "crowded or not", make this "nice" Streeterville spot in the InterContinental a "good place" for a "quality breakfast", a "time-efficient lunch" "or a quick, convenient bite" "if you're shopping on the Mag Mile all day" ("get a window seat" "for people-watching").

Zia's Trattoria *Italian* | 22 | 17 | 20 | $30 |

Edison Park | 6699 N. Northwest Hwy. (bet. Harlem & Touhy Aves.) | 773-775-0808 | www.ziaschicago.com

"A real find" on Edison Park's "Restaurant Row", this "bustling", "rustic Italian eatery" earns enthusiasm for its "fresh, authentic cuisine" and "nice wines" served in a "comfortable" "location for commuters and folk looking for a fine-dining experience on the periphery of the city"; still, a portion of patrons says it "can be very noisy", "service is slow" sometimes and the no-weekend-reservations policy (except for parties of five or more) "makes it a hassle."

NEW ZKF *American* | - | - | - | I |

Bucktown | 1633 N. Milwaukee Ave. (W. Concord Pl.) | 773-278-9600 | www.zkfood.com

Transformed into a full-service American restaurant, Bucktown's former Zoom Kitchen has gone upscale yet maintained its casual atmosphere and traditional faves like the sloppy joe; there's still takeout and curbside pickup, but those who dine in will enjoy the modern setting adorned by works of local artists.

NEW Zocalo *Mexican* | - | - | - | M |

River North | 358 W. Ontario St. (N. Orleans St.) | 312-302-9977 | www.zocalochicago.com

Named for Mexico City's plaza of the presidential palace, this mid-priced Mexican small-plates specialist assumes the onetime Chilpancingo site in River North, where it's serving modern takes on classics like stews, ceviche and a few entrees for bigger appetites; the warm, rustic cantina setting features an open kitchen and a 50-ft. bar pouring flights from a massive collection of tequilas and mezcals.

CHICAGO
INDEXES

Cuisines

Includes restaurant names, neighborhoods and Food ratings. ☑ indicates places with the highest ratings, popularity and importance.

AFGHAN

Kabul House | **Skokie** — 20

AFRICAN

NEW Icosium Kafe | **Andersonville** — -

AMERICAN (NEW)

Adelle's | **Wheaton** — 25
NEW Aigre Doux | **River N** — -
☑ Alinea | **Lincoln Pk** — 28
Allen's | **River N** — 24
Amber Cafe | **Westmont** — 24
Aria | **Loop** — 23
☑ Atwater's | **Geneva** — 21
Avenue M | **Near W** — -
Bank Lane | **Lake Forest** — 23
Bijan's | **River N** — 19
☑ Bin 36/Bin Wine | **multi. loc.** — 20
☑ Blackbird | **W Loop** — 27
Blue Water | **River N** — 22
BOKA | **Lincoln Pk** — 23
NEW Broadway Cellars | **Edgewater** — -
Butter | **Greektown** — 22
Cab's Wine Bar | **Glen Ellyn** — 22
Café Absinthe | **Bucktown** — 23
Café Selmarie | **Lincoln Sq** — 21
Caliterra | **Streeterville** — 23
Canoe Club | **Orland Pk** — 19
Cereality | **multi. loc.** — 16
NEW Chalkboard | **Lincoln Sq** — -
☑ Charlie Trotter's | **Lincoln Pk** — 27
Chef's Station | **Evanston** — 23
Cité | **Streeterville** — 17
NEW Cooper's | **Lakeview** — -
☑ Courtright's | **Willow Spgs** — 26
☑ Crofton on Wells | **River N** — 26
NEW Cru Cafe | **Gold Coast** — -
☑ Custom Hse. | **Printer's Row** — 24
David Burke Prime | **River N** — 22

David's Bistro | **Des Plaines** — 24
Dine | **W Loop** — -
NEW Dodo | **Ukrainian Vill** — -
Emilio's Sunflower | **La Grange** — -
erwin cafe | **Lakeview** — 23
Feast | **Bucktown** — 18
NEW Feed/Beast | **Lincoln Sq** — -
NEW Fiddlehead | **Lincoln Sq** — -
NEW 545 North | **Libertyville** — -
Fixture | **Lincoln Pk** — -
NEW Gage | **S Loop** — -
NEW Gordon Biersch | **Bolingbrook** — -
NEW Graze | **River N** — -
Green Dolphin St. | **Lincoln Pk** — 19
Harvest | **St. Charles** — -
HB | **Lakeview** — 22
Ina's | **W Loop** — 19
Jack's on Halsted | **Lakeview** — 21
Jacky's Bistro | **Evanston** — 23
Jane's | **Bucktown** — 21
Jilly's Cafe | **Evanston** — 23
La Fette | **Old Town** — -
Landmark | **Lincoln Pk** — 21
Lovell's | **Lake Forest** — 20
Magnolia Cafe | **Uptown** — 25
May St. Market | **Near W** — -
Meritage Cafe | **Bucktown** — 22
M. Henry | **Andersonville** — 24
NEW Midtown Kitchen | **Loop** — -
Milk & Honey | **Wicker Pk** — 21
☑ mk | **River N** — 26
Montarra | **Algonquin** — 22
☑ Naha | **River N** — 26
NEW Niche | **Geneva** — -
☑ North Pond | **Lincoln Pk** — 25
One North | **Loop** — 18
NEW Over Easy | **Ravenswood** — -
Park Grill | **Loop** — 19
Parrot Cage | **Far S Side** — -

Pepper Lounge | **Wrigleyville** 22

Philander's | **Oak Pk** 21

NEW Pops/Champ. | **River N** -

Prairie Grass | **Northbrook** 21

Puck's at MCA | **Streeterville** 20

Z Pump Room | **Gold Coast** 21

NEW Quince | **Evanston** -

Rhapsody | **Loop** 21

Ritz-Carlton Café | **Streeterville** -

NEW Room 21 | **S Loop** -

Sage Grille | **Highwood** -

Schwa | **Lincoln Pk** 26

Z Seasons | **Gold Coast** 26

NEW Sequel | **Lombard** -

1776 | **Crystal Lake** 24

Z Signature Rm. | **Streeterville** 18

sola | **Lakeview** -

Z Spring | **Wicker Pk** 27

Stained Glass | **Evanston** 23

State | **Lincoln Pk** -

Tavern | **Libertyville** 23

Think Café | **Bucktown** 24

Tomboy | **Andersonville** 21

NEW Townhouse | **Loop** -

Tweet | **Uptown** 21

Viand Bar | **Streeterville** 23

Z Vie | **W Springs** 27

Volo | **Roscoe Vill** 20

Wolfgang Puck | **Evanston** 18

Z Zealous | **River N** 24

Zest | **Streeterville** 20

AMERICAN (TRADITIONAL)

American Girl | **Gold Coast** 12

Ann Sather | **multi. loc.** 19

Z Atwood Cafe | **Loop** 21

Bandera | **Streeterville** 20

Bar Louie | **multi. loc.** 15

NEW Billy Berk's | **Skokie** -

Billy Goat Tav. | **multi. loc.** 15

Birch River | **Arlington Hts** -

Bongo Room | **multi. loc.** 24

Boston Blackie's | **multi. loc.** 19

Breakfast Club | **W Town** 19

Z Cheesecake Fac. | **multi. loc.** 19

Chicago Firehse. | **S Loop** 18

Clubhouse | **Oak Brook** 21

NEW Cordis Bros. | **Lakeview** -

NEW Depot Diner | **Far W** -

Dine | **W Loop** -

Drake Bros.' | **Streeterville** 17

Edelweiss | **Norridge** 21

Entourage | **Schaumburg** -

Finley's Grill | **Downers Grove** -

Flo | **W Town** 22

Gale St. Inn | **multi. loc.** 20

Glenn's Diner | **Ravenswood** -

Goose Is. Brewing | **multi. loc.** 16

Grace O'Malley's | **S Loop** 17

Green Door Tav. | **River N** 14

Grill on Alley | **Streeterville** 18

Hackney's | **multi. loc.** 18

Hard Rock Cafe | **River N** 13

Hemmingway's | **Oak Pk** 21

Hot Chocolate | **Bucktown** 23

J. Alexander's | **multi. loc.** 20

Joey's Brickhouse | **Lakeview** 18

John's Place | **Lincoln Pk** 18

Kroll's | **S Loop** -

Kuma's Corner | **Logan Sq** -

Lawry's Prime Rib | **River N** 24

Lou Mitchell's | **multi. loc.** 22

Lucca's | **Lakeview** 19

LuxBar | **Gold Coast** 17

L. Woods Lodge | **Lincolnwood** 19

Margie's Candies | **multi. loc.** 23

Medici on 57th | **Hyde Pk** 18

Mike Ditka's | **Gold Coast** 20

Miller's Pub | **Loop** 17

NEW Minnies | **Lincoln Pk** -

Mity Nice Grill | **Streeterville** 18

Mrs. Park's Tav. | **Streeterville** 17

Next Door Bistro | **Northbrook** 21

Nookies | **multi. loc.** 19

Oak Tree | **Gold Coast** 17

Orange | **multi. loc.** 23

Z Original Pancake | **multi. loc.** 23

Parlor | **Wicker Pk**	19
NEW Patty Burger | **Loop**	–
Petterino's | **Loop**	19
Phil & Lou's | **W Loop**	17
P.J. Clarke's | **multi. loc.**	17
Poag Mahone's | **Loop**	17
R.J. Grunts | **Lincoln Pk**	19
Z RL | **Gold Coast**	22
Rock Bottom | **multi. loc.**	16
Rockit B&G | **River N**	19
Z Seasons Café | **Gold Coast**	25
NEW Shor | **S Loop**	–
Sidebar Grille | **Loop**	–
Silver Cloud B&G | **Bucktown**	18
South Gate Cafe | **Lake Forest**	18
South Water Kitchen | **Loop**	17
Stanley's | **multi. loc.**	19
Tavern on Rush | **Gold Coast**	19
312 Chicago | **Loop**	19
Toast | **multi. loc.**	22
Twisted Spoke | **multi. loc.**	18
Weber Grill | **multi. loc.**	19
West Town Tav. | **W Town**	23
White Fence | **Romeoville**	21
Z Wildfire | **multi. loc.**	23
Yard House | **Glenview**	17
NEW Yolk | **S Loop**	–
NEW ZKF | **Bucktown**	–

ARGENTINEAN

El Nandu | **Logan Sq**	21
Tango | **Naperville**	20
Z Tango Sur | **Wrigleyville**	24

ARMENIAN

Sayat Nova | **Streeterville**	20

ASIAN

Alice & Friends | **Uptown**	20
Big Bowl | **multi. loc.**	18
Catch 35 | **multi. loc.**	23
China Grill | **Loop**	20
Chinoiserie | **Wilmette**	20
Flat Top Grill | **multi. loc.**	19
NEW Ginger Asian | **Orland Pk**	–

Karma | **Mundelein**	24
Z Kevin | **River N**	26
LuLu's Dim Sum | **Evanston**	19
NEW Mulan | **Chinatown**	–
Opera | **S Loop**	23
pingpong | **Lakeview**	21
Red Light | **Mkt Dist**	23
NEW Republic | **River N**	–
Z Shanghai Terr. | **River N**	24
Stir Crazy | **multi. loc.**	19
Yoshi's Café | **Lakeview**	23

AUSTRIAN

Glunz Bavarian | **Lincoln Sq**	19
Julius Meinl | **Lakeview**	21

BARBECUE

Carson's Ribs | **multi. loc.**	20
Z Fat Willy's | **Logan Sq**	23
Hecky's | **multi. loc.**	21
NEW Honey 1 BBQ | **Bucktown**	–
Lem's BBQ | **Far S Side**	24
Merle's Smokehse. | **Evanston**	21
Ribs 'n' Bibs | **Hyde Pk**	22
Robinson's Ribs | **multi. loc.**	19
Russell's BBQ | **multi. loc.**	18
Smoke Daddy | **Wicker Pk**	20
NEW Smoque BBQ | **NW Side**	–
Twin Anchors | **Old Town**	22
NEW Uncle John's | **Far S Side**	–
Weber Grill | **multi. loc.**	19

BRAZILIAN

Brazzaz | **River N**	23
Z Fogo de Chão | **River N**	24
Sabor do Brasil | **Orland Pk**	–
Texas de Brazil | **Schaumburg**	–

BRITISH

Red Lion Pub | **Lincoln Pk**	16

CAJUN

Davis St. Fish | **Evanston**	19
Dixie Kitchen | **multi. loc.**	19
Z Heaven on Seven | **multi. loc.**	21
Pappadeaux Sea. | **multi. loc.**	20
Wishbone | **multi. loc.**	21

CHINESE
(* dim sum specialist)

Ben Pao | **River N**	21
Best Hunan | **Vernon Hills**	21
Chens | **Wrigleyville**	23
Dee's | **Lincoln Pk**	19
Dragonfly | **Mkt Dist**	14
Emperor's Choice | **Chinatown**	23
Evergreen | **Chinatown**	22
NEW Fornetto & Mei's | **S Loop**	–
Fornetto Mei | **Gold Coast**	19
Hai Yen | **multi. loc.**	22
Happy Chef Dim Sum* | **Chinatown**	23
Koi | **Evanston**	19
NEW KS Seafood | **Chinatown**	–
Z Lao Sze Chuan | **multi. loc.**	24
Moon Palace | **Chinatown**	21
New Three Happiness* | **Chinatown**	19
Z P.F. Chang's | **multi. loc.**	20
Phoenix* | **Chinatown**	22
Pine Yard | **Evanston**	20
Shine & Morida | **Lincoln Pk**	20
Silver Seafood | **Uptown**	22
Three Happiness* | **Chinatown**	22

COFFEEHOUSES
NEW Gale's Coffee | **Wheeling**	–
Julius Meinl | **Lakeview**	21
Uncommon Grnd. | **Wrigleyville**	21

COFFEE SHOPS/DINERS
Chicago Diner | **Lakeview**	19
NEW Depot Diner | **Far W**	–
Ed Debevic's | **multi. loc.**	14
Eleven City Diner | **S Loop**	–
Glenn's Diner | **Ravenswood**	–
Lou Mitchell's | **multi. loc.**	22
Z Manny's | **multi. loc.**	23
Milk & Honey | **Wicker Pk**	21
Nookies | **multi. loc.**	19
Orange | **multi. loc.**	23
Z Original Pancake | **multi. loc.**	23
Tempo | **Gold Coast**	19

COLOMBIAN
La Fonda | **Andersonville**	19
Las Tablas | **multi. loc.**	21

CONTINENTAL
Café la Cave | **Des Plaines**	24
Le P'tit Paris | **Streeterville**	22
Z Lobby | **River N**	23

COSTA RICAN
Irazu | **Bucktown**	22
NEW Palmito | **Lakeview**	–

CREOLE
Z Heaven on Seven | **multi. loc.**	21
Pappadeaux Sea. | **multi. loc.**	20

CUBAN
Cafe Bolero | **Bucktown**	21
Cafe 28 | **Lakeview**	23
NEW Habana Libre | **W Town**	–
Miramar | **Highwood**	19

DELIS
Bagel | **multi. loc.**	18
Cold Comfort | **Bucktown**	22
Eleven City Diner | **S Loop**	–
Z Manny's | **multi. loc.**	23

ECLECTIC
Aria | **Loop**	23
NEW BB's | **River N**	–
NEW Billy Berk's | **Skokie**	–
Bite Cafe | **Ukrainian Vill**	23
CHIC Cafe | **River N**	20
Chinoiserie | **Wilmette**	20
Deleece | **Wrigleyville**	21
Di Pescara | **Northbrook**	–
Eatzi's | **Lincoln Pk**	18
NEW Erik's | **Highwood**	–
NEW Flatwater | **River N**	–
Flight | **Glenview**	19
foodlife | **Streeterville**	16
NEW Ginger Asian | **Orland Pk**	–
Grand Lux | **River N**	20
Gulliver's Pizza | **Rogers Pk**	17

NEW Hamburger Mary's | **Andersonville**	–
Heartland Cafe | **Rogers Pk**	16
NEW Hunter's | **St. Charles**	–
Jane's | **Bucktown**	21
Kit Kat Lounge | **Wrigleyville**	15
Kitsch'n | **multi. loc.**	17
Lula | **Logan Sq**	25
Mj2 Bistro | **Park Ridge**	–
☑ Moto | **Mkt Dist**	25
Narcisse | **River N**	20
NEW Nosh | **Geneva**	–
Orange | **multi. loc.**	23
Saltaus | **Mkt Dist**	19
Sidebar Grille | **Loop**	–
Slice of Life | **Skokie**	13
Tasting Room | **Mkt Dist**	18
Think Café | **Bucktown**	24
NEW Treat | **Humboldt Pk**	–
Tweet | **Uptown**	21
Twist | **Lakeview**	22
Uncommon Grnd. | **Wrigleyville**	21
Victory's Banner | **Roscoe Vill**	23
Vive La Crepe | **Evanston**	20
Webster Wine | **Lincoln Pk**	17
Zest | **Streeterville**	20

ETHIOPIAN

Ethiopian Diamond | **Edgewater**	24
Mama Desta's | **Lakeview**	18

FILIPINO

Coobah | **Lakeview**	19

FONDUE

Geja's Cafe | **Lincoln Pk**	21
Melting Pot | **multi. loc.**	21

FRENCH

Cafe Matou | **Bucktown**	22
NEW Convito | **Wilmette**	–
Froggy's French | **Highwood**	22
La Fette | **Old Town**	–
la petite folie | **Hyde Pk**	24
Le P'tit Paris | **Streeterville**	22
Le Vichyssois | **Lakemoor**	24

FRENCH (BISTRO)

☑ Barrington Bistro | **Barrington**	27
☑ Bin 36/Bin Wine | **multi. loc.**	20
Bistro Campagne | **Lincoln Sq**	23
Bistro Kirkou | **Lake Zurich**	22
NEW Bistro Monet | **Glen Ellyn**	–
Bistro 110 | **Gold Coast**	20
Bistrot Margot | **Old Town**	21
Bistrot Zinc | **Gold Coast**	20
Café Bernard | **Lincoln Pk**	21
Cafe Central | **Highland Pk**	23
Café le Coq | **Oak Pk**	23
Cafe Pyrenees | **Libertyville**	21
Chez Joël | **Little Italy**	22
NEW Côtes/Rhône | **Edgewater**	–
Cyrano's Bistrot | **River N**	20
D & J Bistro | **Lake Zurich**	25
Hemmingway's | **Oak Pk**	21
Jacky's Bistro | **Evanston**	23
KiKi's Bistro | **River N**	23
NEW Koda | **Far S Side**	–
La Crêperie | **Lakeview**	20
NEW La Petite Amelia | **Evanston**	–
La Sardine | **W Loop**	23
La Tache | **Andersonville**	21
Le Bouchon | **Bucktown**	22
Marché | **Mkt Dist**	20
Miramar | **Highwood**	19
☑ Mon Ami Gabi | **multi. loc.**	22
Pierrot Gourmet | **River N**	21
Retro Bistro | **Mt. Prospect**	25
Shallots Bistro | **Skokie**	21
socca | **Lakeview**	21

FRENCH (BRASSERIE)

☑ Brasserie Jo | **River N**	22

FRENCH (NEW)

☑ Atwater's | **Geneva**	21
☑ Avenues | **River N**	26
Café/Architectes | **Gold Coast**	22
☑ Carlos' | **Highland Pk**	29
CHIC Cafe | **River N**	20

copperblue | **Streeterville**	–
Dining Rm./Kendall | **Near W**	23
Dorado | **Lincoln Sq**	23
🔲 Everest | **Loop**	27
🔲 Gabriel's | **Highwood**	26
Jilly's Cafe | **Evanston**	23
🔲 Kevin | **River N**	26
L'anne | **Wheaton**	20
🔲 Le Français | **Wheeling**	28
🔲 Le Lan | **River N**	26
🔲 Les Nomades | **Streeterville**	28
🔲 Le Titi/Paris | **Arlington Hts**	26
Michael | **Winnetka**	25
Mimosa | **Highland Pk**	23
🔲 NoMI | **Gold Coast**	26
🔲 Oceanique | **Evanston**	27
🔲 one sixtyblue | **Mkt Dist**	25
🔲 Tallgrass | **Lockport**	28
🔲 Tru | **Streeterville**	28
Vive La Crepe | **Evanston**	20
Yoshi's Café | **Lakeview**	23

GERMAN

Berghoff | **multi. loc.**	–
Edelweiss | **Norridge**	21
Glunz Bavarian | **Lincoln Sq**	19
Mirabell | **NW Side**	20

GREEK

Artopolis | **Greektown**	21
Athena | **Greektown**	19
Costa's | **multi. loc.**	21
Greek Islands | **multi. loc.**	21
NEW 9 Muses | **Greektown**	–
OPA Estiatorio | **Vernon Hills**	19
Parthenon | **Greektown**	20
Pegasus | **multi. loc.**	22
🔲 Roditys | **Greektown**	22
Santorini | **Greektown**	21
Venus | **Greektown**	19

HAMBURGERS

Billy Goat Tav. | **multi. loc.**	15
Boston Blackie's | **multi. loc.**	19
Ed Debevic's | **multi. loc.**	14

NEW fRedhots | **Glenview**	–
Goose Is. Brewing | **multi. loc.**	16
Hackney's | **multi. loc.**	18
NEW Hamburger Mary's | **Andersonville**	–
NEW Hop Häus | **River N**	–
NEW Patty Burger | **Loop**	–
Pete Miller | **multi. loc.**	21
P.J. Clarke's | **multi. loc.**	17
Poag Mahone's | **Loop**	17
Twisted Spoke | **multi. loc.**	18
Wiener's Circle | **Lincoln Pk**	20

HAWAII REGIONAL

Roy's | **River N**	24

HOT DOGS

Al's #1 Beef | **multi. loc.**	22
NEW fRedhots | **Glenview**	–
Gold Coast Dogs | **multi. loc.**	19
🔲 Hot Doug's | **NW Side**	25
🔲 Superdawg | **multi. loc.**	22
Wiener's Circle | **Lincoln Pk**	20

INDIAN

Essence of India | **Lincoln Sq**	21
Gaylord Indian | **multi. loc.**	22
Hema's Kitchen | **multi. loc.**	20
🔲 India House | **multi. loc.**	23
Indian Garden | **multi. loc.**	22
Klay Oven | **River N**	20
NEW Marigold | **Uptown**	–
Mt. Everest | **Evanston**	21
Mysore Woodland | **multi. loc.**	17
NEW Radhuni | **Lakeview**	–
Raj Darbar | **Lincoln Pk**	20
Tiffin | **W Rogers Pk**	22
Udupi Palace | **multi. loc.**	23
Vermilion | **River N**	21
Viceroy of India | **multi. loc.**	20

IRISH

Chief O'Neill's | **NW Side**	18
Grace O'Malley's | **S Loop**	17
Irish Oak | **Wrigleyville**	19
Mrs. Murphy | **Lakeview**	21

ISRAELI

Hashalom | **NW Side**	-
Old Jerusalem | **Old Town**	19

ITALIAN

(N=Northern; S=Southern)

NEW Adesso | **Lakeview**	-
NEW Amira | **Streeterville**	-
Angelina | S | **Wrigleyville**	20
Anna Maria | **Uptown**	19
NEW Anteprima | **Andersonville**	-
Antico Posto | **Oak Brook**	23
a tavola | N | **Ukrainian Vill**	23
Aurelio's Pizza | **multi. loc.**	22
NEW Baccalà | N | **Wicker Pk**	-
Bacchanalia | N | **SW Side**	23
Balagio | **Homewood**	22
Ballo | **River N**	19
NEW Barcello's | **Wicker Pk**	-
Basil Leaf | N | **Lincoln Pk**	21
Bella Bacino | **multi. loc.**	21
Bella Notte | S | **Near W**	23
Bruna's | **SW Side**	23
Buona Terra | N | **Logan Sq**	24
NEW Café Bionda | **S Loop**	-
Z Café Spiaggia | **Gold Coast**	24
Caliterra | N | **Streeterville**	23
Campagnola | **Evanston**	23
NEW Carlos & Carlos | N | **Arlington Hts**	-
Carlucci | N | **multi. loc.**	19
Carmine's | **Gold Coast**	21
NEW Chicago Pizza Co. | **Rolling Meadows**	-
Club Lago | N | **River N**	17
Club Lucky | S | **Bucktown**	20
Coco Pazzo | N | **River N**	24
Coco Pazzo | N | **Streeterville**	22
NEW Convito | **Wilmette**	-
Dave's Italian | S | **Evanston**	17
Del Rio | N | **Highwood**	18
Dinotto | **Old Town**	20
Di Pescara | **Northbrook**	-
EJ's Place | N | **Skokie**	19

Enoteca Piattini | S | **Lincoln Pk**	21
NEW Erba | N | **Lincoln Sq**	-
Erie Cafe | **River N**	23
Extra Virgin | **Mkt Dist**	19
Filippo's | **Lincoln Pk**	20
NEW Fiorentino's | S | **Lakeview**	-
Follia | N | **Mkt Dist**	22
NEW Fornetto & Mei's | **S Loop**	-
Fornetto Mei | N | **Gold Coast**	19
Z Francesca's | **multi. loc.**	23
Francesco's | S | **Northbrook**	24
NEW Frasca Pizzeria | **Lakeview**	-
Z Gabriel's | **Highwood**	26
Gene & Georgetti | **River N**	23
Gio | N | **Evanston**	19
Gioco | N | **S Loop**	21
Grotto | **Gold Coast**	18
NEW Gruppo/Amici | **Rogers Pk**	-
Harry Caray's | **multi. loc.**	19
NEW Il Covo | **Bucktown**	-
Il Mulino | **Gold Coast**	-
Jay's Amore | N | **W Loop**	-
La Bocca/Verità | **Lincoln Sq**	18
La Cantina | N | **Loop**	19
La Cucina/Donatella | **Rogers Pk**	22
La Donna | **Andersonville**	19
La Gondola | **Lincoln Pk**	-
La Piazza | **Forest Pk**	25
La Piazza | **Naperville**	-
La Scarola | **Near W**	23
La Strada | N | **multi. loc.**	19
La Vita | N | **Little Italy**	20
Leonardo's | N | **Andersonville**	23
Lucia | **Wicker Pk**	22
Luna Caprese | S | **Lincoln Pk**	25
Z Maggiano's | **multi. loc.**	20
Merlo | N | **multi. loc.**	23
Mia Francesca | **Lakeview**	23
Mimosa | **Highland Pk**	23
Next Door Bistro | **Northbrook**	21
NEW Osteria/Tramonto | **Wheeling**	-
Osteria Via Stato | **River N**	21

Pane Caldo | N | **Gold Coast**	24
Pasta Palazzo | **Lincoln Pk**	22
Philly G's | **Vernon Hills**	22
Phil Stefani's | **River N**	21
Piazza Bella | **Roscoe Vill**	21
Pizza Capri | **multi. loc.**	19
Pizza D.O.C. | **Lincoln Sq**	22
Pompei Bakery | **multi. loc.**	20
Quartino | **River N**	-
Riccardo Tratt. | N | **Lincoln Pk**	-
rist. we | N | **Loop**	18
RoSal's Kitchen | S | **Little Italy**	24
Rose Angelis | **Lincoln Pk**	22
🔲 Rosebud | **multi. loc.**	21
Rosebud Steak | **Gold Coast**	23
Sabatino's | **NW Side**	23
Salvatore's | N | **Lincoln Pk**	21
NEW Sapore/Napoli | **Lakeview**	-
Sapori Tratt. | **Lincoln Pk**	22
Scoozi! | **River N**	21
socca | **Lakeview**	21
NEW Spacca Napoli | **Ravenswood**	-
🔲 Spiaggia | **Gold Coast**	26
Tarantino's | **Lincoln Pk**	21
Terragusto Cafe | **Roscoe Vill**	-
312 Chicago | **Loop**	19
Timo | **Near W**	-
Timpano Chophse. | **Naperville**	-
Tony Rocco's | **River N**	-
Topo Gigio | **Old Town**	20
Tratt. D.O.C. | **Evanston**	-
Tratt. Gianni | **Lincoln Pk**	18
Tratt. No. 10 | **Loop**	23
Tratt. Roma | S | **Old Town**	19
NEW Tratt. 31 | **Near S Side**	-
Tucci Benucch | **Gold Coast**	18
Tufano's Tap | S | **Near S Side**	21
Tuscany | N | **multi. loc.**	22
🔲 Va Pensiero | **Evanston**	26
Via Carducci | S | **Lincoln Pk**	20
Village | **Loop**	19
Vinci | **Lincoln Pk**	22

Vito & Nick's | **Far S Side**	-
Vivere | **Loop**	21
Vivo | **Mkt Dist**	21
Volare | **Streeterville**	23
Zia's Tratt. | **Edison Pk**	22

JAPANESE
(* sushi specialist)

🔲 Agami* | **Uptown**	26
Akai Hana* | **Wilmette**	21
Aki Sushi* | **Wicker Pk**	-
Benihana* | **multi. loc.**	19
NEW Blu Coral* | **multi. loc.**	-
Bluefin* | **Bucktown**	21
Bob San* | **Wicker Pk**	23
Chens* | **Wrigleyville**	23
Chiyo* | **Albany Pk**	-
Coast Sushi* | **Bucktown**	23
Dee's* | **Lincoln Pk**	19
Hachi's Kitchen* | **Logan Sq**	-
Heat* | **Old Town**	25
Indie Cafe* | **Edgewater**	19
Itto Sushi* | **Lincoln Pk**	22
Izumi Sushi* | **Mkt Dist**	23
NEW Jai Yen* | **Lakeview**	-
🔲 Japonais* | **Near W**	24
Kamehachi* | **multi. loc.**	22
NEW Kanok* | **Lakeview**	-
NEW Kansaku* | **Evanston**	-
Katsu* | **NW Side**	26
Kaze Sushi* | **Roscoe Vill**	24
Kizoku Sushi* | **River N**	25
Kohan* | **S Loop**	-
Koi* | **Evanston**	19
Kuni's* | **Evanston**	25
Kyoto* | **multi. loc.**	22
NEW Matsuri* | **Geneva**	-
Matsuya* | **Wrigleyville**	21
Matsu Yama* | **Lakeview**	22
Meiji* | **W Loop**	24
🔲 Mirai Sushi* | **Wicker Pk**	26
Mizu Yakitori* | **Old Town**	-
NEW Ninefish | **Evanston**	-
Oysy* | **multi. loc.**	21

RA Sushi*	**multi. loc.**	19
Ringo*	**Lincoln Pk**	22
Rise*	**Wrigleyville**	20
Ron of Japan*	**multi. loc.**	18
Sai Café*	**Lincoln Pk**	24
NEW Sakuma's*	**Streamwood**	-
Shine & Morida*	**Lincoln Pk**	20
Shiroi Hana*	**Lakeview**	18
Starfish*	**Mkt Dist**	23
Sushi Ai*	**Palatine**	-
Sushi Naniwa*	**River N**	21
Z SushiSamba rio*	**River N**	21
Z sushi wabi*	**Mkt Dist**	26
Swordfish*	**Batavia**	25
Takkatsu	**Arlington Hts**	-
NEW Tamarind*	**S Loop**	-
Tank Sushi*	**Lincoln Sq**	21
NEW Ta Tong*	**Lakeview**	-
NEW Tokyo 21*	**Lincoln Pk**	-
T-Spot Sushi*	**Lakeview**	-
Tsuki*	**Lincoln Pk**	22
Tsunami*	**Gold Coast**	20
NEW Wakamono*	**Lakeview**	-
Wildfish*	**multi. loc.**	25

JEWISH

Bagel	**multi. loc.**	18
Eleven City Diner	**S Loop**	-
Z Manny's	**multi. loc.**	23

KOREAN

(* barbecue specialist)

Jin Ju	**Andersonville**	22
Koryo	**Lakeview**	19
San Soo Gab San*	**NW Side**	21
Woo Lae Oak*	**Rolling Meadows**	19

KOSHER

Shallots Bistro	**Skokie**	21
Slice of Life	**Skokie**	13

LEBANESE

Fattoush	**Lincoln Pk**	23
Kan Zaman	**River N**	21
Maza	**Lincoln Pk**	23

MALAYSIAN

Penang	**Chinatown**	19

MEDITERRANEAN

NEW Amira	**Streeterville**	-
Andies	**multi. loc.**	18
Artopolis	**Greektown**	21
Z Avec	**W Loop**	25
Café/Architectes	**Gold Coast**	22
Café Suron	**Rogers Pk**	-
copperblue	**Streeterville**	-
Cousin's I.V.	**NW Side**	-
Extra Virgin	**Mkt Dist**	19
Z Isabella's	**Geneva**	26
Lucca's	**Lakeview**	19
Z Naha	**River N**	26
Z Pita Inn	**multi. loc.**	24
Scylla	**Bucktown**	25
Shallots Bistro	**Skokie**	21
Z Tizi Melloul	**River N**	21
Turquoise	**Roscoe Vill**	21
Venus	**Greektown**	19
Wave	**Streeterville**	20

MEXICAN

Adobo Grill	**multi. loc.**	21
Brioso	**Lincoln Sq**	19
Cafe 28	**Lakeview**	23
de cero	**Mkt Dist**	21
Don Juan's	**Edison Pk**	21
Dorado	**Lincoln Sq**	23
El Presidente	**Lincoln Pk**	14
Fonda del Mar	**Logan Sq**	-
Z Frontera Grill	**River N**	26
Hacienda Teca.	**Ukrainian Vill**	20
Hot Tamales	**Highland Pk**	21
Irazu	**Bucktown**	22
NEW La Cantina Grill	**S Loop**	-
La Cazuela Mar.	**Rogers Pk**	-
Lalo's	**multi. loc.**	16
Las Palmas	**multi. loc.**	-
La Taberna Tapatia	**Roscoe Vill**	21
Lupita's	**Evanston**	21
Maiz	**Humboldt Pk**	25
NEW Mundial	**Near S Side**	-

Platiyo	**Lakeview**	20
Riques	**Uptown**	21
🅉 Salbute	**Hinsdale**	26
Salpicón	**Old Town**	24
San Gabriel	**Bannockburn**	20
NEW Sol de Mex.	**NW Side**	-
Tecalitlan	**W Town**	23
NEW Tepatulco	**Lincoln Pk**	-
🅉 Topolobampo	**River N**	27
NEW Xel-Há	**River N**	-
Zapatista	**S Loop**	20
NEW Zocalo	**River N**	-

MIDDLE EASTERN

Aladdin's Eatery	**Lincoln Pk**	17
NEW Alhambra	**Mkt Dist**	-
Andies	**multi. loc.**	18
Babylon Eatery	**Bucktown**	17
🅉 Pita Inn	**multi. loc.**	24
Reza's	**multi. loc.**	19
Samah	**Wrigleyville**	-
🅉 Tizi Melloul	**River N**	21

MOROCCAN

Hashalom	**NW Side**	-
Tagine	**Ravenswood**	-

NEPALESE

Mt. Everest	**Evanston**	21

NOODLE SHOPS

Joy Yee's Noodle	**multi. loc.**	21
Penny's Noodle	**multi. loc.**	19

NUEVO LATINO

🅉 Carnivale	**W Loop**	22
Coobah	**Lakeview**	19
Cuatro	**S Loop**	23
NEW DeLaCosta	**River N**	-
Mambo Grill	**River N**	19
Mas	**Wicker Pk**	22
Nacional 27	**River N**	22
Olé Olé	**Andersonville**	-
Rumba	**River N**	18
Sangria	**Lincoln Pk**	16
Vermilion	**River N**	21

PACIFIC NORTHWEST

Meritage Cafe	**Bucktown**	22

PAKISTANI

NEW Radhuni	**Lakeview**	-

PERSIAN

Café Suron	**Rogers Pk**	-
Noon-O-Kabab	**NW Side**	20

PIZZA

Art of Pizza	**Lakeview**	24
Aurelio's Pizza	**multi. loc.**	22
NEW Barcello's	**Wicker Pk**	-
Bella Bacino	**multi. loc.**	21
Bricks	**Lincoln Pk**	21
Chicago Pizza/Oven	**Lincoln Pk**	22
NEW Chicago Pizza Co.	**Rolling Meadows**	-
NEW Coalfire Pizza	**Near W**	-
NEW Crust	**Wicker Pk**	-
Edwardo's Pizza	**multi. loc.**	20
NEW Frasca Pizzeria	**Lakeview**	-
Gio	**Evanston**	19
🅉 Giordano's	**multi. loc.**	21
NEW Gruppo/Amici	**Rogers Pk**	-
Gulliver's Pizza	**Rogers Pk**	17
La Gondola	**Lincoln Pk**	-
🅉 Lou Malnati's	**multi. loc.**	24
My Pie Pizza	**multi. loc.**	21
Nancy's Orig.	**multi. loc.**	21
O'Famé	**Lincoln Pk**	17
Original Gino's	**multi. loc.**	22
Piece	**Bucktown**	22
Pizza Capri	**multi. loc.**	19
Pizza D.O.C.	**Lincoln Sq**	22
Pizzeria Uno/Due	**River N**	22
Pompei Bakery	**multi. loc.**	20
NEW Sapore/Napoli	**Lakeview**	-
NEW Spacca Napoli	**Ravenswood**	-
Tratt. D.O.C.	**Evanston**	-
Vito & Nick's	**Far S Side**	-
Wolfgang Puck	**Evanston**	18

POLISH

Lutnia	**NW Side**	-

RUSSIAN

Russian Tea | Loop — 22

SANDWICHES

Al's #1 Beef | multi. loc. — 22
Bagel | multi. loc. — 18
Berghoff | multi. loc. — -
Cold Comfort | Bucktown — 22
Hannah's Bretzel | Loop — -
Mr. Beef | River N — 23
Potbelly Sandwich | multi. loc. — 20

SCANDINAVIAN

Tre Kronor | NW Side — 24

SCOTTISH

Duke of Perth | Lakeview — 18

SEAFOOD

Z Avenues | River N — 26
Z Bob Chinn's Crab | Wheeling — 23
Canoe Club | Orland Pk — 19
Cape Cod Rm. | Streeterville — 21
Catch 35 | multi. loc. — 23
Chinn's Fishery | Lisle — 22
Davis St. Fish | Evanston — 19
Devon Seafood | River N — -
Don Roth's | Wheeling — 20
Dover Straits | multi. loc. — 18
Drake Bros.' | Streeterville — 17
Emperor's Choice | Chinatown — 23
Erie Cafe | River N — 23
Fonda del Mar | Logan Sq — -
Froggy's French | Highwood — 22
Fulton's | River N — 20
Glenn's Diner | Ravenswood — -
Half Shell | Lakeview — 22
Harbour House | Winnetka — -
Z Hugo's Frog/Fish | multi. loc. — 24
Z Joe's Sea/Steak | River N — 26
Keefer's | River N — 23
NEW KS Seafood | Chinatown — -
La Cantina | Loop — 19
La Cazuela Mar. | Rogers Pk — -
Z Lobby | River N — 23

McCormick/Schmick | multi. loc. — 21
Mitchell's Fish Mkt. | Glenview — -
Nick's Fishmkt. | multi. loc. — 24
Z Nine | W Loop — 22
Z Oceanique | Evanston — 27
Pacific Blue | Glen Ellyn — 25
Pappadeaux Sea. | multi. loc. — 20
Parkers' | Downers Grove — 21
Pete Miller | multi. loc. — 21
Riva | multi. loc. — 18
NEW Sam & Harry's | — -
Schaumburg
Santorini | Greektown — 21
Scylla | Bucktown — 25
Z Shaw's Crab | multi. loc. — 23
Shula's Steak | multi. loc. — 20
Silver Seafood | Uptown — 22
Z Spring | Wicker Pk — 27
Tin Fish | multi. loc. — 22
NEW Tramonto's | Wheeling — -

SMALL PLATES

(See also Spanish tapas specialist)
Z Avec | Med. | W Loop — 25
BOKA | Amer. | Lincoln Pk — 23
Enoteca Piattini | Italian | — 21
Lincoln Pk
Extra Virgin | Italian | Mkt Dist — 19
Fixture | Amer. | Lincoln Pk — -
Flight | Eclectic | Glenview — 19
NEW Graze | Amer. | River N — -
Z Green Zebra | Veg. | W Town — 25
La Taberna Tapatia | Mex. | — 21
Roscoe Vill
Maza | Lebanese | Lincoln Pk — 23
NEW Pops/Champ. | Amer. | — -
River N
Quartino | Italian | River N — -
Sangria | Nuevo Latino | Lincoln Pk — 16
Tango | Argent. | Naperville — 20
Volo | Amer. | Roscoe Vill — 20
Wave | Med. | Streeterville — 20
Webster Wine | Eclectic | — 17
Lincoln Pk
NEW Zocalo | Mex. | River N — -

190   subscribe to zagat.com

SOUL FOOD

Army & Lou's | Far S Side	19

SOUTH AMERICAN

La Peña | NW Side	20
Rinconcito Sudamer. | Bucktown	17
☑ SushiSamba rio | River N	21

SOUTHERN

Army & Lou's | Far S Side	19
NEW Bourbon | Lakeview	–
Dixie Kitchen | multi. loc.	19
☑ Fat Willy's | Logan Sq	23
House of Blues | River N	16
Wishbone | multi. loc.	21

SOUTHWESTERN

Bandera | Streeterville	20
Flo | W Town	22
NEW Taos | Roscoe Vill	–

SPANISH

(* tapas specialist)

Arco/Cuchilleros* | Lakeview	19
NEW Azucar* | Logan Sq	–
NEW Bravo Tapas* | Wicker Pk	–
Cafe Ba-Ba-Reeba!* | Lincoln Pk	22
☑ Café Iberico* | River N	23
Emilio's Tapas* | multi. loc.	21
1492 Tapas* | River N	19
Haro* | SW Side	–
La Tasca* | Arlington Hts	23
☑ Mesón Sabika* | multi. loc.	23
People Lounge* | Wicker Pk	–
Tapas Barcelona* | Evanston	20
Twist* | Lakeview	22

STEAKHOUSES

Avenue M | Near W	–
Benihana | multi. loc.	19
Bogart's Charhse. | multi. loc.	21
Brazzaz | River N	23
NEW Brockway Chop | Palatine	–
Capital Grille | multi. loc.	24
Carmichael Steak | W Loop	22

☑ Chicago Chop | River N	25
David Burke Prime | River N	22
Don Roth's | Wheeling	20
Drake Bros.' | Streeterville	17
EJ's Place | Skokie	19
El Nandu | Logan Sq	21
Entourage | Schaumburg	–
Erie Cafe | River N	23
☑ Five O'Clock | Fox Riv. Grove	26
Fleming's Steak | Lincolnshire	–
☑ Fogo de Chão | River N	24
Fulton's | River N	20
Gene & Georgetti | River N	23
☑ Gibsons | multi. loc.	25
Grill on Alley | Streeterville	18
Grillroom | multi. loc.	17
Grotto | Gold Coast	18
Harry Caray's | multi. loc.	19
☑ Hugo's Frog/Fish | multi. loc.	24
☑ Joe's Sea/Steak | River N	26
Keefer's | River N	23
Kinzie Chophse. | River N	20
Las Tablas | multi. loc.	21
Lawry's Prime Rib | River N	24
Magnum's Steak | multi. loc.	23
Mike Ditka's | Gold Coast	20
Montarra | Algonquin	22
☑ Morton's Steak | multi. loc.	26
Myron & Phil's | Lincolnwood	21
☑ Nine | W Loop	22
Palm, The | multi. loc.	23
Pete Miller | multi. loc.	21
Phil Stefani's | River N	21
rist. we | Loop	18
Ron of Japan | multi. loc.	18
NEW Room 21 | S Loop	–
Rosebud Steak | Gold Coast	23
☑ Ruth's Chris | multi. loc.	24
Sabor do Brasil | Orland Pk	–
Sage Grille | Highwood	–
Saloon Steak | Streeterville	23
NEW Sam & Harry's | Schaumburg	–
NEW Shor | S Loop	–

Shula's Steak	**multi. loc.**	20
Smith & Wollensky	**River N**	22
Stetson's Chop Hse.	**Loop**	23
Sullivan's Steak	**multi. loc.**	23
Tango	**Naperville**	20
Z Tango Sur	**Wrigleyville**	24
Tavern	**Libertyville**	23
Tavern on Rush	**Gold Coast**	19
Texas de Brazil	**Schaumburg**	–
Timpano Chophse.	**Naperville**	–
NEW Tramonto's	**Wheeling**	–
Z Wildfire	**multi. loc.**	23

SWEDISH

Ann Sather	**multi. loc.**	19

THAI

Amarind's	**Far W**	25
NEW Amarit	**Printer's Row**	–
Z Arun's	**NW Side**	28
Indie Cafe	**Edgewater**	19
P.S. Bangkok	**multi. loc.**	20
Ruby of Siam	**multi. loc.**	20
Siam Café	**Uptown**	–
Spoon Thai	**Lincoln Sq**	22
Star of Siam	**River N**	20
NEW Sura	**Lakeview**	–
NEW Ta Tong	**Lakeview**	–
Thai Classic	**Lakeview**	23
Thai Pastry	**Uptown**	22
Vong's	**River N**	21

TURKISH

A La Turka	**Lakeview**	20
Turquoise	**Roscoe Vill**	21

VEGETARIAN

(* vegan)

Aladdin's Eatery	**Lincoln Pk**	17
Alice & Friends*	**Uptown**	20
Andies	**multi. loc.**	18
Blind Faith	**Evanston**	19
Chicago Diner	**Lakeview**	19
Cousin's I.V.*	**NW Side**	–
NEW Dodo*	**Ukrainian Vill**	–
Ethiopian Diamond	**Edgewater**	24
Z Green Zebra	**W Town**	25
Heartland Cafe	**Rogers Pk**	16
Hema's Kitchen	**multi. loc.**	20
Kabul House	**Skokie**	20
Karyn's*	**River N**	19
Karyn's*	**Lincoln Pk**	17
Lake Side Café*	**Rogers Pk**	–
Lula*	**Logan Sq**	25
Mama Desta's	**Lakeview**	18
Maza	**Lincoln Pk**	23
Mysore Woodland	**multi. loc.**	17
Reza's	**multi. loc.**	19
Slice of Life	**Skokie**	13
Tiffin	**W Rogers Pk**	22
Udupi Palace	**multi. loc.**	23
Victory's Banner	**Roscoe Vill**	23

VIETNAMESE

Hai Yen	**multi. loc.**	22
L'anne	**Wheaton**	20
Z Le Colonial	**Gold Coast**	23
Z Le Lan	**River N**	26
NEW Simply It	**Lincoln Pk**	–
NEW Viet Bistro	**Rogers Pk**	–

Locations

Includes restaurant names, cuisines and Food ratings. ☑ indicates places with the highest ratings, popularity and importance.

Downtown

LOOP

Aria	*Amer./Eclectic*	23
☑ Atwood Cafe	*Amer.*	21
Aurelio's Pizza	*Pizza*	22
Berghoff	*German*	–
Billy Goat Tav.	*Amer.*	15
Boston Blackie's	*Hamburgers*	19
Catch 35	*Seafood*	23
Cereality	*Amer.*	16
China Grill	*Asian*	20
☑ Everest	*French*	27
☑ Giordano's	*Pizza*	21
Gold Coast Dogs	*Hot Dogs*	19
Grillroom	*Steak*	17
Hannah's Bretzel	*Sandwiches*	–
☑ Heaven on Seven	*Cajun/Creole*	21
La Cantina	*Italian/Seafood*	19
La Strada	*Italian*	19
McCormick/Schmick	*Seafood*	21
NEW Midtown Kitchen	*Amer.*	–
Miller's Pub	*Pub*	17
☑ Morton's Steak	*Steak*	26
Nick's Fishmkt.	*Seafood*	24
One North	*Amer.*	18
Palm, The	*Steak*	23
Park Grill	*Amer.*	19
NEW Patty Burger	*Hamburgers*	–
Petterino's	*Amer.*	19
Poag Mahone's	*Pub*	17
Potbelly Sandwich	*Sandwiches*	20
Rhapsody	*Amer.*	21
rist. we	*Italian*	18
☑ Rosebud	*Italian*	21
Russian Tea	*Russian*	22
Sidebar Grille	*Eclectic*	–
South Water Kitchen	*Amer.*	17
Stetson's Chop Hse.	*Steak*	23
312 Chicago	*Amer./Italian*	19

NEW Townhouse	*Amer.*	–
Tratt. No. 10	*Italian*	23
Village	*Italian*	19
Vivere	*Italian*	21

RIVER NORTH

NEW Aigre Doux	*Amer.*	–
Allen's	*Amer.*	24
Al's #1 Beef	*Sandwiches*	22
☑ Avenues	*French/Seafood*	26
Ballo	*Italian*	19
Bar Louie	*Amer.*	15
NEW BB's	*Eclectic*	–
Ben Pao	*Chinese*	21
Big Bowl	*Asian*	18
Bijan's	*Amer.*	19
Billy Goat Tav.	*Amer.*	15
☑ Bin 36/Bin Wine	*Amer./French*	20
Blue Water	*Amer.*	22
☑ Brasserie Jo	*French*	22
Brazzaz	*Brazilian/Steak*	23
☑ Café Iberico	*Spanish*	23
Carson's Ribs	*BBQ*	20
☑ Chicago Chop	*Steak*	25
CHIC Cafe	*Eclectic/French*	20
Club Lago	*Italian*	17
Coco Pazzo	*Italian*	24
☑ Crofton on Wells	*Amer.*	26
Cyrano's Bistrot	*French*	20
David Burke Prime	*Steak*	22
NEW DeLaCosta	*Nuevo Latino*	–
Devon Seafood	*Seafood*	–
Ed Debevic's	*Diner*	14
Erie Cafe	*Italian/Steak*	23
NEW Flatwater	*Eclectic*	–
☑ Fogo de Chão	*Brazilian/Steak*	24
1492 Tapas	*Spanish*	19
☑ Frontera Grill	*Mex.*	26
Fulton's	*Seafood/Steak*	20
Gaylord Indian	*Indian*	22

Gene & Georgetti	*Steak*	23
☑ Giordano's	*Pizza*	21
Grand Lux	*Eclectic*	20
NEW Graze	*Amer.*	-
Green Door Tav.	*Amer.*	14
Hard Rock Cafe	*Amer.*	13
Harry Caray's	*Italian/Steak*	19
☑ Heaven on Seven	*Cajun/Creole*	21
NEW Hop Häus	*Hamburgers*	-
House of Blues	*Southern*	16
☑ India House	*Indian*	23
☑ Joe's Sea/Steak	*Seafood/Steak*	26
Kamehachi	*Jap.*	22
Kan Zaman	*Lebanese*	21
Karyn's	*Veg.*	19
Keefer's	*Steak*	23
☑ Kevin	*Asian/French*	26
KiKi's Bistro	*French*	23
Kinzie Chophse.	*Steak*	20
Kitsch'n	*Eclectic*	17
Kizoku Sushi	*Jap.*	25
Klay Oven	*Indian*	20
Lalo's	*Mex.*	16
Lawry's Prime Rib	*Steak*	24
☑ Le Lan	*French/Viet.*	26
☑ Lobby	*Continental/Seafood*	23
☑ Lou Malnati's	*Pizza*	24
☑ Maggiano's	*Italian*	20
Mambo Grill	*Nuevo Latino*	19
Melting Pot	*Fondue*	21
☑ mk	*Amer.*	26
Mr. Beef	*Sandwiches*	23
Nacional 27	*Nuevo Latino*	22
☑ Naha	*Amer.*	26
Narcisse	*Eclectic*	20
Original Gino's	*Pizza*	22
Osteria Via Stato	*Italian*	21
Oysy	*Jap.*	21
☑ P.F. Chang's	*Chinese*	20
Phil Stefani's	*Italian/Steak*	21
Pierrot Gourmet	*French*	21
Pizzeria Uno/Due	*Pizza*	22
NEW Pops/Champ.	*Amer.*	-
Potbelly Sandwich	*Sandwiches*	20
Quartino	*Italian*	-
NEW Republic	*Asian*	-
Reza's	*Mideast.*	19
Rock Bottom	*Amer.*	16
Rockit B&G	*Amer.*	19
☑ Rosebud	*Italian*	21
Roy's	*Hawaiian*	24
Rumba	*Nuevo Latino*	18
☑ Ruth's Chris	*Steak*	24
Scoozi!	*Italian*	21
☑ Shanghai Terr.	*Asian*	24
☑ Shaw's Crab	*Seafood*	23
Smith & Wollensky	*Steak*	22
Star of Siam	*Thai*	20
Sullivan's Steak	*Steak*	23
Sushi Naniwa	*Jap.*	21
☑ SushiSamba rio	*Jap./S Amer.*	21
☑ Tizi Melloul	*Med./Mideast.*	21
Tony Rocco's	*Italian*	-
☑ Topolobampo	*Mex.*	27
Vermilion	*Indian/Nuevo Latino*	21
Vong's	*Thai*	21
Weber Grill	*BBQ*	19
☑ Wildfire	*Steak*	23
NEW Xel-Há	*Mex.*	-
☑ Zealous	*Amer.*	24
NEW Zocalo	*Mex.*	-

STREETERVILLE

NEW Amira	*Italian/Med.*	-
Bandera	*Amer.*	20
Billy Goat Tav.	*Amer.*	15
Boston Blackie's	*Hamburgers*	19
Caliterra	*Amer./Italian*	23
Cape Cod Rm.	*Seafood*	21
Capital Grille	*Steak*	24
☑ Cheesecake Fac.	*Amer.*	19
Cité	*Amer.*	17
Coco Pazzo	*Italian*	22
copperblue	*French/Med.*	-
Drake Bros.'	*Seafood/Steak*	17
Emilio's Tapas	*Spanish*	21
foodlife	*Eclectic*	16
Grill on Alley	*Amer.*	18

Indian Garden	*Indian*	22
Kamehachi	*Jap.*	22
Le P'tit Paris	*Continental/French*	22
Ⓩ Les Nomades	*French*	28
Mity Nice Grill	*Amer.*	18
Mrs. Park's Tav.	*Amer.*	17
Original Gino's	*Pizza*	22
Ⓩ Original Pancake	*Amer.*	23
P.J. Clarke's	*Amer.*	17
Puck's at MCA	*Amer.*	20
Ritz-Carlton Café	*Amer.*	-
Riva	*Seafood*	18
Ron of Japan	*Jap./Steak*	18
Saloon Steak	*Steak*	23
Sayat Nova	*Armenian*	20
Shula's Steak	*Steak*	20
Ⓩ Signature Rm.	*Amer.*	18
Ⓩ Tru	*French*	28
Viand Bar	*Amer.*	23
Volare	*Italian*	23
Wave	*Med.*	20
Zest	*Amer./Eclectic*	20

City North

ANDERSONVILLE/ EDGEWATER

Andies	*Mideast.*	18
Ann Sather	*Amer./Swedish*	19
NEW Anteprima	*Italian*	-
NEW Broadway Cellars	*Amer.*	-
NEW Côtes/Rhône	*French*	-
Ethiopian Diamond	*Ethiopian*	24
Ⓩ Francesca's	*Italian*	23
NEW Hamburger Mary's	*Hamburgers*	-
NEW Icosium Kafe	*African*	-
Indie Cafe	*Jap./Thai*	19
Jin Ju	*Korean*	22
La Donna	*Italian*	19
La Fonda	*Colombian*	19
La Tache	*French*	21
Leonardo's	*Italian*	23
M. Henry	*Amer.*	24
Olé Olé	*Nuevo Latino*	-

Reza's	*Mideast.*	19
Tomboy	*Amer.*	21

DEPAUL/LINCOLN PARK/ SHEFFIELD

Aladdin's Eatery	*Mideast.*	17
Ⓩ Alinea	*Amer.*	28
Basil Leaf	*Italian*	21
Bella Bacino	*Pizza*	21
BOKA	*Amer.*	23
Bricks	*Pizza*	21
Cafe Ba-Ba-Reeba!	*Spanish*	22
Café Bernard	*French*	21
Ⓩ Charlie Trotter's	*Amer.*	27
Chicago Pizza/Oven	*Pizza*	22
Dee's	*Asian*	19
Eatzi's	*Eclectic*	18
Edwardo's Pizza	*Pizza*	20
El Presidente	*Mex.*	14
Emilio's Tapas	*Spanish*	21
Enoteca Piattini	*Italian*	21
Fattoush	*Lebanese*	23
Filippo's	*Italian*	20
Fixture	*Amer.*	-
Geja's Cafe	*Fondue*	21
Goose Is. Brewing	*Pub*	16
Green Dolphin St.	*Amer.*	19
Hai Yen	*Chinese/Viet.*	22
Hema's Kitchen	*Indian*	20
Itto Sushi	*Jap.*	22
J. Alexander's	*Amer.*	20
John's Place	*Amer.*	18
Karyn's	*Veg.*	17
Kyoto	*Jap.*	22
La Gondola	*Italian*	-
Lalo's	*Mex.*	16
Landmark	*Amer.*	21
Las Tablas	*Colombian/Steak*	21
Ⓩ Lou Malnati's	*Pizza*	24
Luna Caprese	*Italian*	25
Maza	*Mideast.*	23
Merlo	*Italian*	23
NEW Minnies	*Amer.*	-
Ⓩ Mon Ami Gabi	*French*	22

My Pie Pizza | *Pizza*	21
Nookies | *Diner*	19
☑ North Pond | *Amer.*	25
O'Famé | *Pizza*	17
Original Gino's | *Pizza*	22
☑ Original Pancake | *Amer.*	23
Pasta Palazzo | *Italian*	22
Penny's Noodle | *Asian*	19
Pizza Capri | *Pizza*	19
Pompei Bakery | *Italian*	20
Potbelly Sandwich | *Sandwiches*	20
P.S. Bangkok | *Thai*	20
Raj Darbar | *Indian*	20
Red Lion Pub | *British*	16
Riccardo Tratt. | *Italian*	-
Ringo | *Jap.*	22
R.J. Grunts | *Amer.*	19
Robinson's Ribs | *BBQ*	19
Rose Angelis | *Italian*	22
Sai Café | *Jap.*	24
Salvatore's | *Italian*	21
Sangria | *Nuevo Latino*	16
Sapori Tratt. | *Italian*	22
Schwa | *Amer.*	26
Shine & Morida | *Chinese/Jap.*	20
NEW Simply It | *Viet.*	-
Stanley's | *Amer.*	19
State | *Amer.*	-
Tarantino's | *Italian*	21
NEW Tepatulco | *Mex.*	-
Toast | *Amer.*	22
NEW Tokyo 21 | *Asian*	-
Tratt. Gianni | *Italian*	18
Tsuki | *Jap.*	22
Via Carducci | *Italian*	20
Vinci | *Italian*	22
Webster Wine | *Eclectic*	17
Wiener's Circle | *Hot Dogs*	20

GOLD COAST

American Girl | *Amer.*	12
Big Bowl | *Asian*	18
Bistro 110 | *French*	20
Bistrot Zinc | *French*	20
Café/Architectes | *French/Med.*	22
☑ Café Spiaggia | *Italian*	24
Carmine's | *Italian*	21
NEW Cru Cafe | *Amer.*	-
Edwardo's Pizza | *Pizza*	20
Fornetto Mei | *Chinese/Italian*	19
☑ Gibsons | *Steak*	25
Grotto | *Italian/Steak*	18
☑ Hugo's Frog/Fish | *Seafood*	24
Il Mulino | *Italian*	-
☑ Le Colonial | *Viet.*	23
LuxBar | *Amer.*	17
McCormick/Schmick | *Seafood*	21
Merlo | *Italian*	23
Mike Ditka's | *Steak*	20
☑ Morton's Steak | *Steak*	26
☑ NoMI | *French*	26
Oak Tree | *Amer.*	17
Pane Caldo | *Italian*	24
P.J. Clarke's | *Amer.*	17
☑ Pump Room | *Amer.*	21
RA Sushi | *Jap.*	19
☑ RL | *Amer.*	22
Rosebud Steak | *Italian/Steak*	23
☑ Seasons | *Amer.*	26
☑ Seasons Café | *Amer.*	25
☑ Spiaggia | *Italian*	26
Tavern on Rush | *Steak*	19
Tempo | *Diner*	19
Tsunami | *Jap.*	20
Tucci Benucch | *Italian*	18

LAKEVIEW/ WRIGLEYVILLE

NEW Adesso | *Italian*	-
A La Turka | *Turkish*	20
Angelina | *Italian*	20
Ann Sather | *Amer./Swedish*	19
Arco/Cuchilleros | *Spanish*	19
Art of Pizza | *Pizza*	24
Bagel | *Deli*	18
Bar Louie | *Amer.*	15
NEW Bourbon | *Southern*	-
Cafe 28 | *Cuban/Mex.*	23

Chens	*Chinese*	23
Chicago Diner	*Diner*	19
Coobah	*Filipino/Nuevo Latino*	19
NEW Cooper's	*Amer.*	–
NEW Cordis Bros.	*Amer.*	–
Deleece	*Eclectic*	21
Duke of Perth	*Pub*	18
erwin cafe	*Amer.*	23
NEW Fiorentino's	*Italian*	–
Flat Top Grill	*Asian*	19
NEW Frasca Pizzeria	*Pizza*	–
Z Giordano's	*Pizza*	21
Goose Is. Brewing	*Pub*	16
Half Shell	*Seafood*	22
HB	*Amer.*	22
Irish Oak	*Pub*	19
Jack's on Halsted	*Amer.*	21
NEW Jai Yen	*Jap.*	–
Joey's Brickhouse	*Amer.*	18
Julius Meinl	*Austrian*	21
NEW Kanok	*Jap.*	–
Kit Kat Lounge	*Eclectic*	15
Koryo	*Korean*	19
La Crêperie	*French*	20
Lucca's	*Amer./Med.*	19
Mama Desta's	*Ethiopian*	18
Matsuya	*Jap.*	21
Matsu Yama	*Jap.*	22
Mia Francesca	*Italian*	23
Mrs. Murphy	*Irish*	21
Nancy's Orig.	*Pizza*	21
Nookies	*Diner*	19
Orange	*Eclectic*	23
NEW Palmito	*Costa Rican*	–
Penny's Noodle	*Asian*	19
Pepper Lounge	*Amer.*	22
pingpong	*Asian*	21
Pizza Capri	*Pizza*	19
Platiyo	*Mex.*	20
Potbelly Sandwich	*Sandwiches*	20
P.S. Bangkok	*Thai*	20
NEW Radhuni	*Indian/Pakistani*	–
Rise	*Jap.*	20

Samah	*Mideast.*	–
NEW Sapore/Napoli	*Pizza*	–
Shiroi Hana	*Jap.*	18
socca	*French/Italian*	21
sola	*Amer.*	–
NEW Sura	*Thai*	–
Z Tango Sur	*Argent./Steak*	24
NEW Ta Tong	*Jap./Thai*	–
Thai Classic	*Thai*	23
T-Spot Sushi	*Jap.*	–
Tuscany	*Italian*	22
Twist	*Eclectic*	22
Twisted Spoke	*Pub*	18
Uncommon Grnd.	*Coffee*	21
NEW Wakamono	*Jap.*	–
Yoshi's Café	*Asian/French*	23

LINCOLN SQUARE/ UPTOWN

Z Agami	*Jap.*	26
Alice & Friends	*Asian*	20
Andies	*Mideast.*	18
Anna Maria	*Italian*	19
Bistro Campagne	*French*	23
Brioso	*Mex.*	19
Café Selmarie	*Amer.*	21
NEW Chalkboard	*Amer.*	–
Dorado	*French/Mex.*	23
NEW Erba	*Italian*	–
Essence of India	*Indian*	21
NEW Feed/Beast	*Amer.*	–
NEW Fiddlehead	*Amer.*	–
Glunz Bavarian	*Austrian/German*	19
Gold Coast Dogs	*Hot Dogs*	19
Hai Yen	*Chinese/Viet.*	22
La Bocca/Verità	*Italian*	18
Magnolia Cafe	*Amer.*	25
NEW Marigold	*Indian*	–
Pizza D.O.C.	*Pizza*	22
Riques	*Mex.*	21
Siam Café	*Thai*	–
Silver Seafood	*Chinese/Seafood*	22
Spoon Thai	*Thai*	22
Tank Sushi	*Jap.*	21

Thai Pastry | *Thai*	22
Tweet | *Eclectic*	21

OLD TOWN

Adobo Grill | *Mex.*	21
Bistrot Margot | *French*	21
Dinotto | *Italian*	20
Flat Top Grill | *Asian*	19
Heat | *Jap.*	25
Kamehachi | *Jap.*	22
La Fette | *Amer./French*	–
Mizu Yakitori | *Jap.*	–
Nookies | *Diner*	19
Old Jerusalem | *Israeli*	19
Salpicón | *Mex.*	24
Topo Gigio | *Italian*	20
Tratt. Roma | *Italian*	19
Twin Anchors | *BBQ*	22

ROGERS PARK/ WEST ROGERS PARK

Café Suron | *Med./Persian*	–
Gold Coast Dogs | *Hot Dogs*	19
NEW Gruppo/Amici | *Pizza*	–
Gulliver's Pizza | *Pizza*	17
Heartland Cafe | *Eclectic/Veg.*	16
Hema's Kitchen | *Indian*	20
Indian Garden | *Indian*	22
La Cazuela Mar. | *Mex./Seafood*	–
La Cucina/Donatella | *Italian*	22
Lake Side Café | *Veg.*	–
Mysore Woodland | *Indian*	17
Tiffin | *Indian*	22
Udupi Palace | *Indian*	23
Viceroy of India | *Indian*	20
NEW Viet Bistro | *Viet.*	–

City Northwest

BUCKTOWN

Babylon Eatery | *Mideast.*	17
Bar Louie | *Amer.*	15
Bluefin | *Jap.*	21
Café Absinthe | *Amer.*	23
Cafe Bolero | *Cuban*	21
Cafe Matou | *French*	22

Club Lucky | *Italian*	20
Coast Sushi | *Jap.*	23
Cold Comfort | *Sandwiches*	22
Feast | *Amer.*	18
NEW Honey 1 BBQ | *BBQ*	–
Hot Chocolate | *Amer.*	23
NEW Il Covo | *Italian*	–
Irazu | *Costa Rican*	22
Jane's | *Amer./Eclectic*	21
Las Palmas | *Mex.*	–
Le Bouchon | *French*	22
Margie's Candies | *Amer.*	23
Meritage Cafe | *Amer.*	22
My Pie Pizza | *Pizza*	21
Piece | *Pizza*	22
Rinconcito Sudamer. | *S Amer.*	17
Scylla | *Seafood*	25
Silver Cloud B&G | *Amer.*	18
Think Café | *Amer./Eclectic*	24
Toast | *Amer.*	22
NEW ZKF | *Amer.*	–

EDISON PARK/ O'HARE AREA

Berghoff | *German*	–
Big Bowl | *Asian*	18
Billy Goat Tav. | *Amer.*	15
Café la Cave | *Continental*	24
Carlucci | *Italian*	19
Z Cheesecake Fac. | *Amer.*	19
David's Bistro | *Amer.*	24
Don Juan's | *Mex.*	21
Fleming's Steak | *Steak*	–
Z Gibsons | *Steak*	25
Z Giordano's | *Pizza*	21
Gold Coast Dogs | *Hot Dogs*	19
Harry Caray's | *Italian/Steak*	19
Kamehachi | *Jap.*	22
Lalo's | *Mex.*	16
Lou Mitchell's | *Diner*	22
Z Morton's Steak | *Steak*	26
Nick's Fishmkt. | *Seafood*	24
Original Gino's | *Pizza*	22
Z Original Pancake | *Amer.*	23

Z Wildfire	*Steak*	23
Zia's Tratt.	*Italian*	22

HUMBOLDT PARK

Maiz	*Mex.*	25
NEW Treat	*Eclectic*	-

LOGAN SQUARE

NEW Azucar	*Spanish*	-
Buona Terra	*Italian*	24
El Nándu	*Argent.*	21
Z Fat Willy's	*BBQ/Southern*	23
Fonda del Mar	*Mex./Seafood*	-
Hachi's Kitchen	*Jap.*	-
Kuma's Corner	*Amer.*	-
Lula	*Eclectic*	25

NORTHWEST SIDE/ RAVENSWOOD

Z Arun's	*Thai*	28
Chief O'Neill's	*Pub*	18
Chiyo	*Jap.*	-
Cousin's I.V.	*Med.*	-
Gale St. Inn	*Amer.*	20
Z Giordano's	*Pizza*	21
Glenn's Diner	*Diner*	-
Hashalom	*Israeli/Moroccan*	-
Z Hot Doug's	*Hot Dogs*	25
Katsu	*Jap.*	26
La Peña	*S Amer.*	20
Las Tablas	*Colombian/Steak*	21
Lutnia	*Polish*	-
Margie's Candies	*Amer.*	23
Mirabell	*German*	20
Nancy's Orig.	*Pizza*	21
Noon-O-Kabab	*Persian*	20
NEW Over Easy	*Amer.*	-
Sabatino's	*Italian*	23
San Soo Gab San	*Korean*	21
NEW Smoque BBQ	*BBQ*	-
NEW Sol de Mex.	*Mex.*	-
NEW Spacca Napoli	*Pizza*	-
Z Superdawg	*Hot Dogs*	22
Tagine	*Moroccan*	-
Tre Kronor	*Scan.*	24

ROSCOE VILLAGE

Kaze Sushi	*Jap.*	24
Kitsch'n	*Eclectic*	17
La Taberna Tapatia	*Mex.*	21
Piazza Bella	*Italian*	21
NEW Taos	*SW*	-
Terragusto Cafe	*Italian*	-
Turquoise	*Turkish*	21
Victory's Banner	*Eclectic*	23
Volo	*Amer.*	20
Wishbone	*Southern*	21

WICKER PARK

Adobo Grill	*Mex.*	21
Aki Sushi	*Jap.*	-
NEW Baccalà	*Italian*	-
NEW Barcello's	*Italian/Pizza*	-
Z Bin 36/Bin Wine	*Amer./French*	20
NEW Blu Coral	*Jap.*	-
Bob San	*Jap.*	23
Bongo Room	*Amer.*	24
NEW Bravo Tapas	*Spanish*	-
NEW Crust	*Pizza*	-
Z Francesca's	*Italian*	23
Lucia	*Italian*	22
Mas	*Nuevo Latino*	22
Milk & Honey	*Amer.*	21
Z Mirai Sushi	*Jap.*	26
Parlor	*Amer.*	19
Penny's Noodle	*Asian*	19
People Lounge	*Spanish*	-
Smoke Daddy	*BBQ*	20
Z Spring	*Amer./Seafood*	27

City South

CHINATOWN

Emperor's Choice	*Chinese*	23
Evergreen	*Chinese*	22
Happy Chef Dim Sum	*Chinese*	23
Joy Yee's Noodle	*Asian*	21
NEW KS Seafood	*Chinese/Seafood*	-
Z Lao Sze Chuan	*Chinese*	24
Moon Palace	*Chinese*	21

NEW Mulan | *Asian*	-
New Three Happiness | *Chinese*	19
Penang | *Malaysian*	19
Phoenix | *Chinese*	22
Three Happiness | *Chinese*	22

FAR SOUTH SIDE

Army & Lou's | *Southern*	19
Greek Islands | *Greek*	21
NEW Koda | *French*	-
Lem's BBQ | *BBQ*	24
Parrot Cage | *Amer.*	-
NEW Uncle John's | *BBQ*	-
Vito & Nick's | *Pizza*	-

HYDE PARK/KENWOOD

Bar Louie | *Amer.*	15
Dixie Kitchen | *Cajun/Southern*	19
Edwardo's Pizza | *Pizza*	20
la petite folie | *French*	24
Medici on 57th | *Amer.*	18
Z Original Pancake | *Amer.*	23
Pizza Capri | *Pizza*	19
Ribs 'n' Bibs | *BBQ*	22

NEAR SOUTH SIDE

Lalo's | *Mex.*	16
NEW Mundial | *Mex.*	-
NEW Tratt. 31 | *Italian*	-
Tufano's Tap | *Italian*	21

PRINTER'S ROW

NEW Amarit | *Thai*	-
Z Custom Hse. | *Amer.*	24
Edwardo's Pizza | *Pizza*	20
Hackney's | *Amer.*	18

SOUTH LOOP

Bar Louie | *Amer.*	15
Billy Goat Tav. | *Amer.*	15
Bongo Room | *Amer.*	24
NEW Café Bionda | *Italian*	-
Chicago Firehse. | *Amer.*	18
Cuatro | *Nuevo Latino*	23
Eleven City Diner | *Diner*	-

NEW Fornetto & Mei's | *Chinese/Italian*	-
NEW Gage | *Amer.*	-
Gioco | *Italian*	21
Grace O'Malley's | *Pub*	17
Kohan | *Jap.*	-
Kroll's | *Amer.*	-
NEW La Cantina Grill | *Mex.*	-
Z Manny's | *Deli*	23
Opera | *Asian*	23
Orange | *Eclectic*	23
Oysy | *Jap.*	21
NEW Room 21 | *Steak*	-
NEW Shor | *Amer.*	-
NEW Tamarind | *Asian*	-
NEW Yolk | *Amer.*	-
Zapatista | *Mex.*	20

SOUTHWEST SIDE

Bacchanalia | *Italian*	23
Bruna's | *Italian*	23
Z Giordano's | *Pizza*	21
Gold Coast Dogs | *Hot Dogs*	19
Haro | *Spanish*	-
Harry Caray's | *Italian/Steak*	19
Lalo's | *Mex.*	16
Z Lou Malnati's | *Pizza*	24
Z Manny's | *Deli*	23
Pegasus | *Greek*	22
Z Superdawg | *Hot Dogs*	22

City West

FAR WEST

Amarind's | *Thai*	25
NEW Depot Diner | *Diner*	-

GREEKTOWN

Artopolis | *Greek/Med.*	21
Athena | *Greek*	19
Butter | *Amer.*	22
Costa's | *Greek*	21
Z Giordano's | *Pizza*	21
NEW 9 Muses | *Greek*	-
Parthenon | *Greek*	20

Pegasus	*Greek*	22
☑ Roditys	*Greek*	22
Santorini	*Greek/Seafood*	21
Venus	*Greek*	19

LITTLE ITALY/ UNIVERSITY VILLAGE

Al's #1 Beef	*Sandwiches*	22
Bar Louie	*Amer.*	15
Chez Joël	*French*	22
☑ Francesca's	*Italian*	23
La Vita	*Italian*	20
Pompei Bakery	*Italian*	20
RoSal's Kitchen	*Italian*	24
☑ Rosebud	*Italian*	21
Tuscany	*Italian*	22

MARKET DISTRICT

NEW Alhambra	*Mideast.*	-
de cero	*Mex.*	21
Dragonfly	*Chinese*	14
Extra Virgin	*Italian/Med.*	19
Flat Top Grill	*Asian*	19
Follia	*Italian*	22
Izumi Sushi	*Jap.*	23
Marché	*French*	20
☑ Moto	*Eclectic*	25
☑ one sixtyblue	*French*	25
Red Light	*Asian*	23
Saltaus	*Eclectic*	19
Starfish	*Jap.*	23
☑ sushi wabi	*Jap.*	26
Tasting Room	*Eclectic*	18
Vivo	*Italian*	21

NEAR WEST

Avenue M	*Amer.*	-
Bella Notte	*Italian*	23
NEW Coalfire Pizza	*Pizza*	-
Dining Rm./Kendall	*French*	23
Hecky's	*BBQ*	21
☑ Japonais	*Jap.*	24
La Scarola	*Italian*	23
May St. Market	*Amer.*	-
Timo	*Italian*	-
Twisted Spoke	*Pub*	18

UKRAINIAN VILLAGE

a tavola	*Italian*	23
Bite Cafe	*Eclectic*	23
NEW Dodo	*Amer.*	-
Hacienda Teca.	*Mex.*	20

WEST LOOP

☑ Avec	*Med.*	25
Bella Bacino	*Pizza*	21
Billy Goat Tav.	*Amer.*	15
☑ Blackbird	*Amer.*	27
Carmichael Steak	*Steak*	22
☑ Carnivale	*Nuevo Latino*	22
Dine	*Amer.*	-
Gold Coast Dogs	*Hot Dogs*	19
Ina's	*Amer.*	19
Jay's Amore	*Italian*	-
La Sardine	*French*	23
Lou Mitchell's	*Diner*	22
Meiji	*Jap.*	24
☑ Nine	*Seafood/Steak*	22
Phil & Lou's	*Amer.*	17
Robinson's Ribs	*BBQ*	19
Stanley's	*Amer.*	19
Wishbone	*Southern*	21

WEST TOWN

Breakfast Club	*Amer.*	19
Flo	*Amer.*	22
☑ Green Zebra	*Veg.*	25
NEW Habana Libre	*Cuban*	-
Tecalitlan	*Mex.*	23
West Town Tav.	*Amer.*	23

Suburbs

SUBURBAN NORTH

Akai Hana	*Jap.*	21
Al's #1 Beef	*Sandwiches*	22
Bagel	*Deli*	18
Bank Lane	*Amer.*	23
Bar Louie	*Amer.*	15
Benihana	*Jap./Steak*	19
Best Hunan	*Chinese*	21
NEW Billy Berk's	*Amer./Eclectic*	-

Blind Faith	*Veg.*	19	Kamehachi	*Jap.*	22
Z Bob Chinn's Crab	*Seafood*	23	NEW Kansaku	*Jap.*	-
Boston Blackie's	*Hamburgers*	19	Karma	*Asian*	24
Cafe Central	*French*	23	Koi	*Asian*	19
Cafe Pyrenees	*French*	21	Kuni's	*Jap.*	25
Campagnola	*Italian*	23	Kyoto	*Jap.*	22
Z Carlos'	*French*	29	Lalo's	*Mex.*	16
Carson's Ribs	*BBQ*	20	NEW La Petite Amelia	*French*	-
Cereality	*Amer.*	16	Z Le Français	*French*	28
Z Cheesecake Fac.	*Amer.*	19	Z Lou Malnati's	*Pizza*	24
Chef's Station	*Amer.*	23	Lovell's	*Amer.*	20
Chinoiserie	*Asian*	20	LuLu's Dim Sum	*Asian*	19
NEW Convito	*French/Italian*	-	Lupita's	*Mex.*	21
Dave's Italian	*Italian*	17	L. Woods Lodge	*Amer.*	19
Davis St. Fish	*Seafood*	19	Z Maggiano's	*Italian*	20
Del Rio	*Italian*	18	Merle's Smokehse.	*BBQ*	21
Di Pescara	*Eclectic/Italian*	-	Z Mesón Sabika	*Spanish*	23
Dixie Kitchen	*Cajun/Southern*	19	Michael	*French*	25
Don Roth's	*Seafood/Steak*	20	Mimosa	*French/Italian*	23
Dover Straits	*Seafood*	18	Miramar	*French*	19
Edwardo's Pizza	*Pizza*	20	Mitchell's Fish Mkt.	*Seafood*	-
EJ's Place	*Italian/Steak*	19	Z Morton's Steak	*Steak*	26
NEW Erik's	*Eclectic*	-	Mt. Everest	*Indian*	21
NEW 545 North	*Amer.*	-	Myron & Phil's	*Steak*	21
Flat Top Grill	*Asian*	19	Next Door Bistro	*Amer.*	21
Flight	*Eclectic*	19	Nick's Fishmkt.	*Seafood*	24
Z Francesca's	*Italian*	23	NEW Ninefish	*Jap.*	-
Francesco's	*Italian*	24	Z Oceanique	*French*	27
NEW fRedhots	*Hot Dogs*	-	OPA Estiatorio	*Greek*	19
Froggy's French	*French*	22	Z Original Pancake	*Amer.*	23
Z Gabriel's	*French/Italian*	26	NEW Osteria/Tramonto		-
NEW Gale's Coffee	*Coffee*	-	*Italian*	
Gale St. Inn	*Amer.*	20	Oysy	*Jap.*	21
Gio	*Italian*	19	Palm, The	*Steak*	23
Gold Coast Dogs	*Hot Dogs*	19	Pete Miller	*Seafood/Steak*	21
Hackney's	*Amer.*	18	Z P.F. Chang's	*Chinese*	20
Harbour House	*Seafood*	-	Philly G's	*Italian*	22
Hecky's	*BBQ*	21	Pine Yard	*Chinese*	20
Hot Tamales	*Mex.*	21	Z Pita Inn	*Mideast.*	24
Jacky's Bistro	*Amer./French*	23	Prairie Grass	*Amer.*	21
J. Alexander's	*Amer.*	20	NEW Quince	*Amer.*	-
Jilly's Cafe	*Amer./French*	23	RA Sushi	*Jap.*	19
Joy Yee's Noodle	*Asian*	21	Ron of Japan	*Jap./Steak*	18
Kabul House	*Afghan*	20	Z Rosebud	*Italian*	21

Ruby of Siam	*Thai*	20	Lalo's	*Mex.*	16
🄩 Ruth's Chris	*Steak*	24	🄩 Lao Sze Chuan	*Chinese*	24
Sage Grille	*Amer.*	–	Las Palmas	*Mex.*	–
San Gabriel	*Mex.*	20	La Strada	*Italian*	19
Shallots Bistro	*French/Med.*	21	La Tasca	*Spanish*	23
Slice of Life	*Eclectic/Veg.*	13	🄩 Le Titi/Paris	*French*	26
South Gate Cafe	*Amer.*	18	Le Vichyssois	*French*	24
Stained Glass	*Amer.*	23	🄩 Lou Malnati's	*Pizza*	24
Stir Crazy	*Asian*	19	🄩 Maggiano's	*Italian*	20
Tapas Barcelona	*Spanish*	20	Magnum's Steak	*Steak*	23
Tavern	*Amer.*	23	Melting Pot	*Fondue*	21
NEW Tramonto's	*Seafood/Steak*	–	Mj2 Bistro	*Eclectic*	–
Tratt. D.O.C.	*Pizza*	–	Montarra	*Amer.*	22
Tuscany	*Italian*	22	🄩 Morton's Steak	*Steak*	26
🄩 Va Pensiero	*Italian*	26	Nancy's Orig.	*Pizza*	21
Vive La Crepe	*Eclectic/French*	20	Original Gino's	*Pizza*	22
🄩 Wildfire	*Steak*	23	🄩 Original Pancake	*Amer.*	23
Wildfish	*Jap.*	25	Pappadeaux Sea.	*Seafood*	20
Wolfgang Puck	*Amer.*	18	🄩 P.F. Chang's	*Chinese*	20
Yard House	*Amer.*	17	Pompei Bakery	*Italian*	20
			Retro Bistro	*French*	25
SUBURBAN NW			🄩 Rosebud	*Italian*	21
Al's #1 Beef	*Sandwiches*	22	Russell's BBQ	*BBQ*	18
Aurelio's Pizza	*Pizza*	22	NEW Sakuma's	*Jap.*	–
🄩 Barrington Bistro	*French*	27	NEW Sam & Harry's	*Steak*	–
Benihana	*Jap./Steak*	19	1776	*Amer.*	24
Big Bowl	*Asian*	18	🄩 Shaw's Crab	*Seafood*	23
Birch River	*Amer.*	–	Shula's Steak	*Steak*	20
Bistro Kirkou	*French*	22	Stir Crazy	*Asian*	19
Boston Blackie's	*Hamburgers*	19	Sushi Ai	*Jap.*	–
NEW Brockway Chop	*Steak*	–	Takkatsu	*Jap.*	–
NEW Carlos & Carlos	*Italian*	–	Texas de Brazil	*Brazilian*	–
🄩 Cheesecake Fac.	*Amer.*	19	Udupi Palace	*Indian*	23
NEW Chicago Pizza Co.	*Pizza*	–	Weber Grill	*BBQ*	19
D & J Bistro	*French*	25	White Fence	*Amer.*	21
Dover Straits	*Seafood*	18	🄩 Wildfire	*Steak*	23
Edelweiss	*German*	21	Wildfish	*Jap.*	25
Entourage	*Amer.*	–	Woo Lae Oak	*Korean*	19
🄩 Five O'Clock	*Steak*	26			
🄩 Francesca's	*Italian*	23	**SUBURBAN SOUTH**		
Gaylord Indian	*Indian*	22	Al's #1 Beef	*Sandwiches*	22
Hackney's	*Amer.*	18	Aurelio's Pizza	*Pizza*	22
🄩 India House	*Indian*	23	Balagio	*Italian*	22
Indian Garden	*Indian*	22	Bogart's Charhse.	*Steak*	21

Dixie Kitchen | *Cajun/Southern* 19

Z Original Pancake | *Amer.* 23

SUBURBAN SW

Al's #1 Beef | *Sandwiches* 22

Aurelio's Pizza | *Pizza* 22

Bar Louie | *Amer.* 15

NEW Blu Coral | *Jap.* -

Bogart's Charhse. | *Steak* 21

Canoe Club | *Amer.* 19

Z Courtright's | *Amer.* 26

NEW Ginger Asian | *Asian/Eclectic* -

Hackney's | *Amer.* 18

Original Gino's | *Pizza* 22

Sabor do Brasil | *Brazilian* -

Z Tallgrass | *French* 28

Tin Fish | *Seafood* 22

SUBURBAN WEST

Adelle's | *Amer.* 25

Amber Cafe | *Amer.* 24

Antico Posto | *Italian* 23

Z Atwater's | *Amer./French* 21

Aurelio's Pizza | *Pizza* 22

Bar Louie | *Amer.* 15

Bella Bacino | *Pizza* 21

Benihana | *Jap./Steak* 19

NEW Bistro Monet | *French* -

Cab's Wine Bar | *Amer.* 22

Café le Coq | *French* 23

Capital Grille | *Steak* 24

Carlucci | *Italian* 19

Catch 35 | *Seafood* 23

Z Cheesecake Fac. | *Amer.* 19

Chinn's Fishery | *Seafood* 22

Clubhouse | *Amer.* 21

Costa's | *Greek* 21

Ed Debevic's | *Diner* 14

Edwardo's Pizza | *Pizza* 20

Emilio's Sunflower | *Amer.* -

Emilio's Tapas | *Spanish* 21

Finley's Grill | *Amer.* -

Flat Top Grill | *Asian* 19

Z Francesca's | *Italian* 23

NEW Gordon Biersch | *Amer.* -

Greek Islands | *Greek* 21

Grillroom | *Steak* 17

Harvest | *Amer.* -

Z Heaven on Seven | *Cajun/Creole* 21

Hemmingway's | *Amer./French* 21

Z Hugo's Frog/Fish | *Seafood* 24

NEW Hunter's | *Eclectic* -

Indian Garden | *Indian* 22

Z Isabella's | *Med.* 26

J. Alexander's | *Amer.* 20

Joy Yee's Noodle | *Asian* 21

Kyoto | *Jap.* 22

Lalo's | *Mex.* 16

L'anne | *Viet.* 20

Z Lao Sze Chuan | *Chinese* 24

La Piazza | *Italian* 25

La Piazza | *Italian* -

Z Lou Malnati's | *Pizza* 24

Z Maggiano's | *Italian* 20

Magnum's Steak | *Steak* 23

NEW Matsuri | *Jap.* -

Melting Pot | *Fondue* 21

Z Mesón Sabika | *Spanish* 23

Z Mon Ami Gabi | *French* 22

Z Morton's Steak | *Steak* 26

Mysore Woodland | *Indian* 17

Nancy's Orig. | *Pizza* 21

NEW Niche | *Amer.* -

NEW Nosh | *Eclectic* -

Original Gino's | *Pizza* 22

Z Original Pancake | *Amer.* 23

Pacific Blue | *Seafood* 25

Pappadeaux Sea. | *Seafood* 20

Parkers' | *Seafood* 21

Pegasus | *Greek* 22

Penny's Noodle | *Asian* 19

Z P.F. Chang's | *Chinese* 20

Philander's | *Amer.* 21

Pompei Bakery | *Italian* 20

Reza's | *Mideast.* 19

Riva | *Seafood* 18

Robinson's Ribs | *BBQ* 19

Rock Bottom | *Amer.* 16

CHICAGO

LOCATIONS

Special Features

Listings cover the best in each category and include restaurant names, locations and Food ratings. Multi-location restaurants' features may vary by branch. ☑ indicates places with the highest ratings, popularity and importance.

ADDITIONS

(Properties added since the last edition of the book)

Adesso | **Lakeview**

Aigre Doux | **River N**

Alhambra | **Mkt Dist**

Amarit | **Printer's Row**

Amira | **Streeterville**

Anteprima | **Andersonville**

Azucar | **Logan Sq**

Baccalà | **Wicker Pk**

Barcello's | **Wicker Pk**

BB's | **River N**

Billy Berk's | **Skokie**

Bistro Monet | **Glen Ellyn**

Blu Coral | **multi. loc.**

Bourbon | **Lakeview**

Bravo Tapas | **Wicker Pk**

Broadway Cellars | **Edgewater**

Brockway Chop | **Palatine**

Café Bionda | **S Loop**

Café Suron | **Rogers Pk**

Carlos & Carlos | **Arlington Hts**

Chalkboard | **Lincoln Sq**

Chicago Pizza Co. | **Rolling Meadows**

Coalfire Pizza | **Near W**

Convito | **Wilmette**

Cooper's | **Lakeview**

Cordis Bros. | **Lakeview**

Côtes/Rhône | **Edgewater**

Cru Cafe | **Gold Coast**

Crust | **Wicker Pk**

DeLaCosta | **River N**

Depot Diner | **Far W**

Dodo | **Ukrainian Vill**

Erba | **Lincoln Sq**

Erik's | **Highwood**

Feed/Beast | **Lincoln Sq**

Fiddlehead | **Lincoln Sq**

Fiorentino's | **Lakeview**

545 North | **Libertyville**

Flatwater | **River N**

Fornetto & Mei's | **S Loop**

Frasca Pizzeria | **Lakeview**

fRedhots | **Glenview**

Gage | **S Loop**

Gale's Coffee | **Wheeling**

Ginger Asian | **Orland Pk**

Glenn's Diner | **Ravenswood**

Gordon Biersch | **Bolingbrook**

Graze | **River N**

Gruppo/Amici | **Rogers Pk**

Habana Libre | **W Town**

Hamburger Mary's | **Andersonville**

Hannah's Bretzel | **Loop**

Honey 1 BBQ | **Bucktown**

Hop Häus | **River N**

Hunter's | **St. Charles**

Icosium Kafe | **Andersonville**

Il Covo | **Bucktown**

Jai Yen | **Lakeview**

Kanok | **Lakeview**

Kansaku | **Evanston**

Koda | **Far S Side**

KS Seafood | **Chinatown**

La Cantina Grill | **S Loop**

La Petite Amelia | **Evanston**

Las Palmas | **multi. loc.**

Marigold | **Uptown**

Matsuri | **Geneva**

Midtown Kitchen | **Loop**

Minnies | **Lincoln Pk**

Mulan | **Chinatown**

Mundial | **Near S Side**

Niche | **Geneva**

Ninefish | **Evanston**

9 Muses | **Greektown**

Nosh | **Geneva**	⌐
Osteria/Tramonto | **Wheeling**	⌐
Over Easy | **Ravenswood**	⌐
Palmito | **Lakeview**	⌐
Patty Burger | **Loop**	⌐
Pops/Champ. | **River N**	⌐
Quince | **Evanston**	⌐
Radhuni | **Lakeview**	⌐
Republic | **River N**	⌐
Room 21 | **S Loop**	⌐
Sakuma's | **Streamwood**	⌐
Sam & Harry's | **Schaumburg**	⌐
Sapore/Napoli | **Lakeview**	⌐
Sequel | **Lombard**	⌐
Shor | **S Loop**	⌐
Siam Café | **Uptown**	⌐
Simply It | **Lincoln Pk**	⌐
Smoque BBQ | **NW Side**	⌐
Sol de Mex. | **NW Side**	⌐
Spacca Napoli | **Ravenswood**	⌐
Sura | **Lakeview**	⌐
Tamarind | **S Loop**	⌐
Taos | **Roscoe Vill**	⌐
Ta Tong | **Lakeview**	⌐
Tepatulco | **Lincoln Pk**	⌐
Tokyo 21 | **Lincoln Pk**	⌐
Townhouse | **Loop**	⌐
Tramonto's | **Wheeling**	⌐
Tratt. 31 | **Near S Side**	⌐
Treat | **Humboldt Pk**	⌐
Uncle John's | **Far S Side**	⌐
Viet Bistro | **Rogers Pk**	⌐
Vito & Nick's | **Far S Side**	⌐
Wakamono | **Lakeview**	⌐
Xel-Há | **River N**	⌐
Yolk | **S Loop**	⌐
ZKF | **Bucktown**	⌐
Zocalo | **River N**	⌐

BREAKFAST

(See also Hotel Dining)

Ann Sather | **multi. loc.**	19
Army & Lou's | **Far S Side**	19
Bagel | **multi. loc.**	18

Billy Goat Tav. | **multi. loc.**	15
☑ Bin 36/Bin Wine | **River N**	20
Bite Cafe | **Ukrainian Vill**	23
Blind Faith | **Evanston**	19
Bongo Room | **Wicker Pk**	24
Breakfast Club | **W Town**	19
Café Selmarie | **Lincoln Sq**	21
Chicago Diner | **Lakeview**	19
Cold Comfort | **Bucktown**	22
David's Bistro | **Des Plaines**	24
Dixie Kitchen | **Evanston**	19
NEW Dodo | **Ukrainian Vill**	⌐
Ed Debevic's | **River N**	14
Flo | **W Town**	22
foodlife | **Streeterville**	16
Harry Caray's | **SW Side**	19
Heartland Cafe | **Rogers Pk**	16
☑ Heaven on Seven | **Loop**	21
Ina's | **W Loop**	19
Irazu | **Bucktown**	22
Kitsch'n | **multi. loc.**	17
Lou Mitchell's | **multi. loc.**	22
Lula | **Logan Sq**	25
☑ Manny's | **multi. loc.**	23
M. Henry | **Andersonville**	24
Milk & Honey | **Wicker Pk**	21
Nookies | **multi. loc.**	19
NEW Nosh | **Geneva**	⌐
Oak Tree | **Gold Coast**	17
Orange | **Lakeview**	23
☑ Original Pancake | **multi. loc.**	23
NEW Over Easy | **Ravenswood**	⌐
Pegasus | **SW Side**	22
Phoenix | **Chinatown**	22
San Soo Gab San | **NW Side**	21
Slice of Life | **Skokie**	13
Tecalitlan | **W Town**	23
Tempo | **Gold Coast**	19
Three Happiness | **Chinatown**	22
Toast | **multi. loc.**	22
Tre Kronor | **NW Side**	24
Uncommon Grnd. | **Wrigleyville**	21
Viand Bar | **Streeterville**	23
Victory's Banner | **Roscoe Vill**	23

Wishbone | **multi. loc.**	21
NEW Yolk | **S Loop**	–

BRUNCH

Adobo Grill | **multi. loc.**	21
American Girl | **Gold Coast**	12
Andies | **Andersonville**	18
Angelina | **Wrigleyville**	20
Ann Sather | **Andersonville**	19
☑ Atwater's | **Geneva**	21
☑ Atwood Cafe | **Loop**	21
Bar Louie | **Evanston**	15
Bistro 110 | **Gold Coast**	20
Bistrot Margot | **Old Town**	21
Bistrot Zinc | **Gold Coast**	20
Bite Cafe | **Ukrainian Vill**	23
Bongo Room | **Wicker Pk**	24
Café/Architectes | **Gold Coast**	22
Café Selmarie | **Lincoln Sq**	21
☑ Café Spiaggia | **Gold Coast**	24
Cafe 28 | **Lakeview**	23
☑ Cheesecake Fac. | **multi. loc.**	19
Chicago Diner | **Lakeview**	19
Clubhouse | **Oak Brook**	21
Coobah | **Lakeview**	19
Davis St. Fish | **Evanston**	19
erwin cafe | **Lakeview**	23
Flo | **W Town**	22
☑ Frontera Grill | **River N**	26
Grand Lux | **River N**	20
Hackney's | **Palos Pk**	18
☑ Heaven on Seven | **multi. loc.**	21
Hemmingway's | **Oak Pk**	21
House of Blues | **River N**	16
Jack's on Halsted | **Lakeview**	21
Jane's | **Bucktown**	21
Jilly's Cafe | **Evanston**	23
John's Place | **Lincoln Pk**	18
Kitsch'n | **multi. loc.**	17
La Crêperie | **Lakeview**	20
La Donna | **Andersonville**	19
La Tache | **Andersonville**	21
☑ Lobby | **River N**	23
Magnolia Cafe | **Uptown**	25

Meritage Cafe | **Bucktown**	22
☑ Mesón Sabika | **Naperville**	23
M. Henry | **Andersonville**	24
Mike Ditka's | **Gold Coast**	20
Milk & Honey | **Wicker Pk**	21
☑ North Pond | **Lincoln Pk**	25
Orange | **Lakeview**	23
☑ Original Pancake | **Lincolnshire**	23
Pizza Capri | **multi. loc.**	19
P.J. Clarke's | **multi. loc.**	17
Platiyo | **Lakeview**	20
☑ Pump Room | **Gold Coast**	21
rist. we | **Loop**	18
Ritz-Carlton Café | **Streeterville**	–
☑ RL | **Gold Coast**	22
Salpicón | **Old Town**	24
☑ Seasons | **Gold Coast**	26
☑ Signature Rm. | **Streeterville**	18
Silver Cloud B&G | **Bucktown**	18
Smith & Wollensky | **River N**	22
South Water Kitchen | **Loop**	17
Stanley's | **Lincoln Pk**	19
☑ SushiSamba rio | **River N**	21
Tavern on Rush | **Gold Coast**	19
312 Chicago | **Loop**	19
Toast | **multi. loc.**	22
Tre Kronor | **NW Side**	24
Tweet | **Uptown**	21
Twisted Spoke | **multi. loc.**	18
Uncommon Grnd. | **Wrigleyville**	21
Viceroy of India | **Lombard**	20
Vinci | **Lincoln Pk**	22
Wishbone | **multi. loc.**	21
Yoshi's Café | **Lakeview**	23

BUFFET

(Check availability)

Andies | **Andersonville**	18
☑ Avenues | **River N**	26
Clubhouse | **Oak Brook**	21
Drake Bros.' | **Streeterville**	17
Edwardo's Pizza | **Oak Pk**	20
Essence of India | **Lincoln Sq**	21
Flat Top Grill | **multi. loc.**	19

NEW Fornetto & Mei's | **S Loop** _-_
Gale St. Inn | **Jefferson Pk** 20
Gaylord Indian | **multi. loc.** 22
Grace O'Malley's | **S Loop** 17
Hackney's | **Palos Pk** 18
Hemmingway's | **Oak Pk** 21
House of Blues | **River N** 16
☑ India House | **multi. loc.** 23
Indian Garden | **multi. loc.** 22
Karyn's | **Lincoln Pk** 17
Klay Oven | **River N** 20
La Fonda | **Andersonville** 19
☑ Lobby | **River N** 23
Mt. Everest | **Evanston** 21
Pappadeaux Sea. | 20
    Arlington Hts
P.S. Bangkok | **Wrigleyville** 20
Puck's at MCA | **Streeterville** 20
NEW Radhuni | **Lakeview** _-_
Raj Darbar | **Lincoln Pk** 20
Reza's | **multi. loc.** 19
RoSal's Kitchen | **Little Italy** 24
Ruby of Siam | **multi. loc.** 20
☑ Seasons | **Gold Coast** 26
NEW Shor | **S Loop** _-_
Siam Café | **Uptown** _-_
☑ Signature Rm. | **Streeterville** 18
Stanley's | **Lincoln Pk** 19
Thai Classic | **Lakeview** 23
Tiffin | **W Rogers Pk** 22
Udupi Palace | **Schaumburg** 23
Venus | **Greektown** 19
Viceroy of India | **multi. loc.** 20

BUSINESS DINING

NEW Aigre Doux | **River N** _-_
☑ Alinea | **Lincoln Pk** 28
NEW Amira | **Streeterville** _-_
Aria | **Loop** 23
☑ Atwood Cafe | **Loop** 21
☑ Avenues | **River N** 26
Balagio | **Homewood** 22
Ben Pao | **River N** 21
Bistro Kirkou | **Lake Zurich** 22

NEW Bistro Monet | **Glen Ellyn** _-_
☑ Blackbird | **W Loop** 27
Blue Water | **River N** 22
☑ Brasserie Jo | **River N** 22
Brazzaz | **River N** 23
NEW Brockway Chop | **Palatine** _-_
Café/Architectes | **Gold Coast** 22
Caliterra | **Streeterville** 23
Capital Grille | **Streeterville** 24
Carlucci | **multi. loc.** 19
Carmichael Steak | **W Loop** 22
Catch 35 | **Loop** 23
☑ Charlie Trotter's | **Lincoln Pk** 27
☑ Chicago Chop | **River N** 25
Coco Pazzo | **River N** 24
☑ Crofton on Wells | **River N** 26
☑ Custom Hse. | **Printer's Row** 24
David Burke Prime | **River N** 22
David's Bistro | **Des Plaines** 24
Devon Seafood | **River N** _-_
Dine | **W Loop** _-_
Drake Bros.' | **Streeterville** 17
Erie Cafe | **River N** 23
☑ Everest | **Loop** 27
Finley's Grill | **Downers Grove** _-_
NEW Flatwater | **River N** _-_
Fleming's Steak | **Lincolnshire** _-_
☑ Fogo de Chão | **River N** 24
Fulton's | **River N** 20
NEW Gage | **S Loop** _-_
Gene & Georgetti | **River N** 23
☑ Gibsons | **multi. loc.** 25
Grill on Alley | **Streeterville** 18
Grillroom | **Loop** 17
Grotto | **Gold Coast** 18
Harry Caray's | **multi. loc.** 19
Il Mulino | **Gold Coast** _-_
☑ Japonais | **Near W** 24
☑ Joe's Sea/Steak | **River N** 26
Karma | **Mundelein** 24
Keefer's | **River N** 23
☑ Kevin | **River N** 26
Kinzie Chophse. | **River N** 20
Lawry's Prime Rib | **River N** 24

Ⓩ Le Colonial | **Gold Coast**	23
Ⓩ Le Français | **Wheeling**	28
Ⓩ Les Nomades | **Streeterville**	28
Ⓩ Le Titi/Paris | **Arlington Hts**	26
LuxBar | **Gold Coast**	17
Magnum's Steak | **multi. loc.**	23
NEW Matsuri | **Geneva**	–
McCormick/Schmick | **Gold Coast**	21
Michael | **Winnetka**	25
NEW Midtown Kitchen | **Loop**	–
Mike Ditka's | **Gold Coast**	20
Ⓩ mk | **River N**	26
Ⓩ Morton's Steak | **multi. loc.**	26
Mrs. Park's Tav. | **Streeterville**	17
Ⓩ Naha | **River N**	26
Nick's Fishmkt. | **multi. loc.**	24
Ⓩ Nine | **W Loop**	22
Ⓩ NoMI | **Gold Coast**	26
One North | **Loop**	18
Ⓩ one sixtyblue | **Mkt Dist**	25
NEW Osteria/Tramonto | **Wheeling**	–
Palm, The | **Loop**	23
Park Grill | **Loop**	19
Petterino's | **Loop**	19
Phil Stefani's | **River N**	21
NEW Quince | **Evanston**	–
Rhapsody | **Loop**	21
rist. we | **Loop**	18
Ritz-Carlton Café | **Streeterville**	–
Ⓩ RL | **Gold Coast**	22
Roy's | **River N**	24
Ⓩ Ruth's Chris | **multi. loc.**	24
Saloon Steak | **Streeterville**	23
NEW Sam & Harry's | **Schaumburg**	–
Ⓩ Seasons | **Gold Coast**	26
NEW Sequel | **Lombard**	–
Ⓩ Shaw's Crab | **multi. loc.**	23
NEW Shor | **S Loop**	–
Sidebar Grille | **Loop**	–
Slice of Life | **Skokie**	13
Smith & Wollensky | **River N**	22
South Water Kitchen | **Loop**	17

Ⓩ Spiaggia | **Gold Coast**	26
Sullivan's Steak | **multi. loc.**	23
Takkatsu | **Arlington Hts**	–
312 Chicago | **Loop**	19
Timpano Chophse. | **Naperville**	–
Ⓩ Topolobampo | **River N**	27
NEW Townhouse | **Loop**	–
NEW Tramonto's | **Wheeling**	–
Tuscany | **multi. loc.**	22
Vivere | **Loop**	21
Vivo | **Mkt Dist**	21
Vong's | **River N**	21
Weber Grill | **River N**	19

BYO

Ann Sather | **Andersonville**	19
Babylon Eatery | **Bucktown**	17
NEW Barcello's | **Wicker Pk**	–
Bite Cafe | **Ukrainian Vill**	23
Café Suron | **Rogers Pk**	–
CHIC Cafe | **River N**	20
Chinoiserie | **Wilmette**	20
NEW Coalfire Pizza | **Near W**	–
Coast Sushi | **Bucktown**	23
Cold Comfort | **Bucktown**	22
NEW Côtes/Rhône | **Edgewater**	–
NEW Dodo | **Ukrainian Vill**	–
Dorado | **Lincoln Sq**	23
El Presidente | **Lincoln Pk**	14
Fattoush | **Lincoln Pk**	23
Fonda del Mar | **Logan Sq**	–
Ⓩ Giordano's | **Edison Pk**	21
NEW Habana Libre | **W Town**	–
Hashalom | **NW Side**	–
HB | **Lakeview**	22
Hecky's | **multi. loc.**	21
Hema's Kitchen | **multi. loc.**	20
NEW Honey 1 BBQ | **Bucktown**	–
NEW Icosium Kafe | **Andersonville**	–
Indie Cafe | **Edgewater**	19
Irazu | **Bucktown**	22
Izumi Sushi | **Mkt Dist**	23

NEW Jai Yen | **Lakeview**	–
Joy Yee's Noodle | **multi. loc.**	21
Kabul House | **Skokie**	20
NEW Kanok | **Lakeview**	–
Kan Zaman | **River N**	21
Karyn's | **Lincoln Pk**	17
La Cazuela Mar. | **Rogers Pk**	–
La Cucina/Donatella | **Rogers Pk**	22
Las Tablas | **multi. loc.**	21
Lucia | **Wicker Pk**	22
Matsu Yama | **Lakeview**	22
Medici on 57th | **Hyde Pk**	18
Melting Pot | **multi. loc.**	21
M. Henry | **Andersonville**	24
NEW Mundial | **Near S Side**	–
My Pie Pizza | **Lincoln Pk**	21
Mysore Woodland | **W Rogers Pk**	17
NEW Ninefish | **Evanston**	–
Nookies | **Old Town**	19
Old Jerusalem | **Old Town**	19
Orange | **multi. loc.**	23
Original Gino's | **Lincoln Pk**	22
NEW Over Easy | **Ravenswood**	–
NEW Palmito | **Lakeview**	–
Parrot Cage | **Far S Side**	–
Penny's Noodle | **Wrigleyville**	19
pingpong | **Lakeview**	21
P.S. Bangkok | **Lincoln Pk**	20
NEW Radhuni | **Lakeview**	–
Riccardo Tratt. | **Lincoln Pk**	–
Rinconcito Sudamer. | **Bucktown**	17
Ringo | **Lincoln Pk**	22
Riques | **Uptown**	21
Robinson's Ribs | **multi. loc.**	19
Ruby of Siam | **Skokie**	20
NEW Sapore/Napoli | **Lakeview**	–
Schwa | **Lincoln Pk**	26
NEW Simply It | **Lincoln Pk**	–
NEW Smoque BBQ | **NW Side**	–
NEW Sol de Mex. | **NW Side**	–
Spoon Thai | **Lincoln Sq**	22

State | **Lincoln Pk**	–
Tagine | **Ravenswood**	–
☑ Tango Sur | **Wrigleyville**	24
NEW Ta Tong | **Lakeview**	–
Terragusto Cafe | **Roscoe Vill**	–
Thai Classic | **Lakeview**	23
Thai Pastry | **Uptown**	22
Think Café | **Bucktown**	24
Tre Kronor | **NW Side**	24
T-Spot Sushi | **Lakeview**	–
Udupi Palace | **W Rogers Pk**	23
NEW Wakamono | **Lakeview**	–
Yard House | **Glenview**	17

CELEBRITY CHEFS
(Listed under their primary restaurants)

☑ Alinea | *Grant Achatz* | **Lincoln Pk**	28
☑ Arun's | *Arun Sampanthavivat* | **NW Side**	28
☑ Avec | *Koren Grieveson* | **W Loop**	25
☑ Avenues | *Graham Elliot Bowles* | **River N**	26
Bistro Campagne | *M. Altenberg* | **Lincoln Sq**	23
Bistro 110 | *Dominique Tougne* | **Gold Coast**	20
☑ Blackbird | *Paul Kahan* | **W Loop**	27
Cafe Matou | *Charlie Socher* | **Bucktown**	22
☑ Charlie Trotter's | *Charlie Trotter* | **Lincoln Pk**	27
☑ Crofton on Wells | *Suzy Crofton* | **River N**	26
NEW Crust | *Michael Altenberg* | **Wicker Pk**	–
NEW DeLaCosta | *Douglas Rodriguez* | **River N**	–
erwin cafe | *Erwin Drechsler* | **Lakeview**	23
☑ Everest | *Jean Joho* | **Loop**	27
☑ Frontera Grill | *Rick Bayless* | **River N**	26
NEW Gale's Coffee | *Gale Gand* | **Wheeling**	–

- Hot Chocolate | *Mindy Segal* | **Bucktown** 23
- Keefer's | *John Hogan* | **River N** 23
- Ⓩ Kevin | *Kevin Shikami* | **River N** 26
- Le Bouchon | *J-C Poilevey* | **Bucktown** 22
- Ⓩ Le Français | *Roland Liccioni* | **Wheeling** 28
- Ⓩ Le Titi/Paris | *M. Maddox* | **Arlington Hts** 26
- Le Vichyssois | *Bernard Cretier* | **Lakemoor** 24
- Mas | *John Manion* | **Wicker Pk** 22
- Michael | *Michael Lachowitz* | **Winnetka** 25
- Ⓩ mk | *Michael Kornick* | **River N** 26
- Ⓩ Moto | *Homaro Cantu* | **Mkt Dist** 25
- Nacional 27 | *Randy Zweiban* | **River N** 22
- Ⓩ Naha | *Carrie Nahabedian* | **River N** 26
- Ⓩ North Pond | *Bruce Sherman* | **Lincoln Pk** 25
- Ⓩ one sixtyblue | *Martial Noguier* | **Mkt Dist** 25
- Opera | *Paul Wildermuth* | **S Loop** 23
- Prairie Grass | *Sarah Stegner & George Bumbaris* | **Northbrook** 21
- NEW Quince | *Mark Hannon* | **Evanston** –
- Red Light | *Jackie Shen* | **Mkt Dist** 23
- Salpicón | *Priscila Satkoff* | **Old Town** 24
- Schwa | *Michael Carlson* | **Lincoln Pk** 26
- Ⓩ Spiaggia | *Tony Mantuano* | **Gold Coast** 26
- Ⓩ Spring | *Shawn McClain* | **Wicker Pk** 27
- Ⓩ Tallgrass | *Robert Burcenski* | **Lockport** 28
- NEW Tepatulco | *Geno Bahena* | **Lincoln Pk** –
- Timo | *John Bubala* | **Near W** –
- Ⓩ Topolobampo | *Rick Bayless* | **River N** 27
- NEW Tramonto's | *Rick Tramonto* | **Wheeling** –
- West Town Tav. | *Susan Goss* | **W Town** 23
- NEW Xel-Há | *Dudley Nieto* | **River N** –
- Ⓩ Zealous | *Michael Taus* | **River N** 24

CHILD-FRIENDLY

(Alternatives to the usual fast-food places; * children's menu available)

- American Girl* | **Gold Coast** 12
- Ann Sather | **multi. loc.** 19
- Antico Posto* | **Oak Brook** 23
- Artopolis | **Greektown** 21
- Bandera* | **Streeterville** 20
- Benihana* | **multi. loc.** 19
- Berghoff | **O'Hare Area** –
- Big Bowl* | **multi. loc.** 18
- NEW Billy Berk's* | **Skokie** –
- Ⓩ Bob Chinn's Crab* | **Wheeling** 23
- Bongo Room | **Wicker Pk** 24
- Breakfast Club | **W Town** 19
- Café Selmarie | **Lincoln Sq** 21
- Carson's Ribs* | **River N** 20
- Cereality | **Loop** 16
- Ⓩ Cheesecake Fac.* | **multi. loc.** 19
- Chicago Pizza/Oven | **Lincoln Pk** 22
- Dave's Italian | **Evanston** 17
- Davis St. Fish* | **Evanston** 19
- NEW Depot Diner | **Far W** –
- Eatzi's | **Lincoln Pk** 18
- Ed Debevic's* | **River N** 14
- Edwardo's Pizza* | **multi. loc.** 20
- Flat Top Grill* | **multi. loc.** 19
- foodlife* | **Streeterville** 16
- NEW Gale's Coffee | **Wheeling** –
- Gold Coast Dogs | **multi. loc.** 19
- Gulliver's Pizza* | **Rogers Pk** 17
- Hackney's* | **multi. loc.** 18
- Hard Rock Cafe* | **River N** 13
- Harry Caray's* | **multi. loc.** 19
- Ⓩ Heaven on Seven* | **multi. loc.** 21
- Hecky's | **Near W** 21
- Ⓩ Hot Doug's* | **NW Side** 25
- House of Blues* | **River N** 16
- Ina's* | **W Loop** 19

John's Place* | **Lincoln Pk** | 18
Joy Yee's Noodle | **multi. loc.** | 21
NEW Kansaku | **Evanston** | -
Kitsch'n* | **Roscoe Vill** | 17
Lawry's Prime Rib* | **River N** | 24
Z Lou Malnati's* | **multi. loc.** | 24
Lou Mitchell's* | **multi. loc.** | 22
LuLu's Dim Sum | **Evanston** | 19
Z Maggiano's* | **multi. loc.** | 20
Z Manny's* | **SW Side** | 23
Margie's Candies* | **Bucktown** | 23
Mity Nice Grill* | **Streeterville** | 18
Oak Tree | **Gold Coast** | 17
OPA Estiatorio | **Vernon Hills** | 19
Orange* | **multi. loc.** | 23
Original Gino's* | **multi. loc.** | 22
Z Original Pancake* | **multi. loc.** | 23
Pegasus | **SW Side** | 22
Z P.F. Chang's | **River N** | 20
Pizza Capri* | **multi. loc.** | 19
Pizza D.O.C. | **Lincoln Sq** | 22
Pizzeria Uno/Due* | **River N** | 22
Potbelly Sandwich | **multi. loc.** | 20
R.J. Grunts* | **Lincoln Pk** | 19
Robinson's Ribs* | **multi. loc.** | 19
Rock Bottom* | **multi. loc.** | 16
Ron of Japan* | **multi. loc.** | 18
Russell's BBQ* | **Elmwood Pk** | 18
NEW Sapore/Napoli | **Lakeview** | -
Sapori Tratt. | **Lincoln Pk** | 22
Scoozi!* | **River N** | 21
Sidebar Grille | **Loop** | -
NEW Smoque BBQ* | **NW Side** | -
Stanley's* | **Lincoln Pk** | 19
Stir Crazy* | **multi. loc.** | 19
Tempo | **Gold Coast** | 19
Timo | **Near W** | -
Toast* | **multi. loc.** | 22
Tratt. D.O.C. | **Evanston** | -
Tucci Benucch* | **Gold Coast** | 18
Tufano's Tap | **Near S Side** | 21
Twin Anchors* | **Old Town** | 22
Uncommon Grnd.* | **Wrigleyville** | 21

White Fence* | **Romeoville** | 21
Wishbone* | **multi. loc.** | 21

CIGARS WELCOME

Ballo | **River N** | 19
Carlucci | **multi. loc.** | 19
Carmine's | **Gold Coast** | 21
Cité | **Streeterville** | 17
Clubhouse | **Oak Brook** | 21
D & J Bistro | **Lake Zurich** | 25
Devon Seafood | **River N** | -
Erie Cafe | **River N** | 23
Fornetto Mei | **Gold Coast** | 19
Froggy's French | **Highwood** | 22
Gale St. Inn | **Mundelein** | 20
Gene & Georgetti | **River N** | 23
Z Gibsons | **multi. loc.** | 25
Goose Is. Brewing | **Lincoln Pk** | 16
Greek Islands | **Lombard** | 21
Green Dolphin St. | **Lincoln Pk** | 19
Green Door Tav. | **River N** | 14
Grillroom | **Loop** | 17
Grotto | **Gold Coast** | 18
Hacienda Teca. | **Ukrainian Vill** | 20
Hackney's | **multi. loc.** | 18
Hard Rock Cafe | **River N** | 13
Harry Caray's | **multi. loc.** | 19
Z Hugo's Frog/Fish | **multi. loc.** | 24
Irish Oak | **Wrigleyville** | 19
Karma | **Mundelein** | 24
Kinzie Chophse. | **River N** | 20
Kizoku Sushi | **River N** | 25
La Strada | **Loop** | 19
Lovell's | **Lake Forest** | 20
Magnum's Steak | **Lombard** | 23
Narcisse | **River N** | 20
Palm, The | **Northbrook** | 23
Parkers' | **Downers Grove** | 21
Philly G's | **Vernon Hills** | 22
Phil Stefani's | **River N** | 21
P.J. Clarke's | **multi. loc.** | 17
Riva | **Streeterville** | 18
Z Rosebud | **Little Italy** | 21
Rumba | **River N** | 18

Restaurant	Location	Score
☑ Ruth's Chris	multi. loc.	24
Saloon Steak	Streeterville	23
Silver Cloud B&G	Bucktown	18
Smith & Wollensky	River N	22
Smoke Daddy	Wicker Pk	20
Stetson's Chop Hse.	Loop	23
Sullivan's Steak	multi. loc.	23
Tavern	Libertyville	23
Tavern on Rush	Gold Coast	19
Topo Gigio	Old Town	20
Tratt. Roma	Old Town	19
Tuscany	multi. loc.	22
Twisted Spoke	multi. loc.	18
Viand Bar	Streeterville	23
Weber Grill	multi. loc.	19
Zia's Tratt.	Edison Pk	22

DANCING

Restaurant	Location	Score
Ballo	River N	19
Dover Straits	multi. loc.	18
Gale St. Inn	Mundelein	20
Hacienda Teca.	Ukrainian Vill	20
Kizoku Sushi	River N	25
La Peña	NW Side	20
Lutnia	NW Side	-
Nacional 27	River N	22
Narcisse	River N	20
☑ Nine	W Loop	22
Phil & Lou's	W Loop	17
☑ Pump Room	Gold Coast	21
Rumba	River N	18
Sayat Nova	Streeterville	20
Venus	Greektown	19

DELIVERY/TAKEOUT
(D=delivery, T=takeout)

Restaurant	Location	Score
Adobo Grill	T	multi. loc.	21
Akai Hana	D, T	Wilmette	21
Aladdin's Eatery	D, T	Lincoln Pk	17
A La Turka	T	Lakeview	20
Andies	D, T	Andersonville	18
Athena	T	Greektown	19
Bella Notte	D, T	Near W	23
Benihana	T	multi. loc.	19

Restaurant	Location	Score
Berghoff	T	multi. loc.	-
Bijan's	T	River N	19
☑ Bob Chinn's Crab	T	Wheeling	23
Cafe Ba-Ba-Reeba!	T	Lincoln Pk	22
☑ Café Spiaggia	T	Gold Coast	24
Coco Pazzo	T	Streeterville	22
☑ Crofton on Wells	T	River N	26
D & J Bistro	T	Lake Zurich	25
Davis St. Fish	T	Evanston	19
Don Juan's	T	Edison Pk	21
Emilio's Tapas	T	multi. loc.	21
erwin cafe	T	Lakeview	23
Filippo's	T	Lincoln Pk	20
foodlife	D, T	Streeterville	16
☑ Francesca's	D, T	multi. loc.	23
Gale St. Inn	D, T	multi. loc.	20
Gene & Georgetti	T	River N	23
☑ Gibsons	T	multi. loc.	25
Gioco	T	S Loop	21
☑ Heaven on Seven	D, T	multi. loc.	21
Hema's Kitchen	D, T	Lincoln Pk	20
☑ Japonais	D, T	Near W	24
☑ Joe's Sea/Steak	T	River N	26
Keefer's	T	River N	23
La Sardine	T	W Loop	23
La Scarola	T	Near W	23
La Tasca	T	Arlington Hts	23
☑ Le Colonial	D, T	Gold Coast	23
Lula	T	Logan Sq	25
L. Woods Lodge	D, T	Lincolnwood	19
☑ Maggiano's	T	multi. loc.	20
Meritage Cafe	T	Bucktown	22
☑ Mesón Sabika	T	multi. loc.	23
Mia Francesca	T	Lakeview	23
☑ Mirai Sushi	T	Wicker Pk	26
☑ Mon Ami Gabi	T	multi. loc.	22
Old Jerusalem	D, T	Old Town	19
Opera	T	S Loop	23
Orange	T	Lakeview	23

Parthenon | T | **Greektown** 20
Penang | D, T | **Chinatown** 19
Pierrot Gourmet | T | **River N** 21
Platiyo | T | **Lakeview** 20
Poag Mahone's | D, T | **Loop** 17
Potbelly Sandwich | D, T | 20
  multi. loc.
Red Light | T | **Mkt Dist** 23
R.J. Grunts | T | **Lincoln Pk** 19
Rock Bottom | T | **multi. loc.** 16
RoSal's Kitchen | T | **Little Italy** 24
☑ Rosebud | D, T | **multi. loc.** 21
☑ Salbute | T | **Hinsdale** 26
Saloon Steak | D, T | 23
  Streeterville
San Soo Gab San | D, T | 21
  NW Side
Scoozi! | T | **River N** 21
☑ Shaw's Crab | D, T | 23
  multi. loc.
Smith & Wollensky | T | **River N** 22
Sullivan's Steak | T | **River N** 23
Sushi Naniwa | D, T | **River N** 21
☑ sushi wabi | D, T | **Mkt Dist** 26
Swordfish | T | **Batavia** 25
Tarantino's | D, T | **Lincoln Pk** 21
☑ Tizi Melloul | T | **River N** 21
Tratt. Roma | D, T | **Old Town** 19
Twin Anchors | T | **Old Town** 22
Village | D, T | **Loop** 19
Volare | D, T | **Streeterville** 23
Yoshi's Café | T | **Lakeview** 23

DINING ALONE

(Other than hotels and places with counter service)
Ann Sather | **multi. loc.** 19
Bar Louie | **multi. loc.** 15
☑ Bin 36/Bin Wine | **River N** 20
Bite Cafe | **Ukrainian Vill** 23
Blind Faith | **Evanston** 19
Blue Water | **River N** 22
Breakfast Club | **W Town** 19
Chicago Diner | **Lakeview** 19
Eatzi's | **Lincoln Pk** 18

Eleven City Diner | **S Loop** –
Extra Virgin | **Mkt Dist** 19
Flat Top Grill | **multi. loc.** 19
foodlife | **Streeterville** 16
Gold Coast Dogs | **W Loop** 19
Heartland Cafe | **Rogers Pk** 16
☑ Hot Doug's | **NW Side** 25
Indie Cafe | **Edgewater** 19
Kaze Sushi | **Roscoe Vill** 24
Kinzie Chophse. | **River N** 20
Kizoku Sushi | **River N** 25
Koi | **Evanston** 19
Kroll's | **S Loop** –
Lula | **Logan Sq** 25
Maiz | **Humboldt Pk** 25
☑ Manny's | **S Loop** 23
Meiji | **W Loop** 24
Mrs. Murphy | **Lakeview** 21
Nookies | **multi. loc.** 19
Oak Tree | **Gold Coast** 17
Penny's Noodle | **multi. loc.** 19
Puck's at MCA | **Streeterville** 20
Reza's | **multi. loc.** 19
Toast | **multi. loc.** 22
Tsuki | **Lincoln Pk** 22
Tweet | **Uptown** 21
Viand Bar | **Streeterville** 23
Wiener's Circle | **Lincoln Pk** 20

ENTERTAINMENT

(Call for days and times of performances)
A La Turka | belly dancing | 20
  Lakeview
American Girl | musical/theater | 12
  Gold Coast
Cafe Bolero | Latin jazz | 21
  Bucktown
Catch 35 | piano | **Loop** 23
☑ Chicago Chop | piano | 25
  River N
Chief O'Neill's | Irish | **NW Side** 18
Costa's | piano | **Oakbrook Terr** 21
Cyrano's Bistrot | cabaret | 20
  River N

Dover Straits | bands | **multi. loc.** 18

Edelweiss | German music | **Norridge** 21

El Nandu | guitar | **Logan Sq** 21

Emilio's Tapas | flamenco | **Lincoln Pk** 21

Geja's Cafe | flamenco | **Lincoln Pk** 21

Green Dolphin St. | jazz | **Lincoln Pk** 19

Hackney's | varies | **multi. loc.** 18

House of Blues | blues | **River N** 16

Irish Oak | Irish/rock | **Wrigleyville** 19

Kit Kat Lounge | varies | **Wrigleyville** 15

Lalo's | DJ/mariachi | **multi. loc.** 16

La Strada | piano | **Loop** 19

La Taberna Tapatia | DJ | **Roscoe Vill** 21

☑ Lobby | jazz | **River N** 23

Lutnia | piano | **NW Side** –

☑ Mesón Sabika | flamenco | **multi. loc.** 23

Myron & Phil's | piano | **Lincolnwood** 21

Nacional 27 | DJ/jazz | **River N** 22

Nick's Fishmkt. | jazz | **Rosemont** 24

Parkers' | jazz/piano | **Downers Grove** 21

Philander's | jazz | **Oak Pk** 21

Philly G's | piano | **Vernon Hills** 22

☑ Pump Room | jazz | **Gold Coast** 21

Rock Bottom | karaoke | **multi. loc.** 16

Rumba | bands/DJ | **River N** 18

Sabatino's | piano | **NW Side** 23

Sayat Nova | DJ | **Streeterville** 20

☑ Shaw's Crab | blues/jazz | **multi. loc.** 23

☑ Signature Rm. | jazz | **Streeterville** 18

Smoke Daddy | blues/jazz | **Wicker Pk** 20

Sullivan's Steak | jazz | **multi. loc.** 23

☑ sushi wabi | DJ | **Mkt Dist** 26

☑ Tizi Melloul | belly dancing | **River N** 21

Uncommon Grnd. | varies | **Wrigleyville** 21

Webster Wine | bands | **Lincoln Pk** 17

FIREPLACES

Adelle's | **Wheaton** 25

Andies | **Andersonville** 18

Ann Sather | **Lakeview** 19

Athena | **Greektown** 19

☑ Atwater's | **Geneva** 21

Bistrot Margot | **Old Town** 21

Boston Blackie's | **Arlington Hts** 19

Café la Cave | **Des Plaines** 24

Carlucci | **Downers Grove** 19

Carson's Ribs | **Deerfield** 20

Chens | **Wrigleyville** 23

Clubhouse | **Oak Brook** 21

Costa's | **multi. loc.** 21

☑ Courtright's | **Willow Spgs** 26

NEW Cru Cafe | **Gold Coast** –

David's Bistro | **Des Plaines** 24

Dee's | **Lincoln Pk** 19

Don Roth's | **Wheeling** 20

Dover Straits | **Mundelein** 18

Edelweiss | **Norridge** 21

EJ's Place | **Skokie** 19

Enoteca Piattini | **Lincoln Pk** 21

Entourage | **Schaumburg** –

Erie Cafe | **River N** 23

Finley's Grill | **Downers Grove** –

☑ Five O'Clock | **Fox Riv. Grove** 26

☑ Francesca's | **multi. loc.** 23

Froggy's French | **Highwood** 22

Gale St. Inn | **Mundelein** 20

Gene & Georgetti | **River N** 23

☑ Gibsons | **multi. loc.** 25

NEW Ginger Asian | **Orland Pk** –

Greek Islands | multi. loc.	21
Green Door Tav. | River N	14
Hacienda Teca. | Ukrainian Vill	20
Hackney's | multi. loc.	18
Half Shell | Lakeview	22
Harbour House | Winnetka	-
Hecky's | Evanston	21
Il Mulino | Gold Coast	-
ⓩ Japonais | Near W	24
John's Place | Lincoln Pk	18
Keefer's | River N	23
Koi | Evanston	19
ⓩ Les Nomades | Streeterville	28
Le Vichyssois | Lakemoor	24
Lovell's | Lake Forest	20
Magnum's Steak | Lombard	23
McCormick/Schmick | Gold Coast	21
Melting Pot | Schaumburg	21
Milk & Honey | Wicker Pk	21
Mrs. Murphy | Lakeview	21
My Pie Pizza | Bucktown	21
Narcisse | River N	20
ⓩ North Pond | Lincoln Pk	25
ⓩ Original Pancake | Lake Zurich	23
Park Grill | Loop	19
Prairie Grass | Northbrook	21
NEW Quince | Evanston	-
Reza's | River N	19
ⓩ RL | Gold Coast	22
Sai Café | Lincoln Pk	24
Santorini | Greektown	21
South Gate Cafe | Lake Forest	18
Stanley's | W Loop	19
Swordfish | Batavia	25
ⓩ Tallgrass | Lockport	28
Tsunami | Gold Coast	20
Uncommon Grnd. | Wrigleyville	21
ⓩ Va Pensiero | Evanston	26
ⓩ Vie | W Springs	27

GAME IN SEASON

NEW Adesso | Lakeview	-
ⓩ Alinea | Lincoln Pk	28
Allen's | River N	24

ⓩ Atwater's | Geneva	21
ⓩ Avenues | River N	26
NEW Azucar | Logan Sq	-
Bank Lane | Lake Forest	23
NEW Barcello's | Wicker Pk	-
ⓩ Barrington Bistro | Barrington	27
Bistro Campagne | Lincoln Sq	23
Bistro Kirkou | Lake Zurich	22
Bistro 110 | Gold Coast	20
Bistrot Margot | Old Town	21
Bistrot Zinc | Gold Coast	20
BOKA | Lincoln Pk	23
ⓩ Brasserie Jo | River N	22
Buona Terra | Logan Sq	24
Cab's Wine Bar | Glen Ellyn	22
Café Absinthe | Bucktown	23
Café Bernard | Lincoln Pk	21
Café/Architectes | Gold Coast	22
Café la Cave | Des Plaines	24
Café le Coq | Oak Pk	23
Cafe Matou | Bucktown	22
Cafe Pyrenees | Libertyville	21
Campagnola | Evanston	23
ⓩ Carlos' | Highland Pk	29
NEW Chalkboard | Lincoln Sq	-
ⓩ Charlie Trotter's | Lincoln Pk	27
Chicago Firehse. | S Loop	18
CHIC Cafe | River N	20
Cité | Streeterville	17
Coco Pazzo | River N	24
copperblue | Streeterville	-
NEW Côtes/Rhône | Edgewater	-
ⓩ Courtright's | Willow Spgs	26
ⓩ Crofton on Wells | River N	26
ⓩ Custom Hse. | Printer's Row	24
Cyrano's Bistrot | River N	20
D & J Bistro | Lake Zurich	25
David's Bistro | Des Plaines	24
de cero | Mkt Dist	21
Emilio's Sunflower | La Grange	-
erwin cafe | Lakeview	23
Froggy's French | Highwood	22

🔲 Frontera Grill	**River N**	26
🔲 Gabriel's	**Highwood**	26
NEW Gage	**S Loop**	–
Glunz Bavarian	**Lincoln Sq**	19
Green Dolphin St.	**Lincoln Pk**	19
Harvest	**St. Charles**	–
HB	**Lakeview**	22
Heartland Cafe	**Rogers Pk**	16
Hemmingway's	**Oak Pk**	21
NEW Hop Häus	**River N**	–
🔲 Hot Doug's	**NW Side**	25
🔲 Isabella's	**Geneva**	26
Jack's on Halsted	**Lakeview**	21
Jilly's Cafe	**Evanston**	23
Karma	**Mundelein**	24
Kaze Sushi	**Roscoe Vill**	24
Keefer's	**River N**	23
🔲 Kevin	**River N**	26
KiKi's Bistro	**River N**	23
La Fette	**Old Town**	–
NEW La Petite Amelia	**Evanston**	–
la petite folie	**Hyde Pk**	24
La Piazza	**Forest Pk**	25
La Piazza	**Naperville**	–
La Sardine	**W Loop**	23
La Scarola	**Near W**	23
La Strada	**Loop**	19
La Tache	**Andersonville**	21
La Tasca	**Arlington Hts**	23
Le Bouchon	**Bucktown**	22
🔲 Le Français	**Wheeling**	28
🔲 Les Nomades	**Streeterville**	28
🔲 Le Titi/Paris	**Arlington Hts**	26
Le Vichyssois	**Lakemoor**	24
Lovell's	**Lake Forest**	20
Meritage Cafe	**Bucktown**	22
Merlo	**Gold Coast**	23
Michael	**Winnetka**	25
Mimosa	**Highland Pk**	23
🔲 mk	**River N**	26
Mrs. Murphy	**Lakeview**	21
NEW Mulan	**Chinatown**	–
🔲 Naha	**River N**	26

Narcisse	**River N**	20
NEW Niche	**Geneva**	–
🔲 North Pond	**Lincoln Pk**	25
🔲 Oceanique	**Evanston**	27
One North	**Loop**	18
🔲 one sixtyblue	**Mkt Dist**	25
Opera	**S Loop**	23
Park Grill	**Loop**	19
Parlor	**Wicker Pk**	19
Philander's	**Oak Pk**	21
🔲 Pump Room	**Gold Coast**	21
Retro Bistro	**Mt. Prospect**	25
🔲 RL	**Gold Coast**	22
Russian Tea	**Loop**	22
🔲 Salbute	**Hinsdale**	26
Salpicón	**Old Town**	24
Saltaus	**Mkt Dist**	19
Sapori Tratt.	**Lincoln Pk**	22
Schwa	**Lincoln Pk**	26
🔲 Seasons	**Gold Coast**	26
NEW Sequel	**Lombard**	–
1776	**Crystal Lake**	24
socca	**Lakeview**	21
Stained Glass	**Evanston**	23
State	**Lincoln Pk**	–
🔲 Tallgrass	**Lockport**	28
Tarantino's	**Lincoln Pk**	21
Think Café	**Bucktown**	24
Timo	**Near W**	–
🔲 Va Pensiero	**Evanston**	26
🔲 Vie	**W Springs**	27
Vivere	**Loop**	21
Volo	**Roscoe Vill**	20

HISTORIC PLACES

(Year opened; * building)

1847	Mesón Sabika*	**Naperville**	23
1858	Don Roth's*	**Wheeling**	20
1865	Crofton on Wells*	**River N**	26
1872	Green Door Tav.*	**River N**	14
1880	West Town Tav.*	**W Town**	23
1881	Twin Anchors*	**Old Town**	22
1885	Red Lion Pub*	**Lincoln Pk**	16
1886	Cold Comfort*	**Bucktown**	22

1890 | Pasta Palazzo* | **Lincoln Pk** 22

1890 | Pizzeria Uno/Due* | **River N** 22

1890 | Sapori Tratt.* | **Lincoln Pk** 22

1890 | Webster Wine* | **Lincoln Pk** 17

1893 | Tavern* | **Libertyville** 23

1895 | Club Lago* | **River N** 17

1897 | Tallgrass* | **Lockport** 28

1900 | Vivo* | **Mkt Dist** 21

1901 | South Gate Cafe* | **Lake Forest** 18

1905 | Carnivale* | **W Loop** 22

1909 | Pompei Bakery | **Little Italy** 20

1911 | Poag Mahone's* | **Loop** 17

1918 | Drake Bros.' | **Streeterville** 17

1918 | Vito & Nick's | **Far S Side** ‒

1920 | Chef's Station* | **Evanston** 23

1921 | Margie's Candies | **Bucktown** 23

1923 | Lou Mitchell's | **W Loop** 22

1927 | Francesca's* | **Edgewater** 23

1927 | Village* | **Loop** 19

1927 | Vivere* | **Loop** 21

1928 | Philander's* | **Oak Pk** 21

1930 | Del Rio* | **Highwood** 18

1930 | Russell's BBQ | **Elmwood Pk** 18

1930 | Tufano's Tap* | **Near S Side** 21

1933 | Bruna's | **SW Side** 23

1933 | Cape Cod Rm. | **Streeterville** 21

1934 | Billy Goat Tav. | **River N** 15

1935 | Miller's Pub | **Loop** 17

1937 | Café le Coq* | **Oak Pk** 23

1938 | Al's #1 Beef | **Little Italy** 22

1938 | Pump Room | **Gold Coast** 21

1939 | Hackney's | **Glenview** 18

1941 | Gene & Georgetti | **River N** 23

1942 | Manny's | **S Loop** 23

1945 | Ann Sather | **Lakeview** 19

1945 | Army & Lou's | **Far S Side** 19

1948 | Superdawg | **NW Side** 22

1954 | White Fence | **Romeoville** 21

1955 | La Cantina | **Loop** 19

1955 | Pizzeria Uno/Due | **River N** 22

HOTEL DINING

Ambassador East Hotel

  🖸 Pump Room | **Gold Coast** 21

Belden-Stratford Hotel

  🖸 Mon Ami Gabi | **Lincoln Pk** 22

Best Western Grant Park Hotel

  NEW Fornetto & Mei's | **S Loop** ‒

Carleton Hotel

  Philander's | **Oak Pk** 21

Crowne Plaza Chicago Metro

  Dine | **W Loop** ‒

Crowne Plaza Hotel

  Karma | **Mundelein** 24

Doubletree Guest Suites Hotel

  Mrs. Park's Tav. | **Streeterville** 17

Doubletree Hotel

  🖸 Gibsons | **Rosemont** 25

Drake Hotel

  Cape Cod Rm. | **Streeterville** 21

  Drake Bros.' | **Streeterville** 17

Embassy Suites Hotel

  P.J. Clarke's | **Streeterville** 17

Fairmont Chicago Hotel

  Aria | **Loop** 23

Four Seasons Hotel

  🖸 Seasons | **Gold Coast** 26

  🖸 Seasons Café | **Gold Coast** 25

Hard Rock Hotel

  China Grill | **Loop** 20

Herrington Inn

  🖸 Atwater's | **Geneva** 21

Hilton Garden Inn

  Weber Grill | **River N** 19

Holiday Inn

  Aurelio's Pizza | **Loop** 22

Homestead Hotel

  NEW Quince | **Evanston** ‒

Hotel Allegro

  312 Chicago | **Loop** 19

CHICAGO

SPECIAL FEATURES

Hotel Blake
  ☑ Custom Hse. | **Printer's Row** 24

Hotel Burnham
  ☑ Atwood Cafe | **Loop** 21

Hotel Monaco
  South Water Kitchen | **Loop** 17

Hyatt Regency
  Stetson's Chop Hse. | **Loop** 23

Hyatt Regency McCormick Pl.
  NEW Shor | **S Loop** —

InterContinental, Hotel
  Zest | **Streeterville** 20

James Chicago Hotel
  David Burke Prime | **River N** 22

Margarita Inn
  ☑ Va Pensiero | **Evanston** 26

Northshore Hotel
  Tapas Barcelona | **Evanston** 20

O'Hare International Ctr.
  Harry Caray's | **Rosemont** 19

Park Hyatt Chicago
  ☑ NoMI | **Gold Coast** 26

Peninsula Hotel
  ☑ Avenues | **River N** 26
  ☑ Lobby | **River N** 23
  Pierrot Gourmet | **River N** 21
  ☑ Shanghai Terr. | **River N** 24

Pheasant Run Resort
  Harvest | **St. Charles** —

Red Roof Inn
  Coco Pazzo | **Streeterville** 22

Renaissance Hotel
  ☑ Ruth's Chris | **Northbrook** 24

Renaissance Schaumburg Hotel
  NEW Sam & Harry's |
    Schaumburg —

Ritz-Carlton Hotel
  Ritz-Carlton Café | **Streeterville** —

Seneca Hotel
  Saloon Steak | **Streeterville** 23

Sheraton Chicago
  Shula's Steak | **Streeterville** 20

Sofitel Chicago Water Tower
  Café/Architectes | **Gold Coast** 22

Swissôtel
  Palm, The | **Loop** 23

Tremont Hotel
  Mike Ditka's | **Gold Coast** 20

W Chicago Lakeshore
  Wave | **Streeterville** 20

Westin Chicago North Shore
  NEW Gale's Coffee |
    Wheeling —
  NEW Osteria/Tramonto |
    Wheeling —
  NEW Tramonto's | **Wheeling** —

Westin Hotel
  Grill on Alley | **Streeterville** 18

Westin River North
  Kamehachi | **River N** 22

Whitehall Hotel
  Fornetto Mei | **Gold Coast** 19

W Hotel
  rist. we | **Loop** 18

Write Inn
  Hemmingway's | **Oak Pk** 21

Wyndham Chicago
  Caliterra | **Streeterville** 23

Wyndham Northwest Chicago
  Shula's Steak | **Itasca** 20

JACKET REQUIRED

☑ Carlos' | **Highland Pk** 29
☑ Charlie Trotter's | **Lincoln Pk** 27
☑ Spiaggia | **Gold Coast** 26
☑ Tru | **Streeterville** 28

LATE DINING

(Weekday closing hour)

☑ Agami | 12 AM | **Uptown** 26
NEW Alhambra | 2 AM |
  Mkt Dist —
Al's #1 Beef | varies | **River N** 22
Andies | varies | **Andersonville** 18
Artopolis | 12 AM | **Greektown** 21
Athena | 12 AM | **Greektown** 19
☑ Avec | 12 AM | **W Loop** 25
Avenue M | 2 AM | **Near W** —

Ballo | 12 AM | **River N** _19_

Bar Louie | varies | **multi. loc.** _15_

NEW BB's | 12 AM | **River N** _-_

Bijan's | 3:30 AM | **River N** _19_

Billy Goat Tav. | varies | **River N** _15_

NEW Bourbon | 2 AM | **Lakeview** _-_

NEW Bravo Tapas | 12 AM | **Wicker Pk** _-_

Carmichael Steak | 12 AM | **W Loop** _22_

Carmine's | 12 AM | **Gold Coast** _21_

Coast Sushi | 12 AM | **Bucktown** _23_

Coobah | 1 AM | **Lakeview** _19_

NEW Cru Cafe | 2 AM | **Gold Coast** _-_

Cuatro | 2 AM | **S Loop** _23_

El Presidente | 24 hrs. | **Lincoln Pk** _14_

Emperor's Choice | 12 AM | **Chinatown** _23_

Evergreen | 12 AM | **Chinatown** _22_

Finley's Grill | 1:30 AM | **Downers Grove** _-_

Fixture | 12 AM | **Lincoln Pk** _-_

NEW Flatwater | 12 AM | **River N** _-_

Flight | 1 AM | **Glenview** _19_

Gene & Georgetti | 12 AM | **River N** _23_

Z Gibsons | varies | **multi. loc.** _25_

Z Giordano's | varies | **SW Side** _21_

Gold Coast Dogs | varies | **multi. loc.** _19_

Greek Islands | varies | **Far S Side** _21_

NEW Gruppo/Amici | 12 AM | **Rogers Pk** _-_

Happy Chef Dim Sum | 2 AM | **Chinatown** _23_

Hard Rock Cafe | 12 AM | **River N** _13_

NEW Hop Häus | 3:30 AM | **River N** _-_

Z Hugo's Frog/Fish | varies | **multi. loc.** _24_

Itto Sushi | 12 AM | **Lincoln Pk** _22_

Kamehachi | varies | **Old Town** _22_

Kit Kat Lounge | 12 AM | **Wrigleyville** _15_

Kuma's Corner | 1 AM | **Logan Sq** _-_

Landmark | 2 AM | **Lincoln Pk** _21_

Z Lao Sze Chuan | varies | **Chinatown** _24_

La Taberna Tapatia | 12 AM | **Roscoe Vill** _21_

Lou Mitchell's | varies | **O'Hare Area** _22_

LuxBar | 1:30 AM | **Gold Coast** _17_

Margie's Candies | varies | **Bucktown** _23_

Melting Pot | varies | **River N** _21_

Miller's Pub | 2 AM | **Loop** _17_

NEW Minnies | 2 AM | **Lincoln Pk** _-_

Nancy's Orig. | varies | **Lakeview** _21_

Narcisse | 1 AM | **River N** _20_

NEW 9 Muses | 1 AM | **Greektown** _-_

Nookies | varies | **Lakeview** _19_

Olé Olé | 12 AM | **Andersonville** _-_

Parlor | 12 AM | **Wicker Pk** _19_

Parthenon | 12 AM | **Greektown** _20_

Pegasus | varies | **multi. loc.** _22_

Penang | 1 AM | **Chinatown** _19_

People Lounge | 1 AM | **Wicker Pk** _-_

Pepper Lounge | 12 AM | **Wrigleyville** _22_

Pete Miller | varies | **Evanston** _21_

pingpong | 12 AM | **Lakeview** _21_

Pizzeria Uno/Due | varies | **River N** _22_

NEW Pops/Champ. | 1 AM | **River N** _-_

Quartino | 1 AM | **River N** _-_

RA Sushi | 1 AM | **multi. loc.** _19_

Reza's | varies | **multi. loc.** _19_

Ribs 'n' Bibs | 12 AM | **Hyde Pk** _22_

Rockit B&G | 2 AM | **River N** _19_

Z Roditys | 12 AM | **Greektown** _22_

Saltaus | 12:30 AM | **Mkt Dist** _19_

Samah | 12 AM | **Wrigleyville** _-_

San Soo Gab San | 24 hrs. | **NW Side** _21_

Santorini | 12 AM | **Greektown** _21_

Silver Seafood | 1 AM | **Uptown** _22_

Z Superdawg | varies | **NW Side** _22_

Z sushi wabi | 12 AM | **Mkt Dist** _26_

NEW Taos | 12 AM | **Roscoe Vill** ⌐

Tasting Room | 12 AM | **Mkt Dist** 18

Tavern on Rush | 12 AM | 19
Gold Coast

Tecalitlan | 12 AM | **W Town** 23

Tempo | 24 hrs. | **Gold Coast** 19

NEW Tokyo 21 | varies | ⌐
Lincoln Pk

Tsuki | 12:30 AM | **Lincoln Pk** 22

Twisted Spoke | 1 AM | **multi. loc.** 18

Webster Wine | 12:30 AM | 17
Lincoln Pk

Wiener's Circle | 4 AM | **Lincoln Pk** 20

MEET FOR A DRINK

(Most top hotels and the following
standouts)

NEW Alhambra | **Mkt Dist** ⌐

Allen's | **River N** 24

Avenue M | **Near W** ⌐

Ballo | **River N** 19

Bandera | **Streeterville** 20

Bar Louie | **multi. loc.** 15

NEW BB's | **River N** ⌐

Bijan's | **River N** 19

Billy Goat Tav. | **multi. loc.** 15

Z Bin 36/Bin Wine | **multi. loc.** 20

Bistro 110 | **Gold Coast** 20

Blue Water | **River N** 22

BOKA | **Lincoln Pk** 23

Z Brasserie Jo | **River N** 22

NEW Bravo Tapas | **Wicker Pk** ⌐

NEW Broadway Cellars | ⌐
Edgewater

Butter | **Greektown** 22

Cab's Wine Bar | **Glen Ellyn** 22

Café/Architectes | **Gold Coast** 22

Canoe Club | **Orland Pk** 19

Z Carnivale | **W Loop** 22

Catch 35 | **Loop** 23

Chief O'Neill's | **NW Side** 18

China Grill | **Loop** 20

Coobah | **Lakeview** 19

NEW Cordis Bros. | **Lakeview** ⌐

NEW Cru Cafe | **Gold Coast** ⌐

Cuatro | **S Loop** 23

NEW DeLaCosta | **River N** ⌐

Dine | **W Loop** ⌐

Di Pescara | **Northbrook** ⌐

Enoteca Piattini | **Lincoln Pk** 21

Entourage | **Schaumburg** ⌐

Extra Virgin | **Mkt Dist** 19

Finley's Grill | **Downers Grove** ⌐

NEW Flatwater | **River N** ⌐

Fleming's Steak | **Lincolnshire** ⌐

Flight | **Glenview** 19

Z Frontera Grill | **River N** 26

Fulton's | **River N** 20

NEW Gage | **S Loop** ⌐

Z Gibsons | **multi. loc.** 25

Goose Is. Brewing | **multi. loc.** 16

NEW Gordon Biersch | ⌐
Bolingbrook

NEW Graze | **River N** ⌐

Green Door Tav. | **River N** 14

Grotto | **Gold Coast** 18

Harry Caray's | **multi. loc.** 19

Z Japonais | **Near W** 24

Z Joe's Sea/Steak | **River N** 26

Keefer's | **River N** 23

Landmark | **Lincoln Pk** 21

LuxBar | **Gold Coast** 17

Mambo Grill | **River N** 19

Marché | **Mkt Dist** 20

McCormick/Schmick | 21
Gold Coast

Meritage Cafe | **Bucktown** 22

NEW Midtown Kitchen | **Loop** ⌐

Mike Ditka's | **Gold Coast** 20

Miramar | **Highwood** 19

Z mk | **River N** 26

NEW Mulan | **Chinatown** ⌐

Nacional 27 | **River N** 22

Z Nine | **W Loop** 22

NEW 9 Muses | **Greektown** ⌐

Z NoMI | **Gold Coast** 26

One North | **Loop** 18

Z one sixtyblue | **Mkt Dist** 25

Osteria Via Stato | **River N** 21

P.J. Clarke's | **Gold Coast**		17
Platiyo | **Lakeview**		20
NEW Pops/Champ. | **River N**		-
Prairie Grass | **Northbrook**		21
Quartino | **River N**		-
Red Light | **Mkt Dist**		23
NEW Republic | **River N**		-
Rhapsody | **Loop**		21
Z RL | **Gold Coast**		22
Rock Bottom | **River N**		16
Rockit B&G | **River N**		19
NEW Room 21 | **S Loop**		-
Rosebud Steak | **Gold Coast**		23
Rumba | **River N**		18
Saltaus | **Mkt Dist**		19
Scoozi! | **River N**		21
Z Shaw's Crab | **multi. loc.**		23
Sidebar Grille | **Loop**		-
Z Signature Rm. | **Streeterville**		18
Smith & Wollensky | **River N**		22
South Water Kitchen | **Loop**		17
Stained Glass | **Evanston**		23
Sullivan's Steak | **River N**		23
NEW Sura | **Lakeview**		-
Z SushiSamba rio | **River N**		21
Tasting Room | **Mkt Dist**		18
Tavern on Rush | **Gold Coast**		19
NEW Tepatulco | **Lincoln Pk**		-
312 Chicago | **Loop**		19
Timpano Chophse. | **Naperville**		-
Z Tizi Melloul | **River N**		21
NEW Tokyo 21 | **Lincoln Pk**		-
NEW Tramonto's | **Wheeling**		-
Tratt. No. 10 | **Loop**		23
Twisted Spoke | **Near W**		18
NEW Viet Bistro | **Rogers Pk**		-
Volo | **Roscoe Vill**		20
Wave | **Streeterville**		20
Webster Wine | **Lincoln Pk**		17
NEW Xel-Há | **River N**		-
Zapatista | **S Loop**		20
NEW Zocalo | **River N**		-

MICROBREWERIES

NEW Brockway Chop | **Palatine**		-
Goose Is. Brewing | **multi. loc.**		16
NEW Gordon Biersch | **Bolingbrook**		-
Piece | **Bucktown**		22
Rock Bottom | **multi. loc.**		16

OUTDOOR DINING

(G=garden; P=patio; S=sidewalk; T=terrace; W=waterside)

Allen's | P | **River N**		24
Arco/Cuchilleros | P | **Lakeview**		19
a tavola | G | **Ukrainian Vill**		23
Athena | G | **Greektown**		19
Z Atwater's | P | **Geneva**		21
Bijan's | S | **River N**		19
Bistro Campagne | G | **Lincoln Sq**		23
Bistro 110 | S | **Gold Coast**		20
Bistrot Margot | S | **Old Town**		21
Z Blackbird | S | **W Loop**		27
Z Brasserie Jo | S | **River N**		22
Cafe Ba-Ba-Reeba! | P | **Lincoln Pk**		22
Carmichael Steak | G | **W Loop**		22
Carmine's | P | **Gold Coast**		21
Chez Joël | P | **Little Italy**		22
Coco Pazzo | P | **Streeterville**		22
Cyrano's Bistrot | S | **River N**		20
Edwardo's Pizza | P | **Printer's Row**		20
Feast | G | **Bucktown**		18
Z Five O'Clock | P, W | **Fox Riv. Grove**		26
NEW Flatwater | P, W | **River N**		-
Flight | P | **Glenview**		19
Z Frontera Grill | P | **River N**		26
Fulton's | P, W | **River N**		20
Greek Islands | P, S | **multi. loc.**		21
Green Dolphin St. | P, W | **Lincoln Pk**		19
Z Isabella's | P | **Geneva**		26
Z Japonais | P | **Near W**		24
John's Place | S | **Lincoln Pk**		18
Kamehachi | P, S | **multi. loc.**		22
Z Le Colonial | S, T | **Gold Coast**		23
Lucca's | G | **Lakeview**		19

Ⓩ Maggiano's | P | **multi. loc.** 20

Mas | S | **Wicker Pk** 22

Meritage Cafe | G | **Bucktown** 22

Ⓩ Mesón Sabika | G, P | **multi. loc.** 23

NEW 9 Muses | S | **Greektown** —

Ⓩ NoMI | G | **Gold Coast** 26

Park Grill | P | **Loop** 19

Pegasus | T | **Greektown** 22

Ⓩ P.F. Chang's | P | **Northbrook** 20

Phil Stefani's | S | **River N** 21

NEW Pops/Champ. | P | **River N** —

Potbelly Sandwich | P | **multi. loc.** 20

Puck's at MCA | P, W | 20
   Streeterville

Ⓩ RL | P | **Gold Coast** 22

Rock Bottom | G, P | **multi. loc.** 16

NEW Room 21 | G | **S Loop** —

Ⓩ Rosebud | P, S, W | **multi. loc.** 21

Salvatore's | G | **Lincoln Pk** 21

Ⓩ Shanghai Terr. | T | **River N** 24

Smith & Wollensky | G, P, T, W | 22
   River N

South Gate Cafe | P, S | **Lake Forest** 18

Ⓩ SushiSamba rio | S | **River N** 21

Tapas Barcelona | G, P | **Evanston** 20

Tavern on Rush | P, S | **Gold Coast** 19

Timo | P | **Near W** —

Tuscany | G, P | **multi. loc.** 22

Twisted Spoke | P | **multi. loc.** 18

Ⓩ Va Pensiero | T | **Evanston** 26

PEOPLE-WATCHING

Adobo Grill | **Old Town** 21

NEW Alhambra | **Mkt Dist** —

American Girl | **Gold Coast** 12

Ⓩ Avec | **W Loop** 25

Avenue M | **Near W** —

Ⓩ Bin 36/Bin Wine | **River N** 20

Bistro 110 | **Gold Coast** 20

Ⓩ Blackbird | **W Loop** 27

BOKA | **Lincoln Pk** 23

Bongo Room | **Wicker Pk** 24

Ⓩ Brasserie Jo | **River N** 22

NEW Bravo Tapas | **Wicker Pk** —

Carmine's | **Gold Coast** 21

Ⓩ Carnivale | **W Loop** 22

Ⓩ Chicago Chop | **River N** 25

Coobah | **Lakeview** 19

NEW Cru Cafe | **Gold Coast** —

Cuatro | **S Loop** 23

NEW DeLaCosta | **River N** —

Entourage | **Schaumburg** —

Ⓩ Gibsons | **Gold Coast** 25

NEW Graze | **River N** —

Ⓩ Green Zebra | **W Town** 25

NEW Hamburger Mary's | —
   Andersonville

Harry Caray's | **River N** 19

Il Mulino | **Gold Coast** —

Ⓩ Japonais | **Near W** 24

Keefer's | **River N** 23

Landmark | **Lincoln Pk** 21

Ⓩ Le Colonial | **Gold Coast** 23

LuxBar | **Gold Coast** 17

Ⓩ Manny's | **S Loop** 23

Marché | **Mkt Dist** 20

Ⓩ Mirai Sushi | **Wicker Pk** 26

Miramar | **Highwood** 19

Ⓩ mk | **River N** 26

Ⓩ Naha | **River N** 26

Narcisse | **River N** 20

Ⓩ Nine | **W Loop** 22

NEW 9 Muses | **Greektown** —

Ⓩ NoMI | **Gold Coast** 26

Opera | **S Loop** 23

Osteria Via Stato | **River N** 21

NEW Pops/Champ. | **River N** —

Quartino | **River N** —

NEW Republic | **River N** —

NEW Room 21 | **S Loop** —

Ⓩ Rosebud | **multi. loc.** 21

Rosebud Steak | **Gold Coast** 23

Saltaus | **Mkt Dist** 19

Scoozi! | **River N** 21

Ⓩ Spring | **Wicker Pk** 27

NEW Sura | **Lakeview** —

Ⓩ SushiSamba rio | **River N** 21

Tavern on Rush | **Gold Coast** 19

NEW Tokyo 21 | **Lincoln Pk**	–
NEW Tramonto's | **Wheeling**	–
Wave | **Streeterville**	20
Zapatista | **S Loop**	20

POWER SCENES

Z Alinea | **Lincoln Pk**	28
Z Avenues | **River N**	26
Capital Grille | **Streeterville**	24
Catch 35 | **Loop**	23
Z Charlie Trotter's | **Lincoln Pk**	27
Z Chicago Chop | **River N**	25
Coco Pazzo | **River N**	24
Z Custom Hse. | **Printer's Row**	24
David Burke Prime | **River N**	22
Entourage | **Schaumburg**	–
Z Everest | **Loop**	27
Fulton's | **River N**	20
Gene & Georgetti | **River N**	23
Z Gibsons | **multi. loc.**	25
Z Hugo's Frog/Fish | **Gold Coast**	24
Il Mulino | **Gold Coast**	–
Keefer's | **River N**	23
Z Le Français | **Wheeling**	28
Z Les Nomades | **Streeterville**	28
Z mk | **River N**	26
Z Morton's Steak | **multi. loc.**	26
Z Naha | **River N**	26
Z NoMI | **Gold Coast**	26
Z RL | **Gold Coast**	22
Z Ruth's Chris | **multi. loc.**	24
Z Seasons | **Gold Coast**	26
Smith & Wollensky | **River N**	22
Z Spiaggia | **Gold Coast**	26
Z Spring | **Wicker Pk**	27
NEW Tramonto's | **Wheeling**	–
Z Tru | **Streeterville**	28

PRIVATE ROOMS

(Restaurants charge less at off times; call for capacity)

Athena | **Greektown**	19
Ben Pao | **River N**	21
Z Brasserie Jo | **River N**	22
Caliterra | **Streeterville**	23

Capital Grille | **Streeterville**	24
Catch 35 | **multi. loc.**	23
Z Charlie Trotter's | **Lincoln Pk**	27
Z Chicago Chop | **River N**	25
Club Lucky | **Bucktown**	20
Costa's | **multi. loc.**	21
Edwardo's Pizza | **multi. loc.**	20
Emilio's Tapas | **Lincoln Pk**	21
Z Everest | **Loop**	27
Z Francesca's | **multi. loc.**	23
Z Frontera Grill | **River N**	26
Z Gabriel's | **Highwood**	26
Gene & Georgetti | **River N**	23
Z Gibsons | **multi. loc.**	25
Gioco | **S Loop**	21
Goose Is. Brewing | **multi. loc.**	16
Greek Islands | **multi. loc.**	21
Z Joe's Sea/Steak | **River N**	26
Kamehachi | **multi. loc.**	22
Keefer's | **River N**	23
Z Mesón Sabika | **Naperville**	23
Z mk | **River N**	26
Z Naha | **River N**	26
Z Nine | **W Loop**	22
Z NoMI | **Gold Coast**	26
Z one sixtyblue | **Mkt Dist**	25
Park Grill | **Loop**	19
Pete Miller | **multi. loc.**	21
Red Light | **Mkt Dist**	23
Rock Bottom | **multi. loc.**	16
Z Rosebud | **multi. loc.**	21
Russian Tea | **Loop**	22
Z Ruth's Chris | **multi. loc.**	24
Scoozi! | **River N**	21
Z Shaw's Crab | **multi. loc.**	23
Smith & Wollensky | **River N**	22
Z Spiaggia | **Gold Coast**	26
Z SushiSamba rio | **River N**	21
Z Tallgrass | **Lockport**	28
312 Chicago | **Loop**	19
Z Tizi Melloul | **River N**	21
Z Topolobampo | **River N**	27
Tratt. Roma | **Old Town**	19
Z Tru | **Streeterville**	28

ℤ Va Pensiero | **Evanston**	26	
Vivo | **Mkt Dist**	21	
ℤ Wildfire | **multi. loc.**	23	

PRIX FIXE MENUS
(Call for prices and times)

ℤ Arun's | **NW Side**	28
ℤ Avenues | **River N**	26
Bank Lane | **Lake Forest**	23
ℤ Bin 36/Bin Wine | **River N**	20
Bistro 110 | **Gold Coast**	20
Caliterra | **Streeterville**	23
ℤ Carlos' | **Highland Pk**	29
ℤ Charlie Trotter's | **Lincoln Pk**	27
ℤ Courtright's | **Willow Spgs**	26
Cyrano's Bistrot | **River N**	20
D & J Bistro | **Lake Zurich**	25
ℤ Everest | **Loop**	27
ℤ Fogo de Chão | **River N**	24
Froggy's French | **Highwood**	22
ℤ Gabriel's | **Highwood**	26
La Sardine | **W Loop**	23
ℤ Le Français | **Wheeling**	28
ℤ Les Nomades | **Streeterville**	28
ℤ mk | **River N**	26
ℤ Moto | **Mkt Dist**	25
ℤ North Pond | **Lincoln Pk**	25
ℤ Oceanique | **Evanston**	27
ℤ Pump Room | **Gold Coast**	21
Red Light | **Mkt Dist**	23
Retro Bistro | **Mt. Prospect**	25
Roy's | **River N**	24
Salpicón | **Old Town**	24
ℤ Seasons | **Gold Coast**	26
ℤ Spiaggia | **Gold Coast**	26
ℤ Spring | **Wicker Pk**	27
ℤ Tallgrass | **Lockport**	28
ℤ Topolobampo | **River N**	27
ℤ Tru | **Streeterville**	28

QUICK BITES

Aladdin's Eatery | **Lincoln Pk**	17
Art of Pizza | **Lakeview**	24
Artopolis | **Greektown**	21
NEW Azucar | **Logan Sq**	–
Babylon Eatery | **Bucktown**	17
Bagel | **multi. loc.**	18
Bar Louie | **multi. loc.**	15
Berghoff | **O'Hare Area**	–
Big Bowl | **multi. loc.**	18
Bijan's | **River N**	19
Billy Goat Tav. | **multi. loc.**	15
ℤ Bin 36/Bin Wine | **multi. loc.**	20
Café Selmarie | **Lincoln Sq**	21
Cereality | **Loop**	16
Chicago Pizza/Oven | **Lincoln Pk**	22
Cold Comfort | **Bucktown**	22
NEW Convito | **Wilmette**	–
NEW Cru Cafe | **Gold Coast**	–
Eleven City Diner | **S Loop**	–
El Presidente | **Lincoln Pk**	14
Extra Virgin | **Mkt Dist**	19
NEW Feed/Beast | **Lincoln Sq**	–
Flat Top Grill | **multi. loc.**	19
foodlife | **Streeterville**	16
NEW Fornetto & Mei's | **S Loop**	–
NEW fRedhots | **Glenview**	–
NEW Gale's Coffee | **Wheeling**	–
Gold Coast Dogs | **multi. loc.**	19
NEW Graze | **River N**	–
Hannah's Bretzel | **Loop**	–
Haro | **SW Side**	–
NEW Honey 1 BBQ | **Bucktown**	–
Hot Chocolate | **Bucktown**	23
ℤ Hot Doug's | **NW Side**	25
Lem's BBQ | **Far S Side**	24
Maiz | **Humboldt Pk**	25
ℤ Manny's | **multi. loc.**	23
NEW Minnies | **Lincoln Pk**	–
NEW Mundial | **Near S Side**	–
Noon-O-Kabab | **NW Side**	20
Oak Tree | **Gold Coast**	17
Old Jerusalem | **Old Town**	19
NEW Patty Burger | **Loop**	–
Pegasus | **SW Side**	22
Penny's Noodle | **multi. loc.**	19
People Lounge | **Wicker Pk**	–
Pierrot Gourmet | **River N**	21
Pompei Bakery | **multi. loc.**	20

Potbelly Sandwich	**multi. loc.**	20
Puck's at MCA	**Streeterville**	20
Quartino	**River N**	–
Russell's BBQ	**Elmwood Pk**	18
Stained Glass	**Evanston**	23
State	**Lincoln Pk**	–
Stir Crazy	**multi. loc.**	19
⚏ Superdawg	**NW Side**	22
Tasting Room	**Mkt Dist**	18
Tempo	**Gold Coast**	19
NEW Uncle John's	**Far S Side**	–
Uncommon Grnd.	**Wrigleyville**	21
Viand Bar	**Streeterville**	23
Webster Wine	**Lincoln Pk**	17
Wiener's Circle	**Lincoln Pk**	20
NEW ZKF	**Bucktown**	–

QUIET CONVERSATION

Akai Hana	**Wilmette**	21
Aria	**Loop**	23
⚏ Arun's	**NW Side**	28
a tavola	**Ukrainian Vill**	23
Bank Lane	**Lake Forest**	23
⚏ Barrington Bistro	**Barrington**	27
Best Hunan	**Vernon Hills**	21
NEW Bistro Monet	**Glen Ellyn**	–
Café Bernard	**Lincoln Pk**	21
Café/Architectes	**Gold Coast**	22
Café la Cave	**Des Plaines**	24
Cafe Matou	**Bucktown**	22
Cafe Pyrenees	**Libertyville**	21
Café Selmarie	**Lincoln Sq**	21
⚏ Café Spiaggia	**Gold Coast**	24
Caliterra	**Streeterville**	23
Cape Cod Rm.	**Streeterville**	21
⚏ Carlos'	**Highland Pk**	29
⚏ Charlie Trotter's	**Lincoln Pk**	27
Chinoiserie	**Wilmette**	20
Cité	**Streeterville**	17
copperblue	**Streeterville**	–
D & J Bistro	**Lake Zurich**	25
Don Roth's	**Wheeling**	20

Dover Straits	**Mundelein**	18
erwin cafe	**Lakeview**	23
⚏ Everest	**Loop**	27
Gale St. Inn	**Mundelein**	20
Gaylord Indian	**multi. loc.**	22
Geja's Cafe	**Lincoln Pk**	21
Hashalom	**NW Side**	–
Itto Sushi	**Lincoln Pk**	22
NEW Jai Yen	**Lakeview**	–
Jilly's Cafe	**Evanston**	23
⚏ Kevin	**River N**	26
Klay Oven	**River N**	20
Kyoto	**multi. loc.**	22
La Crêperie	**Lakeview**	20
La Gondola	**Lincoln Pk**	–
Lawry's Prime Rib	**River N**	24
⚏ Le Français	**Wheeling**	28
Le P'tit Paris	**Streeterville**	22
⚏ Les Nomades	**Streeterville**	28
⚏ Le Titi/Paris	**Arlington Hts**	26
Le Vichyssois	**Lakemoor**	24
Lovell's	**Lake Forest**	20
Lucca's	**Lakeview**	19
NEW Matsuri	**Geneva**	–
Mimosa	**Highland Pk**	23
⚏ North Pond	**Lincoln Pk**	25
⚏ Oceanique	**Evanston**	27
One North	**Loop**	18
Pierrot Gourmet	**River N**	21
⚏ Pump Room	**Gold Coast**	21
NEW Quince	**Evanston**	–
Rhapsody	**Loop**	21
Ritz-Carlton Café	**Streeterville**	–
⚏ RL	**Gold Coast**	22
Ron of Japan	**multi. loc.**	18
Russian Tea	**Loop**	22
Salvatore's	**Lincoln Pk**	21
⚏ Seasons	**Gold Coast**	26
⚏ Seasons Café	**Gold Coast**	25
NEW Sequel	**Lombard**	–
1776	**Crystal Lake**	24
⚏ Shanghai Terr.	**River N**	24
Shiroi Hana	**Lakeview**	18
NEW Shor	**S Loop**	–

Siam Café | **Uptown**	_-_
☑ Signature Rm. | **Streeterville**	18
Slice of Life | **Skokie**	13
South Gate Cafe | **Lake Forest**	18
South Water Kitchen | **Loop**	17
Takkatsu | **Arlington Hts**	_-_
☑ Tallgrass | **Lockport**	28
Tasting Room | **Mkt Dist**	18
Tavern | **Libertyville**	23
Tratt. No. 10 | **Loop**	23
Tre Kronor | **NW Side**	24
☑ Tru | **Streeterville**	28
☑ Va Pensiero | **Evanston**	26
Village | **Loop**	19
Vinci | **Lincoln Pk**	22
Vivere | **Loop**	21
Vong's | **River N**	21
☑ Zealous | **River N**	24

RAW BARS

Blue Water | **River N**	22
☑ Bob Chinn's Crab | **Wheeling**	23
Butter | **Greektown**	22
Cape Cod Rm. | **Streeterville**	21
Cité | **Streeterville**	17
Davis St. Fish | **Evanston**	19
Fulton's | **River N**	20
Half Shell | **Lakeview**	22
☑ Hugo's Frog/Fish | **Gold Coast**	24
Mitchell's Fish Mkt. | **Glenview**	_-_
Pappadeaux Sea. | **Arlington Hts**	20
NEW Pops/Champ. | **River N**	_-_
Riva | **Streeterville**	18
☑ Shaw's Crab | **multi. loc.**	23
Tin Fish | **multi. loc.**	22

ROMANTIC PLACES

NEW Alhambra | **Mkt Dist**	_-_
Avenue M | **Near W**	_-_
☑ Avenues | **River N**	26
NEW Azucar | **Logan Sq**	_-_
☑ Barrington Bistro | **Barrington**	27
Bistro Campagne | **Lincoln Sq**	23

Bistro Kirkou | **Lake Zurich**	22
NEW Bistro Monet | **Glen Ellyn**	_-_
Bistrot Margot | **Old Town**	21
Bistrot Zinc | **Gold Coast**	20
BOKA | **Lincoln Pk**	23
NEW Bravo Tapas | **Wicker Pk**	_-_
Butter | **Greektown**	22
Café Absinthe | **Bucktown**	23
Café Bernard | **Lincoln Pk**	21
Café la Cave | **Des Plaines**	24
Cafe Pyrenees | **Libertyville**	21
Cape Cod Rm. | **Streeterville**	21
☑ Carlos' | **Highland Pk**	29
☑ Charlie Trotter's | **Lincoln Pk**	27
Chez Joël | **Little Italy**	22
Chinoiserie | **Wilmette**	20
Cité | **Streeterville**	17
Coco Pazzo | **River N**	24
copperblue | **Streeterville**	_-_
NEW Côtes/Rhône | **Edgewater**	_-_
☑ Courtright's | **Willow Spgs**	26
☑ Crofton on Wells | **River N**	26
NEW Cru Cafe | **Gold Coast**	_-_
Cuatro | **S Loop**	23
Cyrano's Bistrot | **River N**	20
D & J Bistro | **Lake Zurich**	25
NEW DeLaCosta | **River N**	_-_
Enoteca Piattini | **Lincoln Pk**	21
erwin cafe | **Lakeview**	23
☑ Everest | **Loop**	27
NEW Fiddlehead | **Lincoln Sq**	_-_
NEW Fiorentino's | **Lakeview**	_-_
1492 Tapas | **River N**	19
Froggy's French | **Highwood**	22
Geja's Cafe | **Lincoln Pk**	21
NEW Ginger Asian | **Orland Pk**	_-_
Gioco | **S Loop**	21
Green Dolphin St. | **Lincoln Pk**	19
Grotto | **Gold Coast**	18
NEW Il Covo | **Bucktown**	_-_
Il Mulino | **Gold Coast**	_-_
Jacky's Bistro | **Evanston**	23
☑ Japonais | **Near W**	24

Jilly's Cafe	**Evanston**	23
NEW Kansaku	**Evanston**	-
KiKi's Bistro	**River N**	23
La Crêperie	**Lakeview**	20
Landmark	**Lincoln Pk**	21
La Sardine	**W Loop**	23
La Tache	**Andersonville**	21
Le Bouchon	**Bucktown**	22
Z Le Colonial	**Gold Coast**	23
Z Le Français	**Wheeling**	28
Le P'tit Paris	**Streeterville**	22
Z Les Nomades	**Streeterville**	28
Z Le Titi/Paris	**Arlington Hts**	26
Le Vichyssois	**Lakemoor**	24
Luna Caprese	**Lincoln Pk**	25
NEW Marigold	**Uptown**	-
NEW Matsuri	**Geneva**	-
May St. Market	**Near W**	-
Meritage Cafe	**Bucktown**	22
Z mk	**River N**	26
Z Mon Ami Gabi	**multi. loc.**	22
NEW Mulan	**Chinatown**	-
Nacional 27	**River N**	22
Z Naha	**River N**	26
Narcisse	**River N**	20
NEW Niche	**Geneva**	-
Z NoMI	**Gold Coast**	26
Z Oceanique	**Evanston**	27
Pane Caldo	**Gold Coast**	24
NEW Pops/Champ.	**River N**	-
Z Pump Room	**Gold Coast**	21
NEW Quince	**Evanston**	-
Rhapsody	**Loop**	21
Riccardo Tratt.	**Lincoln Pk**	-
Z RL	**Gold Coast**	22
RoSal's Kitchen	**Little Italy**	24
Z Seasons	**Gold Coast**	26
1776	**Crystal Lake**	24
Z Shanghai Terr.	**River N**	24
Signature Rm.	**Streeterville**	18
sola	**Lakeview**	-
South Gate Cafe	**Lake Forest**	18
Z Spring	**Wicker Pk**	27
Stained Glass	**Evanston**	23

Z Tallgrass	**Lockport**	28
Z Tango Sur	**Wrigleyville**	24
Tasting Room	**Mkt Dist**	18
Tavern	**Libertyville**	23
Z Tizi Melloul	**River N**	21
Topo Gigio	**Old Town**	20
Z Tru	**Streeterville**	28
Z Va Pensiero	**Evanston**	26
Vermilion	**River N**	21
Vinci	**Lincoln Pk**	22
Vivo	**Mkt Dist**	21
Vong's	**River N**	21
Wave	**Streeterville**	20
Webster Wine	**Lincoln Pk**	17
Wildfish	**Arlington Hts**	25
NEW Xel-Há	**River N**	-
NEW Zocalo	**River N**	-

SENIOR APPEAL

Andies	**Uptown**	18
Ann Sather	**multi. loc.**	19
Army & Lou's	**Far S Side**	19
Bacchanalia	**SW Side**	23
Bagel	**multi. loc.**	18
Berghoff	**Loop**	-
Bogart's Charhse.	**multi. loc.**	21
Bruna's	**SW Side**	23
Cape Cod Rm.	**Streeterville**	21
Carson's Ribs	**River N**	20
NEW Chicago Pizza Co.	**Rolling Meadows**	-
NEW Cordis Bros.	**Lakeview**	-
Dave's Italian	**Evanston**	17
Davis St. Fish	**Evanston**	19
Del Rio	**Highwood**	18
Don Roth's	**Wheeling**	20
Dover Straits	**multi. loc.**	18
Edelweiss	**Norridge**	21
Francesco's	**Northbrook**	24
Gale St. Inn	**multi. loc.**	20
Hackney's	**multi. loc.**	18
La Cantina	**Loop**	19
La Gondola	**Lincoln Pk**	-
La Strada	**Loop**	19

Lawry's Prime Rib	**River N**	24
Le P'tit Paris	**Streeterville**	22
Le Vichyssois	**Lakemoor**	24
Lou Mitchell's	**W Loop**	22
Lutnia	**NW Side**	–
Margie's Candies	**Bucktown**	23
Miller's Pub	**Loop**	17
Mirabell	**NW Side**	20
Myron & Phil's	**Lincolnwood**	21
Next Door Bistro	**Northbrook**	21
Nick's Fishmkt.	**multi. loc.**	24
Oak Tree	**Gold Coast**	17
⛁ Original Pancake	**multi. loc.**	23
⛁ Pump Room	**Gold Coast**	21
Ritz-Carlton Café	**Streeterville**	–
⛁ Rosebud	**Loop**	21
Russell's BBQ	**Elmwood Pk**	18
Russian Tea	**Loop**	22
Sabatino's	**NW Side**	23
South Gate Cafe	**Lake Forest**	18
Tre Kronor	**NW Side**	24
Tufano's Tap	**Near S Side**	21
Village	**Loop**	19
White Fence	**Romeoville**	21

SINGLES SCENES

Adobo Grill	**Old Town**	21
Bar Louie	**multi. loc.**	15
BOKA	**Lincoln Pk**	23
⛁ Café Iberico	**River N**	23
⛁ Carnivale	**W Loop**	22
Clubhouse	**Oak Brook**	21
NEW DeLaCosta	**River N**	–
House of Blues	**River N**	16
Landmark	**Lincoln Pk**	21
LuxBar	**Gold Coast**	17
Mike Ditka's	**Gold Coast**	20
Narcisse	**River N**	20
⛁ Nine	**W Loop**	22
NEW 9 Muses	**Greektown**	–
P.J. Clarke's	**Gold Coast**	17
Red Light	**Mkt Dist**	23
Rock Bottom	**multi. loc.**	16
Rockit B&G	**River N**	19

Scoozi!	**River N**	21
Stanley's	**Lincoln Pk**	19
⛁ SushiSamba rio	**River N**	21
Tavern on Rush	**Gold Coast**	19
Wave	**Streeterville**	20

SLEEPERS

(Good to excellent food, but little known)

Amarind's	**Far W**	25
Amber Cafe	**Westmont**	24
Bacchanalia	**SW Side**	23
Balagio	**Homewood**	22
Bite Cafe	**Ukrainian Vill**	23
Bruna's	**SW Side**	23
David Burke Prime	**River N**	22
David's Bistro	**Des Plaines**	24
Dorado	**Lincoln Sq**	23
Fattoush	**Lincoln Pk**	23
Heat	**Old Town**	25
Izumi Sushi	**Mkt Dist**	23
Karma	**Mundelein**	24
Katsu	**NW Side**	26
Kizoku Sushi	**River N**	25
Kyoto	**multi. loc.**	22
La Cucina/Donatella	**Rogers Pk**	22
La Piazza	**Forest Pk**	25
Lem's BBQ	**Far S Side**	24
Leonardo's	**Andersonville**	23
Le P'tit Paris	**Streeterville**	22
Le Vichyssois	**Lakemoor**	24
Lucia	**Wicker Pk**	22
Luna Caprese	**Lincoln Pk**	25
Maiz	**Humboldt Pk**	25
Matsu Yama	**Lakeview**	22
Montarra	**Algonquin**	22
Pacific Blue	**Glen Ellyn**	25
Ringo	**Lincoln Pk**	22
Schwa	**Lincoln Pk**	26
Silver Seafood	**Uptown**	22
Swordfish	**Batavia**	25
Tavern	**Libertyville**	23
Tecatlitlan	**W Town**	23
Thai Classic	**Lakeview**	23
Udupi Palace	**multi. loc.**	23

Viand Bar | **Streeterville**	23
Wildfish | **multi. loc.**	25

TEEN APPEAL

Ann Sather | **multi. loc.**	19
Arco/Cuchilleros | **Lakeview**	19
Aurelio's Pizza | **multi. loc.**	22
Bandera | **Streeterville**	20
Bella Bacino | **multi. loc.**	21
Big Bowl | **multi. loc.**	18
Cereality | **Loop**	16
☑ Cheesecake Fac. | **multi. loc.**	19
Chicago Pizza/Oven | **Lincoln Pk**	22
Eatzi's | **Lincoln Pk**	18
Edwardo's Pizza | **multi. loc.**	20
EJ's Place | **Skokie**	19
Flat Top Grill | **multi. loc.**	19
☑ Giordano's | **multi. loc.**	21
Gold Coast Dogs | **multi. loc.**	19
Grand Lux | **River N**	20
Hackney's | **multi. loc.**	18
Hard Rock Cafe | **River N**	13
Harry Caray's | **River N**	19
☑ Heaven on Seven | **multi. loc.**	21
☑ Hot Doug's | **NW Side**	25
Hot Tamales | **Highland Pk**	21
Ina's | **W Loop**	19
Joy Yee's Noodle | **multi. loc.**	21
Kroll's | **S Loop**	-
☑ Lou Malnati's | **multi. loc.**	24
Lou Mitchell's | **W Loop**	22
LuLu's Dim Sum | **Evanston**	19
L. Woods Lodge | **Lincolnwood**	19
Margie's Candies | **Bucktown**	23
Mity Nice Grill | **Streeterville**	18
My Pie Pizza | **Bucktown**	21
Nancy's Orig. | **multi. loc.**	21
Nookies | **multi. loc.**	19
Original Gino's | **multi. loc.**	22
☑ Original Pancake | **multi. loc.**	23
Penny's Noodle | **multi. loc.**	19
Pizzeria Uno/Due | **River N**	22
Pompei Bakery | **multi. loc.**	20
Potbelly Sandwich | **multi. loc.**	20

R.J. Grunts | **Lincoln Pk**	19
Robinson's Ribs | **multi. loc.**	19
Russell's BBQ | **Elmwood Pk**	18
Stanley's | **Lincoln Pk**	19
Stir Crazy | **Northbrook**	19
☑ Superdawg | **NW Side**	22
Tempo | **Gold Coast**	19
Toast | **multi. loc.**	22
Wiener's Circle | **Lincoln Pk**	20
Wishbone | **multi. loc.**	21

TRENDY

Adobo Grill | **Old Town**	21
☑ Agami | **Uptown**	26
NEW Aigre Doux | **River N**	-
NEW Alhambra | **Mkt Dist**	-
☑ Alinea | **Lincoln Pk**	28
☑ Avec | **W Loop**	25
Avenue M | **Near W**	-
☑ Bin 36/Bin Wine | **multi. loc.**	20
Bistro Campagne | **Lincoln Sq**	23
☑ Blackbird | **W Loop**	27
BOKA | **Lincoln Pk**	23
Bongo Room | **Wicker Pk**	24
NEW Bravo Tapas | **Wicker Pk**	-
Butter | **Greektown**	22
☑ Café Iberico | **River N**	23
☑ Carnivale | **W Loop**	22
NEW Chalkboard | **Lincoln Sq**	-
China Grill | **Loop**	20
Coobah | **Lakeview**	19
NEW Crust | **Wicker Pk**	-
Cuatro | **S Loop**	23
☑ Custom Hse. | **Printer's Row**	24
David Burke Prime | **River N**	22
de cero | **Mkt Dist**	21
NEW DeLaCosta | **River N**	-
NEW 545 North | **Libertyville**	-
NEW Flatwater | **River N**	-
Follia | **Mkt Dist**	22
☑ Frontera Grill | **River N**	26
☑ Gibsons | **Gold Coast**	25

Gioco | **S Loop**	21
NEW Graze | **River N**	-
Z Green Zebra | **W Town**	25
NEW Hamburger Mary's | **Andersonville**	-
Hot Chocolate | **Bucktown**	23
Z Hot Doug's | **NW Side**	25
Z Japonais | **Near W**	24
Landmark | **Lincoln Pk**	21
LuxBar | **Gold Coast**	17
Marché | **Mkt Dist**	20
NEW Marigold | **Uptown**	-
Mas | **Wicker Pk**	22
May St. Market | **Near W**	-
Mia Francesca | **Lakeview**	23
Z Mirai Sushi | **Wicker Pk**	26
Miramar | **Highwood**	19
Z mk | **River N**	26
NEW Mulan | **Chinatown**	-
Z Naha | **River N**	26
Narcisse | **River N**	20
NEW Niche | **Geneva**	-
Z Nine | **W Loop**	22
Z NoMI | **Gold Coast**	26
Olé Olé | **Andersonville**	-
Z one sixtyblue | **Mkt Dist**	25
Opera | **S Loop**	23
Osteria Via Stato | **River N**	21
NEW Pops/Champ. | **River N**	-
Prairie Grass | **Northbrook**	21
Quartino | **River N**	-
Red Light | **Mkt Dist**	23
NEW Republic | **River N**	-
NEW Room 21 | **S Loop**	-
Saltaus | **Mkt Dist**	19
Schwa | **Lincoln Pk**	26
Scylla | **Bucktown**	25
sola | **Lakeview**	-
NEW Spacca Napoli | **Ravenswood**	-
Z Spring | **Wicker Pk**	27
NEW Sura | **Lakeview**	-
Z SushiSamba rio | **River N**	21

Z sushi wabi | **Mkt Dist**	26
NEW Tamarind | **S Loop**	-
NEW Tokyo 21 | **Lincoln Pk**	-
NEW Tramonto's | **Wheeling**	-
Tratt. D.O.C. | **Evanston**	-
Vermilion | **River N**	21
NEW Viet Bistro | **Rogers Pk**	-
Volo | **Roscoe Vill**	20
NEW Wakamono | **Lakeview**	-
Zapatista | **S Loop**	20

VIEWS

Z Atwater's | **Geneva**	21
Z Avenues | **River N**	26
Cité | **Streeterville**	17
Z Courtright's | **Willow Spgs**	26
NEW DeLaCosta | **River N**	-
Drake Bros.' | **Streeterville**	17
Z Everest | **Loop**	27
Z Five O'Clock | **Fox Riv. Grove**	26
NEW Flatwater | **River N**	-
Flight | **Glenview**	19
NEW Fornetto & Mei's | **S Loop**	-
Fulton's | **River N**	20
NEW Gage | **S Loop**	-
Green Dolphin St. | **Lincoln Pk**	19
Z Lobby | **River N**	23
Z NoMI | **Gold Coast**	26
Z North Pond | **Lincoln Pk**	25
OPA Estiatorio | **Vernon Hills**	19
Park Grill | **Loop**	19
Pompei Bakery | **River Forest**	20
Puck's at MCA | **Streeterville**	20
Ritz-Carlton Café | **Streeterville**	-
Riva | **Streeterville**	18
Z Rosebud | **Naperville**	21
Z Seasons | **Gold Coast**	26
Z Shanghai Terr. | **River N**	24
Z Signature Rm. | **Streeterville**	18
Smith & Wollensky | **River N**	22
South Gate Cafe | **Lake Forest**	18
Z Spiaggia | **Gold Coast**	26
Tasting Room | **Mkt Dist**	18
Tavern on Rush | **Gold Coast**	19

VISITORS ON EXPENSE ACCOUNT

☑ Alinea | **Lincoln Pk** 28
☑ Arun's | **NW Side** 28
☑ Avenues | **River N** 26
☑ Blackbird | **W Loop** 27
☑ Bob Chinn's Crab | **Wheeling** 23
Brazzaz | **River N** 23
Caliterra | **Streeterville** 23
Cape Cod Rm. | **Streeterville** 21
Capital Grille | **Streeterville** 24
☑ Carlos' | **Highland Pk** 29
Catch 35 | **Loop** 23
☑ Charlie Trotter's | **Lincoln Pk** 27
☑ Chicago Chop | **River N** 25
Coco Pazzo | **River N** 24
☑ Courtright's | **Willow Spgs** 26
☑ Crofton on Wells | **River N** 26
☑ Custom Hse. | **Printer's Row** 24
David Burke Prime | **River N** 22
Entourage | **Schaumburg** –
☑ Everest | **Loop** 27
Gene & Georgetti | **River N** 23
☑ Gibsons | **multi. loc.** 25
Heat | **Old Town** 25
Il Mulino | **Gold Coast** –
☑ Joe's Sea/Steak | **River N** 26
Keefer's | **River N** 23
☑ Kevin | **River N** 26
Lawry's Prime Rib | **River N** 24
☑ Le Colonial | **Gold Coast** 23
☑ Le Français | **Wheeling** 28
☑ Les Nomades | **Streeterville** 28
☑ Le Titi/Paris | **Arlington Hts** 26
☑ Lobby | **River N** 23
☑ mk | **River N** 26
☑ Morton's Steak | **multi. loc.** 26
☑ Naha | **River N** 26
☑ Nine | **W Loop** 22
☑ NoMI | **Gold Coast** 26
☑ North Pond | **Lincoln Pk** 25
☑ Oceanique | **Evanston** 27
☑ one sixtyblue | **Mkt Dist** 25

Palm, The | **Loop** 23
☑ Pump Room | **Gold Coast** 21
Ritz-Carlton Café | **Streeterville** –
☑ RL | **Gold Coast** 22
Rosebud Steak | **Gold Coast** 23
Roy's | **River N** 24
☑ Ruth's Chris | **multi. loc.** 24
Saloon Steak | **Streeterville** 23
☑ Seasons | **Gold Coast** 26
☑ Shanghai Terr. | **River N** 24
☑ Shaw's Crab | **multi. loc.** 23
☑ Signature Rm. | **Streeterville** 18
Smith & Wollensky | **River N** 22
☑ Spiaggia | **Gold Coast** 26
☑ Spring | **Wicker Pk** 27
☑ Tallgrass | **Lockport** 28
☑ Topolobampo | **River N** 27
NEW Tramonto's | **Wheeling** –
☑ Tru | **Streeterville** 28
Vivere | **Loop** 21
Wave | **Streeterville** 20
☑ Zealous | **River N** 24

WINE BARS

☑ Avec | **W Loop** 25
☑ Bin 36/Bin Wine | **Wicker Pk** 20
NEW Broadway Cellars | **Edgewater** –
Cab's Wine Bar | **Glen Ellyn** 22
Café Bernard | **Lincoln Pk** 21
NEW Cru Cafe | **Gold Coast** –
Cyrano's Bistrot | **River N** 20
Fleming's Steak | **Lincolnshire** –
Flight | **Glenview** 19
NEW Frasca Pizzeria | **Lakeview** –
Meritage Cafe | **Bucktown** 22
Osteria Via Stato | **River N** 21
NEW Pops/Champ. | **River N** –
Quartino | **River N** –
Stained Glass | **Evanston** 23
Tasting Room | **Mkt Dist** 18
NEW Townhouse | **Loop** –
Volo | **Roscoe Vill** 20
Webster Wine | **Lincoln Pk** 17

NEW Aigre Doux | River N – |

Z Alinea | Lincoln Pk 28

Allen's | River N 24

Z Arun's | NW Side 28

Z Avec | W Loop 25

Z Avenues | River N 26

Z Bin 36/Bin Wine | 20
multi. loc.

Bistrot Margot | Old Town 21

Z Blackbird | W Loop 27

Blue Water | River N 22

BOKA | Lincoln Pk 23

Cab's Wine Bar | Glen Ellyn 22

Campagnola | Evanston 23

Capital Grille | Streeterville 24

Z Carlos' | Highland Pk 29

NEW Chalkboard | Lincoln Sq – |

Z Charlie Trotter's | 27
Lincoln Pk

Z Courtright's | Willow Spgs 26

NEW Cru Cafe | Gold Coast – |

Z Custom Hse. | Printer's Row 24

Cyrano's Bistrot | River N 20

NEW DeLaCosta | River N – |

Del Rio | Highwood 18

Z Everest | Loop 27

NEW Fiddlehead | Lincoln Sq – |

Fleming's Steak | Lincolnshire – |

Flight | Glenview 19

Z Fogo de Chão | River N 24

Fornetto Mei | Gold Coast 19

Z Gabriel's | Highwood 26

Geja's Cafe | Lincoln Pk 21

Z Green Zebra | W Town 25

Heat | Old Town 25

Z Isabella's | Geneva 26

Z Japonais | Near W 24

NEW Koda | Far S Side – |

La Sardine | W Loop 23

La Tache | Andersonville 21

Z Le Français | Wheeling 28

Le P'tit Paris | Streeterville 22

Z Les Nomades | Streeterville 28

Z Le Titi/Paris | Arlington Hts 26

May St. Market | Near W – |

Meritage Cafe | Bucktown 22

Michael | Winnetka 25

Miramar | Highwood 19

Z mk | River N 26

Z Moto | Mkt Dist 25

NEW Mulan | Chinatown – |

Z Naha | River N 26

NEW Niche | Geneva – |

Z NoMI | Gold Coast 26

Z North Pond | Lincoln Pk 25

Z Oceanique | Evanston 27

Z one sixtyblue | Mkt Dist 25

NEW Osteria/Tramonto | – |
Wheeling

Pane Caldo | Gold Coast 24

NEW Pops/Champ. | River N – |

NEW Quince | Evanston – |

Rhapsody | Loop 21

Ritz-Carlton Café | Streeterville – |

Salpicón | Old Town 24

Saltaus | Mkt Dist 19

NEW Sam & Harry's | – |
Schaumburg

Z Seasons | Gold Coast 26

1776 | Crystal Lake 24

Z Signature Rm. | Streeterville 18

Smith & Wollensky | River N 22

Z Spiaggia | Gold Coast 26

Z Spring | Wicker Pk 27

Stained Glass | Evanston 23

Z Tallgrass | Lockport 28

Tasting Room | Mkt Dist 18

Z Topolobampo | River N 27

NEW Tramonto's | Wheeling – |

Tratt. No. 10 | Loop 23

Z Tru | Streeterville 28

Z Va Pensiero | Evanston 26

Vivere | Loop 21

Volo | Roscoe Vill 20

Webster Wine | Lincoln Pk 17

West Town Tav. | W Town 23

Z Zealous | River N 24

WORTH A TRIP

MILWAUKEE

Milwaukee Most Popular

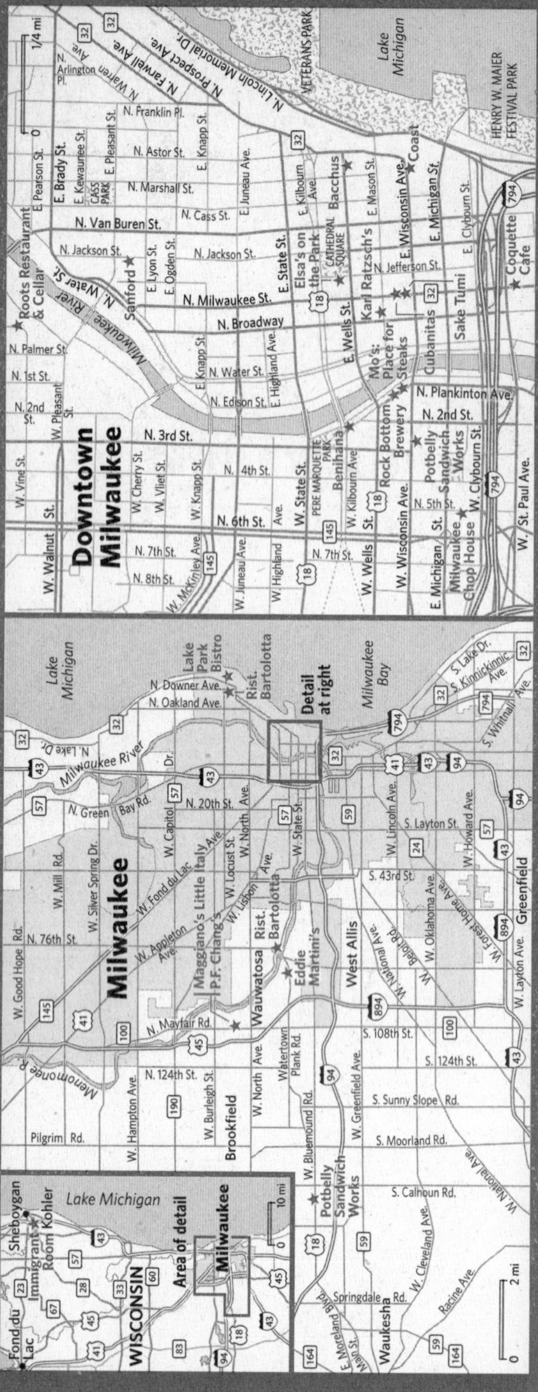

Top Ratings

* Indicates a tie with restaurant above

BY LOCATION

DOWNTOWN
26 Bacchus
25 Osteria del Mondo
Sake Tumi

EAST SIDE
29 Sanford
25 Lake Park Bistro
Tess

NORTH SHORE
25 River Lane Inn
21 Hama
19 North Shore Bistro

OUTLYING AREAS
26 Immigrant Room
25 Riversite, The
23 Mr. B's: Steak

THIRD WARD
25 Coquette Cafe
24 Nanakusa
21 Palms

WEST SIDE
26 Eddie Martini's
24 Singha Thai
20 Edwardo's Pizza

TOP DECOR

27 Bjonda
Lake Park Bistro
26 Sanford
Bacchus
Immigrant Room

25 Coast
24 Sake Tumi
Karl Ratzsch's
Yanni's
Eddie Martini's

TOP SERVICE

28 Sanford
26 Immigrant Room
Bacchus
Riversite, The
Eddie Martini's

25 Dream Dance
Lake Park Bistro
24 Mr. B's: Steak
River Lane Inn
23 Sake Tumi

BEST BUYS

In order of Bang for the Buck rating.

1. Potbelly Sandwich
2. Singha Thai
3. Cubanitas
4. Elsa's on Park
5. Edwardo's Pizza

6. Cempazuchi
7. King & I
8. Knick, The
9. Sake Tumi
10. Rock Bottom Brewery

MILWAUKEE
RESTAURANT
DIRECTORY

NEW Andrew's Restaurant *American*   – | – | – | E

Delafield | Delafield Hotel | 415 Genesee St. (I-94) | 262-646-1600 |
www.delafieldhotel.com

In keeping with its bonny boutique-hotel environs, Colonial-era antiques crowd every inch of wall space inside this stately Delafield New American run by Andrew Ruggeri, who lends his name and west-of-the-city reputation to this spot (he also owns a nearby rustic-Italian restaurant and an Irish pub); though he doesn't man the stoves, Ruggeri does have a hand in planning the seasonal menu.

Bacchus *American*   26 | 26 | 26 | $56

Downtown | Cudahy Towers | 925 E. Wells St. (Prospect Ave.) |
414-765-1166 | www.bacchusmke.com

"Milwaukee arrives" courtesy of this "snazzy" Downtown "in-a-class-by-itself" "jewel" that's "definitely a place to indulge" your taste for New American cuisine (it "doesn't get much better" than this) served within a "posh" setting; even admirers, though, assert that the "over-attentive staff just needs to relax a bit"; P.S. lunch is served in the sun-drenched, glass-enclosed conservatory.

Barossa ☒Ⓜ *American*   20 | 17 | 19 | $35

Fifth Ward | 235 S. Second St. (Oregon St.) | 414-272-8466 |
www.barossawinebar.com

"Fresh", "inventive organic creations" pleasing to "vegetarians and carnivores alike" (e.g. chicken panzanella, a popular item at the "excellent" Sunday brunch) define this "lovely" New American in the Fifth Ward, a "hidden gem" "everyone wants to like" – in part because its "calm, warming" atmosphere makes it "great for social and business dinners"; still, some warn that it "can get pricey depending on what one orders."

NEW Bayou *Cajun/Creole*   – | – | – | M

East Side | 2060 N. Humboldt Blvd. (Commerce Ave.) | 414-431-1511 |
www.bayoumilwaukee.com

N'Awlins goes upscale at this stylish Cajun-Creole hot spot on the East Side, featuring views over the Milwaukee River and a mid-priced menu of fiery Big Easy bites including jambalaya, blackened redfish and a classic Sazerac cocktail; the sprawling waterfront patio (set to debut in summer 2007) will add another 100-plus seats.

Benihana *Japanese/Steak*   19 | 16 | 20 | $34

Downtown | 850 N. Plankinton Ave. (2nd St.) | 414-270-0890 |
www.benihana.com

See review in the Chicago Directory.

Ⓩ Bjonda *Eclectic*   22 | 27 | 23 | $51

Wauwatosa | 7754 Harwood Ave. (Watertown Plank Rd.) |
414-431-1444 | www.bjonda.com

"Save up your dollars for a great night out" at this "classy", "aggressively hip" Wauwatosa Eclectic (No. 1 for Decor in Wisconsin) offering "downtown chic without the drive"; from the "amazing descriptions of the dishes that leave you wondering what delights

your tongue is going to encounter" to the "adorable stools for women's purses", there's an "East Coast influence" (particularly "welcome in the Midwest") that makes for a "fabulous dining experience", especially in the "romantic and private" Skylight Room; N.B. it's brunch-only on Sundays.

Bosley on Brady ⊠Ⓜ Seafood/Steak — — — M
East Side | 815 E. Brady St. (Cass St.) | 414-727-7975 | www.bosleyonbrady.com

Offering a warm departure in the chilly Midwestern clime, this East Side Key West–themed venue sprinkles a Southern coastal influence on its seafood-steakhouse theme, which suits Brady Street's hodgepodge-of-edibles identity; visitors ease into the bright Floridian colors, piped-in smooth jazz and breezy menu (Florida grouper, rib-eye steak, sea scallops) like they're on holiday.

Carnevor ⊠ Steak — — — M
Downtown | 724 N. Milwaukee St. (Mason St.) | 414-223-2200 | www.carnevor.com

Chic meets red meat at this Downtown looker that combines à la carte prime steaks (seafood too), trendy tunes and a cutting-edge, three-level space on throbbing Milwaukee Street; the staff pampers patrons with ultra-attentive 'swarm service' and playful desserts (e.g. doughnut holes with dipping sauces).

Caterina's Italian ▽ 21 15 24 $35
Southwest Side | 9104 W. Oklahoma Ave. (92nd St.) | 414-541-4200 | www.caterinasrestaurant.com

Cat-fanciers of this "casual", "family"-friendly Southwest Side spot insist "if it were Downtown or in the Third Ward you'd never be able to get in", so enamored are they of its "hearty Italian" fare ("as good a value as there is") and "old supper club–style" decor; still, some find it "predictable", with "nothing bad but nothing outstanding either."

Cempazuchi Ⓜ Mexican 21 20 20 $24
East Side | 1205 E. Brady St. (Franklin Pl.) | 414-291-5233 | www.cempazuchi.com

Lovers of "the freshest", "top-notch" margaritas (try the variety of the day) are in paradise at this "wonderful", "muy auténtico" East Side Mexican, where "family recipes" render "not-typical" dishes "bursting with complex flavors" – "including several regional moles", the "best fish tacos in town" and a shrimp sandwich that's "so good [some] would consider it as a deathbed meal"; P.S. the "festive" decor is nearly "as good as the food."

Coast American 20 25 19 $42
Downtown | O'Donnell Park Complex | 931 E. Wisconsin Ave. (Astor St.) | 414-727-5555 | www.coastrestaurant.com

"What a view!" is the consensus on this Downtown New American, whose windows face Lake Michigan and the Milwaukee Art Museum's nationally known Calatrava addition; the menu's coastal concept (for instance, cedar planked walleye) is "imaginative and trendy" to some, "hit-or-miss" to others, but crooners unite in won-

dering "who could resist those decadent, warm popovers?"; P.S. the weather-dependent "outdoor seating is the place to be."

Coquette Cafe Ⓢ *French*   25 | 21 | 23 | $36

Third Ward | 316 N. Milwaukee St. (St. Paul Ave.) | 414-291-2655 | www.coquettecafe.com

"Is this France?" local Europhiles ask about this "lively" "little bit of Paris" in the "newly hippified" Third Ward, "friendly and creative chef" Sanford 'Sandy' D'Amato's source for "hearty", "innovative" French cuisine "at affordable prices"; the "cozy", "casually elegant" atmosphere is "great for a pre-show meal" at one of the nearby theaters; P.S. don't miss D'Amato's adjacent Harlequin Bakery.

Crawdaddy's ⓈⓂ *Cajun/Creole*   21 | 15 | 19 | $29

Southwest Side | 6414 W. Greenfield Ave. (National Ave.) | 414-778-2228 | www.crawdaddysrestaurant.com

Better arrive early at this "always-packed hot spot", a "fun, fun, fun" N'Awlins "gem on the blue-collar" Southwest Side, or "be prepared to wait" for its "creative", "delicious" Cajun-Creole cuisine (think steak Diane with a Cajun twist) since the place "can get very busy" – especially "on weekends"; be warned, as well, that the "vibrant" setting strikes some as "conversational" but others as "uncomfortably noisy."

Cubanitas Ⓢ *Cuban*   23 | 21 | 19 | $23

Downtown | 728 N. Milwaukee St. (bet. Mason St. & Wisconsin Ave.) | 414-225-1760 | www.cubanitas.us

This "trendsetter on a fashionable" street that's become a "Restaurant Row" of sorts, Downtown's "welcoming, lively" Cuban (little sister of Italian Osteria del Mondo) attracts the "young, hip crowd" with "fantabulous" mojitos and "top-flight" food such as sweet or savory plantains served at "easy-on-the-wallet" prices in a "trendy", "modern" "comfortable oasis" of a space; N.B. expect counter service at lunchtime.

Dream Dance ⓈⓂ *American*   25 | 23 | 25 | $59

Downtown | Potawatomi Bingo Casino | 1721 W. Canal St. (16th St.) | 414-847-7883 | www.paysbig.com

They "treat you like royalty" at this "calming, romantic" Downtown "refuge" attached to the Potawatomi Bingo Casino; factor in the "amazing combinations" on chef Jason Gorman's New American menu and "retail-priced wines", and you get a "foodie's heavenly experience, not merely a dream."

Eagan's *Eclectic*   21 | 20 | 21 | $32

Downtown | 1030 N. Water St. (State St.) | 414-271-6900 | www.eagansonwater.com

A "winner all the way", this "cosmopolitan" "standby" with "interesting items" (such as the "fantastic" lobster BLT) on its seafood-focused Eclectic menu occupies a "wonderfully convenient" Downtown location that's close to concert and theater venues, meaning it's "easy to drop by for a [pre- or post-show] snack"; it's also a "great people-watching place", but unimpressed diners still size it up as "good – but nothing special."

	FOOD	DECOR	SERVICE	COST

☒ Eddie Martini's *Steak*   `26` `24` `26` `$54`
West Side | 8612 Watertown Plank Rd. (86th St.) | 414-771-6680 |
www.eddiemartinis.com

"It's back to the '50s" at this "real gem" of a West Side steakhouse
"institution", a classic for "incredible" steaks ("my mouth is watering
just thinking about them") and "unbelievable" martinis that's "popular
with doctors" from the nearby medical complex and other "Milwaukee
bigwigs"; its "sophisticated" "old supper club–like" interior has some
convinced that "Frank and Dean are still with us", but remember that
the "big drinks" are matched by "big tabs", so "bring extra cash."

Edwardo's Natural Pizza *Pizza*   `20` `10` `15` `$17`
Downtown | 700 E. Kilbourn Ave. (Van Buren St.) | 414-277-8080
West Side | 10845 Bluemound Rd. (Hwy. 100) | 414-771-7770
www.edwardos.com

See review in the Chicago Directory.

Elliot's Bistro ●Ⓜ *French*   `20` `18` `20` `$37`
East Side | 2321 N. Murray Ave. (North Ave.) | 414-273-1488 |
www.elliotsbistro.com

"For the French bistro experience in Milwaukee", this "delightful"
East Side "favorite" is "a definite must-do" "complete with an authentic [Gallic] chef", Pierre Briere, whose "traditional" cooking – from
cassoulet to boeuf bourguignon – "rivals that of many Paris bistros";
"great for a dinner date or meeting old friends", it's also a "perfect
spot for weekend brunch."

Elm Grove Inn, The ☒ *American/Eclectic*   `▽ 22` `19` `21` `$40`
Elm Grove | 13275 Watertown Plank Rd. (Elm Grove Rd.) | 262-782-7090 |
www.elmgroveinn.com

Offering a "good selection of [New] American favorites", this "quiet
and inviting" Elm Grove Eclectic is "great for a special evening out"; its
"historic location", a building dating to 1855, has a "cozy, romantic"
atmosphere; some young folk find it all "rather staid", but that's a boon
for seniors ("my grandmother loved it"), who enjoy taking advantage
of the early-bird menu – half-off the second entree from 4–5:30 PM.

Elsa's on the Park ● *American*   `23` `24` `19` `$24`
Downtown | 833 N. Jefferson St. (Wells St.) | 414-765-0615 |
www.elsas.com

"It doesn't get any better than" this "über-hip, trendy" "see-and-be-
seen" American opposite Downtown's Cathedral Square Park feel
fans who favor its "gussied-up versions of old favorites", including
"outstanding burgers" and the "best pork chop sandwiches in town"
(you "can't go wrong with the chicken wings"); P.S. the "lively" vibe
and "awesome drinks" at its "amazing bar" also draw "huge crowds."

Envoy *American*   `-` `-` `-` `M`
Downtown | The Ambassador Hotel | 2308 W. Wisconsin Ave.
(bet. N. 23rd & 24th Sts.) | 414-345-5015 | www.envoymilwaukee.com

A result of the exhaustive renovation of the art deco Ambassador
Hotel, this Downtown New American offers a feeding frenzy from

early in the morning into the evening; menu options range from the casual (a cheeseburger with applewood cheddar and pommes frites) to the fussy (Thai curried rack of lamb with green papaya salad and coconut cream), and after dinner a respectful late-night crowd gathers in the adjacent Envoy Lounge for cocktails and live jazz on weekends.

☑ Five O'Clock Steakhouse 🅂🅼 *Steak* 26 | 12 | 22 | $46
(fka Coerper's 5 O'Clock Club)
Central City | 2416 W. State St. (24th St.) | 414-342-3553 | www.fiveoclocksteakhouse.com

Clock-watchers "can't stop eating once [they] start" tucking into the "enormous portions" of "to-die-for" steaks at this Central City standby; its "kitsch", "time-warp-into-the-'50s" decor "will bring back memories of the classic steakhouse experience of days gone by", and "the servers will make you feel like you're visiting an older relative's house" – though some "don't like" the "required stop at the bar", where you "order a drink and dinner before getting to your table"; N.B. a Suburban Chicago branch opened post-Survey.

Gilbert's *American* - | - | ± | M
Lake Geneva | 327 Wrigley Dr. (Center St.) | 262-248-6680 | www.gilbertsrestaurant.com

"When you want something different from the usual Lake Geneva family-style place", this New American – housed in an 1875 Victorian house with 13 working fireplaces and a "marvelous view" of the water – is "worth the trip!"; work in the fare's largely organic status ("try the vegetarian tasting menu"), including ingredients from the edible garden in summer, and you just may have "one of Wisconsin's finest"; N.B. jacket suggested.

Golden Mast Inn 🅼 *American/German* ▽ 18 | 20 | 19 | $38
Okauchee | W349 N5293 Lacy's Ln. (Lake Dr.) | 262-567-7047 | www.weissgerbers.com/goldenmast

"On a balmy summer evening", a "spectacular" view of Okauchee Lake and a "relaxed" atmosphere "with a tinge of ritziness" will make you "feel at home" at this Weissgerber family–owned German-American; flatterers feel there's "nothing like" its "popular Friday [night] fish fry" that routinely "packs 'em in" (it's "one of the best in the area"), but grumblers grouse that the food overall is "hit-or-miss"; N.B. check out the new semiprivate sunroom that extends over the lake.

Hama *Asian Fusion/Japanese* 21 | 14 | 18 | $34
North Shore | 333 W. Brown Deer Rd. (Port Washington Rd.) | 414-352-5051

Though there's "fresh" raw-fish fare on offer, some folks insist the "non-sushi entrees star" at this "inspired Japanese–Asian" fusion favorite "located in a strip mall" on the North Shore – "as do the spectacular desserts", such as banana fritters and Belgian chocolate mousse; still, some find the kitchen "uneven" and say the "limited space feels tight."

	FOOD	DECOR	SERVICE	COST

Heaven City 🖥M *American*   ▽ 24 | 25 | 25 | $40

Mukwonago | S91 W27850 National Ave./Hwy. ES (Edgewood Ave.) | 262-363-5191 | www.heavencity.com

Founding owner Scott McGlinchey no longer runs this Mukwonago New American reputedly set in gangster Al Capone's "haunted" "old hangout", but many still rank it a "superb" "must-visit" "with excellent food and service", as well as "great atmosphere" – indeed, clairvoyants claim that if you "close the bar, you might be treated to an unforgettable supernatural sideshow"; P.S. the long-running "Tapas Tuesday reigns supreme."

Holiday House *Eclectic*   - | - | - | M

Third Ward | 525 E. Menomonee St. (Jefferson St.) | 414-272-1122

Sib of East Side hangout Tess, this Third Ward Eclectic combines a low-key albeit elegant vibe and an accessible world-fusion menu created by chef-owner Joe Volpe; the window-framed dining room is just paces from Henry Maier Park (the mother of all city outdoor summer festival grounds), and when temps soar the planned sidewalk tables should be a paradise for people-watchers.

NEW Il Mito Enoteca M *Italian*   - | - | - | M

Wauwatosa | 6913 W. North Ave. (N. 69th St.) | 414-443-1414 | www.ilmito.com

Given the inclusion of 'enoteca' in this suburban Wauwatosa Italian hangout's moniker, it's no surprise that alongside hearty, affordable pastas and osso buco, it pours copious amounts of vino from a 150-bottle list; the storefront's warm, wooden setting is also a draw for neighborhood crowds.

Z Immigrant Room & Winery, The 🖥M *American*   26 | 26 | 26 | $64

Kohler | American Club | 419 Highland Dr. (School St.) | 920-457-8888 | www.destinationkohler.com

For "a fine-dining experience of the highest caliber", "gourmets" go to this "wonderful" "Wisconsin treasure" in Kohler's American Club resort, one of the "finest hotels in the Midwest", where the "elegant" New American fare comes with a "nice wine list" and "doting service" ("at these prices, it should be"); "now *this* is a place for romance and privacy" say fans of its six different dining rooms, which "take you back to the old days"; P.S. if the tab's too high, remember that "the prices on bottles and cheese in The Winery [next door] are extremely fair."

Jackson Grill 🖥M *Steak*   23 | 13 | 23 | $41

South Side | 3736 W. Mitchell St. (38th St.) | 414-384-7384

"Don't go or it'll get too crowded" suggest selfish surveyors who "expect to wait" a while before slipping into this "little" South Side "hideaway" for its "small but incredible menu" of "excellent steaks", ribs and seafood; some complain that the "exterior looks like any neighborhood joint" and the interior is decidedly "bland" in the atmosphere department (a patio was added outside last summer), but those who find it "homey and comfortable" insist it breathes "old-style Milwaukee."

	FOOD	DECOR	SERVICE	COST

Jake's Fine Dining ⑤ *Steak* | ▽ 25 | 20 | 22 | $39 |

Brookfield | 21445 W. Gumina Rd. (Capital Dr.) | 262-781-7995 | www.jakes-restaurant.com

"You only have to go once" to this "nostalgic" Brookfield steakhouse – an "established presence on the West Side" since 1967 – "to feel like a regular" thanks to its "wonderful presentation" of "awesome" "comfort food" (filet mignon and signature onion rings) and "comfortable service"; "ask for a seat by" the "huge fireplace" ("a great place on a winter day") or belly up to the bar and "enjoy some fine brandy."

Karl Ratzsch's ⑤ *German* | 24 | 24 | 23 | $38 |

Downtown | 320 E. Mason St. (bet. B'way & Milwaukee St.) | 414-276-2720 | www.karlratzsch.com

"*Das ist gut!*" declare devotees of this "high-caliber" 103-year-old Downtown German, a "traditional favorite" where "authentic" Teutonic cuisine – "nothing says lovin' like schnitzel" or "great sauerbraten" – is served in an "appropriate setting" whose "old-world atmosphere" reminds travelers of "eating in Munich"; less enamored types say it's "heavy, heavy, heavy" (though "worth it once in a while"), but "where else can you get roast goose and a pianist [weekends only] playing 'The Way You Look Tonight'?"

NEW Kil@wat Restaurant *American* | – | – | – | E |

Downtown | Intercontinental Milwaukee Hotel | 139 E. Kilbourn Ave. (N. Water St.) | 414-291-4793 | www.kilawatcuisine.com

With the costly transformation of the former Wyndham Hotel into the Intercontinental Milwaukee comes this hip Downtown New American, bathed in shagadelic shades of green and orange; the moderately priced menu is divided into candescent categories like "Spark" (goat cheese–stuffed peppers), "Sizzle" (shrimp beignets) and "Synergy" (lobster pot pie); N.B. once diners' Kil@wat hours are up, they can nightcap inside the hotel's meditative Zen Den Lounge.

King & I, The *Thai* | 21 | 15 | 18 | $24 |

Downtown | 830 N. Old World Third St. (bet. Kilbourn Ave. & Wells St.) | 414-276-4181 | www.kingandirestaurant.com

"Yul Brynner would certainly have broken a sweat on some of these dishes", so "proceed with caution" when sampling the "delicious Thai food" at this "quick and easy" spot "tucked into an urban corner of Downtown"; its "convenient" location makes it a "great place for a pre-theater dinner."

Knick, The ● *Eclectic* | 22 | 20 | 21 | $27 |

Downtown | Knickerbocker Hotel | 1030 E. Juneau Ave. (Astor St.) | 414-272-0011 | www.theknickrestaurant.com

"There's something for everyone" (from some of the "best appetizers" around to "great burgers" and "entrees that are good as well") on the "huge menu" at this "consistent" Downtown Eclectic that's "the place to be if you want to be seen"; it's "wonderful for Sunday brunch or a hearty lunch", and a "happy-hour favorite" too, with a "lively atmosphere" that attracts a "young and hip crowd" – no wonder the "terrace is a people-watcher's dream."

	FOOD	DECOR	SERVICE	COST

☑ Lake Park Bistro *French* | 25 | 27 | 25 | $50 |

East Side | Lake Park Pavilion | 3133 E. Newberry Blvd. (N. Lake Dr.) |
414-962-6300 | www.lakeparkbistro.com

"It's wonderful to sit by the windows" and revel in the "exquisite"
Lake Michigan view (especially "heavenly" at sunset) at this "treat"
located in Frederick Law Olmsted–designed Lake Park, where "lots of
new twists on old classics" make the "ooh-la-la fabulous French cuisine" "worth every decadent calorie"; factor in a "romantic atmosphere" and staffers who "pay attention to all the details" and it adds
up to a "great place for a special occasion" or "the perfect date."

☑ Maggiano's Little Italy *Italian* | 20 | 19 | 20 | $31 |

Wauwatosa | Mayfair Mall | 2500 N. Mayfair Rd. (North Ave.) |
414-978-1000 | www.maggianos.com
See review in the Chicago Directory.

Mangia *Italian* | 23 | 19 | 20 | $34 |

Kenosha | 5717 Sheridan Rd. (bet. 57th & 58th Sts.) | 262-652-4285
"Excellent for a casual spot", this "not-to-be-missed" "little treasure"
in Kenosha, "midway between Chicago and Milwaukee", is an "oasis"
of "authentic Italian cuisine", with "great pastas", "very good pizzas"
and wood-roasted meats served in a "cozy dining room" – and "without ruining the family budget"; little surprise, then, that it's considered
a place of "proven worth in this rather desolate Downtown area."

NEW Mason Street Grill *American* | – | – | – | E |

Downtown | Pfister Hotel | 425 E. Mason St. (bet. N. Jefferson &
N. Milwaukee Sts.) | 414-298-3131 | www.masonstreetgrill.com
The historic Pfister Hotel's new eatery is a firm departure from its
subterranean predecessors, The English Room and Celia, with a
looser vibe and street-level location (yes, windows!); conceived by
local über-chef Mark Weber, the Traditional American menu hooks
both the suits (wood-grilled dry-aged strip steak) and the jeans
crowds (Monte Cristo sandwich); N.B. for a close-up view of the
open kitchen, eat at the marble-topped bar.

☑ Milwaukee Chop House ⑤ *Steak* | 24 | 22 | 22 | $50 |

Downtown | Hilton Milwaukee City Ctr. | 633 N. Fifth St. (bet. Michigan St. &
Wisconsin Ave.) | 414-226-2467 | www.milwaukeechophouse.com
"Bring your grandparents, grandchildren" and "everyone" in between
to this "top-notch" steakhouse in Downtown's Hilton Milwaukee City
Center, where the "excellent" steak-and-seafood fare is "cooked to
perfection and served piping hot" by an "accommodating staff" in a
"supper club-ish atmosphere"; some complain that it's "inconsistent"
and "a bit pricey for what you get", but most maintain it's "well worth"
the expense and an "overall good place to go for a nice night out."

Mimma's Cafe *Italian* | 22 | 20 | 21 | $40 |

East Side | 1307 E. Brady St. (Arlington Pl.) | 414-271-7337 |
www.mimmas.com
If you "want something that's not on the menu", ask chef and
Sicily native Mimma Megna – "she'll do her magic and make an excep-

tional dish" at this "warm and inviting" Italian with a "classy" interior that "harkens back to the 1920s era"; many report it's "still a favorite" "must-stop" on the East Side, and a "pioneer" that deserves "credit for reviving Brady Street" since it opened in 1989, but others counter that it has "grown into a big", rather "run-of-the-mill" restaurant.

Moceans ⬛ Seafood 21 | 20 | 22 | $50
Downtown | 747 N. Broadway (bet. Mason St. & Wisconsin Ave.) | 414-272-7470 | www.moceans.com

"Part of the 'Mo-pire'" that includes Mo's: A Place for Steaks, this Johnny Vassallo–owned Downtown mecca (whose name rhymes with 'oceans') in Grenadier's old digs mates "great seafood" with "excellent service" "in a quiet romantic setting"; not all fin-feasters are fans, though, with some "disappointed" patrons reporting a "pretentious" vibe, "haughty", "heavy-handed" staffers and fare that's "way" "too expensive."

Mo's: A Place for Steaks ⬛ Steak 23 | 20 | 23 | $53
Downtown | 720 N. Plankinton Ave. (Wisconsin Ave.) | 414-272-0720 | www.mosaplaceforsteaks.com

"You feel like you're in the big city to the south" at this "Chicago"-style steakhouse (and Moceans sibling), a "place to be seen" Downtown dining upon "juicy, tasty and enormous steaks" amid "hip decor" and a "lively" crowd; still, some de-Mo-ters detect some "attitude" and do "not like the à la carte menu", declaring they "need more than meat on the platter" for these "high prices" and dismissing the place as only "for the flashy spender" who doesn't mind "forking over lots of bucks."

Mr. B's: A Bartolotta Steakhouse Steak 23 | 20 | 24 | $49
Brookfield | 17700 W. Capitol Dr. (Calhoun Rd.) | 262-790-7005 | www.mrbssteakhouse.com

Bringing "a bit of the Bartolotta touch" and "consistency" to Brookfield, this cousin of Lake Park Bistro and Bacchus is the "steakhouse of record" for many meat-craving "locals", "wow"-ing with "excellent", "personal service" from a "terrific staff" that transports "mouthwatering" cuts and "great drinks" in a "stylish yet casual" environment; a word of financial warning from veterans to first-timers, though – "remember that this kind of quality comes at a price."

Nanakusa Ⓜ Japanese 24 | 24 | 20 | $42
Third Ward | 408 E. Chicago St. (Milwaukee St.) | 414-223-3200

"Traditional Japanese" "meets urban chic" at this "beautiful, minimalist" Third Ward source for "top-quality sushi" fashioned from "delicious" "fresh" fish, as well as "lovely cooked dishes", all accompanied by "extensive wine and saki offerings"; lauders "love" the "private" 16-seat tatami room that contributes to the "Zen atmosphere", but some say it's "really too bad" that the "service quality doesn't match the quality of the food and decor", while others state that "the high prices keep [them] from returning often."

	FOOD	DECOR	SERVICE	COST

North Shore Bistro *American*   19 | 16 | 18 | $32

North Shore | River Point Village | 8649 N. Port Washington Rd.
(Brown Deer Rd.) | 414-351-6100 | www.northshorebistro.com

A "great place for get-togethers", especially "for a group where everyone wants something different", this "reliable" "suburban hangout"
is a "nice respite on the North Shore", with "good", "consistent"
New American fare and a "friendly" staff; some, though, deem its
cuisine "unremarkable", while others insist its "only failing" is its
"prosaic" "strip-mall" setting.

North Star American Bistro *American*   - | - | - | I

NEW **Brookfield** | 19115 W. Capitol Dr. (Brookfield Rd.) |
262-754-1515
Shorewood | 4515 N. Oakland Ave. (Kensington Blvd.) | 414-964-4663
www.northstarbistro.com

Traditional American cuisine is dished out for lunch and dinner daily
at these cozy, cordial siblings, made all the more palatable by their
unpretentious patina and gentle prices; the menu is rife with classic,
unfussy favorites like bacon and blue cheese burgers, bourbon
salmon and, come Sunday mornings, quiche Lorraine and crème
brûlée French toast.

Osteria del Mondo S *Italian*   25 | 22 | 22 | $48

Downtown | 1028 E. Juneau Ave. (Astor St.) | 414-291-3770 |
www.osteria.com

"Remaining solidly [near] the top of the ladder in Milwaukee", this
Downtown Northern Italian delivers "outstanding meals" courtesy
of chef/co-owner Marc Bianchini, who "never ceases to amaze" with
"elegant fare" that's "inventive" "without being strange"; combined
with "wonderful service" and a "comfortable setting" (including "a
great patio"), it amounts to a "fine-dining" experience that's "not to be
missed"; N.B. a separate cigar lounge and valet parking are available.

Palms Bistro & Bar S M *American*   21 | 20 | 19 | $29

Third Ward | 221 N. Broadway (bet. Buffalo & Chicago Sts.) |
414-298-3000

"Lots of kudos" go to this New American in the Third Ward for its
"excellent preparations" of "bistro-esque food" made from "fresh
ingredients", its "simply elegant Cream City–meets-exotic"-
"simian-themed" decor ("gotta love those monkeys") and its "just-
right service" from a "friendly staff"; all told, it's a "nice stop for a
quick, light bite"; P.S. there's "great outdoor seating in the summer",
and the "expansive upstairs bar is also available for private parties."

Pasta Tree, The M *Italian*   20 | 18 | 20 | $30

East Side | 1503 N. Farwell Ave. (Curtis Pl.) | 414-276-8867 |
www.foodspot.com/thepastatree

"Pastaholics" who've "been dining here for years" praise this "casual" East Side Northern Italian for "imaginative" interpretations of
their "favorite" "comfort food" delivered "piping hot" to the table;
true, not everyone appreciates "practically sitting in the laps of the
people next to you", but supporters defend the space as "romantic,

	FOOD	DECOR	SERVICE	COST

"comfortable" and "cozy (like eating in someone's living room)", swearing "you'll forget that the rest of the diners are even there."

☑ P.F. Chang's China Bistro *Chinese* — 20 | 20 | 19 | $28

Wauwatosa | Mayfair Mall | 2500 N. Mayfair Rd. (North Ave.) | 414-607-1029 | www.pfchangs.com
See review in the Chicago Directory.

Pleasant Valley Inn Ⓜ *American* — ▽ 21 | 17 | 21 | $31

Southwest Side | 9801 W. Dakota St. (99th St.) | 414-321-4321 | www.foodspot.com/pleasantvalleyinn
Though "hidden" on the Southwest Side, this American "gem" in an inn dating to the 1930s "gives you the feeling you're at a supper club in the North woods"; with its "great food and service", it strikes supporters as "a nice neighborhood" spot, but lukewarm sorts cite its "nothing-fancy" decor and "rather basic meat-and-potatoes" fare as evidence that it's "not bad" – but also "not spectacular."

Polonez Ⓜ *Polish* — ▽ 23 | 13 | 21 | $22

South Side | 4016 S. Packard Ave. (Tesch St.) | 414-482-0080 | www.foodspot.com/polonez
"Pierogi power!" proclaim dumpling devotees dedicated to this "true Milwaukee treasure", an "authentic" South Side Polish place proffering "made-from-scratch" fare that's "mm-mm-good" – and "one of the best values in town"; true, it's "not a fancy place", but "the warm personality and service" of owners George and Aleksandra Burzynski put sausage scarfers "at ease"; N.B. it also hosts a Friday night fish fry and Sunday brunch with live accordion music.

Potbelly Sandwich Works *Sandwiches* — 20 | 15 | 18 | $9

Downtown | 135 W. Wisconsin Ave. (Plankinton Ave.) | 414-226-0014
Brookfield | 17800 W. Bluemound Rd. (bet. Brookfield & Calhoun Rds.) | 262-796-9845
www.potbelly.com
See review in the Chicago Directory.

Ristorante Bartolotta *Italian* — 25 | 22 | 23 | $46

Wauwatosa | 7616 W. State St. (Harwood Ave.) | 414-771-7910 | www.bartolottaristorante.com
"You'll think you're in a big city" when visiting the "wonderful" 'Tosa Italian – "a total star of a restaurant", featuring executive chef Juan Urbieta's "varied menu" of "incredible" cuisine ("the risotto is positively orgasmic!"), "excellent service" and "lovely", "cozy atmosphere"; P.S. "reservations are a must", though some suggest the small venue always seems "to be overbooked."

River Lane Inn Ⓢ *Seafood* — 25 | 18 | 24 | $37

North Shore | 4313 W. River Ln. (Brown Deer Rd.) | 414-354-1995
"From [Wednesday] lobster night to the always-changing fish specials on the chalkboard", this "longtime favorite" (sibling to Mequon's Riversite) set in a turn-of-the-century building in an "off-the-beaten-path" North Shore location "still delivers" "consistently

great" seafood ferried by "friendly servers" in a "low-key" setting – no wonder it continues to "attract a crowd" ("regulars love it").

Riversite, The Ⓢ *American* | 25 | 23 | 26 | $46 |

Mequon | 11120 N. Cedarburg Rd. (Mequon Rd.) | 262-242-6050
"The always reliable, elegant sister to the River Lane Inn" on the North Shore, this "very popular" place in Mequon keeps dinner "creative" thanks to "artist"-chef Tom Peschong, whose Traditional American specialties are "superb"; "fabulous warm service" from a "stellar staff" that's "knowledgeable about" the "unbeatable wine list" and a "glorious setting" affording a "great view of the Milwaukee River" also make it "worth the drive."

Rock Bottom Brewery *American* | 16 | 15 | 16 | $22 |

Downtown | 740 N. Plankinton Ave. (bet. Wells St. & Wisconsin Ave.) | 414-276-3030 | www.rockbottom.com
See review in the Chicago Directory.

Roots Restaurant & Cellar *Californian* | 25 | 23 | 21 | $37 |

Brewers Hill | 1818 N. Hubbard St. (Vine St.) | 414-374-8480 | www.rootsmilwaukee.com
A "class act all the way", this "wonderful place" on Brewers Hill "puts together delicious creations" of Californian "comfort food" (using some "organically grown local produce" from co-owner Joe Schmidt's 67-acre Cedarburg farm) in "surprisingly inventive combinations that really work"; "perched above the city", its bi-level location also offers "drop-dead views" of Downtown Milwaukee, so "whether upstairs or down" expect an "always-enjoyable" experience; N.B. the Cellar offers a less-formal menu.

Saffron Indian Bistro Ⓜ *Indian* | ▽ 25 | 14 | 20 | $24 |

Brookfield | 17395D-1 W. Blue Mound Rd. (bet. Brookfield & Calhoun Rds.) | 262-784-1332
"Your palate will thank you for the exotic trip" after a visit to this "unassuming and unpretentious" Brookfield strip-mall spot serving "lots of uncommon but delicious specialties from India" that offer an "innovative" respite from the "Americanized" fare at some other subcontinental venues – indeed, the "food is much nicer than the appearance of the restaurant would suggest"; P.S. don't miss the "great buffet" featured daily at lunch.

Sake Tumi Ⓢ *Asian* | 25 | 24 | 23 | $34 |

Downtown | 714 N. Milwaukee St. (bet. Mason St. & Wisconsin Ave.) | 414-224-7253 | www.sake-milwaukee.com
"Don't let the corny", *Laugh-In*-style name "fool you into thinking this isn't a high-quality experience" advise addicts "hooked" on this "amazing" Asian, an "absolute must" Downtown whose "ambitious and well-executed menu has something for everyone" – from "trendy" fusion dishes to traditional Japanese and Korean BBQ fare; also, the "lively dining room" and "fun", "swanky" upstairs Buddha Lounge are "where the beautiful people go to eat sushi" and revel in a "cool vibe."

| | FOOD | DECOR | SERVICE | COST |

☑ Sanford ☒ *American* · 29 | 26 | 28 | $66
East Side | 1547 N. Jackson St. (Pleasant St.) | 414-276-9608 |
www.sanfordrestaurant.com

"Words can't describe" the "world-class" experience at this "hits-
on-all-cylinders" East Side New American "gem" that's definitely "in
a league by itself" (as evidenced by the fact that it's ranked No. 1 for
both Food and Service in Wisconsin); eponymous toque-owner
Sandy D'Amato gets "all the details right" – from the "sophisticated" "gourmet" fare, to the "unbeatable" service provided by
"friendly caring staffers" who can "feel your table's mood", to the
"intimate", "ultramodern" dining room; P.S. "try the chef's
'Surprise'", an "especially fabulous seven-course" tasting menu.

Sebastian's ☒ *American* · - | - | - | M
Caledonia | 6025 Douglas Ave. (5 Mile Rd.) | 262-681-5465 |
www.sebastiansfinefood.com

A "way-off-the-beaten-path" setting adds to the "best-kept secret
status" of this "friendly place" that's "worth the drive" to Caledonia
for its "outstanding" New American cuisine and "surprisingly stunning dining room"; fans feel "it's unfortunate that this fine restaurant is disadvantaged by its location", as it "stacks up favorably
against many in larger metropolitan areas."

Singha Thai *Thai* · 24 | 13 | 18 | $19
West Side | 2237 S. 108th St. (Lincoln Ave.) | 414-541-1234
Singha Thai II *Thai*
Downtown | 780 N. Jefferson St. | 414-226-0288
www.singhathairestaurant.com

"Delicious food" at a "good value" makes for a "great Thai" experience at this West Side "favorite" "hidden in a strip mall"; to be sure,
the "uninspired", "no-ambiance" decor keeps some diners away, but
folks who flip for the "authentic" fare ("their pad Thai is a favorite")
insist the "picturesque" cuisine more than compensates; N.B. the
Downtown branch opened post-Survey.

Social, The *American* · 22 | 21 | 19 | $30
Fifth Ward | 170 S. First St. (Pittsburgh Ave.) | 414-270-0438 |
www.the-social.com

With "more room and better parking", the "new location" of this
Fifth Ward spot that "moved into a remodeled factory" "is more
ambitious" than its old Walker's Point digs, but its New American
menu is "still very good" – including such "unique offerings" as its
trademark "to-die-for macaroni and goat cheese", which "puts
mom's to shame"; "you won't be as close to the kitchen as before",
note social-ites, but "fun decor" and "more table choices make
up for it."

Taqueria Azteca ☒ *Mexican* · ▽ 21 | 16 | 21 | $22
South Side | 119 E. Oklahoma Ave. (Chase Ave.) | 414-486-9447

"Try the chalkboard specials", "amazing guacamole" and, of course,
"those wonderful margaritas" at this "solid" source for "nonstandard
Mexican" fare whose "unique offerings" feature a fusion of European

flavors; its "great patio" also helps make it a "treat", leading some to call it "the emerald of the South Side."

Tess *Eclectic*   25 | 17 | 22 | $37

East Side | 2499 N. Bartlett Ave. (Bradford Ave.) | 414-964-8377
Savoring the "can't-miss" Eclectic menu of "excellent food" "from both land and sea" "while sipping a cocktail" at this "quiet, romantic bistro" adds up to the "perfect neighborhood night" for many East Siders; some say the decor of its "small, intimate" dining room is merely "so-so", but the "fabulous patio" "has the feel of a New Orleans courtyard" – too bad it's only open "in summer."

Third Ward Caffe 🛅 Ⓜ *Italian*   ▽ 20 | 16 | 17 | $36

Third Ward | 225 E. St. Paul Ave. (bet. B'way & Water St.) | 414-224-0895 |
www.foodspot.com/thirdwardcaffe
Caffe-klatchers who "enjoy" this "pleasant" Third Warder "time and time again" claim it's an "ideal place to go before the theater" or "for a pasta fix" anytime thanks to a kitchen turning out "good, quick" Northern Italian meals; others see it as "uneven" – but either way, it's "been around forever" (well, since 1982) so it "must be doing something right."

Three Brothers Ⓜ🛱 *Serbian*   23 | 15 | 20 | $29

South Side | 2414 S. St. Clair (Russell Ave.) | 414-481-7530
"Bring an appetite" to this "delightful old-world tavern" in a former Schlitz brewery, a 51-year-old South Side "institution" (still run by the Radicevic family) that's "like hanging out at your grandma's kitchen table" – if, that is, your nana made "lovingly presented" burek, goulash and other "traditional" Serbian dishes; there's certainly "no pretense" to the "rustic and homespun" (some say "dumpy") interior, but most find it "fun and kitschy"– just "don't expect it to be fast."

Yanni's 🛅 *Steak*   22 | 24 | 21 | $49

Downtown | 540 E. Mason St. (Jackson St.) | 414-847-9264
This "cosmopolitan" Downtown steakhouse strikes supporters as a "great" restaurant thanks to its "beautiful decor", "clubby atmosphere", "excellent steaks" and servers who "try very hard" to ensure a good experience; critics for whom "the jury's still out", however, say they "wouldn't rush back", calling it "too expensive for what it is" and insisting that the "over-attentive staff needs to relax a bit."

Zarletti 🛅 *Italian*   20 | 19 | 19 | $32

Downtown | 741 N. Milwaukee St. (Mason St.) | 414-225-0000
A real "find", this "solid" site is a "great addition" to Downtown's Restaurant Row (aka Milwaukee Street), serving "inventive Italian" cuisine – "if you want sketti and meatballs, go elsewhere" – in a "surprisingly metro" "cappuccino-colored interior" that still manages to "feel like a neighborhood place."

MILWAUKEE
INDEXES

Cuisines

Includes restaurant names, neighborhoods and Food ratings. ☑ indicates places with the highest ratings, popularity and importance.

AMERICAN (NEW)

NEW Andrew's | **Delafield**	-
Bacchus | **Downtown**	26
Barossa | **Fifth Ward**	20
Coast | **Downtown**	20
Dream Dance | **Downtown**	25
Elm Grove Inn | **Elm Grove**	22
Envoy | **Downtown**	-
Gilbert's | **Lake Geneva**	-
Heaven City | **Mukwonago**	24
☑ Immigrant Room | **Kohler**	26
NEW Kil@wat | **Downtown**	-
North Shore Bistro | **N Shore**	19
Palms Bistro | **Third Ward**	21
☑ Sanford | **E Side**	29
Sebastian's | **Caledonia**	-
Social | **Fifth Ward**	22

AMERICAN (TRADITIONAL)

Elsa's on Park | **Downtown**	23
Golden Mast | **Okauchee**	18
Jackson Grill | **S Side**	23
NEW Mason St. Grill | **Downtown**	-
North Star Amer. | **multi. loc.**	-
Pleasant Valley Inn | **SW Side**	21
Riversite | **Mequon**	25
Rock Bottom | **Downtown**	16

ASIAN FUSION

Hama | **N Shore**	21

CAJUN

NEW Bayou | **E Side**	-
Crawdaddy's | **SW Side**	21

CALIFORNIAN

Roots | **Brewers Hill**	25

CHINESE

☑ P.F. Chang's | **Wauwatosa**	20

CREOLE

NEW Bayou | **E Side**	-
Crawdaddy's | **SW Side**	21

CUBAN

Cubanitas | **Downtown**	23

ECLECTIC

☑ Bjonda | **Wauwatosa**	22
Eagan's | **Downtown**	21
Elm Grove Inn | **Elm Grove**	22
Holiday House | **Third Ward**	-
Knick | **Downtown**	22
Tess | **E Side**	25

FRENCH

Coquette Cafe | **Third Ward**	25
☑ Lake Park Bistro | **E Side**	25

FRENCH (BISTRO)

Elliot's Bistro | **E Side**	20

GERMAN

Golden Mast | **Okauchee**	18
Karl Ratzsch's | **Downtown**	24

HAMBURGERS

Elsa's on Park | **Downtown**	23

INDIAN

Saffron Indian | **Brookfield**	25

ITALIAN

(N=Northern)

Caterina's | **SW Side**	21
NEW Il Mito Enoteca | **Wauwatosa**	-
☑ Maggiano's | **Wauwatosa**	20
Mangia | **Kenosha**	23
Mimma's Cafe | **E Side**	22
Osteria/Mondo | N | **Downtown**	25
Pasta Tree | N | **E Side**	20
Rist. Bartolotta | **Wauwatosa**	25
Third Ward Caffe | N | **Third Ward**	20
Zarletti | **Downtown**	20

JAPANESE

(* sushi specialist)

Benihana* | **Downtown**	19
Hama | **N Shore**	21
Nanakusa* | **Third Ward**	24
Sake Tumi | **Downtown**	25

KOREAN

(* barbecue specialist)

Sake Tumi* | **Downtown**   25

MEXICAN

Cempazuchi | **E Side**   21
Taqueria Azteca | **S Side**   21

PIZZA

Edwardo's Pizza | **multi. loc.**   20

POLISH

Polonez | **S Side**   23

SANDWICHES

Potbelly Sandwich | **multi. loc.**   20

SEAFOOD

Bosley on Brady | **E Side**   -
Eagan's | **Downtown**   21
Jackson Grill | **S Side**   23
Moceans | **Downtown**   21
River Lane Inn | **N Shore**   25

SERBIAN

Three Brothers | **S Side**   23

STEAKHOUSES

Benihana | **Downtown**   19
Bosley on Brady | **E Side**   -
Carnevor | **Downtown**   -
Z Eddie Martini's | **W Side**   26
Z Five O'Clock | **Central City**   26
Jackson Grill | **S Side**   23
Jake's | **Brookfield**   25
Z Milwaukee Chop | **Downtown**   24
Mo's: Steak | **Downtown**   23
Mr. B's: Steak | **Brookfield**   23
Yanni's | **Downtown**   22

THAI

King & I | **Downtown**   21
Singha Thai | **multi. loc.**   24

Locations

Includes restaurant names, cuisines and Food ratings. **Z** indicates places with the highest ratings, popularity and importance.

Milwaukee

BREWERS HILL

Roots | *Calif.* — 25

CENTRAL CITY

Z Five O'Clock | *Steak* — 26

DOWNTOWN

Bacchus | *Amer.* — 26
Benihana | *Jap./Steak* — 19
Carnevor | *Steak* — -
Coast | *Amer.* — 20
Cubanitas | *Cuban* — 23
Dream Dance | *Amer.* — 25
Eagan's | *Eclectic* — 21
Edwardo's Pizza | *Pizza* — 20
Elsa's on Park | *Amer.* — 23
Envoy | *Amer.* — -
Karl Ratzsch's | *German* — 24
NEW Kil@wat | *Amer.* — -
King & I | *Thai* — 21
Knick | *Eclectic* — 22
NEW Mason St. Grill | *Amer.* — -
Z Milwaukee Chop | *Steak* — 24
Moceans | *Seafood* — 21
Mo's: Steak | *Steak* — 23
Osteria/Mondo | *Italian* — 25
Potbelly Sandwich | *Sandwiches* — 20
Rock Bottom | *Amer.* — 16
Sake Tumi | *Asian* — 25
Singha Thai | *Thai* — 24
Yanni's | *Steak* — 22
Zarletti | *Italian* — 20

EAST SIDE

NEW Bayou | *Cajun/Creole* — -
Bosley on Brady | *Seafood/Steak* — -
Cempazuchi | *Mex.* — 21
Elliot's Bistro | *French* — 20
Z Lake Park Bistro | *French* — 25
Mimma's Cafe | *Italian* — 22
Pasta Tree | *Italian* — 20
Z Sanford | *Amer.* — 29
Tess | *Eclectic* — 25

FIFTH WARD

Barossa | *Amer.* — 20
Social | *Amer.* — 22

NORTH SHORE

Hama | *Asian Fusion/Jap.* — 21
North Shore Bistro | *Amer.* — 19
River Lane Inn | *Seafood* — 25

SOUTH SIDE

Jackson Grill | *Steak* — 23
Polonez | *Polish* — 23
Taqueria Azteca | *Mex.* — 21
Three Brothers | *Serbian* — 23

SOUTHWEST SIDE

Caterina's | *Italian* — 21
Crawdaddy's | *Cajun/Creole* — 21
Pleasant Valley Inn | *Amer.* — 21

THIRD WARD

Coquette Cafe | *French* — 25
Holiday House | *Eclectic* — -
Nanakusa | *Jap.* — 24
Palms Bistro | *Amer.* — 21
Third Ward Caffe | *Italian* — 20

WEST SIDE

Z Eddie Martini's | *Steak* — 26
Edwardo's Pizza | *Pizza* — 20
Singha Thai | *Thai* — 24

Outlying Areas

BROOKFIELD

Jake's | *Steak* — 25
Mr. B's: Steak | *Steak* — 23
North Star Amer. | *Amer.* — -
Potbelly Sandwich | *Sandwiches* — 20
Saffron Indian | *Indian* — 25

CALEDONIA

Sebastian's | *Amer.* — -

DELAFIELD

NEW Andrew's | *Amer.* — -

ELM GROVE

Elm Grove Inn | *Amer./Eclectic* 22

KENOSHA

Mangia | *Italian* 23

KOHLER

Z Immigrant Room | *Amer.* 26

LAKE GENEVA

Gilbert's | *Amer.* –

MEQUON

Riversite | *Amer.* 25

MUKWONAGO

Heaven City | *Amer.* 24

OKAUCHEE

Golden Mast | *Amer./German* 18

SHOREWOOD

North Star Amer. | *Amer.* –

WAUWATOSA

Z Bjonda | *Eclectic* 22
NEW Il Mito Enoteca | *Italian* –
Z Maggiano's | *Italian* 20
Z P.F. Chang's | *Chinese* 20
Rist. Bartolotta | *Italian* 25

MILWAUKEE

LOCATIONS

Special Features

Listings cover the best in each category and include restaurant names, locations and Food ratings. Multi-location restaurants' features may vary by branch. **Z** indicates places with the highest ratings, popularity and importance.

ADDITIONS
(Properties added since the last edition of the book)

Andrew's | **Delafield**	-
Bayou | **E Side**	-
Il Mito Enoteca | **Wauwatosa**	-
Kil@wat | **Downtown**	-
Mason St. Grill | **Downtown**	-
North Star Amer. | **multi. loc.**	-

BRUNCH

Eagan's | **Downtown**	21
Elliot's Bistro | **E Side**	20
Golden Mast | **Okauchee**	18
Knick | **Downtown**	22
Polonez | **S Side**	23
Tess | **E Side**	25

BUFFET
(Check availability)

Eagan's | **Downtown**	21
King & I | **Downtown**	21
Polonez | **S Side**	23
Saffron Indian | **Brookfield**	25

BUSINESS DINING

NEW Andrew's | **Delafield**	-
Bacchus | **Downtown**	26
Z Bjonda | **Wauwatosa**	22
Carnevor | **Downtown**	-
Coast | **Downtown**	20
Coquette Cafe | **Third Ward**	25
Eagan's | **Downtown**	21
Z Eddie Martini's | **W Side**	26
Elm Grove Inn | **Elm Grove**	22
Envoy | **Downtown**	-
Jake's | **Brookfield**	25
Karl Ratzsch's | **Downtown**	24
NEW Kil@wat | **Downtown**	-
Knick | **Downtown**	22
Z Lake Park Bistro | **E Side**	25
NEW Mason St. Grill | **Downtown**	-
Z Milwaukee Chop | **Downtown**	24
Mo's: Steak | **Downtown**	23
Mr. B's: Steak | **Brookfield**	23

North Shore Bistro | **N Shore**	19
North Star Amer. | **Brookfield**	-
Rist. Bartolotta | **Wauwatosa**	25
River Lane Inn | **N Shore**	25
Riversite | **Mequon**	25
Roots | **Brewers Hill**	25
Saffron Indian | **Brookfield**	25
Yanni's | **Downtown**	22

CELEBRITY CHEFS
(Listed under their primary restaurants)

NEW Il Mito Enoteca | *Michael Feker* | **Wauwatosa**	-
Jackson Grill | *Jimmy Jackson* | **S Side**	23
NEW Mason St. Grill | *Mark Weber* | **Downtown**	-
Mimma's Cafe | *Mimma Megna* | **E Side**	22
Osteria/Mondo | *Marc Bianchini* | **Downtown**	25
Riversite | *Tom Peschong* | **Mequon**	25
Z Sanford | *Sandy D'Amato* | **E Side**	29

CHILD-FRIENDLY
(Alternatives to the usual fast-food places; * children's menu available)

Benihana* | **Downtown**	19
Z Bjonda* | **Wauwatosa**	22
Caterina's | **SW Side**	21
Cempazuchi | **E Side**	21
Coast* | **Downtown**	20
Edwardo's Pizza* | **multi. loc.**	20
Gilbert's* | **Lake Geneva**	-
Golden Mast* | **Okauchee**	18
Hama | **N Shore**	21
Karl Ratzsch's* | **Downtown**	24
Knick | **Downtown**	22
Z Lake Park Bistro* | **E Side**	25
Z Maggiano's* | **Wauwatosa**	20
Mangia* | **Kenosha**	23
Mimma's Cafe | **E Side**	22
Palms Bistro | **Third Ward**	21
Pasta Tree | **E Side**	20
Z P.F. Chang's | **Wauwatosa**	20

Pleasant Valley Inn* | **SW Side** 21

Potbelly Sandwich* | **Downtown** 20

Rist. Bartolotta | **Wauwatosa** 25

River Lane Inn | **N Shore** 25

Rock Bottom* | **Downtown** 16

Taqueria Azteca* | **S Side** 21

Tess | **E Side** 25

Third Ward Caffe | **Third Ward** 20

CIGARS WELCOME

Carnevor | **Downtown** –

Elm Grove Inn | **Elm Grove** 22

Elsa's on Park | **Downtown** 23

Gilbert's | **Lake Geneva** –

Golden Mast | **Okauchee** 18

Heaven City | **Mukwonago** 24

Osteria/Mondo | **Downtown** 25

Yanni's | **Downtown** 22

DELIVERY/TAKEOUT

(D=delivery, T=takeout)

Benihana | T | **Downtown** 19

☑ Bjonda | T | **Wauwatosa** 22

Cempazuchi | T | **E Side** 21

Crawdaddy's | T | **SW Side** 21

Elsa's on Park | T | **Downtown** 23

Hama | T | **N Shore** 21

Knick | T | **Downtown** 22

☑ Maggiano's | T | **Wauwatosa** 20

Mimma's Cafe | T | **E Side** 22

Nanakusa | T | **Third Ward** 24

North Shore Bistro | T | **N Shore** 19

Palms Bistro | T | **Third Ward** 21

Pasta Tree | T | **E Side** 20

Polonez | T | **S Side** 23

Potbelly Sandwich | D, T | **multi. loc.** 20

River Lane Inn | T | **N Shore** 25

Rock Bottom | T | **Downtown** 16

Roots | T | **Brewers Hill** 25

Singha Thai | T | **W Side** 24

Taqueria Azteca | T | **S Side** 21

Third Ward Caffe | T | **Third Ward** 20

DINING ALONE

(Other than hotels and places with counter service)

Benihana | **Downtown** 19

☑ Bjonda | **Wauwatosa** 22

Cempazuchi | **E Side** 21

Coquette Cafe | **Third Ward** 25

Cubanitas | **Downtown** 23

Hama | **N Shore** 21

Lake Park Bistro | **E Side** 25

Nanakusa | **Third Ward** 24

North Shore Bistro | **N Shore** 19

Potbelly Sandwich | **Downtown** 20

Rock Bottom | **Downtown** 16

Singha Thai | **W Side** 24

ENTERTAINMENT

(Call for days and times of performances)

Coast | varies | **Downtown** 20

Elm Grove Inn | classical guitar | **Elm Grove** 22

Gilbert's | jazz | **Lake Geneva** –

Golden Mast | jazz | **Okauchee** 18

☑ Immigrant Room | piano | **Kohler** 26

Karl Ratzsch's | piano | **Downtown** 24

North Shore Bistro | jazz | **N Shore** 19

Rock Bottom | karaoke | **Downtown** 16

FIREPLACES

☑ Bjonda | **Wauwatosa** 22

Coast | **Downtown** 20

Elm Grove Inn | **Elm Grove** 22

Gilbert's | **Lake Geneva** –

Golden Mast | **Okauchee** 18

Heaven City | **Mukwonago** 24

Jake's | **Brookfield** 25

Sebastian's | **Caledonia** –

GAME IN SEASON

Barossa | **Fifth Ward** 20

☑ Bjonda | **Wauwatosa** 22

Coast | **Downtown** 20

Coquette Cafe | **Third Ward** 25

Dream Dance | **Downtown** 25

☑ Eddie Martini's | **W Side** 26

Elliot's Bistro | **E Side** 20

Elm Grove Inn | **Elm Grove** 22

Gilbert's | **Lake Geneva** –

Golden Mast | **Okauchee** 18

Heaven City | **Mukwonago** 24

Holiday House | **Third Ward** –

☑ Immigrant Room | **Kohler** 26

Jake's | **Brookfield** 25

HISTORIC PLACES

(Year opened; * building)

1855 | Elm Grove Inn* | **Elm Grove** 22

1875 | Gilbert's* | **Lake Geneva** –

Taqueria Azteca | P | **S Side** 21
Tess | P | **E Side** 25
Third Ward Caffe | S | **Third Ward** 20

PEOPLE-WATCHING

Bacchus | **Downtown** 26
☒ Bjonda | **Wauwatosa** 22
Carnevor | **Downtown** -
Coast | **Downtown** 20
Coquette Cafe | **Third Ward** 25
Cubanitas | **Downtown** 23
Eagan's | **Downtown** 21
☒ Eddie Martini's | **W Side** 26
Elsa's on Park | **Downtown** 23
Envoy | **Downtown** -
NEW Kil@wat | **Downtown** -
Knick | **Downtown** 22
☒ Maggiano's | **Wauwatosa** 20
NEW Mason St. Grill | **Downtown** -
Mimma's Cafe | **E Side** 22
Mo's: Steak | **Downtown** 23
Nanakusa | **Third Ward** 24
North Shore Bistro | **N Shore** 19
Palms Bistro | **Third Ward** 21
Pasta Tree | **E Side** 20
☒ P.F. Chang's | **Wauwatosa** 20
Rist. Bartolotta | **Wauwatosa** 25
River Lane Inn | **N Shore** 25
Rock Bottom | **Downtown** 16
Sake Tumi | **Downtown** 25
☒ Sanford | **E Side** 29
Three Brothers | **S Side** 23
Yanni's | **Downtown** 22

POWER SCENES

Bacchus | **Downtown** 26
Carnevor | **Downtown** -
☒ Eddie Martini's | **W Side** 26
Envoy | **Downtown** -
☒ Lake Park Bistro | **E Side** 25
NEW Mason St. Grill | **Downtown** -
Mo's: Steak | **Downtown** 23
Mr. B's: Steak | **Brookfield** 23
North Star Amer. | **Brookfield** -
Yanni's | **Downtown** 22

PRIVATE ROOMS

(Restaurants charge less at off times; call for capacity)
☒ Bjonda | **Wauwatosa** 22
Coast | **Downtown** 20

Coquette Cafe | **Third Ward** 25
☒ Eddie Martini's | **W Side** 26
Edwardo's Pizza | **W Side** 20
Elm Grove Inn | **Elm Grove** 22
Gilbert's | **Lake Geneva** -
Golden Mast | **Okauchee** 18
Hama | **N Shore** 21
Heaven City | **Mukwonago** 24
☒ Immigrant Room | **Kohler** 26
☒ Maggiano's | **Wauwatosa** 20
Mangia | **Kenosha** 23
Mimma's Cafe | **E Side** 22
Mr. B's: Steak | **Brookfield** 23
Nanakusa | **Third Ward** 24
Osteria/Mondo | **Downtown** 25
Polonez | **S Side** 23
River Lane Inn | **N Shore** 25
Riversite | **Mequon** 25
Rock Bottom | **Downtown** 16
Sebastian's | **Caledonia** -

PRIX FIXE MENUS

(Call for prices and times)
☒ Bjonda | **Wauwatosa** 22
Elliot's Bistro | **E Side** 20
Gilbert's | **Lake Geneva** -
☒ Immigrant Room | **Kohler** 26

QUICK BITES

Cubanitas | **Downtown** 23
Edwardo's Pizza | **multi. loc.** 20
Elsa's on Park | **Downtown** 23
Hama | **N Shore** 21
Knick | **Downtown** 22

QUIET CONVERSATION

NEW Andrew's | **Delafield** -
Barossa | **Fifth Ward** 20
☒ Bjonda | **Wauwatosa** 22
Bosley on Brady | **E Side** -
Dream Dance | **Downtown** 25
☒ Eddie Martini's | **W Side** 26
Elliot's Bistro | **E Side** 20
Elm Grove Inn | **Elm Grove** 22
Envoy | **Downtown** -
Golden Mast | **Okauchee** 18
Jake's | **Brookfield** 25
Karl Ratzsch's | **Downtown** 24
NEW Kil@wat | **Downtown** -
☒ Milwaukee Chop | **Downtown** 24

North Star Amer. | **Brookfield**	-
Osteria/Mondo | **Downtown**	25
Pasta Tree | **E Side**	20
Polonez | **S Side**	23
Riverite | **Mequon**	25
☑ Sanford | **E Side**	29
Third Ward Caffe | **Third Ward**	20

RAW BARS

Benihana | **Downtown**	19
Eagan's | **Downtown**	21
Moceans | **Downtown**	21

ROMANTIC PLACES

Golden Mast | **Okauchee**	18
NEW Il Mito Enoteca | **Wauwatosa**	-
☑ Immigrant Room | **Kohler**	26
☑ Lake Park Bistro | **E Side**	25
Mimma's Cafe | **E Side**	22
Osteria/Mondo | **Downtown**	25
Pasta Tree | **E Side**	20
Riverite | **Mequon**	25
Third Ward Caffe | **Third Ward**	20
Three Brothers | **S Side**	23
Zarletti | **Downtown**	20

SENIOR APPEAL

NEW Andrew's | **Delafield**	-
Elm Grove Inn | **Elm Grove**	22
Envoy | **Downtown**	-
Golden Mast | **Okauchee**	18
☑ Immigrant Room | **Kohler**	26
Jake's | **Brookfield**	25
Karl Ratzsch's | **Downtown**	24
North Star Amer. | **multi. loc.**	-
Pleasant Valley Inn | **SW Side**	21
Polonez | **S Side**	23
Riverite | **Mequon**	25
Three Brothers | **S Side**	23

SINGLES SCENES

Barossa | **Fifth Ward**	20
NEW Bayou | **E Side**	-
☑ Bjonda | **Wauwatosa**	22
Carnevor | **Downtown**	-
Crawdaddy's | **SW Side**	21
Cubanitas | **Downtown**	23
Eagan's | **Downtown**	21
Elsa's on Park | **Downtown**	23

Holiday House | **Third Ward**	-
Knick | **Downtown**	22
Mo's: Steak | **Downtown**	23
Nanakusa | **Third Ward**	24
Palms Bistro | **Third Ward**	21
Rock Bottom | **Downtown**	16
Sake Tumi | **Downtown**	25
Social | **Fifth Ward**	22

SLEEPERS

(Good to excellent food, but little known)

Elm Grove Inn | **Elm Grove**	22
Heaven City | **Mukwonago**	24
Jake's | **Brookfield**	25
Polonez | **S Side**	23
Saffron Indian | **Brookfield**	25

TEEN APPEAL

Edwardo's Pizza | **multi. loc.**	20
☑ Maggiano's | **Wauwatosa**	20
☑ P.F. Chang's | **Wauwatosa**	20
Potbelly Sandwich | **Downtown**	20
Rock Bottom | **Downtown**	16

TRENDY

Bacchus | **Downtown**	26
Barossa | **Fifth Ward**	20
NEW Bayou | **E Side**	-
☑ Bjonda | **Wauwatosa**	22
Carnevor | **Downtown**	-
Cempazuchi | **E Side**	21
Coast | **Downtown**	20
Cubanitas | **Downtown**	23
☑ Eddie Martini's | **W Side**	26
Elsa's on Park | **Downtown**	23
NEW Kil@wat | **Downtown**	-
Knick | **Downtown**	22
☑ Lake Park Bistro | **E Side**	25
☑ Maggiano's | **Wauwatosa**	20
Mo's: Steak | **Downtown**	23
Palms Bistro | **Third Ward**	21
☑ P.F. Chang's | **Wauwatosa**	20
Rist. Bartolotta | **Wauwatosa**	25
Sake Tumi | **Downtown**	25
☑ Sanford | **E Side**	29
Social | **Fifth Ward**	22
Zarletti | **Downtown**	20

VIEWS

NEW Andrew's | **Delafield**	-
Bacchus | **Downtown**	26

NEW Bayou | E Side	-
Coast | Downtown	20
Gilbert's | Lake Geneva	-
Golden Mast | Okauchee	18
Heaven City | Mukwonago	24
Knick | Downtown	22
Pleasant Valley Inn | SW Side	21
Riversite | Mequon	25
Sebastian's | Caledonia	-

VISITORS ON EXPENSE ACCOUNT

Barossa | Fifth Ward	20
Coquette Cafe | Third Ward	25
Cubanitas | Downtown	23
Eagan's | Downtown	21
Edwardo's Pizza | multi. loc.	20
NEW Il Mito Enoteca | Wauwatosa	-
King & I | Downtown	21
Knick | Downtown	22
Z Maggiano's | Wauwatosa	20
North Shore Bistro | N Shore	19
North Star Amer. | multi. loc.	-
Polonez | S Side	23
Rock Bottom | Downtown	16
Saffron Indian | Brookfield	25
Singha Thai | W Side	24
Social | Fifth Ward	22
Taqueria Azteca | S Side	21

WINE BARS

Barossa | Fifth Ward	20
NEW Il Mito Enoteca | Wauwatosa	-

Z Immigrant Room | Kohler	26
Osteria/Mondo | Downtown	25
Pasta Tree | E Side	20

WINNING WINE LISTS

Bacchus | Downtown	26
Barossa | Fifth Ward	20
Carnevor | Downtown	-
Coquette Cafe | Third Ward	25
Dream Dance | Downtown	25
Z Lake Park Bistro | E Side	25
Mangia | Kenosha	23
NEW Mason St. Grill | Downtown	-
Z Milwaukee Chop | Downtown	24
Osteria/Mondo | Downtown	25
Rist. Bartolotta | Wauwatosa	25
Z Sanford | E Side	29

WORTH A TRIP

Caledonia	
Sebastian's	-
Kenosha	
Mangia	23
Kohler	
Z Immigrant Room	26
Lake Geneva	
Gilbert's	-
Mukwonago	
Heaven City	24
Okauchee	
Golden Mast	18

Wine Vintage Chart

This chart, based on our 0 to 30 scale, is designed to help you select wine. The ratings (by **Howard Stravitz,** a law professor at the University of South Carolina) reflect the vintage quality and the wine's readiness to drink. We exclude the 1987, 1991–1993 vintages because they are not that good. A dash indicates the wine is either past its peak or too young to rate.

Whites	86	88	89	90	94	95	96	97	98	99	00	01	02	03	04	05
French:																
Alsace	–	–	26	26	25	24	24	23	26	24	26	27	25	22	24	25
Burgundy	25	–	23	22	–	28	27	24	23	26	25	24	27	23	25	26
Loire Valley	–	–	–	–	–	–	–	–	–	–	24	25	26	23	24	25
Champagne	25	24	26	29	–	26	27	24	23	24	24	22	26	–	–	–
Sauternes	28	29	25	28	–	21	23	25	23	24	24	28	25	26	21	26
California:																
Chardonnay	–	–	–	–	–	–	–	–	–	24	23	26	26	27	28	29
Sauvignon Blanc	–	–	–	–	–	–	–	–	–	–	–	27	28	26	27	26
Austrian:																
Grüner Velt./Riesling	–	–	–	–	–	25	21	28	28	27	22	23	24	26	26	26
German:	–	25	26	27	24	23	26	25	26	23	21	29	27	25	26	26

Reds	86	88	89	90	94	95	96	97	98	99	00	01	02	03	04	05
French:																
Bordeaux	25	23	25	29	22	26	25	23	25	24	29	26	24	25	23	27
Burgundy	–	–	24	26	–	26	27	26	22	27	22	24	27	24	24	25
Rhône	–	26	28	28	24	26	22	24	27	26	27	26	–	25	24	–
Beaujolais	–	–	–	–	–	–	–	–	–	–	24	–	23	27	23	28
California:																
Cab./Merlot	–	–	–	28	29	27	25	28	23	26	22	27	26	25	24	24
Pinot Noir	–	–	–	–	–	–	–	24	23	24	23	27	28	26	23	–
Zinfandel	–	–	–	–	–	–	–	–	–	–	25	23	27	22	–	–
Oregon:																
Pinot Noir	–	–	–	–	–	–	–	–	–	–	–	26	27	24	25	–
Italian:																
Tuscany	–	–	–	25	22	24	20	29	24	27	24	26	20	–	–	–
Piedmont	–	–	27	27	–	23	26	27	26	25	28	27	20	–	–	–
Spanish:																
Rioja	–	–	–	–	26	26	24	25	22	25	24	27	20	24	25	–
Ribera del Duero/Priorat	–	–	–	–	26	26	27	25	24	25	24	27	20	24	26	–
Australian:																
Shiraz/Cab.	–	–	–	–	24	26	23	26	28	24	24	27	27	25	26	–